NAFTA
IN A NUTSHELL

By

RALPH H. FOLSOM
University Professor of Law
University of San Diego

WEST
GROUP

ST. PAUL, MINN.
1999

PREFACE

Nearly six years on, NAFTA is important and exciting. It is the big first step in North American integration. No lawyer or business operating in North America can escape NAFTA's significance. NAFTA also represents the future, a blending of national legal and business cultures and traditions.

It has been a genuine pleasure to prepare this Nutshell on NAFTA. I hope that students, lawyers, government officials and people in business will find it a useful introduction. In preparing this Nutshell, I have attempted to address the interests not only of North Americans, but also persons located outside the region who worry about NAFTA's externalities.

I have followed the established Nutshell style and omitted most citations. This style creates a book that reads easily. For those who wish citations and much more coverage than a Nutshell permits, please see R. Folsom and W. D. Folsom, *NAFTA Law and Business* (1999) published by Kluwer Law International. This book is a professional treatise featuring contributions from distinguished attorneys and business persons actively working with NAFTA. It is supplemented annually. I am grateful for permission from Kluwer to adapt some of the material I wrote for that treatise to this Nutshell.

Students and professors who enjoy this Nutshell will be happy to learn that the West Group has agreed to publish the first ever coursebook on NAFTA. This problem-oriented coursebook will be released shortly after the millennium. Its co-authors will be Professors Michael Gordon (Florida), David Lopez (St. Mary's) and myself.

Your comments and suggestions concerning any of these books are most welcome.

RALPH H. FOLSOM

San Diego
May, 1999

ACKNOWLEDGMENTS

Special thanks is due my assistant, Rosemary Getty, whose tireless enthusiasm and skilled talents at USD have been priceless to me for many years. Thank you Rosemary!

I also wish to thank my brother, W. Davis Folsom, Professor of Business Studies at the University of South Carolina (Aiken). Brother Davis has extensively tutored me about the economics of NAFTA and opened many doors to understanding. We initially collaborated with pleasure on *Understanding NAFTA and Its International Business Implications* (1996), an interdisciplinary Matthew-Bender/Irwin publication written just after NAFTA came online.

Lastly, I very much appreciate the support of the West Group, particularly Mr. Doug Powell who heads their legal education division. It was he who first shared my enthusiasm for this project. He also authorized an extra allotment of pages that permitted reproduction of much of the NAFTA agreement and its labor and environmental side accords in the Appendices.

*

OUTLINE

OUTLINE

TABLE OF CASES

References are to Pages

TABLE OF CASES

XVI

NAFTA

IN A NUTSHELL

*

CHAPTER 1

PRE–NAFTA

Economically speaking, NAFTA is about the elimination of boundaries between Mexico, Canada and the United States. The political borders between these countries remain firmly in place. In other words, NAFTA has little if any political agenda. This contrasts with the European Union which very much is engaged in a process of integration that blurs boundaries among its member states politically as well as economically. NAFTA is thus a simpler agreement, with limited goals and means.

Canada and the United States

Integrating the economies of Canada, Mexico and the United States is a theme that has reverberated throughout North American history. Canada and the United States, for example, have been discussing free trade for nearly two centuries. In the years after the United States Revolution, Canadians were concerned that they might be annexed. Free trade with the United States thus became a preferred alternative whenever annexation raised its ugly head. Such forces reached their peak in the mid–1800s when Lord Elgin, Governor of Canada under British rule, successfully negotiated a free trade agreement with the United States. This agreement, the Elgin–Marcy Treaty of 1854, established free trade for nearly all goods and also provided for mutual access to fisheries. This was, of course, the period of the Civil War in the United States which ultimately caused the U.S. to abrogate the Elgin–Marcy Treaty in 1866. This was done because Great Britain had generally exhibited sympathies with the South and in particular had permitted Confederates to construct and repair ships in British Canada.

Canada obtained independence from Britain in 1867 by Act of Parliament. The United States and the Dominion of Canada periodically considered renewing free trade relations after the Civil War. Late in the Nineteenth Century these negotiations broke down and both nations enacted highly protective tariffs intended to foster local manufacturing. In 1911, the United States took the initiative and proposed free trade. An agreement was actually reached which the United States Congress ratified, but manufacturing interests in Canada successfully defeated it in the Canadian Parliament.

The trend towards protectionism continued throughout the 1920s and 1930s as both Canada and the United States sought to remedy their economic depressions through trade restraints. Freer trade between the countries was not revived until 1935 when Congress adopted the Reciprocal Trade Agreements Act. Under this Act, President Roosevelt negotiated a substantial reduction in tariffs applicable to Canada–U.S. trade. This agreement was part of Roosevelt's broader "good neighbor policy." This policy even led to secret talks about free trade after World War II. Yet another agreement for free trade was reached, but Canadian Prime Minister King removed his support at the last minute and thus killed the deal.

In the ensuing decades, Canada and the United States participated in the General Agreement on Tariffs and Trade (GATT 1947). This participation diverted both countries from free trade initiatives while generally enhancing trade opportunities through tariff reductions. As long as the GATT provided a reasonably successful alternative, there was little movement in the direction of free trade. One exception, however, was the United States–Canada Automobile Pact of 1965. Broadly speaking, the Auto–Pact permitted free trade in new automobiles and original equipment automotive parts. Over time, the Auto–Pact led to substantial integration of the Canadian and U.S. automotive industries.

The GATT continued to provide an alternative to free trade through the Tokyo Round of negotiations (1973–1979). The Tokyo Round attempted for the first time to reduce nontariff trade barriers. It was not until the Uruguay Round of GATT negotiations commenced in 1986 that Canada and the United States had cause to become concerned about improving their trade relations. This concern arose quickly because the Uruguay Round negotiations seemed endless and fraught with controversy. It appeared that there might not even be a successful conclusion to the Uruguay Round.

It was this prospect, perhaps more than any other influential factor, that pushed negotiations on free trade between Canada and the United States. Each nation appreciated that their willingness to agree to free trade would act as a spur to the Uruguay Round in which they had vested interests. In addition, it did not hurt that President Reagan was in power and that he found a conservative ally in Canadian Prime Minister Mulroney. Both countries also recognized that the European Community, having launched in 1987 its campaign for a Europe without internal frontiers, was on the verge of creating the world's largest integrated market. A free trade agreement would raise the ante in this rivalry.

In sum, after over a century of nearly agreeing to free trade, all of the stars were properly aligned for agreement between Canada and the United States. The Canada–United States Free Trade Agreement (CFTA) took effect January 1, 1989. There was very little expectation at that time that CFTA would ultimately be expanded to include Mexico. Indeed, the CFTA Agreement made no provision for accession of new members. Nevertheless, as we now know, the NAFTA Agreement arrived in 1994 and traces many of its provisions to CFTA.

Mexico and the United States

United States trade relations with Mexico prior to NAFTA were quite different from those with Canada. There were no repeated attempts and experiments at free trade across the border. Moreover,

Mexico did not participate in the GATT until 1986. The history of Mexico-U.S. trade relations was instead much more confrontational and protectionist. Mexican independence from Spain in 1821 was followed by periods of conflict with the United States. Texas became the center of controversy in the 1830s and resulted in what the Mexicans call the "War of North American Invasion." This war actually saw U.S. forces occupying Mexico City and resulted in the Treaty of Guadalupe Hildalgo in 1848. Under this treaty, Mexico conveyed roughly one-third of its lands to the United States including large parts of what are now the states of California, Arizona, New Mexico, Utah, Colorado and Nevada. Even to this day, the Treaty of Guadalupe Hildalgo remains a deeply felt loss to most Mexicans.

In the years after the Mexican–American War, Mexico entered a period of instability. In 1876, Porfirio Diaz took power and he dominated Mexico until 1911. It was under his rule that foreign investors obtained major concessions in railroads, mining and petroleum. Apart from commodities, there was relatively little trade between Mexico and the United States during this time.

The Diaz regime was repressive and led to economic extremes. While the Mexican elite, foreign investors and the Roman Catholic Church did well, most Mexicans were hungry and resentful. This resentment exploded in 1910 for a period of seven years during the Mexican Revolution. Many deaths preceded the adoption in 1917 of a new constitution for the Federal Republic of Mexico. Dr. Guillermo Margadant, Mexico's distinguished legal historian, has referred to the 1917 Constitution as "a multilateral declaration of war, directed against the large land holders, the bosses, the clergy and mining companies". *An Introduction to the History of Mexican Law (1983)*. This Constitution, much amended over time, remains in effect and influenced a variety of provisions in the NAFTA agreement. Apart from agrarian and land reform, foreigners were a principal focus of revolutionary change in Mexico. In 1938 President Cardenas nationalized all foreign oil company interests in Mexico. In many ways, including symbolically, this nationalization was perceived as a declaration of Mexican economic independence. PEMEX, the state oil and gas monopoly of Mexico, is a direct descendant of the 1938 nationalization.

After World War II, Mexico pursued policies of import substitution and foreign investment control. The goal of these policies was to raise tariff and other trade barriers on imports to levels that caused Mexican suppliers to prevail. Behind this protective wall, Mexican industry was sheltered from world competitive forces. Government involvement in the economy grew. While Mexico is not a member of OPEC, the rise in oil prices in the 1970s financed development and paid for the costs of economic isolation. They also greased the wheels of corruption at a level that was shocking even by Mexican standards. In 1981, when oil prices fell dramatically, the Mexican holiday from reality was over.

In rapid succession Mexico's peso was severely devalued, trading in dollars was suspended, Mexico's banks were nationalized, and payment on its national debt became doubtful. Under the influence of the International Monetary Fund, and increasingly out of a perception of self interest, Mexico abandoned its policy of import substitution and loosened its foreign investment controls. It adopted instead the goal of export promotion and embraced for the first time global trade law by joining the GATT in 1986. This was a watershed decision for Mexico and certainly a prerequisite to participation with Canada and the United States in North American free trade.

When Canada and the United States agreed to free trade in 1989, Mexico's President Salinas looked at his alternatives. He first turned towards Europe, but found little interest in an economic partnership across the Atlantic. President Salinas then expressed a desire to negotiate a free trade agreement with the United States. He was influenced in part by the popularity of the idea among the Mexican people, a popularity that remains strong to this day. President Bush, without extensive consultations with Canada, agreed.

From the United States perspective, separate free trade agreements with Canada and Mexico were an option. From the Canadian perspective, however, participation in trilateral North American free trade negotiations was essential. The Canadians were afraid that some of their hard won CFTA benefits might be diluted if they failed to join in the negotiations. Their participation was thus initially defensive, but over time they realized that NAFTA offered the chance to revisit and take up issues of importance to Canada.

Professor Michael Gordon has astutely observed that the United States agenda for NAFTA went beyond what was negotiated in the agreement. *See* 56 Modern L.Rev. 157 (1993). He suggests that the U.S. had and continues to have unwritten NAFTA objectives concerning Mexico. Broadly speaking these are goals of "containment" of what he refers to as the "Mexican Problem." The first objective is the hope that an open and growing Mexican economy will help stem the tide of illegal migration to the United States. On this theme, President Salinas is said to have remarked that the U.S. had a choice, either to take Mexican goods under NAFTA or Mexican people without it.

Professor Gordon also suggests that the U.S. had and has long-term interests in Mexico's abundant energy reserves. This agenda item found its way into the agreement, but certainly not with the terms and conditions preferred by the United States. *See* Chapter 4. Thirdly, Professor Gordon believes that the U.S. feared the concentration of power in Mexico. Politically this fear focused on decades of single party rule. Economically this fear centered on extreme disparities in wealth. Concentration of power in Mexico has always (as Porfirio Diaz learned and Chiapas illustrates) provided a ready recipe for violence and revolt. The United

States hoped that mixing NAFTA into the recipe might reduce the risk of instability south of the border. Of course this agenda item was never put in writing and barely whispered when NAFTA took shape.

Merging Economies

NAFTA is primarily about the integration of the Canadian, Mexican and United States economies. Each of these economies has different characteristics, but on balance and taken together they are quite complementary. The United States, of course, is the giant in the middle with nearly 300,000,000 people driving an extremely consumer-oriented, high-tech economy. The United States has a post-industrial society where services comprise the large majority of economic activity. Computers, telecommunications, banking, insurance, engineering and fast food are just some of the wide ranging services for which the U.S. is well known. Keeping the massive U.S. economy going requires importation of many commodities, particularly energy. The United States is an energy-dependent nation, and one reason for the complementarity of the North American economies is the fact that Canada and Mexico have energy surpluses.

Canada has barely 30,000,000 people, most living along the United States border, in what is geographically the third largest nation in the world. Canada possesses great natural resources and the exportation of these resources has always been a key ingredient in its economy. Canada is also an industrial nation, producing a wide range of goods including automobiles under the 1965 Canada–United States Auto Pact. Comparatively speaking, Canada has more of a producer-driven economy. The Province of Ontario, located roughly in the center of Canada north of the Great Lakes, is the economic powerhouse of the nation. Canada's western provinces and Quebec along with the Maritime provinces in the east have long harbored a certain resentment of the economic and financial power exercised by Ontario. It is perhaps not surprising therefore that CFTA and NAFTA have been more popular in the east and west of Canada than in the central and more economically dominant province of Ontario.

Mexico has a developing economy. This contrasts sharply with the mature economies of its northern neighbors. Some 100,000,000 Mexicans, most of them struggling to rise out of poverty, hope that NAFTA will help them realize their economic aspirations. Poverty in Mexico has been growing. Since the 1994–95 peso devaluation, more than 4 million Mexicans have entered extreme poverty (defined as earning less than $2 a day). Workers living in moderate poverty ($3 a day) have also been increasing rapidly in number. Both groups, taken together, now constitute two-thirds of all Mexicans. These trends, and the desperation and instability that accompanies them, drive migrants north and encourage adoption of the U.S. dollar as Mexico's currency.

Mexico's energy exports dominate its trade relations and national budget. Every $1 change in the price of oil equates with roughly $1 billion in national revenues. Comparatively speaking, Mexico's large, inexpensive and increasingly skilled labor force is a principal asset. Mexico relies heavily upon foreign investment capital, more than half of which comes from the United States.

It is often difficult to appreciate from inside the United States how economically *dependent* Canada and Mexico are upon the United States market. Both nations ship the large majority of their exports to the United States. United States investors predominate in Canada with U.S.-owned subsidiaries playing a critical role in Canada's industrial economy. If United States investors are less visible in Mexico, that is only because restrictive foreign investment controls have historically been pursued.

NAFTA promises to increase the dependence of the Canadian and Mexican economies upon the United States. Given such dependence, it is understandable that Canada and Mexico view NAFTA as a kind of insurance policy. NAFTA greatly diminishes the risk that the United States might in a worse case scenario erect tariff or other trade and investment barriers that would be extremely damaging to their economies. In dealing with the giant in the middle, there is a certain alliance of Canadian and Mexican interests.

Different Legal Traditions

The economic integration of North America under the NAFTA agreement depends upon law for its implementation. Each country naturally brings with it different legal traditions that affect the operational reality of NAFTA. Yet certain common legal themes resonate. Canada, Mexico and the United States are, for example, all federal states. But their federalism is by no means uniform. Mexico probably has the most centrist tradition of federalism. Although there has been some relaxation of the federal government's powers in modern Mexico, most Mexican states are relatively powerless. Thus, in implementing NAFTA, legal activity at the federal level in Mexico usually suffices.

In contrast, Canada has a weak federal tradition. Among other areas, the federal government shares labor and environmental law jurisdiction with the provinces. This has meant that implementation in Canada of the side agreements on North American Labor and Environmental Cooperation have been dependent upon provincial action. Such implementation has arrived slowly. It was not until 1997, for example, that the Labor Cooperation Agreement actively applied to Canada.

The United States, with a strong federal power balanced against a history of states' rights, lies in the middle of these traditions of federalism. State regulation of products and services that may be freely traded under NAFTA can result in significant barriers. That is one reason why the NAFTA Implementation Act of 1993 provides (for the first time in connection with any U.S. treaty) that the states must be informed and permitted to participate in trade matters affecting their interests. While the states cannot alter NAFTA law, which is supreme, they are entitled to significant procedural rights to participate in the defense of state laws that are challenged under NAFTA. *See* Section 102(b)(1)(B) of the NAFTA Implementation Act.

Other legal traditions impact affect NAFTA more obliquely. In Mexico and in Quebec there are strong Civil Law traditions originating in continental Europe. These traditions contrast with the Common Law heritage found generally in the United States and English-speaking Canada. In Quebec and Mexico, for example, one can find a range of Civil Law Codes and comparatively weak traditions of precedent. The tradition of judicial lawmaking found in Common Law legal systems is much diminished in Mexico and to a lesser extent in Quebec. Thus it is perhaps not surprising that United States courts have been more willing to aggressively reject NAFTA and its Implementation Act. For example, the U.S. Court of International Trade ruled that the country of origin marking requirements specified by the NAFTA Implementation Act did not supplant traditional United States legal doctrine in that area. *CPC International, Inc. v. United States,* 933 F.Supp. 1093 (C.I.T. 1996) reversed on appeal *Bestfoods, Inc. v. United States,* 165 F.3d 1371 (Fed.Cir. 1999).

A third legal tradition that provides some contrast between the three NAFTA partners is as much political as constitutional. Both Canada and the United States have mature multiparty democracies and strong commitments to the rule of law. Mexico, on the other hand, has been ruled by a single party (the Partido Revolucionario Institucional or PRI) for about 70 years. Indeed Mexico now has the dubious distinction of possessing the longest running single party government on the globe. This often has made it difficult to distinguish between the party and the state. However, significant political change is under way in Mexico as competing parties have captured a number of state governorships, control of Mexico City, and control collaboratively of the Mexican Congress. All of this change has been influenced by the spotlight that NAFTA has focused upon Mexican politics since 1994. It is not at all clear that the PRI will retain power in Mexico's presidential elections in the year 2000.

More generally, the NAFTA spotlight has contributed to the challenge of ruling Mexico by law. It is always important to remember that Mexico is a developing nation not just in an economic sense but also in terms of its legal system. It is no secret that political and legal corruption permeate Mexican government. Prior to NAFTA, corruption in Mexico was that of a distant neighbor. Since 1994 the increased visibility of corrupt practices under the NAFTA spotlight has arguably helped Mexico improve its rule of law. While there is nothing in the NAFTA agreement that requires such developments, they appear to be a byproduct of North American integration.

Dean Stephen Zamorra has suggested that Mexican law is undergoing "Americanization". *See* 24

Law & Policy in International Business 391 (1993).
Multiparty politics and growing integrity in the
Mexican legal system are certainly part of that
process. But as Dean Zamora emphasizes, there are
important cultural differences at work. For example, Mexican society stresses cooperation and is
communautarian, while U.S. society stresses competition and glorifies individual freedom. In Mexico's
culture, people may feel more comfortable with
authoritarian styles of government than competitive
and responsive models of democracy. Similarly, in
the economic sector, the cooperative, authoritarian
tradition of "El Pacto" between business, government and labor violates free market principles. El
Pacto agreements have held down prices and wages
as part of inflation control programs. Dean Zamora
suggests that pushing U.S.-style solutions on Mexico without acknowledging its different cultural bases may not only be imperialistic, but also counter-
productive in the sense that the solutions will not
work.

The Private Sector

In the preceding sections we have focused upon
the history and growth of intergovernmental trade
relations, economies and legal traditions in North
America. In this section we turn to the private
business sector and its historical relationships prior
to NAFTA. Two broad and significant trends
emerge from this picture. In Canada, with its dependence upon U.S. corporate investment, a large
number of so-called "branch plants" were established. These branch plants were often subsidiaries

of U.S. multinational corporations created for Canada's small market because of tariff and other trade restraints. Such plants provided significant employment opportunities to Canadians, but their economies of scale were limited and therefore typically the costs of production in the Canadian market were higher than in the United States. One of the pronounced trends under NAFTA has been the closure of Canadian branch plants by U.S. corporations. Many U.S. companies have folded their Canadian production needs into their United States manufacturing facilities. This has generated some highly visible unemployment and hostility to NAFTA in Canada.

A second historical trend prior to NAFTA involves Mexico. In Mexico, since the 1960s, but particularly after the devaluation of the Mexican peso in 1982 and again in 1994–95, assembly plant production centers have proliferated. These are known as "maquiladoras" and they provide an enormous source of hard currency earnings and employment. Many maquiladoras are owned by U.S. companies. Others are owned by Mexican, Japanese and Korean investors. They have taken advantage of Mexico's inexpensive labor by shifting production of assembly goods to maquiladoras. Over a million Mexicans, many of them younger women, are now employed in assembly plants making electronics, automotive parts, furniture and apparel among other labor intensive products and services (such as sorting grocery coupons and operating phone banks).

Mexico, quite understandably, wished to preserve the maquiladora program that existed prior to NAFTA. Canada and the United States, on the other hand, were concerned that foreign companies might use maquiladoras as "export platforms" into the NAFTA free trade area. Under the NAFTA agreement, a compromise was reached which encourages continued use of Mexican maquiladoras and allows free trading of maquiladora products provided those goods meet the rules of origin that govern NAFTA trade. In other words, maquiladora products can be free traded only if they are deemed "North American". Classic Japanese "screwdriver plants," using primarily Asian components, for example, will not qualify for free trade. Resolving issues of product origin thus becomes a central legal concern for NAFTA attorneys and their clients. *See* Chapter 4. Most maquiladora producers have in place strategies for compliance with the NAFTA rules of origin so that their products may be freely traded.

Conclusion

This brief historical perspective on CFTA and NAFTA has hopefully prepared you for the more detailed law of North American integration that follows. It is important to remember that these free trade agreements emerged from different contexts and traditions that help explain their contents and implementation. History also gives us a sense of the expectations and hopes of the parties and economic actors seeking to benefit from North American free trade.

CHAPTER 2

CFTA

North American economic integration began in earnest when Canada and the United States concluded a broad free trade agreement in 1989. Without intending to do so, the Canada–United States Free Trade Agreement (CFTA) laid the foundations for NAFTA. In the United States, CFTA was almost a non-event. In Canada, the agreement was much contested. Special Parliamentary elections focused on CFTA kept the Mulroney government in power, which was critical to Canadian ratification of the agreement.

NAFTA did not repeal the Canada–United States Free Trade Agreement. The CFTA agreement continues to govern selected areas of trade (as specified in NAFTA). Officially, the United States and Canada have "suspended" their 1989 agreement. If NAFTA failed or either Canada or the United States withdrew from it, CFTA would come out of suspended animation and continue to bind the two countries. Understanding the CFTA agreement is important because it served as the model upon which NAFTA was built. In some areas, the terms of NAFTA are identical or nearly so. In others, minor or major changes were made which are best understood as attempts at improving upon the early experience of free trade. NAFTA insights can still be drawn from CFTA even as it lies in suspended animation.

The Canada–United States Free Trade Agreement was limited in its scope and purposes, stopping well short of the depth of coverage found in the Treaty of Rome establishing the European Community. *See* R. Folsom, *European Union Law in a Nutshell*. Nevertheless, the CFTA agreement is lengthy and relatively complex. It is comprised of eight Parts that are divided into a total of twenty-one Chapters. Each chapter is comprised of various Articles and accompanying Annexes. Above all CFTA was a pragmatic agreement.

Core Commitments—Federalism, Supremacy and Nondiscrimination

Chapter One of the Agreement contains a listing of CFTA objectives. Internal trade barriers on goods *and* services are to be eliminated, fair competition facilitated and investment opportunities liberalized. Effective procedures to administer CFTA, to resolve disputes, and cooperation to expand and enhance the benefits of the agreement were also listed as objectives.

In realizing these objectives, Canada and the U.S. promised to "ensure that all necessary measures are taken in order to give effect to [CFTA's] provisions, including their observance ... by state, provincial and local governments." (Article 103). This obligation was a major commitment, particularly for

Canada since it has a relatively weak federal system of government with the provinces retaining considerable power. Binding the two federal governments to free trade was relatively simple. Binding their political subdivisions has proven more difficult.

Canada and the United States affirmed their existing bilateral and multilateral trade agreements. They self-servingly declared their agreement consistent with Article 24 of the original (pre-Uruguay Round) General Agreement on Tariffs and Trade (GATT 1947). Article 24 governs the establishment of free trade areas by GATT signatories, and CFTA did indeed ultimately pass examination by a GATT working party.

If there are inconsistencies between CFTA and existing trade agreements, CFTA is supreme. (Article 104). Under this supremacy rule, for example, conflicts with the GATT 1947 agreement would apparently result in regional rules prevailing. This potential was somewhat minimized by incorporating by reference into CFTA various GATT provisions, including the 1979 Procurement Code and Articles III, XI and XX of the GATT 1947.

There are a number of specific exceptions to CFTA supremacy, some limited in scope, if conflicts arise with the following agreements: (1) the GATT rules on antidumping and countervailing duties; (2) the GATT rules on balance of payments problems; (3) the OECD Code of Liberalization of Capital Movements; (4) the Income Tax Convention between Canada and the U.S.; and (5) the International Monetary Fund Agreement. In addition, it is generally specified that CFTA is *not* supreme on agriculture, emergency trade relief, wine and spirits, trade in goods, energy, tariff waivers and investment matters. These exceptions had less impact than their numbers imply.

Canada and the United States broadly promised to grant "national treatment" on investment and trade matters. Each side thus agreed to treat the other's investors and traders in the same manner as their own, a general promise not to discriminate on grounds of nationality. In addition, Article III of the GATT 1947 agreement, along with its interpretative notes, was specifically incorporated into CFTA. Article III stipulates national treatment for goods on taxation, fees and charges, distribution or sale requirements, transport rules, and domestic sourcing (among other matters). Furthermore, the existing GATT interpretations of Article III were to be applied under CFTA. Several Article III disputes subsequently went to binding arbitration under Chapter 18 of CFTA (below).

A state or provincial treatment rule was also created. Regarding like, directly competitive or substitutable goods, treatment that is no less favorable than the most favorable treatment that the state or province grants to any goods is required. Hence, unlike at the federal level, this rule was not one of identical treatment, but a variation on most-favored-nation (MFN) treatment. The states and provinces were obliged to treat goods from the other country in the best manner they treated goods coming from anywhere, including their own state or province. Arguably, this duty provided greater protection from nondiscrimination than simply national treatment.

Trade in Goods

Part Two of the Canada–United States Free Trade Agreement, covered in Chapters 3 through 12, governs free trade in goods. This central goal must be measured against a history of substantial free trade in goods prior to 1989. Canada, for example, had been exporting more than 75 percent of its goods to the U.S. on a duty-free basis prior to the CFTA agreement and the balance were entering the United States at an average 5 percent tariff. Hence, tariffs were not really a significant trade relationship.

Both countries were much more concerned with nontariff trade barriers (NTBs), such as health, safety, environmental, and technical product regulations. NTBs sometimes excluded goods totally from either market and each country sometimes applied international trade remedies to limit the cross-border flow of goods. With its commanding dependency on access to the U.S. market, this Part of the CFTA agreement was critical to Canada. Conversely, the United States was ready to make concessions on trade in goods in order to obtain benefits on trade in services and cross-border investment.

Tariffs and Quotas

Canada and the United States agreed to a phased elimination of the tariffs applicable to their trade in goods. Article 401 created a schedule for import tariff removals starting in 1989 and ending in 1998. This schedule was not subsequently altered by NAFTA. Schedule A goods immediately became duty free on January 1, 1989. Schedule B goods became duty free after 5 years of 20 percent annual reductions on January 1, 1993. Schedule C goods became duty free on January 1, 1998 after 10 years of 10 percent annual reductions. Schedule C goods included the most tariff-sensitive, such as agricultural products, textiles and clothing. Thus, at this writing, trade between Canada and the United States is virtually free of tariffs.

Export taxes (tariffs) were prohibited at the outset of the CFTA agreement. Canada and the U.S. also agreed not to employ "customs user fees" which function like tariffs. The United States phased out its existing fees as applied to Canadian goods. In addition, private sector requests for accelerated tariff reductions ahead of the timelines in the CFTA Schedules were allowed. Companies and industries filed a surprising number of petitions for acceleration with their governments. Canadian and United States officials then met and decided which tariffs to reduce on an accelerated basis. Considerable acceleration in tariff removals were achieved under CFTA and this innovative process has continued under NAFTA.

The CFTA agreement, unlike the customs union of Europe, did not embrace the creation of a common external tariff. In other words, the United States and Canada retained their own tariffs on goods entering their markets. Goods from the rest of the world are still, even after NAFTA, subject to United States or Canadian (not CFTA or NAFTA) tariffs.

Nevertheless, certain external tariff tensions were addressed in CFTA. These primarily concerned foreign goods that entered Canada or the United States and were subsequently shipped to the other country. The widespread practice of "drawback" under customs law was the main issue. The refunding of tariffs that manufacturers pay on imported goods after they are exported, or incorporated or consumed in the production of goods subsequently exported, is the essence of drawback. Drawback can take the form of waivers or reductions in such duties. Either way, manufacturers have lower costs because of the customs refund. Supporters of drawback argue that the imported goods have really not come to rest, merely passed through, and therefore should be beneficially tariffed.

Canada and the United States recognized that drawbacks created problems for their free trade agreement. Manufacturers obtaining them could sell at lower costs than competitors not benefiting from drawback. To solve this problem, Canada and the United States agreed to extensively eliminate drawbacks on goods they trade, and were scheduled have done so by 1996. However, this commitment was notably altered by the NAFTA agreement of 1994. *See* Chapter 4.

Another external tariff tension that CFTA remedied was waivers of tariffs triggered by "performance requirements." Such requirements were primarily found in Canadian law. Often a Canadian manufacturer had to incorporate a minimum amount of Canadian content, purchase or substitute Canadian goods, and maintain minimum export percentages. Manufacturers meeting Canadian performance requirements were recipients of drawback or tariff waivers as an investment incentive. This resulted in an unfair advantage for Canadian manufacturers competing under CFTA with United States companies that did not obtain comparable benefits. Article 405 of CFTA prohibited new or expanded tariff waivers based upon performance requirements (i.e., a "standstill" was stipulated). For all but Auto Pact goods, tariff waivers were eliminated in 1998.

Regarding trade quotas and their equivalents, Canada and the United States agreed to apply Article XI of the GATT 1947. Thus most quotas were banned, excepting notably agricultural, fishery or marketing quotas. Several Article XI disputes were arbitrated under Chapter 18 of CFTA.

The Origin of Goods

Free trade agreements like CFTA and NAFTA have a critical problem. Since Canada and the United States did not establish a common external tariff, other nations in theory could ship their goods into the country with the lowest tariff and then benefit from free trade. If so, third party goods could "free ride" on CFTA. To prevent this, Canada and the United States crafted rules to decide which goods came from their countries and allowed only those goods to be freely traded. All other goods are subject to national tariffs and trade restraints as they cross the border.

The CFTA "rules of origin" became one of the most complex and controversial of the agreement's provisions. Canada and the United States, with different legal traditions in this area, undertook a pathbreaking set of rules of origin. To start, they agreed that all goods "wholly obtained or produced" within either or both of their nations could be freely traded. Since this rule applies mainly to minerals, agricultural goods and fish, it was not difficult to obtain.

Manufactured goods, not so clearly Canadian or United States in origin, were another story. In the global economy, with multinationals producing goods and parts in many nations, it is hard to ascertain which products come from where. In the United States, the origin of goods has typically been decided under the doctrine of "substantial transformation." *See Anheuser-Busch Brewing Ass'n v. United States,* 207 U.S. 556 (1908). If in the process of manufacture a material or part was "substantially transformed" into a new product, then its foreign origin was lost. The material or part so transformed originated as a matter of law in the country of transformation.

Unfortunately, the doctrine of substantial transformation in U.S. customs law has many imprecisions. Canada and the United States, each having recently adopted the Harmonized Tariff System (HTS) of classification of goods, moved in a different direction. Under Article 301 of CFTA, they agreed as a general rule that whenever items of third party origin were transformed to a degree that their tariff classification under the HTS changed, then those items originated in Canada or the United States. But packaging, combining or diluting goods of third party origin was insufficient. The core CFTA rule of origin was therefore linked to changes in HTS tariff classifications. This approach embodied the idea but provided more precision than the doctrine of substantial transformation.

Canadian legal traditions and priorities were the primary source of additional CFTA "content" rules of origin. The CFTA content rules of origin applied only to trade in selected (but quite a large number) goods. These rules generally had to be satisfied *in addition to* the basic rule of change in tariff classification. In a few instances, the content origin of the goods sufficed for free trade.

Canada and the United States agreed, in most circumstances, on a 50 percent CFTA content rule. The value of materials originating in Canada or the United States plus the direct cost of processing performed in either or both countries had to exceed

50 percent of the value of the goods crossing the border. Only if this content rule was satisfied could many goods be freely traded under CFTA. Thus companies whose economic contribution to the region was less significant could not participate in free CFTA trade.

The 50 percent CFTA content rule of origin proved difficult to apply. In one noted case, it became especially controversial regarding Honda automobiles. *See Cantin and Lowenfeld,* 87 Amer.J.Int'l Law 375 (1993). The dispute centered on how to treat third party content that was "rolled up." Honda–U.S. exported auto engines with 10 percent third party content to Honda–Canada. Since the value of the engines was 90 percent United States in origin, when Honda–Canada installed the engines in its automobiles, it "rolled up" (treated as American) the 10 percent third party content when it subsequently shipped the autos to the United States. Canada took the position that the engines were 100 percent American in origin. But U.S. Customs ruled that the 10 percent third-party engine value could not be rolled up in this manner, which meant that overall the autos did not meet the 50 percent CFTA content rule. They therefore could not be freely traded and were subject to United States tariffs. The *Honda* case reverberated in the NAFTA negotiations. Important changes were later made in the North American rules of origin for automobiles. *See* Chapter 4.

Special rules of origin for textiles and clothing were created under CFTA and then tightened under

NAFTA. Demanding "fabric-forward" production requirements were stipulated so as to exclude third party textile goods from CFTA free trade. Certain fabrics (like silk) were exempt from these special CFTA origin requirements.

Product Standards

Canada and the United States focused on technical product standards as nontariff trade barriers in Chapter 6 of their agreement. Unusually, and importantly, Chapter 6 did not apply to state, provincial or local governments. The GATT Code on Technical Barriers to Trade of 1979 was affirmed by the two countries. This Code provided that federal technical standards and product certification systems could not be used to create obstacles to trade, and foreign goods had to be treated no less favorably on standards than domestic goods. Coverage of process and production methods (PPMs) was omitted from the 1979 Code.

Under CFTA, "standards-related measures" (SRM) (including production processes) and "product approval procedures" were subject to free trade goals. (Article 603). If the demonstrable purpose of standards was to achieve legitimate domestic objectives without excluding goods fulfilling those objectives, then CFTA's terms were met. Otherwise, a disguised obstacle to Canada–United States trade might occur and breach the treaty. Regarding each other's standards and certification systems, Canada and the United States generally granted mutual recognition. This approach meant that most goods certified as meeting technical standards by Canada or the United States could be freely traded.

A separate and detailed Chapter 7 was created for agricultural, food and beverage products. For these goods, a unification or harmonization approach was adopted for both standards and inspection procedures. In further contrast, CFTA's harmonized "sanitary and phyto-sanitary" (SPS) rules were made binding on state, provincial and local governments.

Free Trade Exceptions

Article 1201 of CFTA incorporated Article XX of the GATT 1947 agreement. Article XX creates general exceptions to the free movement of goods. These exceptions, however, may not be used in ways constituting "a means of arbitrary or unjustifiable discrimination" or "a disguised restriction on international trade."

The exceptions to international free trade in goods found in Article XX of the GATT include restraints of trade justified on grounds of public morals, prison labor, protection of human, animal or plant life or health, compliance with laws and regulations which are compatible with the GATT, and protection of national historic or artistic treasures. Article XX also exempts international restraints of trade undertaken to conserve natural resources (jointly undertaken with restraints on the domestic sector), to adhere to intergovernmental commodity agreements or domestic price stabilization programs, and in response to supply shortages.

Canada attempted to invoke Article XX to conserve Pacific salmon and herring as exhaustible natural resources by means of "landing" requirements. A CFTA dispute settlement panel ruled against Canada, finding that these requirements were enacted to restrain trade as well as conserve the species. CDA–89–1807–01. The panel doubted that the alleged conservation benefits were sufficiently large to justify the commercial inconvenience of landing *all* salmon and herring caught in Canada's Pacific waters. Despite this ruling, and CFTA Commission efforts at compromise, Canada has continued to impose limited landing requirements as Canadian fisherman assert excessive catches by U.S. boats.

A second group of general exceptions to free trade borrowed from the GATT deal with "national security." Article 2003 of CFTA was essentially lifted from Article XXI of the GATT 1947 agreement. Under it, restrictions on the flow of security-related information, actions to protect national security interests (such as non-proliferation of nuclear weapons), and United Nations peace and security obligations were recognized exceptions to CFTA free trade. However, there was a special agreement regarding energy goods. Such goods could not be restricted except as necessary to: (1) supply the Canadian or United States military when facing domestic armed conflicts; (2) fulfill critical defense contracts; (3) implement nuclear non-proliferation agreements; or (4) respond to direct threats of disruption in the supply of nuclear defense materials. This proviso reinforced the general CFTA commitments made to free trade in energy discussed below.

Canadian Cultural Industries

Canada has a long history of supporting cultural industries through investment, financial, tax and other governmental acts. The free trade agreement between Canada and the United States excluded "cultural industries" from its scope, and this exclusion has been retained under NAFTA. The argument for this exclusion is not to keep American culture out, but instead to assure a Canadian presence as well. Indeed, Canada maintains that it has neither attempted nor succeeded in keeping out American cultural products. That certainly seems right. Over 90 percent of Canada's movie screens and more than 80 percent of its news and TV broadcasts are U.S.–controlled. Books of U.S. origin occupy 60 percent of all Canadian shelf space and U.S. magazines take 80 percent of the English-language market.

Cultural industries are defined in CFTA and NAFTA as those engaged in publishing, distributing or selling:

- books, periodicals and newspapers (except their printing or typesetting);

- films or videos; audio or video music recordings; or printed or machine readable music;

- public radio communications;
- radio, television and cable TV broadcasting; and
- satellite programming and broadcasting network services. (Article 2012).

One practical effect of securing the cultural industries exclusion was to insulate Canada's broadcasting regulations from regional scrutiny. In Canada, content requirements and airtime rules are an important means by which the Canadian Radio–Television and Telecommunications Commission (CRTC) restricts the amount of foreign broadcast material. Current broadcasting regulations employ a quota system mandating Canadian content for a minimum of 60 percent of all programming and 50 percent of prime time. Comparable quotas apply to films, broadcast TV, cable TV and satellite transmissions. "Canadian content" is calculated under a points system traditionally requiring that the producer be Canadian and that at least 6 of 10 key creative positions be filled by Canadians. In addition, most production and distribution expenses must be paid to Canadians.

The requirements for radio are similar and focus on the nationality of the composer and performer, and the location and performance of the selection. The government also provides subsidies and tax incentives for national broadcasting enterprises which have financial difficulty in complying with content quotas. Furthermore, investment regulations effectively limit U.S. ownership or control of

Canadian cultural enterprises. For example, in 1996 Canada refused to permit Borders to open a super-bookstore in Toronto even after securing a Canadian partner as a majority owner. Ironically, although these economically driven rules ensure a national presence in broadcasting, they do not guarantee Canadian cultural content. Moreover, there is a thriving gray market for dishes aimed at U.S. satellites. More broadly, the Internet promises to undermine Canada's cultural industry trade restraints in ways that will likely avoid even the most determined regulator.

In contrast, there is no cultural industry exclusion under NAFTA applicable to Mexico–United States free trade. Integration of U.S.-Mexican cultural industries is occurring. In 1996, for example, the United States and Mexico reached agreement allowing companies in either country to compete for provision of satellite services, including direct-to-home and direct broadcast services. Each country retains the right to impose "reasonable" ownership, content and advertising regulations, but Mexico (unlike Canada) will not impose local content requirements.

There are exceptions and qualifications to the general exclusion of Canadian cultural industries from CFTA and NAFTA free trade. Tariff reductions were specified under CFTA for film, cassettes, records, cameras, musical instruments and the like. Additional tariff reductions were agreed to in NAFTA. Responding to a United States complaint about

Canadian cable TV "pirates," copyright royalties must be paid when U.S.-sourced free transmissions are retransmitted to the Canadian public by cable. In addition, no alteration or non-simultaneous retransmission of such broadcasts is permitted without the permission of the copyright holder. Likewise, no retransmission of cable or pay TV can occur without such authorization.

Occasionally, United States investors may acquire a Canadian cultural industry company by merger or acquisition. If ordered to divest, the U.S. investor must be paid open market value by Canada. Apart from these exceptions, the Canadian cultural industry exclusion covers the entire gamut of the NAFTA agreement. It applies goods, services, investment, intellectual property, and dispute settlement.

Canada's cultural industry exception to free trade comes with a price. The United States can unilaterally implement retaliation for cultural industry protection. The U.S. can undertake "measures of equivalent commercial effect" against acts that would have been "inconsistent" with CFTA but for the cultural industries exclusion. (Article 2005.2). There is no need to utilize CFTA's dispute settlement procedures prior to retaliation, which can be anything except a violation of the free trade agreement. The United States could, for example, pursue "Section 301" investigations and unilateral retaliation under the Trade Act of 1974. *See* R. Folsom, M. Gordon and J. A. Spanogle, *International Trade and Investment in a Nutshell*. Each year the United

States Trade Representative (USTR) must identify new Canadian acts, policies and practices affecting cultural industries.

Both Canada and the United States have sought to minimize the potential for cultural industry disputes through negotiations. The "successful" resolution of the Country Music Television (CMT) dispute in 1995 is often cited as an example. CMT of Nashville had, in the absence of a Canadian competitor, been licensed as a Canadian cable TV distributor. When a competitor emerged, CMT's license was revoked by the CRTC. CMT then petitioned the USTR for Section 301 relief, and an investigation was commenced. Intergovernmental negotiations resulted in the creation of a partnership of the two competitors, which was then licensed by the CRTC.

Cultural industry disputes have also been diverted from CFTA by using the World Trade Organization as an alternative forum. In March of 1997, a WTO Dispute Settlement Panel ruled that Canada's taxes, import regulations and postal subsidies concerning magazines violated the GATT 1994 agreement. WT/DS31/R, 3–14–97. This longstanding dispute centered on *Sports Illustrated*. Canada was seeking to protect and ensure "Canadian issues" of periodicals and prevent the export of its advertising revenues. The United States overcame culturally-based Canadian policies by electing to pursue WTO remedies, although Canada's compliance was disputed. In May of 1999, a settlement was reached. United States publishers may now wholly–own Canadian magazines. In addition, Canada will permit U.S. split–run editions without Canadian editorial content. Such editions may contain Canadian advertisements not in excess of 12 percent by lineage (rising to 18 percent in several years).

Professor Oliver Goodenough has thoughtfully analyzed Canada's preoccupation with culture. *See* 15 Ariz. J. Int'l & Comp. Law 203 (1998). He believes that the cultural industry exclusion reflects a weak national identity and that a principal purpose is to rally Canadians around their flag in a "recurring pageant of threat and defense." Professor Goodenough notes that the "war" against Hollywood is primarily protective of Anglophone Canada. Francophone Canada, with a healthy cultural identity, has already demonstrated a resilience to U.S. and Anglophonic Canadian influences.

Reaching into the literature on "culture transmission theory," Professor Goodenough finds that most foreign influences will "bounce off" healthy cultures without government intervention or, at the very least, compartmentalize such influences in ways which separate them from hearth and home. He concludes that Canada is "defending the imaginary to death" and if it continues to press its cultural protection policies: "[I]t will indeed be to the death, a death brought about not by 'invasion' from the south, but by the incomparably better claims to culturally-based nationhood possessed by Francophone Quebec and by the First Nation Peoples. Rather than acting as a rallying cry for national preservation, cultural protection provides the intellectual basis for a break-up of Canada.''

Procurement

The GATT Procurement Code of 1979, along with past (1986) and future (1995) amendments, was incorporated by reference into CFTA. The agreement, however, surpassed the Code as it existed in 1989 in several important ways. The number of goods eligible for free procurement trade was increased, the value of eligible contracts decreased to $25,000 U.S. and its equivalent in Canadian dollars, and a general rule of most-favored-treatment for goods with at least 50 percent cost-based CFTA origin was established. Canada and the United States also agreed to create opportunities to challenge procurement awards before administrative authorities, a remedy followed in NAFTA and the 1995 WTO Procurement Code.

Temporary Import Restraints

In a step well ahead of the rest of the world, Canada and the United States agreed to dramatically reduce their rights to take unilateral, temporary action against import surges. When such surges cause or threaten serious injury to domestic producers of similar or competing products, Article XIX (the "escape clause") of the GATT permits taking relief in the form of tariffs, quotas, voluntary trade restraints or other protection measures. Nations impacted by such relief can retaliate equivalently. Prior to 1998, Canada and the United States significantly limited each other's right to pursue *bilateral* escape clause relief. After 1997, CFTA totally eliminated bilateral escape clause relief except with the other's unlikely consent. This ban continues in effect under NAFTA.

A different type of escape clause relief (known as "global actions") can be undertaken when the trade involves third parties. If global actions are taken under the GATT, neither Canada nor the United States may restrict imports from the other unless they are "substantial" and "contributing importantly" to injury or its threat. (Article 1102).

While the huge amount of trade between Canada and the United States is not always harmonious, CFTA has virtually taken Canada–United States trade out of escape clause proceedings. In contrast, NAFTA establishes a number of escape clauses to insure against the possibility of import surges from Mexico. Temporary import restraints are even subject to a special "understanding" supplementing NAFTA. *See* Chapter 4.

Wine, Beer and Spirits

The barriers to trade in alcoholic beverages between the United States and Canada presented a complex regulatory maze. Beer was so difficult that little agreement was reached and existing restraints were retained on both sides of the border. Wine and spirits were dissected under Chapter 8 of CFTA and these rules remain in force under NAFTA.

Nondiscriminatory national treatment and most-favored sub-national treatment on licensing the sale of wine and spirits is required. Wine and spirits licensing must be undertaken using normal commercial considerations without causing disguised barriers to trade. Prompt, fair and objective appeals from administrative boards are to be made available to applicants from either side of the border. Furthermore, pricing decisions by public distributors must be nondiscriminatory, but may reflect actual cost-of-service differentials between handling domestic and imported wines or spirits. Canadian price mark-ups above those levels were removed between 1989 and 1995.

Regulations governing the distribution of wine and spirits are also subject to general national and most-favored treatment rules. Certain traditional exceptions continue in force. For example, Ontario and British Columbia oblige private sellers to favor wines originating in their provinces. And Quebec still requires food stores to sell wine bottled in that province. Canada did eliminate longstanding blending requirements on U.S. bulk distilled spirits, and the exclusive right to sell products labeled Bourbon Whiskey and Canadian Whiskey was recognized. Under NAFTA, exclusivity was also extended to Tennessee Whiskey and Mexican Tequila and Mezcal.

The extensive CFTA dismantling of restrictive trade regulations governing wine and spirits contrasts with the coverage of beer. Restrictive and discriminatory beer practices in effect on October 4, 1987 were retained. Only new restraints had to conform to the national and most-favored treatment obligations. Notably, Canada and the United States reserved their GATT rights and obligations for wine, spirits *and* beer. The GATT subsequently provided a venue to challenge some of the trade restraints on beer preserved by CFTA. *See* GATT Doc. DS17/R (Oct. 16, 1991); BISD395/206 (June 19, 1991). Ontario, for example, maintained "warehouse charges" and "environmental" taxes that mostly hit U.S. beer. The United States at one point slapped a 50 percent tariff on Ontario beer. By filing GATT complaints and engaging in negotiations, both countries largely succeeded in removing restraints of trade on beer. Hopefully this will at last resolve the Canada–U.S. "beer wars."

Energy

Canada exports large amounts of oil, gas, coal, electricity and uranium to the United States. This helps meet the energy-hungry needs of the United States. Thus the CFTA provisions on trade in energy goods contained in Chapter 9 were unusually significant. Similar provisions have been retained under NAFTA, but there is a dispute about their meaning if an energy crisis occurs. *See* Chapter 4.

The Canadian National Energy Board (NEB) regulates trade in energy goods by licensing surplus exports. The NEB has the power to regulate the price of Canadian energy imports and exports, determining whether prices are "just and reasonable." The United States perceived this price regulation as constituting minimum export price controls. Article 902(2) of the CFTA agreement bans such price controls. CFTA also disallows charging higher than domestic prices for energy exports. Furthermore, since Canada taxes the export of energy goods, Article 903 prohibits discriminatory taxation. Export taxes and fees are permissible only if they are imposed domestically, and Canada has adjusted export taxes on energy as a consequence.

Perhaps most importantly for the national security of the United States, Canadian law authorizes the NEB to restrain energy exports in times of crisis, as Canada did during the world oil shocks of the 1970s. Article 904(a) of CFTA is less than a model of clarity but seems to remove this authorization as it might apply to exports to the United States. Canada appears obliged in a crisis to maintain the prior proportion of exports to domestic production. The standard proportions among the various energy exports to the United States should also be maintained. The only exception to these duties is if sharing under the International Energy Program is imposed.

Motor Vehicles

Under their bilateral Auto Pact of 1965, Canada and the United States substantially embraced free trade in new automobiles and OEM parts. The Auto Pact was retained under CFTA (and NAFTA) subject to some changes. Tariffs on auto parts traded between Canada and the United States were extinguished. Canada's historic blockage of the importation of used vehicles from the United States was also eliminated. The United States adopted the more rigorous 50 percent regional content test of origin found in CFTA, but permitted manufacturers to average their value content over 12 months.

On the Canadian side, the Auto Pact was limited under CFTA to the Big Three and by special exception CAMI (a General Motors–Suzuki joint venture). No other manufacturers (including various Japanese companies) could acquire preferential Auto Pact status. They and other manufacturers had to meet the general CFTA rule of origin content requirements. Canada further agreed to abolish tariff refunds and waivers for non-Auto Pact producers. But Canada retained its sales to production performance ratio obligations and various "Canadian value-added" content rules for Auto Pact companies.

By 1998 the United States and Canada had removed virtually all tariffs on automotive goods.

Services

The United States, with many highly competitive service providers, sought a general commitment to free trade in services from Canada. Chapters 14 and 17 of CFTA make it clear that the U.S. failed to obtain free trade in services as a general rule. Substantial free trade in "covered" services was all that could be agreed. Annex 1408 of the CFTA agreement lists the services subject to its free provision rules. This list included some glaring omissions, such as transportation, that were not remedied until NAFTA.

Service providers and service seekers acquired benefits under CFTA. The "provision" of covered services included the right to be located in one country and service clients in the other. Provision embraced production, distribution, sale, purchase, marketing, delivery and use of covered services. Provision also included access to and use of domestic distribution systems. Beneficiaries could establish a "commercial presence" to distribute, market, deliver or facilitate covered services, such as establishing a sales agency or branch office in the other country. The right to invest in order to provide covered services was also protected. Indeed, almost *any* activity associated with the provision of covered services was allowed, including the organization, control, operation, maintenance and disposition of companies, branches, agencies, offices or other facilities to conduct business, as well as borrowing money and handling property.

Who could provide services was clarified in Article 201 of the CFTA agreement. Canadian and United States nationals *and* enterprises principally carrying on business in either country were the main beneficiaries. Such businesses had to be incorporated or otherwise constituted under Canadian or United States laws. The Agreement's focus on principal place of business meant that Canadian or U.S.

businesses owned or controlled by individuals or companies from other nations benefited from free trade in CFTA-covered services. Denial of these third party benefits was possible only if the service was provided "indirectly." This exception functioned like a rule of origin. It ensured that only service providers with substantial businesses in Canada or the United States could partake of free trade.

Cross-border CFTA service providers and seekers received "no less favorable" treatment than nationals and enterprises under Canadian and United States laws. For each federal government, national treatment was the general rule. Each state, province or local government was obliged to grant most-favored treatment to service providers and seekers. Ironically, while California could give less than most-favored treatment to New York service providers, it could not do so to Canadians. Since CFTA's beneficiaries included enterprises principally carrying on business in Canada or the United States, third party subsidiaries qualified for national and most-favored services treatment.

There were significant exceptions to the CFTA standards for service providers. Canada and the United States indefinitely retained (in their 1989 form) inconsistent statutes and regulations. Furthermore, Article 1402.3 allowed for deviations in treatment for prudential, fiduciary, health and safety or consumer protection reasons. Any such different treatment had to be "equivalent in effect" to that applied domestically for the same reasons. No deviation could require the establishment of a commercial presence in order to provide services in the other country. And, borrowing from GATT 1947 language relating to goods, no deviation (including tax laws), could serve as a means to "arbitrary or unjustifiable discrimination" or a "disguised restriction" on CFTA trade in services.

Canada and the United States retained their own licensing and certification systems for services. They agreed that these systems should "relate principally to competence or the ability to provide" covered services. (Article 1403) Licensing and certification could not discriminatorily impair or restrain access. Existing inconsistent statutes and regulations were indefinitely retained, but no new licensing or certification statute or regulation could require a commercial presence, arbitrarily discriminate, or disguise a trade restraint.

Financial Services

The provisions of Chapter 17 of CFTA reflect the complexity and sensitivity of the financial services sector. For purposes of Chapter 17, "financial services" were defined so as to exclude securities underwriting and sales of insurance policies. Insurance services were generally a covered service under Chapter 14 of CFTA.

Each country made commitments to alter specific statutes and regulations to benefit the other's financial sector. These commitments were retained under NAFTA. Canada made commitments on financial services in three key sectors:

(1) greater U.S. ownership of Canadian banks;

(2) deregulation of U.S.-controlled foreign bank subsidiaries; and

(3) reduced application of Canada's foreign investment control laws.

The United States also made three major commitments on financial services:

(1) permission for U.S. banks to underwrite Canadian debt;

(2) extension of future U.S. Glass–Steagall Act (48 Stat. 162) amendments to Canadian-controlled financial institutions; and

(3) a promise not to restrict interstate branching rules.

The Canadian commitments allow United States residents and U.S. companies controlled by such persons to acquire Canadian banks and federally regulated trust, loan and life insurance companies. However, no one person may own more than 10 percent of a Schedule A bank class of securities. Limits on the total domestic assets of banking subsidiaries controlled by U.S. citizens or permanent residents were removed, as were restraints on the transfer of loans from subsidiaries to their parent companies. Moreover, new branches of U.S.-controlled banking subsidiaries may be opened without getting the approval the Minister of Finance. More broadly, Canada agreed not to apply its investment review powers over U.S. financial institutions in a manner that would be inconsistent with the "aims" of Chapter 17.

The United States commitments permit federally regulated U.S. banks to underwrite and market the debt of Canada, its political subdivisions, and the debt of Canadian agencies backed by full faith and credit. This authority is an exception to the general prohibition against U.S. banks dealing in securities contained in the Glass–Steagall Act of 1933. Canadian public debt has been more readily sold in the United States as a consequence. If the U.S. amends the Glass–Steagall Act or its regulations at any future time (a longstanding issue), Canadian-controlled financial institutions must be given equal treatment. For these limited purposes, a financial institution controlled directly or indirectly by persons who ordinarily reside in Canada suffices. In the event of federal regulation of interstate branches, the United States agreed not to adopt or apply any laws that would be more restrictive on Canadian banks than those in force at the state level on October 4, 1987.

These commitments not withstanding, Canada and the United States publicly expressed mutual dissatisfaction with treatment of financial institutions in the other's country. Both promised no reduction in existing rights and privileges, except if the benefits from future deregulation of financial markets are not extended to each other absent "normal regulatory and prudential considerations."

Canada and the United States now give each other notice and an opportunity to comment on proposed financial regulations. Consultation between the Canadian Department of Finance and the U.S. Treasury Department is frequent. Such consultations generally displace regional dispute settlement procedures.

Investment

Chapter 16 of CFTA governed laws, regulations and policies generally affecting cross-border investment by Canadian or United States investors. However, financial services, cultural industries, transportation services, government procurement and services not covered by CFTA did not benefit from Chapter 16. CFTA created a rule of national treatment at the federal level and most-favored treatment at lower levels of government. Such rules covered establishing new businesses, acquiring or selling existing ones, and conducting business operations.

The investment rules of CFTA applied *only* to United States and Canadian nationals, governments and enterprises they controlled. This differed from CFTA free trade in services which benefited third party providers established or principally doing business in Canada or the United States. Nevertheless, it was forbidden to require that shareholders include nationals of either country. Nor could investors be forced due to nationality to divest a qualified investment.

Perhaps most importantly, Canada undertook to amend its 1985 Investment Canada Act (ICA). The ICA normally applied to foreign acquisitions of Canadian businesses worth more than 5 million Canadian dollars. CFTA did not suspend the ICA's application to U.S. acquisitions of existing Canadian businesses, but it did alter the thresholds triggering Canadian review. Only direct acquisitions or sales of Canadian companies subject to CFTA that exceed $150 million Canadian dollars could be reviewed by Canada's investment authorities. Indirect acquisitions of Canadian businesses were not reviewable unless they fell in the economic sectors excluded from CFTA. These commitments were continued under NAFTA.

The United States cannot trigger dispute settlement about any Canadian decision under the ICA regarding an acquisition by a U.S. investor. Significantly from the point of view of existing U.S. investors in Canada, the $150 million threshold also triggers a "right of exit." Canadian investments below that amount can be sold to non-Canadians without ICA review.

Performance requirements were a central focus of CFTA's investment rules. They could not be imposed as a condition to allowing or operating an investment. Article 1603 prohibited (for CFTA investors) performance requirements on exports, obligations to substitute or purchase local goods or services, and domestic content minimums. Even so, certain types of performance requirements (notably employment, technology transfer, or research and development obligations) were permissible for CFTA investors. With third party investors, any performance requirement could be used, provided this did not have a "significant impact" on trade between Canada and the United States.

Direct or indirect nationalization or expropriation of investments held by each other's investors was banned by CFTA. The only exception was for non-discriminatory public purposes in accordance with due process of law and upon payment of prompt, adequate and effective compensation at fair market value. Cross-border CFTA investors were free to transfer their profits, dividends, royalties, fees, interest and other earnings or proceeds from the sale or liquidation of their investments. Canada or the United States could prevent such transfers (acting equitably, without discrimination and in good faith) under their bankruptcy, insolvency, creditors' rights, securities, criminal, currency transfer reporting, tax withholding or court judgment enforcement laws. New tax or subsidy rules were allowed provided they did not arbitrarily or unjustifiably discriminate between Canadian or U.S. investors, or function as a disguised restriction on the CFTA benefits of those investors.

Movement of Business Persons

Chapter 15 of CFTA governed *temporary* entry for business persons engaged in trading goods or services, or cross-border investors. Similar provisions can be found under NAFTA. Four groups of persons were granted preferential treatment: (1) business visitors; (2) professionals; (3) traders and (substantial) investors; and (4) intra-company transferees. In the event of disputes concerning the entry of business persons, all available appeals in Canada or the United States had to be first pursued. Only if there was a pattern of restrictive practices was dispute settlement under Chapter 18 of CFTA an option.

All four categories were exempted from labor certification or employment validation tests demonstrating in advance that a local person could not fulfill the needs that these business persons temporarily met. On the other hand, all such business persons had to meet the standard national security, public health and safety requirements for entry. Except for business visitors, employment authorization prior to entering the other country was required. Tens of thousands of Canadian professionals took advantage of CFTA to head south for employment in the United States.

CFTA Dispute Settlement

Dispute settlement under NAFTA has replaced comparable procedures first established under CFTA. Chapter 18 of CFTA employed consultations and if necessary arbitration to settle most kinds of disputes. Chapter 19 of CFTA utilized special binational panels to resolve antidumping and countervailing duty disputes. All of the CFTA dispute settlement decisions, including those cited in this chapter, have been reproduced and analyzed in R.

Folsom, M. Gordon and J. A. Spanogle, *Handbook of NAFTA Dispute Settlement*.

None of CFTA's dispute settlement procedures were mandatory. For example, disputes that could be resolved under CFTA, the GATT 1947 agreement, or the GATT Tokyo Round Codes could be pursued in either forum. Practically speaking, forum shopping as between Chapters 18 and 19 and the GATT (now WTO) was perfectly acceptable. However, once an avenue of relief was chosen by the complaining party, the dispute had to be resolved there exclusively.

One reason behind this legitimization of forum shopping was the sorry state of GATT and GATT Code dispute settlement procedures in 1989. "Working-groups" or panels composed of experts who were not from the nations in dispute issued a "report." This report made findings of fact, rendered conclusions of law, and made remedial recommendations which were forwarded to the GATT Council. Lengthy, cumbersome and subject to a consensus vote in the GATT Council, GATT dispute settlement in 1989 was not really binding as each nation could negate the panel's ruling. Even if the process worked, compliance was essentially voluntary.

The GATT (now WTO) does offer political advantages as a dispute settlement forum. Its membership of over 130 nations frequently means that others will join in the dispute, thus raising visibility and pressure. This was true for CFTA in 1989 and remains true for NAFTA today. However, NAFTA has complicated the forum selection process. *See* Chapter 8.

Chapter 18 Dispute Settlement

Dispute settlement under Chapter 18 of the CFTA agreement applied in most instances, but notably not concerning financial services. The Canada–United States Trade Commission (TC) was the center of the Chapter 18 dispute settlement process. International trade representatives of Canada and the United States or their designees constituted the CFTA Trade Commission, which was aided by Secretariats in Ottawa and Washington, D.C. There were three stages to Chapter 18 dispute settlement: (1) Bilateral Consultations; (2) Trade Commission Review; and (3) Binding Arbitration.

The CFTA Trade Commission has since 1994 largely been supplanted by the NAFTA Trade Commission. The CFTA Commission provided a forum to discuss CFTA disputes. Consultations always preceded Commission deliberations. Questions of implementation, interpretation, application, allegedly inconsistent action, or "nullification and impairment" of benefits expected under the CFTA agreement fell within its jurisdiction. The CFTA Commission had the power to delegate its responsibilities to ad hoc committees and working-groups. It could also obtain the advice of nongovernmental individuals or groups. The Commission promulgated its own rules and procedures and functioned by cooperative consensus.

Notice as far in advance as possible was required of any proposed law with the potential to materially affect the operation of CFTA. With or without notice, Canada and the United States undertook to consult in good faith and "make every attempt" at a mutually satisfactory resolution. A meeting of the CFTA Trade Commission became mandatory only if no resolution was had within 30 days. The Commission then sought to resolve the dispute promptly, relying at its discretion on mediators acceptable to both sides.

For most disputes the CFTA Commission could refer the matter to binding arbitration only by mutual agreement. If no consensus was reached to refer the dispute to arbitration, the fallback was to appoint a panel of experts. Only in disputes concerning emergency escape clause proceedings was binding arbitration mandatory. The Commission could set the terms for arbitration of CFTA disputes, but unless it directed otherwise an arbitration panel was established following the provisions of Article 1807. Under Article 1807, two panelists were chosen by each side with the fifth member (absent agreement) chosen by lot. A list of qualified panelists was established by the Commission. The confidential arbitration panel set its own procedural rules, including a hearing and the right of reply.

An innovative provision of CFTA authorized the submission of memoranda by the governments of Canada and the United States acting jointly if possible, or singly if not, to courts or administrative tribunals in either country. Memoranda on interpretative issues could be submitted whenever the governments of Canada or the United States considered it meritorious. Such submissions could only concern issues of interpretation, but they could be requested by a national court or tribunal entertaining CFTA issues in litigation. This little used request authority resembled somewhat the advisory ruling procedure followed in Europe as between national courts and the European Court of Justice.

A related authority can be found in Chapter 20 of the NAFTA agreement. Article 2020 authorizes the NAFTA Commission to forward "agreed interpretations" to national judicial and administrative bodies. If no agreed interpretation can be reached, individual member state opinions can be submitted. All such submissions are *not* binding upon the national court or tribunal considering how to interpret NAFTA.

Arbitration Decisions under Chapter 18

Chapter 18 of CFTA resulted in five binding arbitrations. Other trade disputes were taken to the GATT, and some contentious issues resolved during the NAFTA and Uruguay Round negotiations.

In the first Chapter 18 arbitration panel, the United States complained against Canadian landing requirements for fish (mostly salmon) caught in their waters. A prior GATT panel ruling against Canadian fish export controls had led to the landing requirements. The CFTA arbitration panel ruled with one dissent in favor of the United States argument that the requirements unfairly increased the burden of exporting Canadian fish in violation of GATT Article XI and were not excepted under GATT Article XX (discussed above). CDA–89–1807–01. Canada accepted the panel's findings. A mutually satisfactory settlement was then reached, but salmon fishing in the Northwest remains a remarkably divisive issue to this day.

The second arbitration panel under Chapter 18 upheld United States limits on the sale of undersized lobsters. By a split vote, argued under GATT Articles III and XI, the panel decided that since both Canadian and United States lobsters were affected there was no unlawful trade restraint. USA–89–1807–01. The third CFTA panel upheld, contrary to a U.S. Customs Service ruling, Canada's practice of including certain interest payments in the costs of production of automobiles. USA–92–1807–01. This dispute arose when Canada determined CFTA content in ascertaining origin under Article 304. The panel followed the Vienna Convention of the Law of Treaties in interpreting CFTA even though the United States is not a party to that Convention.

The fourth arbitration panel generally agreed with Canada's interpretation of Article 701.3 of the CFTA agreement. CDA–92–1807–01. Minimum pricing of durum wheat for sale to the United States was at issue. This dispute was surrounded by U.S. perceptions of unfair subsidization of Canadian wheat exports. Once again, the Vienna Convention was invoked to interpret CFTA. Canadian wheat exports have remained the center of considerable controversy, trade complaints and intergovernmental memoranda of understanding imposing tariff rate quotas.

The fifth and final CFTA arbitration panel concerned Puerto Rico's refusal to allow entry of "improperly certified" long-life milk from Quebec. USA–93–1807–01. Articles III and XI of the GATT were disputed. This panel generally supported the U.S. position that it was entitled to enforce its standards against Canadian goods. The panel suggested that if both countries were essentially using the same inspection standards then entry should have been allowed as a matter of good faith so as to avoid nullification and impairment of CFTA trade benefits. Ongoing equivalency discussions between the two trade partners were recommenced.

Chapter 19 Dispute Settlement

Dispute settlement under CFTA Chapter 19 was limited to two types of international trade law actions: antidumping and countervailing duty proceedings. Both are GATT-authorized and regulated. *See* R. Folsom, M. Gordon, J.A. Spanogle, *International Trade and Investment in a Nutshell.* Such proceedings are typically commenced at the request of industries that face import competition and can ultimately result in the imposition of special tariffs on imported goods. Antidumping duties apply to imported goods or services sold at below home country prices that injure or threaten domestic industries. Countervailing duties apply to imported goods that have benefited from export or specific domestic governmental subsidies and have injured or threaten national industries. Thus antidumping actions challenge private sector price discrimination while countervailing duty actions question governmental acts. The amount of retaliatory tariff duties is the margin of the dump or the level of subsidy determined to exist. Many antidumping duty proceedings (the most prevalent) are "settled" when the exporter agrees to raise its prices. *See* the *Tomatoes Dispute* in Chapter 8. Countervailing duty disputes may also be settled by intergovernmental accords. *See* the *Softwood Lumber Agreement* (below).

Antidumping and countervailing duty actions had been frequently used by the United States to impede entry of Canadian goods. Chapter 19 thus attempted to respond to critical Canadian concerns.

Canada and the United States had long acknowledged through the GATT the unfairness of dumping and subsidy practices. Unlike the European Union, they were unwilling to eliminate internal utilization of these trade remedies. GATT Codes on antidumping and countervailing duties provided the basic ground rules, but GATT dispute settlement was inadequate in the 1980s. Most importantly, each party was distrustful of judicial review in the other's courts of administrative antidumping and countervailing duty determinations. The end result was a unique form of dispute settlement under Chapter

19 of CFTA that was largely replicated in NAFTA, but exists nowhere else in the world.

Under Chapter 19, binational panels of mutually approved experts (mostly international trade lawyers and law professors) ultimately decided antidumping and countervailing duty disputes. Prior to CFTA, the final resolution of such disputes had been in the national courts. Each country selected two panelists with an additional panelist chosen by mutual agreement. Each side had four opportunities to reject the other side's proposed panelists. No cause for rejection was required. A majority of the panelists had to be lawyers in good standing.

The administrative proceedings of Canada and the United States determining the existence of dumping or a countervailable subsidy remained in place. These decisions are made by the International Trade Administration (Commerce Dept.) in the United States and by the Deputy Minister of National Revenue for Customs and Excise in Canada. Likewise, the national proceedings used to decide if there has been material injury (or its threat) to a domestic industry were also retained. These decisions are made by the U.S. International Trade Commission and the Canadian Import Tribunal.

All Chapter 19 proceedings were pursued under the laws of Canada and the United States, neither of which was substantively changed by CFTA. The critical change was the remarkable surrender of judicial sovereignty accomplished by Chapter 19. After CFTA, all final national administrative determinations in antidumping or countervailing duty proceedings were only "appealable" by interested parties to a quasi-judicial binational CFTA panel.

When an antidumping or subsidy proceeding came before a CFTA panel, the legal principles that would have been used by a court in the importing country controlled. For binational panels reviewing final U.S. determinations this meant that U.S. Supreme Court and Federal Circuit Court of Appeal (but not Court of International Trade) decisions were binding precedent. By its terms, CFTA provided that previous panel decisions were not to be treated as precedent. NAFTA also retains these rules.

There were no new CFTA standards for review. With much controversy, each panel proceeded to apply the different standards of judicial review traditionally found in the law of Canada and the United States. For example, Canada's standards of review under the Federal Court Act § 28(1) are failure to observe principles of natural justice, jurisdictional abuse, errors in law, and pervasive, capricious or insupportable erroneous findings of fact. The standards of the U.S. Tariff Act of 1930 §§ 516A(b)(1)(A) and (B) are findings or conclusions unsupported by substantial evidence in the record or otherwise not in accordance with law.

There were over fifty Chapter 19 panel decisions, with more than two-thirds of them reviewing U.S. antidumping and countervailing duty determinations. Not surprisingly, trade in steel products garnered first place in the pursuit of market protection. The U.S. steel industry, in particular, has a long history of resorting to antidumping and countervailing duties to obtain shelter from import competition. Many observers have noted that the mere filing of AD and CVD complaints can produce some breathing room for domestic industries.

Most Chapter 19 panel decisions under CFTA were rendered in less than a year. Technically, these decisions either affirmed the final determination under review or, reversing, referred the determination back to the relevant administrative tribunal. It was up to that tribunal to take appropriate action. If it did not, and a second panel review took place, the agency was typically instructed to act in a not inconsistent manner by the second or (infrequently) third panel. The only further review, a final appeal by Canada or the United States (not the interested parties) of a panel decision, could come before an "Extraordinary Challenge Committee."(ECC) Such Committees were composed of three mutually acceptable judges.

ECC review of binational Chapter 19 panel decisions was intended to be truly extraordinary. In fact, there were only three such reviews (see below) between 1989 and 1994. All of them were raised by the United States. Many believe these challenges were politically motivated, in part to persuade Congress to extend fast track trade agreements authority to the President and in part to assuage key private sector interests. Challenges to CFTA (and

NAFTA) panel decisions are allowed only in limited circumstances such as if a panel member engaged in gross misconduct, was biased, or had a serious conflict of interest. Challenges can also be raised if the panel departed seriously from a fundamental rule of procedure or it manifestly exceeded its powers, authority or jurisdiction. The challenger has the duty to prove that the error alleged materially influenced the panel's decision and threatened the integrity of the review process.

Binational Panel and Extraordinary Challenge Committee Decisions Under Chapter 19

Chapter 19 dispute settlement under CFTA in the five years prior to NAFTA was voluminous. With a few exceptions, most analyses of these decisions suggest an objective and not terribly politicized process. But the ability of binational panels to expertly rule under Canadian and United States law has been hotly contested. A prominent U.S. judge involved in the infamous *Softwood Lumber* dispute wrote a blistering dissent. *See* ECC–94–1904–01–USA (Wilkey, J.) excerpted in Chapter 8. Some administrative determinations had to be repeatedly reviewed by CFTA panels before compliance was achieved. One must wonder whether Chapter 19, which was intended to reduce trade tensions and suspicions, did not instead intensify Canada–U.S. antidumping and countervailing duty disputes.

Appeals to CFTA Extraordinary Challenge Committees demonstrated limited opportunities for relief. For example, the first Extraordinary Challenge

Committee decision concerned U.S. countervailing duties on Canadian exports of pork. ECC–91–1904–01–USA. The initial binational panel decision questioned the substantiality of the evidence supporting the International Trade Commission's domestic injury determination. Upon reconsideration, the ITC found a threat of material injury to the U.S. domestic pork industry for a second time. A second binational panel decision ruled that the ITC had exceeded its notice for the proceedings, and issued specific evidentiary instructions to the ITC.

The ITC's next decision bitterly denounced the second binational panel's ruling. The ITC asserted that the panel's decision violated fundamental principles of the CFTA Agreement and contained egregious errors of U.S. law. Nevertheless, the ITC acquiesced. It determined no threat of material injury expressly (and only) because of the binding nature of the CFTA panel's decision. The United States Trade Representative alleged gross error and sought review by Extraordinary Challenge Committee of the panel's *Pork* rulings. The Committee unanimously held that there was no gross error even if some of the panel determinations might not have followed U.S. rules of evidence. The Committee did caution panels not to rely on evidence not appearing in the record of the national proceedings.

The second extraordinary challenge concerned exports of live swine from Canada. EEC–93–1904–01–USA. Once again the Committee unanimously ruled against the challenge, although it did acknowledge that the panel may have made errors of law.

The bitterly disputed binational panel decisions on U.S. countervailing duty actions against Canadian exports of softwood lumber did not conclude with the third Extraordinary Challenge Committee proceeding in 1994 from which Judge Wilkey so vigorously dissented. Trade tensions and negotiations continued. Canada, the victor before the Challenge Committee (*See* Chapter 8), appeared to realize that it might lose the next time around if changes in U.S. countervailing duty law were recognized. Indeed, these changes were undertaken specifically for that purpose. In 1996, a "settlement" was reached.

The 1996 Softwood Lumber Agreement applies to Alberta, British Columbia, Ontario and Quebec. It committed Quebec, for example, to raising its "stumpage" (timbering) fees. British Columbia (the largest exporter) promised to impose taxes on shipments of lumber to the U.S. above designated levels starting at 9 billion board feet. In addition, the Canadian federal government will impose taxes if exports exceed 14.7 billion board feet. The U.S. government and forest industry, in turn, pledged not to commence a countervailing duty action for 5 years so long as the agreement is followed.

The legal and political controversy surrounding Chapter 19 panel decisions under CFTA sometimes blurs their practical consequences for tariffs and trade between the two countries. A careful reconstruction of that impact has been undertaken by a leading international trade attorney. *See Mercury,* 15 N.W. J. Int'l Law & Bus. 525 (1995). This study demonstrates that Canadian exporters were disproportionate beneficiaries in terms of Chapter 19 outcomes.

CHAPTER 3

GETTING TO NAFTA

Mexico, like Canada, is extremely dependent on market access to the United States. In 1993, just prior to NAFTA, approximately 75 percent of its exports went to the U.S. The Canada–United States Free Trade Agreement (CFTA) and European reluctance to favor Mexican trade prompted President Carlos Salinas to request free trade relations with the United States. President Bush was quick to support this goal, but most Canadians were less enthusiastic. In the end, the Canadians correctly calculated that they could not afford to ignore negotiations that might dilute or adversely impact the benefits they had obtained under CFTA. Initially defensive in their approach, the Canadians soon realized that they too had much to gain in negotiating NAFTA.

In an era when free trade was still a positive political issue in the United States, Congress authorized "fast track" negotiations. Under such negotiations, Congress must vote up or down on trade agreements without amending them. Congress was willing to authorize fast track negotiations because the President promised to keep it heavily involved during the NAFTA negotiations.

Negotiations to create a North American Free Trade Area for Canada, Mexico and the United States commenced in July of 1991. These negotiations moved along smoothly. About a year later, the NAFTA agreement was in final form. President Bush, running for reelection in November of 1992, notified Congress of his intent to sign the NAFTA agreement. This notice ensured a vivid political debate on the merits of free trade during the election.

Multi-millionaire Ross Perot, running as an independent, virulently attacked NAFTA. Governor Bill Clinton of Arkansas generally supported NAFTA, but promised to negotiate better protection for workers and the environment. After Clinton defeated Bush in the November 1992 elections, lame-duck President Bush signed the NAFTA agreement on behalf of the United States. This agreement, as did CFTA, allows any member to withdraw after 6 months notice.

Ratifying NAFTA

Ratification of the NAFTA agreement became hostage to Governor Clinton's campaign promises. Negotiations were re-opened in the Spring of 1993 after Clinton became President. Two "side or supplemental agreements" emerged from these negotiations. The first concerned labor rights and working conditions while the second focused on the environment. *See* Chapters 9 and 10. In addition, an "understanding" on protective relief from import surges was concluded. The original NAFTA agreement negotiated by President Bush, and the side agreements and understanding negotiated by President Clinton, were sent to Congress under fast track procedures in the Fall of 1993.

In a remarkable display of hostility, the NAFTA agreement was vigorously opposed in Congress. Ross Perot, Ralph Nader, unions, environmental groups, the religious and political right, the Congressional Black Caucus, and many others blasted NAFTA. But for the success of Vice President Al Gore in debating Ross Perot on national television, NAFTA might have failed in Congress. The final vote in the House of Representatives was 234 to 200, followed by a 61 to 38 affirmation in the Senate of the NAFTA Implementation Act of 1993. This Act, Public Law No. 103–182 (107 Stat. 2057), was accompanied by President Clinton's Statement of Administrative Action which provides a useful summary of required changes in United States law. The Implementation Act expressly provides that the NAFTA agreement does not modify U.S. law except as provided for by the Act.

Prime Minister Mulroney of Canada presciently secured approval of NAFTA prior to the Canadian elections in the Fall of 1993. Mulroney's Conservative Party was subsequently drummed out of office on a tide of anti-NAFTA sentiment. In Mexico, on the other hand, President Salinas had little difficulty in obtaining ratification of NAFTA from his PRI-controlled legislature.

Interpreting NAFTA

NAFTA's statement of objectives is important because Canada, Mexico and the United States have agreed to "interpret and apply" NAFTA in light of those objectives. The objectives of NAFTA are listed in Article 102 and include:

- The elimination of barriers to trade in and facilitation of cross-border movement of goods and services;

- promotion of conditions of fair competition;

- the increase "substantially" of investment opportunities;

- the provision of adequate and effective protection and enforcement of intellectual property rights;

- the creation of effective procedures for the implementation and application of the Agreement, for its joint administration, and for the resolution of disputes; and

- the establishment of a framework for further trilateral, regional and multilateral cooperation to expand and enhance the benefits of NAFTA.

The NAFTA partners also agreed to interpret the agreement in accordance with "applicable rules of international law." The reference to international law as an interpretive guide is somewhat ambiguous. International law on interpreting and applying treaties, conventions and international agreements is notably embodied in the Vienna Convention on the Law of Treaties. 8 Int'l Legal Mat. 769. The

United States has not joined in this agreement, but generally follows its principles. More broadly, the reference to international law as an interpretive guide may embrace general principles of international law widely accepted in the world community.

NAFTA, The Uruguay Round and Other International Agreements

The NAFTA agreement affirms each nation's rights and obligations under GATT 1947 and other international agreements, but a general rule of NAFTA supremacy is created in Article 103. Annex 300–B reinforces this rule of supremacy when there are inconsistencies with the Multifiber Arrangement Regarding International Trade in Textiles. However, this Arrangement, which permits extensive use of quotas in world textile trade, will be phased out by 2005 under the WTO Agreement on Textiles and Clothing (1995). In some instances, provisions of the GATT 1994 agreement are incorporated by specific reference into NAFTA. This is notably the case with GATT Articles III (National Treatment), XI (Quotas) and XX (Exceptions).

If conflicts emerge with other trade agreements, NAFTA prevails unless the NAFTA agreement provides otherwise. In some cases, the agreement does exactly that. Provisions of the CFTA agreement, for example, are frequently retained to govern Canada–U.S. and sometimes even Canada–Mexico trade relations. Annex 608.2 provides that NAFTA is not supreme over the Agreement on An International Energy Program. Article 2103 provides similarly for international tax conventions. Article 104 makes it clear that NAFTA will *not* prevail over the following environmental and conservation agreements:

1. The Washington Convention on International Trade in Endangered Species (1973, 1979);

2. The Montreal Protocol on Substances that Deplete the Ozone Layer (1987, 1990);

3. The Basel Convention on Control of Transboundary Movements of Hazardous Wastes and Their Disposal (1989);

4. The Canada–U.S. Agreement Concerning Transboundary Movements of Hazardous Waste (1986); and

5. The Mexico–U.S. Agreement on Cooperation for the Protection and Improvement of the Environment in the Border Area (1983).

NAFTA was implemented prior to final completion of the Uruguay Round of GATT negotiations and the creation of the World Trade Organization in 1995. NAFTA's relationship to the WTO Uruguay Round agreements is complex and less than clear, especially on the issue of which prevails in the event of conflict. Negotiated largely in parallel time frames, each influenced the other, but significant differences exist. NAFTA covers temporary entry for business persons, state trading and competition policy, which the Uruguay Round does not. The Uruguay Round covers customs valuation and pre-shipment inspection, which NAFTA does not.

On market access, investment and most services, NAFTA goes further and faster than the Uruguay Round WTO agreements. There is significant overlap on intellectual property where NAFTA's leading edge was particularly influential. The WTO Agreement on Agriculture, on the other hand, exceeded by a good measure NAFTA's trade opening initiatives. The Uruguay Round also addressed basic telecommunications, which was mostly omitted from NAFTA. The WTO has (since 1997) fostered an information technology tariff reduction agreement, but Mexico does not participate.

NAFTA Chapters and WTO Agreements

The NAFTA Chapters chart below indicates the closest parallel WTO agreements.

NAFTA	WTO AGREEMENTS
Chapter 3, Trade in Goods	General Agreement on Tariffs and Trade 1994, Agreement on Textiles and Clothing
Chapter 4, Rules of Origin	Agreement on Rules of Origin
Chapter 5, Customs Procedures	No parallel, but see Customs Valuation Code
Chapter 6, Energy and Basic Petrochemicals	No parallel
Chapter 7, Agriculture and SPS Measures	Agreement on Agriculture, Agreement on SPS Measures
Chapter 8, Emergency Action	Agreement on Safeguards
Chapter 9, Product and Service Standards	Agreement on Technical Barriers to Trade

NAFTA	WTO AGREEMENTS
Chapter 10, Procurement	Agreement on Government Procurement (optional)
Chapter 11, Investment	Agreement on Trade–Related Investment Measures (TRIMs)
Chapter 12, Cross–Border Trade in Services	General Agreement on Trade in Services (GATS)
Chapter 13, Enhanced Telecommunications	See GATS, Basic Telecommunications Covered
Chapter 14, Financial Services	See GATS
Chapter 15, Competition Policy, Monopolies and State Enterprises	No parallel, but see Understanding on Interpretation of GATT Article XVII
Chapter 16, Temporary Entry for Business Persons	No parallel
Chapter 17, Intellectual Property	Agreement on Trade–Related Aspects of Intellectual Property Rights (TRIPs)
Chapter 18, Administrative Provisions	Not applicable
Chapter 19, Antidumping and Countervailing Duty Dispute Settlement	No parallel, but see DSU and Agreement on Implementation of GATT Article VI
Chapter 20, Dispute Settlement	Understanding on Rules and Procedures Governing the Settlement of Disputes (DSU)
Chapter 21, Exceptions	See GATT Articles XX, XXI and Understanding on GATT Balance of Payments Provisions
Agreement on Environmental Cooperation	No parallel
Agreement on Labor Cooperation	No parallel

CHAPTER 4

GOODS

With the implementation of NAFTA, the United States enjoys free trade with the two biggest purchasers of U.S. goods. Canada was always the largest buyer of U.S. goods, and Mexico quickly surpassed Japan to become number two in the first year of NAFTA's operation. This Chapter will analyze the most important areas of growth in North American trading of goods.

NAFTA combines with CFTA to create a North American free trade area for goods. Phased tariff removals are the means to this end. Article 302 of NAFTA prohibits all parties from increasing tariffs or establishing new tariffs on North American goods. This provision had the practical effect of ensuring that many Mexican goods could continue to enter the United States on a duty free basis. This most often occurred prior to NAFTA under the U.S. program of generalized tariff preferences (GSP). The GSP program, with many exceptions and controls, grants duty free entry to goods from over 100 developing nations. *See* R. Folsom, M. Gordon and J.A. Spanogle, *International Trade and Investment in Nutshell*. After President Reagan "graduated" Hong Kong, Singapore, South Korea and Taiwan from the U.S. program in 1989, Mexico had ranked number one in GSP duty free imports. The United States GSP program no longer applies to Mexico.

Tariffs and Customs

Mexico has the highest average tariffs, the U.S has the lowest, and Canada falls in the middle. NAFTA preserved the 1998 deadline for the elimination of tariffs on goods traded between Canada and the United States. This gave Canadian exporters short-term market access advantages compared to their Mexican competitors who do not get full duty-free access to the U.S. until 2003. NAFTA phases out most tariffs on North American goods by 2003. By 2008, essentially all North American trade in goods is duty free. Four stages lead to this result, subject to agreement upon accelerated two-way or three-way tariff reductions.

The tariffs in effect on January 1, 1991 are the baseline. Prior to NAFTA, Mexico's average applied tariff on U.S. goods was 10 percent, while the comparable U.S. tariff on Mexican goods was 4 percent. Tariffs on Schedule A goods, about half of all U.S. exports to Mexico, were dissolved immediately in 1994. Schedule B goods were subject to 20 percent annual tariff reductions to January 1, 1998. Schedule C goods are being reduced 10 percent annually to January 1, 2003. Finally, tariffs on Schedule C+ goods are being removed at a 6.66 percent annual rate to January 1, 2008. Schedule C+ accommodates highly sensitive goods such as corn and beans into Mexico and orange juice and sugar into the United States. A few goods such as orange juice and furniture are not subject to straight-line tariff phase outs. Their tariffs are irregularly removed over time in so-called "kinky curves."

General customs fees, which are quasi-tariffs, were eliminated under CFTA in 1994. Health and safety inspection fees can be collected. The U.S. customs user fee was eliminated on Mexico–United States trade in North American goods on July 1, 1999. As under CFTA, *export* taxes or tariffs are generally prohibited. However, Mexico can employ them to keep essential foodstuffs like corn, flour and milk in the country. Since these products have traditionally been subsidized in Mexico, United States or Canadian buyers might otherwise deplete them. Mexico can also apply export charges temporarily to foodstuffs in short supply.

Canada, Mexico and the United States have retained their national tariffs for purposes of third party trade. NAFTA does, however, move slightly in the direction of a common external tariff. For example, semiconductors and local area network data processing equipment have had a common external tariff of zero and been freely traded since 1994. Article 308 coordinates the external tariffs for automatic data processing goods and parts. By 2004, these tariffs will be uniform. This means that nearly all computer imports will be treated as originating under NAFTA and can be freely traded.

Customs tariff refunds (drawback) and tariff waivers are addressed under NAFTA. Canada and the United States were scheduled to eliminate most drawbacks in 1996. This commitment was altered by Article 303 of NAFTA. The new approach limited drawbacks on Canada–United States trade. Drawbacks will be similarly limited in 2001 for Mexico–United States trade. Essentially, NAFTA provides that drawbacks are not authorized on goods originating in North America which pass duty free across borders. Drawbacks are permitted on non-originating goods. They can also be used with originating goods not yet subject to duty free treatment up to the lesser of the amount of tariff due upon crossing a NAFTA border or the amount of duties originally paid upon importation.

The net result is that by 2003, when most originating goods will circulate duty free within NAFTA, drawbacks are basically prohibited. This could have significant consequences. Canada and Mexico may ultimately lower their external tariffs to those of the United States so as to avoid penalizing manufacturers in their countries who can no longer receive tariff refunds. If this happens, and there have already been unilateral tariff changes of this kind in Canada and Mexico, a common NAFTA external tariff could evolve without formal agreement.

NAFTA also bans new tariff waivers which are tied to performance requirements. The types of performance requirements that are prohibited include: 1) Export minimums; 2) local content; 3) local substitution or purchase minimums; 4) trade balancing export to import ratios; and 5) mandatory foreign exchange inflows. Mexico is not obliged to participate except by way of Annex 304.1. In that Annex Mexico promised not to disproportionately alter existing tariff waivers. Mexico also agreed to freeze the list of goods to which it traditionally grants such waivers. However, all Mexican tariff waivers must be eliminated by 2001.

Impact on Maquiladoras

The NAFTA regime on drawbacks and tariff waivers is important to Mexico's export-driven maquiladora assembly plants (discussed in Chapter 1). Many maquiladoras have historically relied on tariff refunds and waivers on inputs. Under NAFTA, by 2001, Mexico must stop the beneficial application of tariff refunds and waivers to assembly plants if NAFTA free trade is desired. Full Mexican tariffs will apply to imported components, which will make it more difficult for goods assembled with components from outside NAFTA to qualify for NAFTA free trade.

Many Asian manufacturers using Mexican assembly plants will be impacted. As the drafters of NAFTA intended, there should be no preferentially tariffed "export platforms" into Canada or the United States. Some such manufacturers have already switched to North American suppliers for their assembly plant inputs. Others, notably from Japan and Korea, have arranged for their home country suppliers to join them in production in Mexico. Components from these loyal affiliates generally avoid the origin problems created under

NAFTA as Mexican customs refunds and waivers are eliminated. They also add to the North American content of the assembled goods ... the key to accessing NAFTA (*see Regional Value Content* below).

As the North American content of Asian and other maquiladora operations rises to meet NAFTA's rules of origin governing free trade, greater access to the Mexican market is available. Traditionally, sales of maquiladora products in Mexico have been limited. Starting in 1994, amendments to Mexico's Maquiladora Decree permit such sales to increase based upon percentages of prior year individual maquiladora exports from Mexico. In 1994, for example, this percentage was 55%, rising 5% annually to 75% in 1998 and scheduled to be 85% in the year 2000. By 2001, maquiladoras may sell their entire production in Mexico if they choose. This schedule is coordinated with Mexico's phase-out of customs duty drawback and waivers on imported components.

Regulatory and Tax Treatment, Quotas

NAFTA, like CFTA, incorporates by reference the national treatment duties of Article III of the GATT 1947 agreement. Each federal government must generally treat North American goods in the same manner as its own goods. Article 301 further requires states, provinces and local governments to treat goods from NAFTA partners as favorably as they treat goods from anywhere, including their own jurisdiction. These treatment duties affect taxes, fees, sale or distribution requirements, usage regulations and a range of other laws. Specific exceptions, many of which are derived from GATT grandfather rights, are listed in Annex 301.3.

Incorporation of GATT Article III makes it a part of NAFTA. This means that the countries may pursue NAFTA versus World Trade Organization (WTO) dispute settlement. It seems likely that WTO and NAFTA panel reports on Article III issues will remain consistent. Article III arbitration decisions under CFTA Chapter 18 suggest a close adherence to GATT principles. *See* Chapter 2.

The restrictive rules on use of trade quotas and price controls embodied in Article XI of the GATT 1947 agreement are also incorporated by reference into NAFTA. Under CFTA, they were simply affirmed. As with Article III, NAFTA dispute settlement is now an option on trade quota or price control issues. Mexico has 10 years from 1994 to eliminate its import licensing regime. Import and export quotas or restraints applied to goods from other nations will be honored by the NAFTA partners.

NAFTA provides for quota relief on a variety of specific goods. Textile quotas on originating goods are generally removed. On non-originating textile goods, quotas are gradually phased out. Agricultural and food product quotas are reduced in number, and energy quotas are discouraged. Quotas on motor vehicles and their parts are phased out. Most other traditional North American trade quotas are retained.

Export restraints justified under Articles XI or XX of the GATT are subjected to special additional rules applicable to CFTA (but not NAFTA) trade. These special rules require maintaining historically proportionate supplies, not pricing exports above domestic levels, and not disrupting normal channels of supply. These rules are found in NAFTA, but do not apply to Mexico. Mexico can therefore apply trade quotas and other export restraints subject only to GATT 1947 rules. Canada and the United States may restrain exports to Mexico under those same rules.

Rules of Origin

Free trade only applies to goods that originate in North America. Non-originating goods are subject to the normal tariffs of Canada, Mexico and the United States. Origin determinations are thus critical to NAFTA traders. There are Uniform NAFTA Regulations governing rules of origin and customs procedures, including a common Certificate of Origin.

Article 401 of the NAFTA agreement starts with the primary rule that all goods wholly obtained or produced entirely inside NAFTA originate there. Such goods fall under NAFTA Preference Criterion A. Article 415 authorizes free trade in goods made from materials that "originate" exclusively within NAFTA, Preference Criterion C.

Article 401 adopts the change of tariff classification rule initiated in CFTA. *See* Chapter 2. Subject to various exceptions, goods produced in one or more of the three countries with non-originating materials may be freely traded when all such materials (excepting a *de minimis* amount) undergo a change in tariff classification based upon the Harmonized Tariff System (HTS). Ordinarily this requires a change at the HTS product classification level and is known as Preference Criterion B. This Criterion is the most commonly used of all NAFTA's rules of origin for goods.

Meeting the change in tariff classification rule of origin is sometimes insufficient to allow free trading. Some goods must *also* contain a minimum "regional value content" (discussed below) to qualify under Preference Criterion B. For example, footwear, chemicals and automobiles fall in this category. There are fewer such content requirements under NAFTA than under CFTA. Electronics and machinery are generally exempt.

Article 401 also permits certain assembly goods that do not undergo a change in tariff classification to be freely traded if their regional value content is sufficient. This is NAFTA Preference Criterion D. For goods with very small non-originating content, NAFTA creates a "de minimis" rule of origin. Article 405 generally permits free trade in goods whose non-originating value is 7 percent or less. Such goods, in other words, are treated as originating in North America and may be freely traded.

Here are two U.S. Customs Service examples of goods that qualify for free trade under NAFTA Criterion B:

Example 1

Frozen pork meat (HTS heading 0203) is imported into the U.S. from Hungary and combined with spices imported from the Caribbean (HTS subheadings 0907–0910). Then, the spiced meat is mixed with cereals grown and produced in the U.S. to make fresh pork sausage (HTS heading 1601).

The Annex 401 rule of origin for HTS heading 1601 states:

"A change to heading 1601 through 1605 from any other chapter." Since the frozen meat is classified in Chapter 2 and the spices are classified in Chapter 9, these non-NAFTA-originating materials meet the tariff shift requirement. Note that one does not need to consider whether the cereal meets the applicable tariff shift requirement, as the cereal is itself NAFTA-originating.

In conclusion, the fresh pork sausage is originating under NAFTA.

Example 2

A manufacturer purchases inexpensive textile watch straps made in Taiwan (HTS heading 9113), to be assembled with originating mechanical watch movements (HTS heading 9108) and originating cases (HTS heading 9112). The value of the straps is less than seven percent (7%) of the total cost of the final watch (HTS heading 9102).

The rule of origin under Annex 402 for HTS heading 9102 states:

> "A change to heading 9101 through 9107 from any other chapter; A change to heading 9101 through 9107 from 9114, whether or not there is also a change from any other chapter, provided there is a regional value content of not less than:
>
> a) 60 percent where the transaction value method is used, or
>
> b) 50 percent where the net cost method is used."

Remember that only nonoriginating materials need to meet the required tariff shift requirement, and, in this case, the textile straps are the only nonoriginating component. As the value of the straps is less than seven percent (7%) of the total cost of the finished watch, the de minimis rule applies, and the finished watch is originating under NAFTA.

Regional Value Content

Article 402 establishes NAFTA's "top down" regional content valuation methods. These methods represent a change from CFTA's "bottom up" measurement of value for purposes of determining the origin of goods. There are two NAFTA regional content valuation methods: transaction value and net cost value.

In most instances, the importer seeking to qualify goods for duty free treatment under NAFTA can elect between the transaction value or net cost methods. The net cost method is generally thought to be the more difficult rule of origin. For most transactions among related parties, the net cost method must be used. Manipulation of prices in transfers among corporate affiliates might otherwise take advantage of NAFTA's transaction value method. The net cost method must also be followed if Customs rules the transaction value method "unacceptable."

The NAFTA *transaction value method* follows the GATT Customs Valuation Code of 1979 to which Canada, Mexico and the United States adhere. This method starts with an analysis of the F.O.B. price paid, including as a rule commissions, transport costs to the point of direct shipment, royalties on the goods, and manufacturing proceeds upon resale. Profits are included in the transaction value method of establishing the origin of goods as part of the price paid. The value of non-originating materials is then subtracted to arrive at the regional value content of the goods expressed in percentage terms. Normally, this percentage must be at least 60 percent in order to free trade the goods under NAFTA.

The NAFTA *net cost method* starts with a product's net cost to determine its regional value content. The value of non-originating materials is then subtracted. For NAFTA purposes, net cost is defined as total cost less expenses of sales promotion, marketing, after-sales service, royalties, shipping and packing, non-allowable interest charges and other "excluded costs." There are three authorized methods of allocating costs in calculating net cost. (Article 402.8) The producer gets to elect among these methods (provided the allocation of all costs is consistent with the Uniform NAFTA Regulations on Rules of Origin and Customs Procedures).

A regional content of 50 percent or more calculated on a net cost basis qualifies most goods for free trade under NAFTA. For light duty motor vehicles and their parts, a regional value content rising to 62.5 percent in 2002 is required. Other automotive goods must possess 60 percent regional content by 2002. Automotive goods must be valued on a net cost basis.

The *value of non-originating materials* (VNM) is excluded under both methods when determining the NAFTA origin of goods. This value is usually based on transaction values. If necessary, alternative values as determined under the GATT Customs Valuation Code of 1979 are used. "Intermediate materials" fabricated by producers are generally treated as originating, a rule which benefits vertically integrated producers.

NAFTA embraces an "all or nothing" roll up approach to non-originating materials that resolves some of the disputes that emerged under CFTA. In sum, the value of non-originating materials in components used to produce a good that is North American in origin is excluded from the VNM calculation in assessing regional content. This means that for both the transaction value and net cost methods, these materials are excluded in the determination of non-originating value. However, a tracing requirement for automobiles is added. This requirement is a prodigy of the *Honda* case discussed in Chapter 2. The value of non-originating automotive materials must be traced back through suppliers. Such non-originating values are excluded when determining the origin of automobiles.

Components that do not originate in NAFTA but possess some originating materials, on the other hand, are rolled down on the same all or nothing basis. In other words, these originating materials are included in the determination of non-originating value. However, a nonintegrated producer may "accumulate" such originating material when calculating the regional value content of finished goods.

A diagram of the transaction (TV) and net cost (NC) methods of calculating regional value content percentages is provided in Article 402 of the agreement. For these purposes VMC equals the value of non-originating material.

$$\text{Regional Value Content} = \frac{TV - VNM}{TV} \times 100$$

$$\text{Regional Value Content} = \frac{NC - VNM}{NC} \times 100$$

Textiles and Apparel

Like automobiles, textiles and apparel have unique rules of origin. Special production requirements are created that protect North American manufacturers. There is a "yarn forward" rule. This requires: (1) use of North American spun yarns; (2) to make North American fabrics; (3) that are cut and sewn into clothing in North America. Similarly, cotton and man-made fiber yarns have to be "fiber forwarded" for North American free trade.

These "triple transformation" rules of origin have already had substantial impact. Mexican imports (heavily comprised of U.S. content) have increasingly displaced East Asian apparel. Furthermore, Mexico raised its tariffs on non-NAFTA textiles in the wake of its 1995 financial crisis, while continuing NAFTA tariff reductions. The margin of preferential access to Mexico for Canadian and United States textiles was thus magnified. Exports of U.S. textile components to Mexico have also been enhanced by greater allowance under NAFTA of maquiladora apparel sales inside Mexico. Despite Mexico's recession, and a weakening Canadian economy, textile and apparel trade inside NAFTA is booming.

Silk, linen and other fabrics that are scarce in North America are excepted from NAFTA's triple transformation rules, but must still be cut and sewn in North America. Textile products with less than 7 percent non-originating material measured by weight can also be freely traded. This amount is treated as *de minimis*. Some non-qualifying textiles and clothing may be preferentially traded under quotas within NAFTA. U.S. manufacturers have complained about Canadian exports of wool suits under preferential quotas.

Electronics

NAFTA created some unique rules of origin for electronics products. These rules are based on changes in tariff classifications that contain particular components. For example, in order to qualify for free trade color television sets with screens over fourteen inches must contain a North American-made color picture tube. Since 1999, color television sets must also contain, among other things, North American amplifiers, tuners and power suppliers.

For a video cassette recorder to qualify for preferential treatment under NAFTA, it must contain a North American circuit board. For a microwave oven, all the major parts, except the magnetron, must be made in the North American countries. Computers must contain a North American motherboard. Computer monitors, like color television sets, must contain a North American color picture tube to be considered NAFTA originating.

The initial impact of NAFTA on the electronics and computer industries has been significant. United States, Japanese and Korean investment in electronics production facilities in Mexico has grown rapidly, especially in the manufacture of those components that convey NAFTA origin. Mexican purchases of U.S. electronic components and finished goods produced in maquiladoras is up substantially.

Exporting From Mexico to Latin America

Mexico presently has free trade agreements with Bolivia, Chile, Colombia, Costa Rica, Venezuela and Nicaragua. It is negotiating others within Latin America. These agreements create an opportunity for producers of goods in Mexico, especially in maquiladoras, to enjoy duty free status in Latin American as well as North American trade. The key to seizing this opportunity are the rules of origin under Mexico's free trade agreements. These rules are complex and not entirely uniform. They roughly track the NAFTA rules of origin with most transaction value regional content requirements ranging between 45 and 55 percent.

Proof of Origin

NAFTA exporters are legally obligated to provide importers with a certificate of origin. A common customs form has been created for these purposes. In the United States, this is Customs Service Form CF–434. Its Canadian and Mexican counterparts are essentially identical. Exporters can sign the certificate in reliance upon written representations from producers of goods. In practice, however, exporters often contract with producers to shift the duty to sign NAFTA origin certificates directly to them. However, producers cannot be forced to sign NAF-

TA certificates of origin since the ultimate legal duty to prove origin rests with exporters.

Producers most often bear the bulk of the burden of keeping the records necessary to prove NAFTA origin. Five years is the normal retention period. Record keeping is especially difficult when regional value contents are involved. Tracing the content of automotive parts is perhaps the most onerous burden. For some traders, especially of technology goods, proof of NAFTA origin is a burden that outweighs the benefits of compliance. They sometimes elect to just simply pay most-favored-nation (MFN) tariffs which (after the Uruguay Round of GATT negotiations) average about 3 percent for the United States. Canada's MFN rates average about 4 percent, while Mexico currently averages about 13 percent (subject to the right to raise its MFN tariffs significantly). Naturally, the lower the relevant MFN tariff, the more likely traders are to pay that tariff instead of documenting NAFTA status.

Importers rely on certificates of NAFTA origin when they declare goods eligible for regional tariff benefits. The importing country can question the exporter or producer, or review their records in their presence, in any instance where NAFTA tariff preferences are sought. Customs service notice of an intent to conduct a verification of NAFTA origin proceeding is required. The consent of the exporter or producer is also needed, but if withheld NAFTA tariff benefits can be denied. The producer is entitled to have two observers at any on-site customs inspection.

NAFTA importers and exporters can obtain advance rulings from customs services before shipping goods across borders. It is not certain whether competitors may gain access to advance rulings and lodge protests. All customs service determinations on NAFTA origin, whether by advance ruling or not, can be reviewed and appealed. Such appeals must include at least one level of administrative review above the customs office making the initial determination. Thereafter judicial or quasi-judicial review of the final administrative decision is required. In the United States, judicial review of NAFTA origin decisions is taken to the Court of International Trade.

Country of origin marking requirements, such as those of the United States (19 U.S.C. § 1304), are permitted on NAFTA-originating goods. Marking in English, French or Spanish must generally be allowed. The origin of goods for marking purposes is not always governed by the same law as origin for purposes of NAFTA tariff benefits. This reality was well illustrated in the *CPC International* decision of the U.S. Court of International Trade. 933 F.Supp. 1093 (1996). The CIT ruled that the NAFTA Implementation Act required meeting both the NAFTA Marking Rules and the traditional "substantial transformation" test of origin. On appeal, however, the Federal Circuit reversed, affirming that the tariff-shift NAFTA approach exclusively governs

U.S. country of origin marking requirements. *Best-foods v. United States,* 165 F.3d 1371 (Fed.Cir. 1999).

Procurement

Chapter 10 of NAFTA governs procurement of services and goods by state enterprises and governments. Since Mexico, unlike Canada and the United States, has not signed the GATT/WTO Procurement Code, the provisions of Chapter 10 give Canadian and United States suppliers of goods and services priority status in Mexican procurement. NAFTA's procurement rules apply if three criteria are met: (1) the purchasing entity is covered; (2) the goods or services also are covered; and (3) the value of the contract meets designated thresholds. If these criteria are met, then Canadian, Mexican and United States suppliers are free to compete on procurement.

NAFTA's special access rules on procurement do not apply universally. Generally speaking, for example, military and national security procurement is excluded. And not all civil government procurement is covered; only those purchasing entities listed in the Annexes to Chapter 10 are included. These Annexes hoped to list state and provincial entities, another expansion upon the CFTA rules, but their participation was "voluntary" and left to further negotiations. United States and Canadian minority and small business set-aside programs are also excluded.

NAFTA's procurement rules apply to some government enterprises (e.g., parastatal Mexican enterprises, Canadian Crown Corporations, the Tennessee Valley Authority). These states enterprises are phased into NAFTA's procurement rules through 2002. For example, PEMEX and the Mexican Federal Electricity Commission (CFE) procure billions of dollars of goods and services annually. In 1994, 50 percent of their purchases were opened to competitive NAFTA bidding and U.S. firms have since won PEMEX and CFE contracts. The balance is being brought under NAFTA by 2003.

Goods and construction services listed in the Annexes to Chapter 10 are subject to competitive NAFTA bidding. For example, pre-erection site work, civil engineering and construction equipment rentals are listed in Annex 1001.16–3 and therefore included. Transport, data processing, basic telecommunications, research and development, ship repair, management and other services are expressly excluded. But, apart from construction services, unless specifically excluded, services are subject to competitive NAFTA procurement. The United States has complained that Canada has interpreted its exception for services procurement too broadly.

Canada and the United States had agreed in CFTA to a threshold of $25,000 U.S. for federal goods procurement. NAFTA extended this agreement. The threshold for civil procurement between Mexico and the United States is $50,000 U.S. for goods and services. The threshold for construction services is $6.5 million U.S. The $50,000 and $6.5 million thresholds for covered services and construction services also apply between Canada and the United States.

The contract thresholds for government enterprises are higher: $250,000 U.S. for goods and services, and $8 million U.S. for construction services. These contract thresholds apply, for example, to PEMEX and CFE.

Bid procedures are detailed at great length in the NAFTA agreement. NAFTA rules mandate notice of bid information, product specifications, qualifications for bidders, etc. Government and state enterprise agencies must accord national and most-favored treatment to NAFTA bidders. Discrimination on grounds of national origin, or foreign affiliation or ownership of the supplier, is prohibited. Procurement of local content or purchase "offsets," used frequently in Canada and Mexico, are also prohibited. So are technical specifications that create unnecessary obstacles to trade. And the normal rules of product origin must be employed.

NAFTA bidders must be given an opportunity to challenge the results or any feature of the procurement process in an impartial forum. However, bids by service suppliers owned or controlled by non-NAFTA nationals that lack substantial business activity in a NAFTA nation can be rejected.

Motor Vehicles

Canada and the United States have a long tradition of free automotive trade and investment under their 1965 Auto Pact. CFTA and NAFTA made only a few changes to this relationship. The more demanding NAFTA rules of origin were substituted, notably the 62.5 percent regional value content requirement for passenger autos and light trucks (60 percent for other vehicles and parts). These content rules take full effect in 2002 and must be calculated on a net cost basis traced back through suppliers.

The market forces pushing a voluntary harmonization of external tariffs are well illustrated in the Canadian auto sector. NAFTA continued the preferential trade terms of the Canada–U.S. Auto Pact, but only for Auto Pact beneficiaries. Toyota and Honda Canada are not such beneficiaries, but had been receiving duty drawback and production-based customs duty remissions on auto parts which effectively matched Auto Pact benefits. When NAFTA required the elimination of these duty drawback and remission programs at the end of 1995, Honda and Toyota faced a 2.5 percent tariff on auto parts imported for assembly in Canada. The Canadian government, shortly after Honda and Toyota announced plans for expanded assembly plants, removed the 2.5 percent tariff in an effort at maintaining the costs of assembly in Canada.

Automotive investment and trade have been controlled by the Mexican federal government for many years. The 1989 presidential Decree for Development and Modernization of the Automotive Industry and related 1990 implementing regulations were in place as NAFTA was negotiated. Mexico may keep this Decree in force until 2003. Mexico's refusal to allow importation of used vehicles remains effective until 2009. Thereafter, used auto imports are phased in over ten years based on the age of the vehicle.

Pre–NAFTA auto manufacturers in Mexico included Ford, General Motors, Chrysler, Volkswagen and Nissan. These producers are gradually being relieved of "trade balancing" export obligations as a precondition to importing, but get to retain their exclusive import rights until 2003. Mexico is also gradually reducing the percentage of Mexican value that auto manufacturers must add to vehicles until, by 2003, there will be no Mexican value-added requirement. As a result, fewer auto parts will need to be purchased from Mexican "national suppliers." In addition, auto components manufactured in Mexican maquiladoras are now treated as Mexican in origin, and United States and Canadian investors can wholly own Mexican auto parts suppliers. All limits on the importation of autos tied to sales volumes in Mexico have been removed.

Other Mexican automotive trade and investment restraints have been altered by NAFTA. The Auto Transportation Decree of 1989 regulating the production and importation of buses and trucks has been repealed. Since 1999 Mexico no longer requires its manufacturers to limit imports to 50 percent of Mexican production. Non-manufacturers have been able to import more buses and trucks under quotas auctioned by the Mexican government. These quotas corresponded to progressively higher percentages of Mexican production. Since 1999 they too have disappeared.

Mexico and the United States have different auto tariff obligations. Mexico reduced its passenger automobile tariffs by 50 percent in 1994, and is phasing out the remainder by 2003. On light trucks, it cut tariffs immediately by 50 percent, phasing out the remainder by 1998. For all other vehicles, Mexico phases out its tariffs by 2003. In contrast, the United States has removed all tariffs on Mexican passenger automobiles. The United States has also phased out tariffs on Mexican light trucks. All other United States tariffs on motor vehicles from Mexico are scheduled to be phased out by 2003. On auto parts, Mexico and the U.S. removed certain tariffs in 1994. They phased out most others over 5 years, and have promised to eliminate all tariffs on auto parts by 2003.

The United States minimum corporate fuel average economy rules (CAFE rules) provide a good example of United States regulations with trade restraining potential. No alteration in these standards is required by NAFTA. However, the United States agreed to permit inclusion of Mexican auto parts and vehicles under its CAFE regulations. Canadian parts and autos with at least 75 percent of their value added in Canada are classified as domestic and included under CAFE. Mexican goods will be equally treated by 2004.

Motor vehicles and their components are by far the most significant trade sector under NAFTA. This significance helps explain the level of detail in the NAFTA agreement concerning motor vehicles, especially their rules of origin (*supra*). Despite Mexico's financial crisis and ensuing recession, U.S. and Canadian exports of motor vehicles have exploded. Shipments of completed vehicles to Mexico increased by well over 500 percent in the first three years of NAFTA. Moreover, contrary to some expectations, the bulk of new investment in auto production facilities since 1994 has been in the United States, not Mexico. Investment in auto parts production in Mexico, on the other hand, has skyrocketed. A surprisingly large share of the production of auto parts is being done by Mexican industrial conglomerates.

Energy Goods

Like cultural industries for Canada in the CFTA negotiations, energy was non-negotiable for Mexico. Chapter 6 of NAFTA deals with trade in energy and basic petrochemical goods. It opens with a most unusual sentence: "The Parties confirm their full respect for their Constitutions." This is an oblique reference to the revolutionary Mexican Constitution of 1917 that reserved ownership and development of natural resources to the state. Today this constitutional clause is most evident in PEMEX, the state oil, gas and basic petrochemical monopoly. CFE, the state electricity monopoly, also embodies revolutionary state ownership principles. In 1992, prior to

NAFTA, the private sector was allowed to invest in electrical generation facilities provided the energy produced was self-consumed or sold to CFE.

NAFTA Annex 602.3 demonstrates what "full respect" for the Mexican Constitution means. In it, Mexico reserves to its state a lengthy list of strategic activities: Exploration, exploitation, and refining of crude oil and natural gas; production of artificial gas and basic petrochemicals; pipelines; foreign trade in and transport, storage and distribution of the same; virtually the entire supply of electricity to the public in Mexico; and nuclear energy.

No private Canadian, Mexican or United States investment is permitted in these areas. However, it should be noted that basic petrochemicals include ethane, propane, butanes, pentanes, hexanes, heptanes, carbon black feedstocks and napthas. Compared to past Mexican law, this is a narrow definition. NAFTA investors may participate in all secondary and non-reserved basic petrochemicals, but there has been a slowdown in privatization of such opportunities. Transportation, distribution and storage of natural gas were opened to private investors (including foreigners) in 1995 and several U.S. companies have successfully bid on such opportunities. In 1999, Mexico launched a major structural reform of its electricity sector, including privatization of power companies. Amendments to Mexico's constitutional law will be required.

Cross-border trade in energy services is possible only by permit of the Mexican government. Cross-

border trade in natural gas and basic petrochemicals is similarly allowed with PEMEX through regulated supply contracts. In some cases, Mexico will
permit performance clauses in energy service contracts. Mexico's traditional opposition to sharing oil
and gas ownership rights in PEMEX drilling contracts continues.

Mexico has allowed 100 percent foreign ownership of new coal mines. Existing joint ventures can
now become wholly-owned by NAFTA investors.
Mexican tariffs on coal were completely removed at
the outset. NAFTA nationals may own or operate
electricity companies when the production is for the
owner's use. Excess electricity must be sold to CFE
at rates agreed upon by contract. Co-generation is
another possibility when electricity is generated by
industrial production. Once again, excess supplies
go to CFE at agreed rates. Independent power production plants located in Mexico can be owned and
operated by NAFTA nationals, but CFE gets the
electricity. This has been done by leasing foreign-
owned plants to CFE. In the border region, CFE
may contract to sell electricity to United States
utilities.

NAFTA incorporates by reference the GATT 1947
provisions relating to quotas and other restraints on
trade in energy and petrochemical goods. Presumably, this applies to GATT Articles XI, XX and XXI.
As in other areas, this incorporation permits utilization of NAFTA dispute settlement.

In addition, other rights and obligations relating to energy goods are established by NAFTA. There is an express prohibition of import or export price controls that applies to all parties. In times of energy crises, Canadian (but not Mexican) restraints must be proportionate to past export/domestic utilization ratios. Crisis restraints may not push export prices higher than those charged domestically. And the normal channels of supply must be maintained. Mexico is also exempted from the NAFTA rules on restraining trade in energy goods for reasons of national security, but is required to adhere to the general NAFTA rules on national security trade restraints.

Canada and Mexico are important sources of United States energy imports. With oil embargoes in mind, energy security was a major goal for the United States in negotiating NAFTA. Nevertheless, the United States was unable to obtain the same degree of energy security from Mexico that it secured from Canada. Moreover, Canada unilaterally issued in 1993 a declaration interpreting NAFTA as *not* requiring Canadian energy crisis exports at any given level or proportion.

Energy export licensing is permissible under NAFTA. Export taxes and other charges can be used only if they apply to energy goods consumed domestically. The regulation of energy is subject to NAFTA's general national and most-favored treatment duties. The more specific rules of Chapter 6 on trade restraints and export taxes also apply.

NAFTA nations must "seek" to ensure that energy regulation does not disrupt contractual relationships "to the maximum extent practicable." They must provide for "orderly and equitable" implementation of regulatory measures.

State Monopolies and Enterprises

Article 1502 of NAFTA deals with federal (but not state or provincial) monopolies such as PEMEX, CFE, and Petro–Canada. Designating or maintaining federal monopoly providers or purchasers of goods or services in any economic sector is authorized under NAFTA. Such monopolies may or may not be state-owned enterprises. But all federal government monopolies, and all privately-owned monopolies designated after January 1, 1994, must act consistently with NAFTA when exercising "governmental authority." This means that when they issue trade licenses, approve contracts, impose quotas, or levy fees or charges, monopoly enterprises fall within NAFTA's reach.

Furthermore, monopolies must act solely in accordance with commercial considerations. Hence, for example, PEMEX decisions about pricing, quality, availability, marketability, transport and other terms and conditions of purchase or sale must be commercially justifiable. Federal monopolies must give the better of national or most-favored-nation treatment to NAFTA investors, service-providers and sellers of goods. Monopoly positions should not be used to engage in anticompetitive practices in non-monopolized markets to the disadvantage of

NAFTA investors. For example, discrimination in the provision of monopoly goods or services, cross-subsidization, and predatory conduct are prohibited.

All of these rules attempt to get federal monopolies to behave as if they were subject to market forces and competition law. Acting "in accordance with commercial considerations" is even defined as acting consistent with practices of privately-held enterprises. The only exception is procurement for governmental purposes. More generally, NAFTA commits each nation to enforcement of business competition law (referred to as antitrust law in the United States) against private sector trade restraints. For Mexico, this commitment resulted in the adoption of the Federal Law of Economic Competition (June, 1993). This law prohibits monopolies, monopolistic practices (price fixing, market division) and anticompetitive concentrations (mergers and acquisitions).

All state enterprises owned or controlled by a NAFTA government are subject to Article 1503. Unlike monopolies, Article 1503 embraces state or provincial government enterprises, e.g., Hydro–Quebec. All governments must ensure that state enterprises act consistently with Chapters 11 (Investment) and 14 (Financial Services) when exercising governmental authority. Expropriation, for example, would fall within this rule. Like monopolies, state enterprises must sell to NAFTA investors by giving them the better of national or most-favored-nation treatment, but are generally not subjected to the same level of scrutiny as federal monopolies.

Agricultural Goods

Trade in agricultural goods and food products is always sensitive. Canada and the U.S. undertook only token changes in CFTA, not the least because each has powerful farm lobbies. Mexico's large *ejido* communal land program is oriented towards subsistence farming and constitutionally protected. This makes change in agriculture hyper-sensitive. Nevertheless, agricultural free trade between the United States and Mexico was substantially advanced by NAFTA. Relatively little progress was made on the northern front where the CFTA rules on agricultural trade were retained under NAFTA. These rules reduced quota, import license and other agricultural nontariff trade barriers in only a limited way.

Agricultural export subsidies are generally restrained under NAFTA. However, this restraint does not apply to Mexico–United States agricultural trade. Notice and consultation must precede any subsidization and a Working Group on Agricultural Subsidies monitors this volatile area. It is deemed "inappropriate" for one NAFTA partner to subsidize agricultural goods unless there are subsidized imports entering that market from a non-member country. The NAFTA partners have promised to collaborate on retaliatory measures against the offending third-party. It is significant that NAFTA reserves for all partners the right to apply countervailing tariffs against subsidized agricultural imports. Canada, for example, has assessed countervailing tariffs on United States corn.

Mexico and the United States undertook more diffuse agricultural trade reform. Approximately half of all Mexico–U.S. agricultural trade immediately became duty-free. The United States and Mexico also converted agricultural quotas, import licenses and other nontariff trade barriers into tariffs ("tariffication"). Equivalent restrictive tariffs or tariff-rate quotas (TRQs) replaced these restraints. Tariff rate quotas adjust the level of applicable tariffs according to the volume of imports, generally rising with import volume.

Duty free entry at lower import volumes often accompanies TRQs. The amount of duty free agricultural goods entering Mexico and the United States has been increased by 3 percent annually. Nearly all tariffs on Mexico–U.S. agricultural goods are scheduled to be eliminated by 2004. By 2009 tariffs for even the most sensitive agricultural items, such as corn and dry beans entering Mexico, become duty free. Government data indicates that trade in agricultural goods has been moderately expanding in both directions.

The sensitivity of U.S.-Mexico agricultural trade is reflected in emergency protective measures that apply until 2004. Under this provision, Mexico and the United States may impose tariffs at designated import "trigger" levels. The lower of the tariff rate in effect on July 1, 1991 or the importing nation's current most-favored-nation tariff can be assessed when imports surge for the remainder of the growing season or calendar year. The trigger levels increase yearly until 2004 when they can no longer be invoked as temporary protection on agricultural trade. Use of this special provision forecloses the option of NAFTA's general "escape clause" (below).

In pursuing a tariffication process, Mexico and the United States acted in advance of the WTO Agreement on Agriculture (1995). Under that Agreement, Canada and the United States were obligated to do likewise. When Canada tariffied (using TRQs) a number of agricultural quotas at levels measured in hundreds of percent, the United States filed a complaint under NAFTA. This complaint was the first under Chapter 20 to go to arbitration. A panel of five arbitrators unanimously ruled that Canada's tariffication and tariff levels were consistent with its NAFTA obligations. CDA–95–2008–01.

Food Standards (SPS)

Section B of Chapter 7 of NAFTA concerns food regulations ... so-called "Sanitary and Phytosanitary Measures" (SPS). SPS regulations govern the protection of human, animal or plant life or health. They are focused on risks associated with animal or plant pests or diseases, food additives, and food contaminants (such as toxins). There is a WTO agreement on SPS Measures which tracks NAFTA quite closely. All SPS measures that directly or indirectly affect NAFTA trade are covered, including SPS acts of nongovernmental entities. Each

NAFTA member must secure compliance by state or provincial governments with the NAFTA SPS regime. Canada, Mexico and the United States have retained their inspection and approval procedures for food products. Agricultural and food products that fail national SPS requirements may be banned from those markets.

Since each nation may adopt, maintain or apply any necessary SPS regulation, trade in food products continues to be a heavily controlled field. NAF-TA authorizes "appropriate" levels of protection. In other words, each nation establishes its own SPS risk management tolerance. The appropriateness of SPS protection includes an assessment of lost production, lost sales and other economic injury. The cost-effectiveness of alternative approaches to limited risks must be reviewed. The agreement's broad objective of minimizing negative trade impact is also to be considered. Lastly, SPS rules should reflect variable conditions, such as allowing imports from disease-free regions. Arbitrary or unjustifiable SPS discrimination is prohibited by NAFTA agreement. Each country has promised to only adopt necessary levels of SPS protection, and no SPS regulation may be applied with the intent or effect of creating a disguised restraint on trade.

Chapter 7 attempts to minimize the potential for SPS regulations to block NAFTA trade in a variety of ways. All SPS regulations must be based on scientific principles derived from a "risk assessment". They must be eliminated when there is no longer any scientific basis for continuance. Risk assessments focus on the adverse potential of a pest or disease or the presence of additives or contaminants in foodstuffs. They must take into account relevant risk assessment techniques and methodologies developed by international or North American standardizing organizations, relevant scientific evidence, and relevant processes and production methods. Risk assessments must also consider relevant inspection, sampling and testing methods, the prevalence of relevant diseases or pests (including the existence of pest-free or disease-free areas or areas of low pest or disease prevalence), relevant ecological and other environmental conditions, and relevant treatments, such as quarantines.

NAFTA mandates use of international SPS standards so long as there is no reduction in protection levels. SPS protection that surpasses international standards is expressly permitted. The SPS rules of the Codex Alimentarius Commission, the International Office of Epizootics, the International Plant Protection Convention and the North American Plant Protection Convention are specifically supported. Harmonized SPS regulations may and have been negotiated through the NAFTA Committee on Sanitary and Phytosanitary Measures. Canadian and United States SPS regulations, for example, are broadly compatible. More immediately, national SPS regulations are treated as equivalent if the exporting country can objectively demonstrate that its regulations achieve the importing country's chosen level of protection. Scientific evidence evaluated under NAFTA's risk assessment methods must be used to resolve issues of equivalency resulting in a written report.

SPS inspection and control procedures applicable to NAFTA trade must be administered as done domestically. Such procedures must be transparent and available for review by NAFTA traders. New or modified SPS regulations affecting NAFTA must be preceded by public notice and often a statement of objectives and reasons. Such notice must highlight variances from international standards. An opportunity for written comment must be available and, upon request, discussion. All of these procedural requirements are reinforced by official NAFTA "inquiry points" in each country. These centers respond to questions and provide information regarding SPS regulations, inspection and approval procedures, risk assessments and related subjects.

Product and Service Standards–Related Measures (SRM)

Chapter 9 of the NAFTA agreement is titled "Standards–Related Measures." SRM embrace standards, technical regulations and conformity assessment procedures. All of these terms are defined. Standards are voluntary, technical regulations are mandatory, and conformity assessment procedures determine if standards or technical regulations have been fulfilled.

Chapter 9 of NAFTA concerns service and product standards and technical regulations and certifications of compliance. Adherence to the GATT Agreement on Technical Barriers to Trade of 1979 (the GATT Standards Code) was affirmed (but not incorporated by reference) in Chapter 9. However, this Code has been superseded by the WTO Agreement on Technical Barriers to Trade (1995) upon which Chapter 9 was largely modeled. All other international agreements of Canada, Mexico and the United States affecting the regulation of goods were also affirmed. By specific provision in Chapter 9, these include the Washington Convention on International Trade in Endangered Species of Wild Fauna and Flora (1973, 1979), the Montreal Protocol on Substances that Deplete the Ozone Layer (1987, 1990), the Canada–U.S. Agreement on Movement of Transboundary Hazardous Waste (1986) and the Mexico–U.S. Agreement on Cooperation for the Protection and Improvement of the Environment in the Border Area (1983).

With relatively few qualifications (notably a duty not to discriminate), NAFTA permits use of product and service standards and regulations as nontariff trade barriers. Article 904 recognizes the right of each country to adopt, maintain or apply SRMs based on "legitimate objectives." Protection of domestic industries is specifically excluded as a legitimate objective. "Legitimate objectives" is defined in Article 915 as including "sustainable development" as well as safety, health, environmental and consumer protection. "Sustainable development" is not defined in the NAFTA agreement. At a minimum, it refers to Mexico's economic development goals.

More generally, the term is often used to connote development that is *environmentally* sustainable. Thus, all the NAFTA partners may enact SRM that promote sustainable development. The level of protection of all of these interests is left to each NAFTA member-state and is preserved for all levels of government. The power to prohibit the importation of nonconforming goods or services from a NAFTA partner is expressly reserved.

All legitimate objectives for product or service SRM should (where appropriate) be reviewed in light of: (1) fundamental climatic or geographical factors; (2) technological or infrastructural factors; or (3) scientific justification. "Assessments of risk" may be employed (but are not required) when evaluating legitimate trade regulatory objectives. Thus NAFTA's SRM rules, unlike its SPS rules, are not firmly linked to science. When utilized, assessments of risk "may" take into account available scientific evidence or technical information, intended end uses, methodology, or environmental conditions. Such assessments are strongly encouraged in establishing appropriate levels of national standards protection. In determining these levels, arbitrary or unjustifiable distinctions between similar goods or services must not be made if disguised restrictions on NAFTA trade, or discriminations between goods or services posing the same level of risk and providing similar benefits, result.

NAFTA requires SRM to be administered without discrimination under national and most-favored-nation treatment rules. But each member need only "seek" to ensure observance of these rules by state or provincial (not local) governments. Likewise, they need only seek compliance by nongovernmental standards organizations. Adoption of international SRM (such as the numerous International Standards Organization rules) is required except when inappropriate or ineffective to meet a nation's legitimate regulatory objectives. In a provision dear to environmentalists, NAFTA specifically provides that levels of protection that are higher than internationally mandated may be chosen.

No SRM creating unnecessary obstacles to NAFTA trade are permissible. No unnecessary obstacle to trade exists for these purposes if the demonstrable purpose of the SRM is to achieve a legitimate objective and goods meeting that objective are not excluded. The NAFTA partners promised to work jointly towards enhanced and compatible SRM. They agreed to treat each other's technical regulations and certification tests as equivalent when they adequately fulfill the importing partner's legitimate objectives, a commitment not found in the WTO Technical Barriers Agreement. The 1993 CFTA dispute settlement arbitration on Puerto Rican regulations governing the importation of long-life milk from Quebec stands for the principle that each partner must give the others the chance to prove equivalency. *See* Chapter 2.

Testing and approval procedures (conformity assessments) are subject to minimum procedural requirements. The licensing of product testing in the other countries must be on terms that are no less favorable than applied domestically. Lastly, there are extensive notification, publication, information-sharing, information center, and technical cooperation duties intended to keep standards issues transparent. Further review, discussion and consultation is anticipated in a special NAFTA "Committee on Standards–Related Measures."

This professor believes that the Achilles Heel of NAFTA rests in its SPS and SRM provisions. We know from decades of experience in the European Union that as tariffs decline, nontariff trade barriers take on major importance. In NAFTA, unlike Europe or even portions of CFTA, there is no commitment to uniform harmonization or mutual recognition of standards and certifications. Indeed, NAFTA's express reservation of the right to block trade in goods or services that do not meet diverse national SPS or SRM moves in exactly the opposite direction. The primary hope is that NAFTA's numerous cooperative Committees can reach agreement.

That said, in the early years of NAFTA, there have been comparatively few SPS or SRM disputes of major consequence. For example, Mexico was supposed to have issued its standard for terminal attachment telephone equipment by January 1, 1995. Negotiations within the NAFTA Telecommunications Standards Subcommittee (TSSC) were prolonged by divisions of interest in market opening versus market protection. More than 2 years later, under U.S. pressure, the telecom standard was finally promulgated. Known in Mexico as a "norma," the standard contains 13 mandatory parameters and applies to telephones, fax machines, modems and other end-user devices.

CFTA, where some standards disputes went to arbitration, seems to have facilitated considerable cross-border recognition of SPS and SRM. In addition, NAFTA and the WTO Technical Barriers Agreement (1995) and the WTO SPS Agreement (1995) have moved all three NAFTA partners towards greater recognition of international standards. If NAFTA manages to avoid the European experience, that would be a major achievement.

Exceptions to Free Trade

Every chapter of NAFTA has specific exceptions to it. Chapter 21, labeled "Exceptions," is of wider application. For example, information flows adverse to law enforcement can be restrained under NAFTA. So can flows that affect personal privacy or financial information rights. Perhaps the best known exception is that for Canadian cultural industries which was extended to Canadian–Mexican trade. *See* Chapter 2. This exception does not apply to Mexico–United States trade.

In addition, Chapter 21 incorporates by reference into NAFTA Article XX of the GATT 1947 (and its interpretative notes). Article XX, previously discussed in Chapter 2, authorizes restraint on international trade in the name of public morality, public health, protection of intellectual property, conservation of natural resources and so forth. Article 2101 of NAFTA seeks to clarify Article XX of the GATT. It declares environmental health protection a legitimate reason to restrain NAFTA trade. So is conservation of living and non-living exhaustible natural resources. The health protection exception contained in Article XX of the GATT is specifically replaced by NAFTA's provisions on sanitary and phytosanitary (SPS) regulations (above). It was also agreed that all health, safety and consumer protection laws must be consistent with NAFTA. They may not be administered in arbitrary or unjustifiably discriminatory ways. Nor may they amount to a disguised restriction on NAFTA trade.

The NAFTA national security exceptions to free trade follow those created in CFTA. As a general rule, NAFTA does not impact national tax laws. However, Article 301 (national treatment) applies to tax regulations "to the same extent as does Article III of the GATT." Article III bans discriminatory taxation of imported goods and frequently applies to sales, excise and value-added taxes. Income, capital gains taxation, and corporate capital taxation, if applied to a particular service, must also be given national treatment.

Articles 2103.2 through 2103.6 indicate that international tax conventions prevail over NAFTA. This might, for example, authorize performance requirements that would otherwise be prohibited by NAFTA. The most recent relevant conventions are the 1980 Canada–United States Tax Convention, the 1992 Canada–Mexico Tax Convention, and the 1994 Mexico–United States Tax Convention.

NAFTA, with an eye towards Mexico, governs the extent to which balance of payments problems justify restraints of trade. Article 2104 legitimizes use of quotas, surcharges and the like only if authorized by the International Monetary Fund. This makes it unlikely that NAFTA nations can restrain payments on current transactions, dividends, royalties and the like. Capital transfers, on the other hand, are not subject to IMF controls. Mexico can therefore restrain major capital outflows.

Temporary Import Restraints (Escape Clauses)

Canada and the United States severely limited their ability to bilaterally protect their markets when imports surge and cause or threaten serious injury to a domestic industry. *See* Chapter 2. These limitations continue in force. Chapter 8 of NAFTA, governing Mexico and the United States, substantially reproduces the CFTA provisions on emergency import protection. Bilateral escape clause action is possible if there is a threat of serious domestic industry injury until 2003. For Schedule C+ goods which become duty free in 2008, bilateral relief can be applied for a maximum of four (not just three) years. Another variation from CFTA protective relief permits advancing the scheduled NAFTA tariff reductions to later dates, but no later than final duty free dates under the Agreement.

Article 802 of NAFTA applies to all three countries when global escape clause proceedings are pursued. To start, there is a rebuttable presumption that NAFTA goods will be excluded from global actions. Rebuttal is possible if the NAFTA imports are a "substantial share" of total imports, and those NAFTA imports "contribute importantly" to serious domestic industry injury or its threat. "Substantial share" is defined as "normally" including only the five largest supplier-nations. In other words, imports from Canada, Mexico or the United States must be in the top five for any global escape clause relief to apply. Furthermore, NAFTA imports with growth rates that are appreciably lower than the growth rate from all sources will "normally" not be considered to "contribute importantly" to injury. If initially excluded from escape clause global actions, NAFTA imports may later be included should a surge in NAFTA trade occur.

Global escape clause remedies may not reduce the flow of goods across NAFTA borders below levels corresponding to a recent representative time period plus reasonable growth. The exporting NAFTA partner may in turn pursue substantially equivalent compensatory action. Lastly, NAFTA details in Article 803 and Annex 803.3 procedures that must be followed in bilateral or global emergency protective proceedings. These procedures do not differ substantially from those already used in United States law as administered by the U.S. International Trade Commission.

The Corn Broom Case

In its first application of Section 302 of the NAF-TA Implementation Act (a global escape clause proceeding), the U.S. International Trade Commission found in 1996 that the elimination of tariffs on Mexican corn brooms resulted in a surge of imports that were the substantial cause of serious injury or its threat to the U.S. broom industry. No. NAFTA–302–1. The ITC subsequently recommended tariff increases starting at 12 percent above the MFN level declining to 3 percent above that level in the fourth year of relief. This recommendation concerned brooms from Mexico and other nationsexcepting only Canada and Israel. No. TA–201–65, ITC Pub. 3984. Aug. 1996.

President Clinton decided against tariff increases, but instructed the USTR to attempt to negotiate solutions with Mexico and other countries while the Labor, Commerce and Agriculture Departments developed an adjustment plan for the U.S. corn broom industry. Mexico, meanwhile, requested consultations under NAFTA Chapter 20 dispute resolution. Late in 1996, President Clinton deemed the negotiations a failure and imposed substantial tariffs and tariff-rate-quotas (TRQs) on broom imports from Mexico and other countries for 3 years. Mexico, in turn, raised tariffs on U.S. wine, brandy, bourbon, whiskey, wood office and bedroom furniture, flat glass, telephone agendas, and chemically-pure sugar, fructose and syrup products. This retaliation was deemed by Mexico "substantially equivalent" to the U.S. broom tariff surcharges valued at roughly $1 million annually.

Early in 1998, the NAFTA Chapter 20 arbitration panel ruled in Mexico's favor. USA–97–2008–01. Specifically, the panel ruled that the ITC had failed to explain why plastic brooms were not directly competitive with corn brooms, and therefore part of the U.S. domestic industry injury analysis. U.S. officials indicated they would comply, but then took nine months to terminate the safeguards in a decision that does not cite the NAFTA arbitration as a reason for termination. Mexico subsequently removed its retaliatory tariffs.

Special Escape Clauses

Textile and apparel goods, some agricultural goods, frozen concentrated orange juice and major household appliances benefit from special escapes from import competition under NAFTA. Many of these provisions were created to secure passage of NAFTA through the United States Congress. For example, textile and apparel goods are subject to a unique import protection scheme found in Annex 300–B. Standard bilateral escape clause relief on originating goods is possible under less demanding conditions until 2003. For non-originating goods, until 2003, quotas may be used as remedies by the United States or Mexico. The most important alteration probably concerns decision-making: the U.S. International Trade Commission does not participate. Instead, the Interagency Committee for the Implementation of Textile Agreements (CITA), thought to be more pro-industry, is the body that determines escape clause relief for textiles and apparel under NAFTA.

A special provision located in Article 703 benefits U.S.-grown chili peppers, eggplants, watermelons, tomatoes, onions and other agricultural goods. These may be protected using tariff-rate-quotas. The United States NAFTA Implementation Act, in Section 309, protects against imports of frozen concentrated orange juice from Mexico until 2007. Additional tariffs apply if the futures price for OJ falls below historic levels for five consecutive days. Once this happens, tariffs on Mexican OJ imports are "snapbacked" to the lower of the present or July 1, 1991 most-favored-nation rates. These tariffs are eliminated when the average historic price level is exceeded for five days. This statistically driven protective mechanism, a monument to Florida politicians, has frequently been triggered.

The President's Statement of Administrative Action (SAA) accompanying the NAFTA Implementation Act contains yet another special escape from import competition. This time the beneficiaries are United States producers of major household appliances. It is thought that this Statement, and its arcane rules of operation under Chapter 8 escape clause relief, secured critical votes in the House of Representatives for the passage of NAFTA.

CHAPTER 5

SERVICES

The United States is the world's largest exporter of services. Needless to say, it was keenly interested in advancing North American free trade in services. NAFTA does so in a manner that clearly exceeds the WTO General Agreement on Services (GATS) (1995).

A major shift in approach to trade in services was made by NAFTA. Instead of following CFTA's "positive list" for coverage of services, NAFTA employs a "negative list." Under CFTA only services listed in the agreement were included. Under NAFTA all services are covered unless specifically excluded. In other words, there is a presumption of coverage and services unknown at this time qualify for NAFTA free trade.

NAFTA negatively lists sectors that cannot be freely traded. These include most legal, procurement, maritime, general aviation, basic telecommunications, cultural industry, and government-produced (health, social security and law enforcement) services. All of the services covered in the CFTA agreement are subject to NAFTA free trade, including financial services. NAFTA's approach extends free trade to aircraft repair, specialty air, land

123

transport, intermodal terminal, warehousing, maritime port and enhanced telecommunication services. However, some services are restricted by NAFTA quotas (even zero quotas). The United States, for example, imposes quotas on NAFTA provision of radio communication, cable TV, natural gas transport, postal and national park concession services. Overall, NAFTA's initial impact on services trade has been mixed, and perhaps a bit disappointing to the United States.

Service Provider Rights

The right to "provide" covered services across borders is guaranteed by NAFTA. This right includes the production, sale, purchase, payment, transport and delivery of services. Furthermore, no beneficiary is obliged to maintain an office or other local presence in a second or third NAFTA country. The beneficiaries of this right include nationals of NAFTA countries and incorporated enterprises that principally carry on business within NAFTA. This means that most service companies owned by third party investors (e.g., Europeans, Asians and Latin Americans) principally doing business in NAFTA are also beneficiaries. The only general exceptions are third parties from countries with whom there are no diplomatic relations or trade embargoes (e.g., Cuba). In addition, regarding financial services, Canada has reserved the right to exclude all third party providers regardless of their business operations inside NAFTA.

Chapter 12 creates two standards for dealing with NAFTA service providers. NAFTA beneficiaries are entitled to the better of the two standards. First, under Article 1202, federal governments must grant national treatment to NAFTA service providers. Secondly, under Article 1203, federal governments must accord most-favored-nation treatment to NAFTA beneficiaries. State or provincial governments must give NAFTA beneficiaries the most favorable treatment they grant any service provider from their country.

The rights and treatment standards granted service providers under NAFTA are qualified by various quotas and "reservations." These reservations permit each nation to continue to apply certain pre-NAFTA restraints or discriminations. However, such "non-conforming" laws cannot be amended so as to further conflict with NAFTA.

Licensing and Certification

Article 1210 of NAFTA governs licensing and certification of service providers, notably professionals. It provides for use of objective and transparent criteria under the least burdensome regulations necessary to maintain quality services. Disguised restrictions on cross-border trade in services are prohibited.

Mutual recognition of national professional licenses is not mandatory. However, professional service providers must be allowed to prove that their education, experience, licenses or certifications justify licensure. "Professional services" are defined in NAFTA as services provided by persons whose right to practice necessitates specialized post-secondary education or equivalent training or experience. This definition excludes, for example, most trades-persons and vessel or aircraft crew. Since 1996, there have been no citizenship or permanent residency obligations for professional service providers. Retaliatory equivalent requirements are authorized in the same professional services sector should a NAFTA nation fail to honor this rule.

Annex 1210.5 creates a general duty to process applications for professional licenses and certification in a reasonable time. The applicant must be informed of the final determination, but there is no right to challenge or appeal the outcome. Canada, Mexico and the United States agreed to develop mutually acceptable licensing and certification criteria based upon recommendations from professional bodies. Education standards, examinations, experience or training requirements, rules of professional conduct or ethics, professional development and re-certification, practice scopes, local knowledge needs, and consumer protection all fall within the ambit of such recommendations. While long-term permanent licensing and certification of NAFTA professionals is the goal, temporary short-term licensing may also occur.

The first professional group under NAFTA to enjoy mutual recognition of educational, experience and exam backgrounds is engineers. In June of

1995, mutual recognition was achieved through negotiations of the Canadian Council of Professional Engineers, the Mexican Comite Mexicano para la Practica Internacional de la Ingeniera and the U.S. Council for International Engineering Practice. Both temporary and permanent licensing of engineers are subject to mutual recognition. Canada and Mexico have formally ratified the agreement. In the United States, however, licensing is subject to state law and only Texas had ratified the mutual recognition pact as of 1997.

Foreign Legal Consultants

Mexico has a unified national licensing system for attorneys (Abogados). Canada licenses its attorneys (Barristers and Solicitors) on a provincial basis. The 50 states of the United States and the District of Columbia do likewise. While the traditional perception that business lawyers are not fungible is open to challenge in a regional economy, it is reasonable to conclude that the services of Canadian, Mexican and United States lawyers cannot generally be substituted.

Professor James Smith has argued that United States and Mexican legal traditions, constitutions and political systems are so "markedly different" that legal training and law practice in one country is more likely to "hinder rather than aid" in understanding each other's legal systems. 1 U.S.-Mexico L.J. 85 (1993) Certainly the different Civil and Common Law legal traditions and ethical rules found in Quebec, the rest of Canada (ROC), Mexico, and among the states of the United States support this conclusion. On balance the broad exclusion of legal services from NAFTA seems justified, though less so for international business attorneys.

Against this background, NAFTA sought an alternative to mutual licensing of lawyers based on their national certifications. This alternative, the licensing of "foreign legal consultants," proved agreeable. A number of U.S. states had already authorized licensing foreign legal consultants primarily in order to retain opportunities for U.S. lawyers practicing abroad, especially in France. New York, California, Florida, Texas, Alaska, Connecticut, the District of Columbia, Georgia, Hawaii, Illinois, Michigan, New Jersey, Ohio, Oregon and Washington had done so prior to NAFTA. British Columbia, Ontario and Saskatchewan also licensed foreign legal consultants. Mexico had no experience with such licensure, but promised to do so under NAFTA for jurisdictions granting reciprocal rights to Mexican attorneys.

In Section B of Annex 1210.5, the NAFTA partners agreed to promote the licensing of foreign legal consultants. This, of course, is ultimately a decision for the states and provinces of the U.S. and Canada. It was also agreed that such consultants would be permitted to practice or advise on the laws of their home jurisdiction. It is unclear whether this includes the right to practice "international law" as a foreign legal consultant. One could argue that since the law of NAFTA is by implementation part of the law of Canada, Mexico and the United States that foreign legal consultants should at a minimum be able to advise on it.

The issue of just what law a foreign legal consultant can practice has split U.S. states. Alaska, California, Connecticut, Florida, Georgia and Texas only permit foreign legal consultants to advise on the law of their home jurisdictions. Nearly all the other participating states follow the Model Rule of the American Bar Association which permits practice of law except that of the licensing state and the United States.

Land Transportation

CFTA omitted land transportation from its scope. NAFTA Annex 1212 brings most cross-border bus, trucking and railroad services into the North American free trade and investment regime. Thus the bulk of all transport used in North American trade is covered, but implementation of the agreement in this area has proven hard to achieve.

In 1997, contrary to the NAFTA agreement, Mexico and the United States failed to establish border-free commercial trucking in contiguous states. At present, Mexican and U.S. trucks may service only narrow border bands in each country, and there is no further authority provided in the NAFTA Implementation Act. This failure is ongoing and centers on United States perceptions of inadequate Mexican safety regulations for trucks and their personnel and inadequate U.S. border-state enforcement capacity. Moreover, the powerful reality of Teamsters Union hostility to Mexican trucking in the United States cannot be ignored. Indeed, the Teamsters actually announced the U.S. refusal to implement the agreement in 1997 prior to the Department of Transportation.

Mexico's initial response was to exclude 53–foot U.S. trailer trucks. By 1998, Mexico's patience and cooperative efforts were exhausted. It invoked its right to Chapter 20 arbitration of the dispute. Complete cross-border point-to-point trucking is supposed to begin in 2000. Mexico has allowed minority NAFTA ownership of its cross-border trucking companies, and increasing ownership opportunities are scheduled for the future. By 2003, complete ownership in Mexican trucking companies should be permitted.

Vehicles and equipment used in NAFTA cross-border transport may enter and exit on any route. Such routes must, however, reasonably relate to economic and prompt departure by the transport company. If different points of entry and departure are used, bonds or penalties may not be imposed. Specifically, no release from obligations or bonds imposed upon entry may be denied due to exit from another point. Furthermore, shipping containers need not return on the same carrier or vehicle used for entry.

Bus transportation has also proven to be a difficult area to implement under NAFTA. Tour and charter bus operators have been free to provide cross-border services since 1994. But scheduled bus services, which were due for similar treatment in 1997, have fallen victim to the ongoing Mexico–U.S. safety disputes. Mexico has also taken bus transportation to Chapter 20 arbitration. Ownership of Canadian, Mexican or United States bus companies by investors from NAFTA is not anticipated until 2003.

Cross-border railway services were mostly unrestrained even prior to NAFTA. The NAFTA agreement specifically guarantees the right to market rail services in the region. The right to operate trains inside NAFTA with the owner's locomotives is also guaranteed, as is the right to construct and own rail terminals as well as finance railroad infrastructure. The big news in the railway sector is the privatization sale of major Mexican lines to the United States investors and their partners. Nothing in NAFTA required privatization of Mexico's railways. Indeed, there was every indication that Mexico intended to preserve state ownership. Then the peso collapsed late in 1994. Railway privatization suddenly seemed a prudent way to fill state coffers in a time of need. It did not hurt that railway unions were not closely allied with Mexico's dominant political party, the PRI.

The first privatization in December 1996 was of the Northeast Railway, the most significant carrier of goods between Mexico and the United States. It went to a consortium of Kansas City Southern Industries and the shipping company Transportacion Maritima Mexicana for a remarkable $1.4 billion. The second came in mid–1997 when Union Pacific Corp. joined Empresas Ingenieros Civiles Asocidos and Grupo Industrial Minera Mexico (the majority owner) in purchasing the Pacific North Railway for $396 million. The Mexican government retained 20 percent ownership in the Pacific North Railway. Late in 1997, Mexico privatized three short lines, including a 44–mile link between Tijuana and Tecate just below the California border. Railtex of San Antonio joined Grupo Proxima to bid on that maquiladora-centered line, but Grupo Morphy prevailed at just over $10 million. Grupo Morphy, however, failed to meet its payment obligations and the line is expected to go back up for bid.

Enhanced Telecommunications

Cross-border services and investment in basic telecommunications and public networks are not authorized by NAFTA. Nevertheless, the privatization of TELMEX (with a 10 percent U.S. partner) and Mexico's participation in the WTO agreement on basic telecommunications have made a difference. Mexico now allows 49 percent foreign ownership in wireline services, and 100 percent ownership in cellular and private leased-line services. AT & T, MCI and other long distance U.S. carriers have invested heavily in the Mexican market.

One key issue is what local network connection rates TELMEX can charge these carriers. This issue was first subject to intense private negotiations which failed. In 1996, the Mexican Ministry of Communications and Transport (SCT) set rates following "international norms." These rates were viewed by U.S. companies as providing TELMEX with a subsidy for its inexpensive local phone services. Likewise, they increased the incentive to invest in new telecommunications infrastructure so as to be able to avoid connecting through TELMEX entirely. The rates were reduced significantly in 1998, but not before TELMEX had turned the competitive tables by establishing very effective long distance services in the United States targeted at Mexicans and Mexican–Americans calling "home."

Chapter 13 of NAFTA creates North American rules for much of the "enhanced" telecommunications industry. Enhanced or value-added telecommunications services are defined in the agreement as those employing computer processing applications that act on customer-transmitted information, provide customers with information, or involve customer interaction with stored information. Such services include, for example, voice mail, cellular phone, fax, paging systems and electronic mail services. It is noteworthy that the enhanced telecommunications provisions of NAFTA are supreme if inconsistencies with any other part of the agreement arise.

The NAFTA rules on enhanced telecommunications can be summarized as follows. Domestic and international public telecommunications networks and services must be made available on reasonable, nondiscriminatory terms and conditions. Providers of enhanced or value-added telecommunications services, information services, and internal corporate communication systems specifically benefit from this provision. Access terms must generally be reasonable and allow leasing private lines, attachment of equipment to public networks, switching, signalling and processing functions, and selection of operating protocols. All national licensing rules and procedures governing NAFTA telecommunications providers must be transparent, expeditiously applied and nondiscriminatory. A review of the financial solvency and ability of providers to meet technical regulations is anticipated. Furthermore, unlike many utilities, enhanced telecommunications providers need not cost-justify their rates, make mandatory interconnections, nor provide services to the public. Investment by North Americans in enhanced telecommunications companies has been essentially free of restrictions since 1995.

NAFTA also sets some general rules for public telecommunications networks. Transport rates, for example, must be based on actual economic costs, but cross-subsidization between services is permissible. A flat-rate basis must be used to price privately leased circuits. Standards for equipment attached to public networks are authorized only to prevent technical damage or interference, to prevent billing problems, or to guarantee safety. Mutual reciprocity for equipment test results undertaken in each NAFTA country is the rule and there is agreement on promoting international standards for compatibility. In this regard, the delayed arrival of Mexico's telecom standards was discussed in Chapter 4. Mexico's acceptance of U.S. telecommunications test data was also delayed until 1997.

Public telecommunications monopolies are not prohibited by NAFTA provided they do not engage in anticompetitive conduct regarding enhanced services. The agreement specifically prohibits cross-subsidization, predatory behavior and discriminatory access terms in the enhanced telecommunications sector. Each NAFTA government must provide effective access to the information necessary for companies and users to benefit from NAFTA's enhanced telecommunications regime. Specifically, information on public network tariffs and contract terms, interface requirements, standards organizations, attachment conditions and licensing controls must be provided.

General Exceptions

For the most part, the general exceptions to NAFTA free trade in goods discussed in Chapter 4 also apply to trade in services. For example, all of the national security, balance of payments and cultural industries exceptions apply to services. However, the Article XX GATT exceptions do not apply to services.

More specifically, Chapter 21 of the NAFTA agreement reaffirms each nation's right to restrain trade in services in order to secure compliance with health, safety and consumer protection regulations. As with goods, such regulations must be NAFTA consistent, and cannot constitute a means of arbitrary or unjustifiable discrimination, or a disguised restraint on NAFTA trade.

On taxation, the national and most-favored-nation and most-favored state or provincial treatment standards that govern services, financial services and investment apply to the purchase or consumption of services except as otherwise specified. For both goods and services, the use of performance requirements in conjunction with taxation is limited. NAFTA's rules concerning expropriation also govern services taxation.

Financial Services

The NAFTA provisions on financial services differ from services generally. Cross-border provision of financial services is not fully ensured by NAFTA. Indeed each partner retained existing cross-border restraints absent a specific commitment to do otherwise. Greater freedoms were allowed to invest in the financial services sectors of each country, especially Mexico.

Investment and trade in financial services (including insurance and securities) are governed by Chapter 14 of NAFTA. The prior commitments made by Canada and the United States to each other under CFTA were retained. *See* Chapter 2. While the Canadians extended to Mexico the financial services commitments made to the United States under CFTA, the United States CFTA commitments have not been fully extended to Mexico.

For example, United States banks may not underwrite Mexican debt.

Mexico nationalized its banks in the early 1980s and then proceeded to privatize them to Mexicans (only) in the early 1990s. Foreign competition was relatively unknown in Mexico's financial services sector prior to NAFTA. Citibank, for example, stood alone in offering banking services in Mexico. Since 1994 Canadian and United States investors have been able to establish or purchase Mexican-chartered financial institutions. However, for most financial services this right has been subject (until the year 2000) to single firm and NAFTA aggregate capital and market share limits.

The limits have fluctuated according to the amount of capital and assets in Mexico's financial system. Warehousing, bonding, foreign exchange and mutual fund management investments are not subject to any limits. If Mexico were to invoke certain bank or securities safeguard rights, these limits could be extended to 2004. After Mexico's peso crisis of 1994–95 the limits were relaxed, and commitments made in 1998 as part of Mexico's bailout of FOBAPROA (its $60 billion repository of dud bank loans) suggest their elimination.

The Mexican market limitations on NAFTA investors proscribed in the financial services Chapter are as follows.

(1) For banking, the aggregate market share limits are 8 to 15 percent until 2000 with individual market share caps of 1.5 percent. Between

2000 and 2004, if the aggregate capital of NAFTA commercial banks operating in Mexico reaches 25 percent, special consultations to consider potential adverse effects and possible remedial action (including market share limits) may be held. After 2007, no market share caps are permissible. Canadian and United States banks cannot acquire Mexican banks if the result is a 4 percent or greater market share. This prohibition was intended to protect Mexico's largest banks from North American takeovers.

(2) For securities, factoring and leasing, the limits are 4 percent individually until 2000 and, in the aggregate, 10 rising to 30 percent by 2000.

(3) Insurance industry limits until 2000 vary with the nature of the investment and investment vehicle. Since 1996, pre-NAFTA investments may be wholly owned. New investments are subject until 2000 to individual market share caps of 1.5 percent and aggregate caps of 6 to 12 percent. New joint venture insurance investors can since 1998 own 51 percent, but must wait until 2000 to own 100 percent. By then, the Mexican insurance and brokerage industries are totally open to NAFTA investors and any takeover of a Mexican company may occur.

(4) "Limited scope financial institutions" that do not accept deposits can be established in Mex-

ico. Such companies typically provide consumer, commercial, mortgage lending or credit card services. They are generally subject to aggregate asset limits until 2000, but auto finance companies are exempt from this requirement.

Assuming Mexico's capital and market share limits are not an obstacle, a bank or securities company established in Mexico by NAFTA investors can create a holding company in order to offer most financial services. In this respect, NAFTA investors enjoy equal treatment with Mexican-owned financial firms. The range of possible services is quite wide since Mexico permits financial group holding companies to engage in banking, foreign exchange, securities, leasing, insurance, mutual fund management, factoring, bonding, warehousing and other services.

Certain limitations that apply to Mexican-owned financial institutions also apply to NAFTA investors. For example, the investor must already offer the type of financial services it seeks to establish or acquire in Mexico. All investments in Mexican financial services must be wholly-owned, except for insurance joint ventures with Mexican partners. Banks and securities firms may not be affiliated with Mexican industrial or commercial companies, although affiliations with firms operating outside Mexico are possible.

Canadian banks have been expanding south under CFTA and NAFTA. In the United States they operate primarily through branches, although the Bank of Montreal does business through a U.S. banking subsidiary. Canadian banks have also moved significantly into Mexico using representative offices. United States banking, insurance and securities presence in Mexico has also been growing. Most major U.S. money center banks and securities firms have established subsidiaries in Mexico.

Treatment of Financial Services Providers

The NAFTA provisions on treatment of financial services providers cover a wide gamut. The leading articles are the following: (1) Article 1403 (establishment of financial institutions); (2) Article 1404 (cross-border trade); (3) Article 1405 (national treatment); (4) Article 1406 (most-favored-nation treatment); (5) Article 1407 (new financial services and data processing); and (6) Article 1408 (senior management and boards of directors). All of these provisions are subject to various reservations and specific commitments found in Article 1409. For example, Article 1409 grandfathers certain pre-existing national financial services regulations ("nonconforming measures").

First-time NAFTA financial services investors must ordinarily be given entry. They may, however, be obliged to incorporate and be regulated locally. Purchasers of financial services may obtain services when they cross borders as visitors, and providers can solicit their business without a license to do business locally.

A general rule of national treatment governs the provision of financial services. This rule extends to existing and new investors as well as cross-border NAFTA providers. Establishing, acquiring, expanding, managing, conducting, operating, selling or otherwise disposing of financial institutions and investments are embraced within the scope of the general rule of national treatment. State and provincial governments must grant home state treatment, in like circumstances, to NAFTA investors in financial institutions.

NAFTA governments must provide "equal competitive opportunities" for financial services providers. (Article 1405.5) Specifically, NAFTA financial institutions may not be disadvantaged in their ability to provide services in competition under like circumstances with local financial institutions. For these purposes, differences in market share, profitability or size do not alone establish a denial of equal competitive opportunities. However, such differences can represent evidence of such a denial.

Article 1406 of the NAFTA agreement establishes a general most-favored-nation treatment obligation. However, if a NAFTA partner recognizes the "prudential" (public interest licensing and control) regulations of a non-NAFTA country, most-favored-nation treatment is not automatic. An opportunity to demonstrate equivalent prudential regulations or to negotiate a comparable arrangement is all that NAFTA requires. The NAFTA nations did promise to work towards uniform prudential regulations for financial institutions.

Since uniformity is often absent and mutual recognition was not agreeable, each NAFTA nation can adopt its own set of "reasonable" prudential regulations governing protection of investors, depositors, market participants, policy holders, fiduciary beneficiaries and the like. Maintaining the soundness and integrity of financial institutions and each country's financial system is also an authorized basis for prudential regulation, as is control of monetary transfers between parties related or affiliated to financial institutions or service providers. So too nondiscriminatory public regulation in pursuit of monetary, credit or exchange rate policies is allowed.

NAFTA financial institutions must be permitted to offer, in like circumstances, any *new* financial services or products similar to those of domestic institutions. Prior authorization of such new services may be required. Electronic transfer of data required by NAFTA financial institutions operating across borders is protected. Member states cannot mandate senior managers and other essential personnel of a particular nationality, but can stipulate that a simple majority (but not more) of the board of directors of NAFTA financial institutions be composed of its nationals or residents. This latter stipulation can be imposed even if it impairs the NAFTA investor's ability to control its investment.

Securing the benefits of NAFTA on financial services typically involves applying for national authorizations. Such applicants receive procedural protections under Article 1411. NAFTA governments must clarify their application requirements and keep applicants informed regarding the status of their applications. Perhaps most significantly, the authorities must "whenever possible" reach a decision on "completed" applications within 120 days. Applications are not complete until all relevant hearings are held and all necessary information is received.

Some cross-border provision of financial services is rather ambiguously subject to rights "in principle." These ambiguities reflect fundamental differences found in Canadian, Mexican and United States regulation of financial services that were unresolved when NAFTA came into force. For example, financial service-providers establishing a commercial presence in any NAFTA nation should "in principle" be allowed to choose the form of their investment. In banking, however, Canada and Mexico require foreign banks to establish local subsidiaries not branches (which are thought to be harder to regulate than subsidiaries). The United States generally permits either.

Providing a full range of financial services through separate institutions, expanding geographically, and nondiscriminatory ownership of local financial institutions are also NAFTA "principles." The first of these principles clearly reflects U.S.

banking law restraints on dealing in securities under the Glass–Steagall Act of 1933. Mexico and Canada generally follow the "universal banking" model which permits financial institutions to engage in banking, trust and loan, insurance and securities services. The second principle was aimed at United States interstate banking restraints that were largely removed under the Interstate Banking and Branching Efficiency Act of 1994. The third principle demonstrates disappointment with Mexican restraints on foreign ownership of banks and Canadian requirements for foreign bank subsidiaries.

Financial Services Dispute Settlement

The NAFTA Financial Services Committee is in charge of Chapter 14. This Committee includes representatives from the Canadian Department of Finance, the Mexican Secretaria de Hacienda y Credito Publico and the U.S. Treasury Department. On insurance matters, however, the Department of Commerce represents the United States.

The NAFTA Financial Services Committee will review any issue referred to it by a NAFTA government. Such intergovernmental disputes are preceded by member state consultations. If a dispute is not resolved by consultation or Committee review, Chapter 20 NAFTA dispute settlement procedures can be invoked. *See* Chapter 8. The only variations are that the Chapter 20 panelists are likely to be experts in financial services, and the normal Chapter 20 remedies may be limited.

The Financial Services Committee will also review certain private investment disputes concerning financial services, so-called investor-state disputes. *See* Chapter 6. This occurs when a member state claims exclusion from arbitration of the dispute on the basis of Article 1410 (prudential regulation, national monetary policy). In such a case, the arbitration tribunal set up under Chapter 11 refers the exclusion issue for resolution by the Financial Services Committee. The Committee then decides whether Article 1410 provides a valid defense to the investor's claim and its decision is final and binding. If for any reason the Committee fails to render its decision within 60 days, the arbitration tribunal generally rules on the exclusion issue. However, if a member state requests a dispute settlement panel under Chapter 20, then this panel decides the issue.

No particularly prominent financial services disputes have emerged as yet under NAFTA.

NAFTA Business Visas

Preferential visa treatment for business visitors, traders, investors, intracompany transferees, and certain professionals is established by NAFTA. Only Canadian, Mexican and United States citizens can benefit from these nonimmigrant entry rights. Spouses who accompany NAFTA visa entrants may not work without individual permission. Since many of the beneficiaries are service providers or investors, treatment of these provisions has been placed in this chapter. Please take note, however, that NAFTA's temporary entry rules are not limited to services.

NAFTA permits temporary duty free entry of certain goods accompanying business persons crossing borders on NAFTA visas. Such persons may bring with them professional equipment, press or television broadcasting and film equipment, sports goods, commercial samples, advertising films, and display or demonstration goods. These "tools of trade" are temporarily admitted on a duty free basis. Their origin and the existence or nonexistence of domestically produced competitive or substitutable items are irrelevant to exercise of this right.

However, customs duty bonds for nonoriginating goods, return responsibilities, and prohibitions against soliciting, selling or leasing such goods or equipment may apply. Failure to adhere to any of these conditions results in payment of the relevant tariff. Commercial solicitation samples of negligible value and printed packets of advertising materials enter duty free regardless of their origin and may remain in the country of entry.

NAFTA dispute settlement under Chapter 20 regarding entry rules can be triggered only when a pattern of practice is found and all available national administrative remedies have been exhausted. There is a tumultuous dispute over the legality under NAFTA of 1996 Helms–Burton LIBERTAD Act (110 Stat. 785) restraints on entry into the United States of persons who traffic in Cuban confiscated goods. The United States maintains that management consultants and lawyers, are also beneficiaries of NAFTA's preferential visa regime. Temporary entry is available only to members of professions listed in Appendix 1603.D.1 to Annex 1603. Standard public safety, national security and labor dispute reviews apply. As between Canada and the United States, no pre-entry labor screens are used. But such screens do apply to Mexican professionals entering the United States.

There are no United States limits for Canadians on temporary entry professional employee visas (so-called TN visas). The United States has restricted to 5,500 annually the number of such visas available to Mexican professionals. However, these 5,500 visas are in addition to whatever other professional visas Mexicans can obtain in the normal course of immigration law. The United States is obliged to eliminate this quota in 2003. Canada and Mexico have the option of imposing comparable limits on professional employee entrants, but have elected not to do so.

Proof by Canadians at time of entry into the United States of citizenship, educational credentials (and licensing if necessary), and a professional job in its offices to obtain a TN visa. United States professionals seeking entry to Canada can just as easily do the same. Tens of thousands of Canadian professionals have entered and remain (by renewal of their TN visas) in the United States in this

such restraints are exempt as national security measures. Canada and Mexico argue that they directly contravene the temporary entry rights enshrined in Chapter 16 of NAFTA. They have lodged a complaint under Chapter 20, which has not gone to arbitration only because President Clinton repeatedly has suspended application of Helms–Burton in pursuit of an intergovernmental agreement on trade with Cuba.

Business Visitors

NAFTA increases the number of Canadian, Mexican and United States citizens able to obtain temporary entry visas. NAFTA also increases the types of permissible activities of business visitors. For example, temporary entry visas are available for purposes of research and design, purchasing, production, marketing, sales, distribution and after-sales service. Such visas may also be had by persons providing general services, including credentialed professionals, managers, supervisors, financial services personnel, public relations officers, advertising staff, tourist leaders, tour bus operator and translators. One of the requirements for temporary business visitor visas is non-remuneration in the country of entry. For this reason, there are no pre-entry employment validation or labor certification screening procedures in connection with NAFTA business visitor visas (B–1 visas in the United States).

Numerical limits on the number of NAFTA business visitors are banned. However, entry may be barred for reasons of public safety or national security. Normally, business visitors need only prove citizenship, document their scheduled NAFTA business activities, and offer evidence that they are not seeking to enter the local labor market. Oral declaration at the border as to source of remuneration, principal place of business, and predominant outside accrual of profits are usually sufficient to meet these criteria.

The administration of business visitor visas differs among the member states. Canadian business visitors can cross United States borders without advance visas. United States business visitors to Canada may do likewise. Mexicans, however, must obtain advance business visitor visa approvals to enter Canada and the United States. Similarly, Canadian and United States business visitors must get visas in advance of going to Mexico.

Traders and Investors

NAFTA traders and investors also enjoy preferential temporary entry visas. "Traders" are defined as persons employed to carry on substantial trade in goods or services principally between NAFTA countries. "Investors" are defined person employed to establish, develop, administer or provide advice or key technical services to the operation of an investment to which a substantial amount of capital has been or is in the process of being committed. For both categories, preferential NAFTA treatment is available only if the person concerned acts in a capacity that is supervisory, executive or involves essential skills. In practice, these provisions have

chiefly benefited Canadians and Mexicans entering the United States. The NAFTA agreement gave treaty trader and investor status to Mexicans for the first time.

Standard public safety and national security exceptions apply to NAFTA traders and inves Pre-entry labor certification screening is not sary, and there are no numerical limits to temporary entry visas (E–1 and E–2 visas United States). However, by special provis visas may be denied if settlement of a cur dispute or employment of persons invol dispute would be adversely affected.

Intracompany Transferees

NAFTA further benefits executives employees with specialized knowl services to their employer or its sub ate in another NAFTA country. S obtain special "intracompany tr rary entry visas. Public safety, na labor dispute reviews apply. Th labor certification screens nor to intracompany transferee States these are known as States, but not Canada and of employment for the sar during one of the three pr

Professionals

Credentialed profess employed profession

Mexicans must apply in advance for TN visa status and quota qualification. In no year since 1994, however, has the Mexican quota been filled. The reason is that TN visas are harder to use as a springboard for permanent resident alien status (a "Green Card") which in turn can lead to naturalization as a U.S. citizen. Mexican professionals have demonstrably preferred H–1B visas (a traditional category not related to NAFTA) which can relatively easily lead to green cards and ultimately citizenship.

CHAPTER 6

INVESTMENT

The cross-border investment rules established in 1989 by Canada and the United States were reviewed in Chapter 2. NAFTA expands upon these rules with special emphasis on relaxation of Mexico's foreign investment controls. These controls find their roots in the revolutionary 1917 Mexican Constitution and the nationalization of foreign oil and gas interests in 1937. Under Mexican regulation of foreign investment since the 1940s, some industries were reserved for state ownership while others could only be owned by Mexicans. Foreigners were ordinarily allowed to invest in less sensitive industries, but often subject to mandatory joint venture requirements with majority Mexican ownership.

In 1973, Mexico promulgated an Investment Law that mandated more use of joint ventures if approved by the National Foreign Investment Commission. This Law was the most restrictive of its kind in Mexican history. By the 1980s, after years of mismanagement and corruption while awash in petroleum dollars, Mexico had a massive national debt problem. Foreign investment regulations issued by Presidential decree in 1989 shifted significantly towards allowance of wholly-owned subsidiaries. However, the regulations conflicted with the

1973 Investment Law. These uncertainties were finally resolved in 1993 as a direct consequence of NAFTA when Mexico adopted a new Law on Foreign Investment.

The 1993 Law is much more permissive of foreign investment without prior approval of by the Mexican Investment Commission. Although adopted on the eve of NAFTA, the new Law opens many of the same doors to all investors, not just those from NAFTA. Investment opportunities based upon the NAFTA agreement that are not generally available include the suspension of many performance requirements, the phased removal of market share caps on financial services, and reduced thresholds triggering Investment Commission review.

Acquisitions or sales of existing Mexican companies are generally subject to Commission review if exceeding $25 million U.S. This threshold increases to $150 million U.S. for NAFTA investors by 2003. It is presently $50 million U.S. and will become $75 million U.S. in 2000. For NAFTA investors, no permission from the National Commission is required to invest on a wholly-owned basis, or acquire or sell Mexican companies, whose values fall below this threshold.

NAFTA Investment Rights

In an unusual provision, Article 1112 subordinates all of Chapter 11 on investment to the rest of the NAFTA agreement. In other words, if there are inconsistencies between Chapter 11 and other parts of the NAFTA agreement, those other parts are supreme. That said, NAFTA provides investors and their investments with a number of important rights.

Canadian, Mexican and United States citizens, permanently resident aliens, and other designated persons are eligible to benefit from NAFTA's investment rules. In addition, most private and public, profit and nonprofit businesses "constituted or organized" under Canadian, Mexican or United States law also qualify. This coverage specifically includes businesses operating as corporations, partnerships, trusts, sole proprietorships, joint ventures and business associations.

Furthermore, in a notable change from CFTA, it is not necessary for such businesses to be owned or controlled by Canadian, Mexican or U.S. nationals or enterprises. As with services, this means that businesses owned by anyone which are "constituted or organized" inside NAFTA benefit from the agreement *provided* they carry on substantial business activities in North America. Thus Asians, Europeans and Latin Americans (for example) can invest in North America and benefit from NAFTA. Exceptions are made for NAFTA businesses owned or controlled by third parties from countries lacking diplomatic relations with or economically embargoed by Canada, Mexico or the United States.

Beneficiaries of NAFTA rights enjoy a broad definition of "investment." This definition includes most stocks, bonds, loans, and income, profit or asset interests. Real estate, tangible or intangible (intellectual) business property, turnkey or construction contracts, concessions, and licensing and franchising contracts are also generally included. However, under Annex III, each member state reserves certain economic activities to its state or domestic investors. Mexico has done so under its 1993 Foreign Investment Law. For purposes of Chapter 11, investment is defined so as to exclude claims to money arising solely from commercial contracts for the sale of goods or services, or trade financing, and claims for money that do not involve the interests noted above.

Treatment of Investors and Investments

The NAFTA agreement establishes a so-called "minimum standard of treatment" for NAFTA investors and investments which is "treatment in accordance with international law," including "fair and equitable treatment and full protection and security." (Article 1105.) For example, if losses occur due to armed conflict or civil strife, NAFTA investors and investments must be accorded nondiscriminatory treatment in response.

Beyond this minimum, NAFTA investors and their investments are entitled to the better of national or most-favored-nation treatment from federal governments. Such treatment rights extend to establishing, acquiring, expanding, managing, conducting, operating, and selling or disposing of investments. From state or provincial governments, NAFTA investors and their investments are entitled to receive the most-favored treatment those

governments grant their own investors and investments. Along these lines, United Parcel Service
found Mexico lacking when it was initially limited
to using smaller vans than Mexican competitors.
UPS persuaded the United States to lodge a complaint under Chapter 20 (see Chapter 8) which led
to intergovernmental consultations followed by
NAFTA Commission mediation. These efforts lasted
many months but eventually UPS got permission to
use smaller vans.

Article 1102 of NAFTA prohibits requiring minimum levels of equity holdings by nationals of the
host government. No investor can be forced on
grounds of nationality to sell or dispose of a qualified investment. Mandatory appointment of senior
managers on the basis of nationality is also contrary
to NAFTA. However, it is permissible to require
boards of directors and corporate committees with
majorities from one nationality or residence, provided this does not materially impair the investor's
ability to exercise control. Canadian law often
makes such stipulations. Residency requirements
are generally authorized if there is no impairment
of the rights of NAFTA investors.

Article 1106 of NAFTA prohibits various investment performance obligations, including tax-related
measures, in a scope that surpasses the WTO
Agreement on Trade–Related Investment Measures
(TRIMS) (1995). Requirements relating to exports,
domestic content, domestic purchases, trade balancing of foreign exchange inflows or earnings, im-

port/export ratios, technology transfers, and regional or global sales exclusivity ("product mandates") are broadly prohibited. All other types of investment-related performance requirements, such as employment and research and development obligations, are not prohibited and therefore presumably lawful.

Article 1106.3 of NAFTA further prohibits conditioning the receipt or continued receipt of "an advantage" (e.g., a government subsidy or tax benefit) on compliance with requirements relating to domestic content, domestic purchases, domestic sales restraints or trade balancing. But "advantages" can be given when the requirements concern production location, provision of services, training or employing workers, constructing or expanding facilities, or carrying out research and development locally.

By way of exception, domestic content or purchase requirements *and* advantages can be linked to investor compliance with: (1) Laws and regulations that are consistent with NAFTA; (2) laws necessary to protect human, animal or plant life or health; or (3) laws needed to conserve living or non-living exhaustible natural resources. However, such requirements cannot be applied arbitrarily or unjustifiably, and may not constitute a disguised restraint on trade or investment.

All monetary transfers relating to NAFTA investments are to be allowed "freely and without delay." (Article 1109) Such transfers must be possible in a "freely usable currency" at the market rate of exchange prevailing in spot transactions on the transfer date. For these purposes, monetary transfers specifically include profits, dividends, interest, capital gains, royalties, management, technical assistance and other fees, returns in kind, and funds derived from the investment. Sale or liquidation proceeds, contract payments, compensatory payments for expropriation and NAFTA dispute settlement payments are also encompassed.

Requiring investment-related monetary transfers or penalizing them is prohibited. However, such transfers can be controlled in an equitable, nondiscriminatory and good faith application of bankruptcy, insolvency, creditors' rights, securities, criminal, currency reporting and satisfaction of judgment laws. Whereas tax withholding was a justifiable basis for restricting monetary transfers under CFTA, this is not the case under NAFTA. Special restraints may arise in connection with balance of payments problems and taxation laws.

Expropriation

Article 1110 of NAFTA generally prohibits direct or indirect nationalization or expropriation of NAFTA investments. Measures "tantamount" to nationalization or expropriation, such as creeping expropriation or confiscatory taxation, are also prohibited. Expropriation, nationalization or tantamount measures may occur for public purposes on a nondiscriminatory basis in accordance with due process of law and NAFTA's "minimum level of treatment" (above).

Any authorized expropriation must result in payment of compensation without delay. The amount of payment must be equivalent to the fair market value of the investment immediately prior to expropriation. In valuing the investment, going concern value, asset value (including declared tax values of tangible property) and other appropriate factors must be considered. It has been suggested that case law developed in connection with the Iran–United States Claims Tribunal provides insight into what "fair market value" is likely to mean under NAFTA. *See Levin and Martin*, 1996 NAFTA: Law and Business Review of the Americas (Summer).

Payment must be made in a manner that is fully realizable, such as in a "G7" currency (U.S. dollars, Canadian dollars, EUROS, British pounds sterling, Japanese yen). Interest at a commercially reasonable rate must also be included. If payment is made in Mexican pesos, this amount must be calculated as of the expropriation date in a G7 currency plus interest.

Certain governmental acts are not expropriatory. For example, NAFTA specifies that nondiscriminatory measures of general application that impose costs on defaulting debtors are not tantamount to expropriation of a bond or loan *solely* for that reason. Compulsory licensing of intellectual property rights is not expropriatory. Revocation, limitation or creation of such rights as allowed by Chapter 17 of NAFTA is also deemed not an expropriation.

These provisions embody an historic change in Mexico's position on expropriation law. Without explicitly saying so, Mexico has essentially embraced the U.S. position that under "international law" expropriation of foreign investments requires "prompt, adequate and effective" compensation. Mexico had specifically rejected this standard in negotiating a settlement of its oil and gas (and land) expropriations in the 1930s. Down through the years Mexico adamantly clung to its view that compensation would only be paid according to Mexican law. For investors protected under NAFTA (which are not just Canadian and U.S. investors), Chapter 11 represents the dawn of a new era.

Exceptions and Reservations

Annexes I–IV of the NAFTA agreement reveal a host of investment-related reservations and exceptions. Many pre-existing, non-conforming regulations were grandfathered though most (not including basic telecommunications, social services and maritime services) are subject to a standstill agreement intended to avoid relapses into greater protection. In contrast, regulations promoting investment "sensitive to environmental concerns" are expressly authorized. Mexico's tradition of assessing the environmental impact of foreign investments will therefore continue. There is also a formal recognition that creating exceptions to environmental laws to encourage NAFTA investors to establish, acquire, expand or retain their investments is inappropriate. However, NAFTA's Chapter 20 dispute settlement mechanism cannot be invoked concerning this "commitment." Only intergovernmental consultations are mandatory.

Other investment-related exceptions concern government procurement, subsidies, export promotion, foreign aid and preferential trade arrangements. These exceptions apply mostly to the rules on nondiscriminatory treatment and performance requirements. Most general exceptions to NAFTA, such as for Canadian cultural industries, also apply to its investment rules. The general national security exception, for example, allows the United States to block the acquisition of U.S. companies by foreigners (including Canadians and Mexicans) under "Exon–Florio" regulations (50 U.S.C. App. § 2170).

Arbitration of Investor–State Disputes

NAFTA has created a highly innovative and increasingly controversial investment dispute settlement system. This system provides a way for investors to challenge governmental and state enterprise acts. Remarkably, investors may not only assert claims as individuals, but also on behalf of NAFTA enterprises they own or control directly or indirectly. (Article 1117). This authorization avoids one of international law's most famous problems ... "standing to sue" when the investor's only loss or damage is injury to its investment abroad. *See Belgium v. Spain (the "Barcelona Traction Case")*, 1970 Int'l Court of Justice 3 (preliminary objections).

Chapter 20 NAFTA dispute settlement does not apply to "investor-state disputes." Such disputes are instead subject to binding arbitration, another major concession on the part of Mexico which has always adhered to the "Calvo Doctrine." That doctrine (widely followed in Latin America) requires foreign investors to forego protection by their home governments, be treated as Mexican nationals, and pursue legal remedies exclusively in Mexico. *See* Article 27 of the Mexican Constitution.

Individual investors claiming that a government has breached NAFTA investment or state enterprise obligations, or that one of its monopolies has done so, commence the dispute resolution process. All claims are filed against the federal government even when it is state, provincial or local government action that is being challenged. This can sometimes place Canada, Mexico and the United States in the awkward position of defending sub-central governmental acts. *See Metalclad* and *Loewen* below.

The investor must allege that the breach of NAFTA caused loss or damage. Such claims must be asserted no later than three years after the date when knowledge of the alleged breach and knowledge of the loss or damage was first acquired or should have been first acquired. However, decisions by the Canadian or Mexican foreign investment control commissions, national security actions, and Canadian cultural industry reservations cannot be the basis for such a claim. Moreover, a host of reservations and exceptions deny access to NAFTA's investor-state arbitration remedy. *See* Chapter

11B. Even so, as outlined below, the number of claims being filed is rising, some claims are producing unexpected results, and the process itself is under dispute.

Before submitting a claim to arbitration, individual investors must give 90 days advance notice to the host country. Such notice must include an explanation of the issues, their factual basis and remedies sought. Claimants must also consent in writing to arbitrate under the procedures established in the NAFTA agreement. They must waive in writing their rights to initiate or continue any other damages proceedings. Individual investors need not, however, waive their rights to injunctive, declaratory or other extraordinary relief (not involving damages). These remedies may not be awarded through NAFTA arbitration of investor-state disputes.

The NAFTA nations consented in advance to the submission of investor claims to arbitration under NAFTA procedures. Furthermore, they agreed not to assert insurance payments or other investor indemnification rights as a defense, counterclaim, right of setoff or otherwise.

The investor submitting a claim to arbitration against a NAFTA state ordinarily can elect between the following arbitration rules:

- The ICSID Convention* if both member states adhere. This is impossible at present since only the United States has ratified ICSID;

* The Convention on the Settlement of Investment Disputes between States and Nationals of Other States (1966). The Con-

- The Additional Facility Rules of ICSID provided one member state (i.e., the United States) adheres to the ICSID Convention; or
- The U.N.-derived UNCITRAL Arbitration Rules.

NAFTA investor-state tribunals have three panelists. The investor and the state each choose one arbitrator. If possible, the third presiding panelist is chosen by agreement. The ICSID Secretary–General selects the presiding arbitrator if agreement is not reached within 90 days. That person is chosen from a consensus roster of acceptable names, but may not be a national from either side of the dispute.

Investor-state tribunals must decide the dispute in accordance with the NAFTA agreement and "applicable rules of international law." The responding state may raise defenses based upon reservations or exceptions contained in Annexes I–IV to the NAFTA agreement. In such instances, the NAFTA Commission (not the arbitration panel) will ordinarily issue a binding ruling on the validity of such a defense. Defenses based upon permissible regulation of monetary transfers by financial institutions are generally decided by the NAFTA Financial Services Committee.

By agreement of the parties, the investor-state arbitration tribunal can obtain expert reports on factual issues concerning environmental, health, safety or other scientific matters. The tribunal may

vention is administered through the World Bank in Washington, D.C. and has been ratified by over 130 nations.

also order temporary relief measures to preserve rights or the full effectiveness of its jurisdiction. It may, for example, order the preservation of evidence. The tribunal cannot, however, order attachment or enjoin governmental regulations that are being challenged.

NAFTA investor-state tribunals are authorized to award investors or NAFTA enterprises actual damages and interest, or restitution of property, or both. If the award is to an enterprise, any person may *also* pursue relief under "applicable domestic law." If restitution is ordered, the responsible member state may provide monetary damages and interest instead.

The award of the tribunal is binding only on the parties. It is specifically not "precedent" in future NAFTA arbitrations. NAFTA investor-state arbitration awards are supposed to be honored. Should this not occur, the investor may seek enforcement of the award and NAFTA nations have agreed to provide the means of enforcement. The NAFTA investor-state dispute settlement system meets the various requirements of the ICSID Convention, its Additional Facility Rules, the New York Convention on Recognition and Enforcement of Foreign Arbitral Awards (1958), and the Inter–American Convention on International Commercial Arbitration (1975). Should it become necessary to judicially enforce an investor-state arbitration award, the New York Convention provides the most likely recourse as all three nations adhere to it.

If there is no compliance with the award and enforcement proceedings fail, the investor's government may as a last recourse commence dispute settlement under Chapter 20 of NAFTA. *See* Chapter 8. This panel rules on whether noncompliance inconsistent with the NAFTA agreement has occurred and can recommend compliance. If compliance still does not follow, benefits granted under NAFTA to the noncomplying nation may be suspended.

Early Investor Claims Against States Under NAFTA

Investors have not hesitated to invoke the innovative investor-state arbitration procedures authorized under Section B of Chapter 11 of NAFTA. Since there are no NAFTA public disclosure requirements, and the arbitration process and award are confidential, it is difficult to ascertain which investor-state arbitrations are underway and what they concern. Most information about these disputes is obtained through securities filings or press releases issued by the claimant, although Canada has adopted a policy of making public notices of intent to file investor-state claims. Many of the investors allege state action that is "tantamount to expropriation." This is a claim that Article 1110 authorizes and one which could be construed to fit many fact patterns. Canada is actively seeking to restrictively "clarify" this and other Chapter 11B provisions.

The following claims have reportedly been filed:

1. Metalclad Corp. of California acquired a hazardous waste site operated by a Mexican company in Guadalcazar, San Luis Potosi subject to various federal approvals all of which were obtained. State and local opposition to opening the site after an expensive clean-up resulted in the denial of a building permit in a newly created "ecological zone." Metalclad claims this amounts to expropriation and denial of national treatment benefits under NAFTA. It seeks $90 million U.S. in damages.

2. Signa SA of Mexico claims that the Canadian government is wrongfully preventing it from entering the Canadian market for pharmaceuticals. Signa and its Canadian partner seek to make generic versions of Bayer's CIPRO antibiotic. Signa seeks $50 million Canadian in damages.

3. Ethyl Corp. of the USA claimed $250 million U.S. damages against the Canadian government as a consequence of 1997 federal legislation banning importation or interprovincial trade of the gasoline additive, MMT. Canada was the first country to ban MMT as a pollution and health hazard, although California has also done so. MMT is a manganese-based octane enhancer alleged to interfere with the proper functioning of catalytic converters. Ethyl Corp. is the sole producer of MMT in North America. Ethyl claimed that the new law was tantamount to expropriation, violated NAFTA's national treatment standards and constituted an unlawful Canadian-content performance requirement (because the

ban would favor Canadian ethanol as a substitute for MMT).

A dispute resolution panel under Canada's Agreement on Internal Trade struck down the interprovincial trade ban. In 1998, Canada withdrew its ban on MMT and paid $13 million to Ethyl Corp. Ethyl then withdrew its $250 million arbitration claim. Canada noted the current lack of scientific evidence documenting MMT harm, an apparent abandonment of the "precautionary principle." Environmentalists have decried evidence of NAFTA's negative impact, and Europeans have cited *Ethyl* as good reason to reject multilateral investment guarantee agreements in the OECD (Organization for Economic Cooperation and Development). Both groups believe Chapter 11 has created a privileged class of "supercitizens" who are a threat to state sovereignty.

4. USA Waste claims that Acapulco, the state of Guerrero and the Mexican federal government have unlawfully appropriated its 15–year concession agreement to provide waste removal services to Acapulco. USA Waste claims $60 million U.S. in damages, largely as a result of nonpayment and failure of the federal BANOBRAS Bank to meet payment guarantees.

5. The Loewen Group of Canada was held liable by a jury in 1995 for $500 million in a Mississippi breach of a funeral services contract suit. The case was settled for $150 million after the Mississippi Supreme Court required posting a $625 million

bond prior to appealing the jury's verdict, a sum in excess of Loewen's net worth. In 1998, Loewen filed a claim under NAFTA alleging discrimination, denial of the minimum NAFTA standard of investor treatment, and uncompensated expropriation. This claim, like that of Ethyl Corp., is destined for controversy. Among other things, it challenges the discretion of American juries in awarding punitive damages. Note that it does so in a forum that does not give the American Trial Lawyers Association an opportunity to respond.

6.   Sun Belt Water Co. of Santa Monica, California contracted to supply Canadian water (yes, water) to parched California towns. Sun Belt also contracted with Snowcap Waters of Fanny Bay, British Columbia to obtain the water. However, the B.C. provincial government placed a moratorium on bulk water exports by container ships. In ensuing litigation, British Columbia settled with Snowcap but not Sun Belt. That company then served notice that it was filing an investor-state claim under NAFTA alleging that it had not received "fair and equitable treatment" (the minimum standard). Sun Belt asserts $300 million U.S. in damages.

This claim revisits an old theme ... will Canada allow the export of water resources? Canada possesses about 20 percent of the world's fresh water supplies. Southern California has been locked for decades in water wars with Northern California and users of the Colorado River. Query, however, whether Sun Belt has an "investment" protected by NAFTA?

7. Pope and Talbot, Inc. of Portland, Oregon claims that the 1996 Softwood Lumber Agreement (see Chapter 2) violates the national treatment, most-favored-nation treatment, minimum treatment, and performance requirements rules of NAFTA. The claim asserts that the company's British Columbia subsidiary was the victim of discrimination because the Canadian export restraints required under that Agreement applied only to four Canadian provinces. Pope & Talbot seek $20 million U.S. in compensation from the Canadian government.

8. S.D. Myers of Ohio claims that Canada's 1995 *export* ban on polychlorinated byphenyls (PCBs) damaged its hazardous waste disposal business by $10 to $20 million U.S. S.D. Myers alleges that the ban constitutes a measure tantamount to expropriation (Article 1110), violates Article 1105 because it is not being treated in accordance with international law, and violates Article 1106 concerning performance requirements. In 1997, on the very day that a U.S. Court ordered the EPA to control the importation of PCBs, Canada lifted its export ban. The EPA has since established a regulatory permit process for PCB imports.

CHAPTER 7

INTELLECTUAL PROPERTY

There was no coverage of intellectual property under CFTA. In contrast, Chapter 17 of the NAFTA agreement contains a comprehensive set of rules for North American intellectual property rights. NAF-TA's provisions on intellectual property are closely related, but somewhat more extensive than those of the WTO Agreement on Trade–Related Intellectual Property Rights (TRIPs) (1995). Both NAFTA and TRIPs stipulate that whichever agreement affords the broadest protection of intellectual property will prevail. While its primary impact has been on Mexico, Canada and the United States also amended their intellectual property laws after NAFTA.

Prior to 1991, Mexico had a Technology Transfer Commission with a veto power over most intellectual property licensing and franchising agreements. The Commission also controlled in detail the terms and conditions of technology transfer agreements. It even decided the level of acceptable royalties. Commissions of this kind are best understood by remembering that developing nations like Mexico are basically technology importers. While Mexico needed technology, it did not wish to pay excessively for what was not always at the cutting edge. So it, like most of Latin America, empowered the Technology

Transfer Commission to get better terms. What happened instead was that technology transfers to Mexico slowed to a trickle.

In 1991, well prior to NAFTA, Mexico abolished the Commission and most technology transfer controls. Licensors and licensees became free to bargain over the terms and conditions of their agreements. However, Mexico's patent, copyright, trademark and trade secret laws remained (by United States standards) less than fully protective of intellectual property rights. This was of concern because many Mexican patents and copyrights, for example, are owned by U.S. corporations and investors. NAFTA brought fundamental alterations to Mexican law in these areas. In 1994, Mexico joined the Patent Cooperation Treaty. Obtaining Mexican patents is now as simple as checking a box designating Mexico as a country in which protection is desired.

General Obligations

Specific commitments on patents, copyrights, trademarks, trade secrets and other intellectual property rights are made in the NAFTA agreement. These are discussed individually below. NAFTA also contains some general intellectual property rights obligations. Many of these obligations have counterparts under the TRIPS agreement. For example, except for secondary use of sound recordings, there is a general rule of national treatment.

There is also a general duty to protect intellectual property adequately and effectively, as long as barriers to legitimate trade are not created. At a minimum, this duty necessitates adherence to NAFTA Chapter 17. This general duty also embraces adherence to the substantive provisions of: The Geneva Convention of Phonograms (1971); the Berne Convention for the Protection of Literary and Artistic Works (1971); the Paris Convention for the Protection of Industrial Property (1967); and the 1978 or 1991 versions of the International Convention for the Protection of New Varieties of Plants. Protecting intellectual property rights more extensively than these Conventions is expressly authorized.

The process of intellectual property rights enforcement is covered in detail under NAFTA. Speaking generally, these provisions require fair, equitable, and not unnecessarily complicated, costly or time-consuming enforcement procedures. Written notice, independent legal counsel, the opportunity to substantiate claims and present evidence, and protection of confidential information are stipulated for civil enforcement proceedings. Overly burdensome mandatory personal appearances cannot be imposed.

Remedies to enjoin infringement (new to Mexico), prevent importation of infringing goods, and order payment for damages and litigation costs must exist. However, proof of knowing infringement or reasonable grounds for such knowledge is an acceptable criterion. Recovery of profits or liquidated damages must be available when copyright or sound recording infringement is involved. Disposition of infringing or counterfeit goods outside the ordinary channels of commerce or even by destruction is anticipated by NAFTA. All administrative intellectual property rights decisions must be reviewable by a court of law.

Counterfeiting

Criminal penalties are required under NAFTA for willful trademark counterfeiting or copyright piracy undertaken on a commercial scale. For United States law on point, see the Trademark Counterfeiting Act of 1984 (18 U.S.C. § 2320 et seq.). When the counterfeit or pirated goods come from outside the region, those affected must be given the opportunity to bar importation and possibly obtain their destruction or other satisfactory disposal.

Despite strong provisions in NAFTA to fight counterfeiting and promote protection of intellectual property, Mexico is seen by some as still not measuring up. Annual submissions by the International Intellectual Property Alliance to the USTR under Special 301 procedures document the ineffectiveness of Mexico's anti-piracy law enforcement. Hundreds of millions of dollars of fake tapes, videos, CDs, software and the like can be found in Mexican marketplaces and the amount is increasing. Prosecutions and border controls to combat counterfeiting have been limited. Some 2500 government raids in 1998 netted just 35 convictions with no fines in excess of $1,000.

Mexico's Customs Law of 1996 placed border controls in the hands of the Mexican Institute of Industrial Property (IMPI) for the first time. This Institute was created in 1993 specifically for the task of enforcing Mexican intellectual property rights. Unlike the U.S. Patent and Trademark Office, the IMPI has the power to enforce patent owners rights against actual and potential infringers. It can prevent commercialization of an infringing product including its removal from the stream of commerce. Mexico also has had, since 1993, a multi-departmental Anti–Piracy Commission.

In June of 1998, the U.S. and Mexico reached agreement on new measures to combat counterfeiting in Mexico. These include a national anti-piracy campaign, tax crimes against counterfeiters, expeditious search and seizure and arrest warrants, and increased administrative enforcement resources. Whether these measures will stem the tide of counterfeit goods in Mexico remains to be seen.

Gray Market Trading

One important intellectual property rights issue that NAFTA does not speak to is gray market trading. Gray market goods consist of goods produced abroad with authorization which are imported without authorization. Trade in gray market goods has exploded in recent years, often because of sharply fluctuating currency exchange rates. Such fluctuations create opportunities to import and sell the "real thing" at a discount from local price levels. K Mart, Wal–Mart and other retailers have devoted significant resources to gray market trading. Consumers, as a rule, are only too happy to benefit from this form of price competition.

Manufacturers and their authorized distributors, on the other hand, are frequently upset with gray marketeers. They often call such traders "free riders." That is to say, some manufacturers and authorized distributors believe that gray marketeers are benefiting from but not paying their fair share of advertising, promotional, service, warranty and other associated costs. In a general sense, manufacturers worry that gray market goods will dilute their brand names. Some manufacturers will not do warranty work on gray market goods (cameras and Mercedes Benz autos, for example).

To stem the tide of gray market imports, manufacturers ordinarily turn to intellectual property rights that accompany the goods. Most goods, for example, are trademarked. United States law concerning the use of intellectual property rights as import barriers has a checkered history. The most important legislation in this complex area is the Genuine Goods Exclusion Act of 1922 (19 U.S.C. § 1526). This Act bars unauthorized importation of goods bearing trademarks owned by U.S. citizens. Such persons or companies may register their marks with the U.S. Customs Service which is empowered to seize the offending goods.

For a variety of reasons, including the legislative history of the Act, the U.S. Customs Service created two exceptions to the general rule against importing trademarked gray market goods. These are known as the "common control" and "authorized use" exceptions. Under these exceptions, gray market goods can enter the U.S. market if the trademark in question is under common ownership or control, or its use on the goods was authorized by the U.S. owner. Practically speaking, these exceptions allowed entry to most gray market goods until 1988. In that year, the U.S. Supreme Court ruled that only the common control (not the authorized use) exception was a reasonable administrative interpretation of the Act. *K Mart Corp. v. Cartier*, 486 U.S. 281 (1988). Even so, United States law remains relatively open to gray market trading. More so, for example, than Canadian law.

The question that gray market trading poses for NAFTA is the same as has been debated for decades in Europe. Should national intellectual property rights be allowed to function as trade barriers inside the region? Europe, especially the European Court of Justice, has by and large said not. *See* R. Folsom, *European Union Law in a Nutshell*. In the European Union, free trade interests usually trump national intellectual property rights.

Under NAFTA, there is no clear answer. Chapter 17 takes pains to expand and protect national intellectual property rights, and specifically addresses the issue of counterfeiting, but not gray market trading. The relevant law of each nation remains intact, but some have argued that NAFTA's free trade rules (*see* Chapter 4) should and perhaps will trump national intellectual property rights, much as has happened in Europe. *See especially Miller*, 16 Loyola L.A. Entertainment L.J. 475 (1996) and the discussion of the U.S. copyright "first sale doctrine" below.

Patents

Article 1709 of NAFTA assures the availability of patents "in all fields of technology." New products and processes resulting from an inventive step that are capable of industrial application are patentable. Patents for pharmaceuticals, computer software, microorganisms and microbiological processes, plant varieties, and agricultural chemicals were specifically included under NAFTA and caused changes in Mexican law. In addition, protection for layout designs of semiconductor integrated circuits was provided by Article 1710. All patent rights must be granted without discrimination as to field of technology, country of origin, and importation or local production of the relevant products. Since the United States still awards patents on a first-to-invent (not first-to-file) basis, activities in Canada and Mexico now count for purposes establishing the date of invention.

NAFTA specifically reserves the right to *deny* patents for diagnostic, therapeutic and surgical methods, transgenic plants and animals, and for essentially biological processes that produce plants or animals. If commercial exploitation might endanger public morality or "ordre public" (state security) no patents need be granted. Patent denials to protect human, animal or plant life or health, or to avoid serious injury to nature or the environment, are also justifiable under NAFTA.

It was agreed that patents in NAFTA nations would run either for 20 years from the date of filing of the patent application, or 17 years from the grant of patent rights (the traditional U.S. approach). However, the subsequent TRIPs agreement stipulates a 20–year patent term from the date of filing. Canadian, Mexican and United States patent laws now follow this rule. Under NAFTA, patent owners generally possess the right to prevent others from making, using or selling the invention without their consent. No mention is made of the right to block infringing or unauthorized imports. If the patent covers a process, this includes the right to prevent others from using, selling or *importing* products obtained directly from that process. Assignment or transfer of patents, and licensing contracts for their use and exploitation, are also expressly protected.

On the touchy subject of compulsory licensing, which is not authorized under U.S. law, governments may allow limited nonexclusive usage without the owner's authorization if the invention has not been used or exploited locally through production or importation. This is generally permissible only after reasonable attempts at securing a license. However, under emergency, competition law or public noncommercial circumstances, no prior attempt at securing a license is required. In all cases of compulsory licensing, there is a duty to adequately remunerate the patent owner. Significant changes in Canadian compulsory licensing of pharmaceuticals were made in 1993. These changes caused some pharmaceutical prices to rise in Canada.

Apart from compulsory licensing, NAFTA authorizes "limited exceptions" to exclusive patents rights. Such exceptions may not "unreasonably conflict" with the normal exploitation of the patent. Nor may they "unreasonably prejudice" the owner's "legitimate interests." It is not clear how this broad authorization will be construed or applied.

Copyrights

The NAFTA provisions on copyrights promote uniformity in North America. Canada, Mexico and the United States promised extensive protection of copyrights, sound recordings, program-carrying satellite signals and industrial designs. Copyrights are available on all works of original expression. These include books, articles, choreography, photographs, paintings, sculpture, films, videos, records, tapes, CDs and other traditionally copyrighted materials. In most instances, copyrights must be granted for at least 50 years. (The United States now grants 70–year copyrights.) Computer programs and data compilations which constitute intellectual creations are subject to copyrights. *See Feist Publications, Inc. v. Rural Telephone Service Co.*, 499 U.S. 340 (1991). Article 1707 requires criminal sanctions for makers and sellers of unauthorized decoding devices, and civil sanctions for unauthorized receivers of satellite signals.

Copyright holders also receive the rights enumerated in the Berne Convention for the Protection of Literary and Artistic Works (1971). However, translation and reproduction licenses permitted by the Berne Convention are not allowed under NAFTA if these needs could be fulfilled voluntarily by the copyright holder but for national laws. In addition, Article 1704.2 specifically conveys to copyright holders:

1. Control over importation of unauthorized copies;

2. first public distribution rights over the work (whether by sale, rental or otherwise);

3. control over communication of the work to the public; and

4. control over commercial rental of computer programs.

If the original or a copy of a computer program is put on the market, this does not exhaust rental rights. Despite the specific reference to control over unauthorized imports in Article 1704.2, it is doubtful whether NAFTA can be construed so as to block free trade in copyrighted goods after their first sale. The "first sale doctrine" limits an owner's rights to control copyrighted goods to their first sale or transfer. Thereafter, the goods can be freely exchanged. *See Quality King Distributors, Inc. v. L'Anza Research International, Inc.,* 523 U.S. 135 (1998).

Licensing and conveyance of copyrights, royalties and the like are freely transferable under NAFTA. Assignment of works of creation to employers by employees is also protected. However, Article 1705.5 somewhat vaguely allows limits or exceptions in "special cases" that do not conflict with "normal exploitation" of the work. Presumably, "fair use" of copyrighted material falls within this provision. These exceptions may not unreasonably prejudice the owner's legitimate interests.

Trademarks

Trademarks are found on most products, and service and other marks are commonly used. The pervasiveness of marks arguably makes them the most important of NAFTA's intellectual property provisions. Such marks help make markets work by signaling attributes, qualities, price levels and other relevant information. The NAFTA provisions on marks foster uniform law. They stop short, however, from establishing a regional trademark as the Europeans have done. *See* EU Council Regulation 40/94.

Canada, Mexico and the United States agreed to register trademarks, service marks, collective organizational marks and certification marks. All of these marks must be capable of distinguishing goods or services. Internationally "well-known" marks are given special protections against pirates. Whether a mark is "well-known" turns upon knowledge of it in the sector of the public normally dealing with the goods or services. A reasonable opportunity to petition to cancel trademark registrations must be granted. In contrast, a reasonable opportunity to oppose registration applications is not mandatory under NAFTA. The nature of the goods or services *per se* cannot justify a refusal to register.

To apply for protection, there is no requirement of prior usage on goods or services. However, if actual usage does not occur within 3 years, Chapter 17 provides that registration may be denied. Immoral, deceptive, scandalous and disparaging marks, and those that falsely suggest a connection with or contempt of persons, institutions, beliefs or national symbols can be denied registration. No registration of words in English, French or Spanish that generically designate goods or services is permitted. Registration of marks indicating geographic origin can be rejected if "deceptively misdescriptive."

Trademark registrations must be valid for at least 10 years. They can be renewed indefinitely provided use is continuous. If circumstances beyond the owner's control justify non-use, registrations can be continued. For all these purposes, the NAFTA nations agreed that use is continued when undertaken by franchisees or licensees.

NAFTA trademark owners can prevent persons from using identical or "similar" signs on identical or similar goods or services if this would cause a "likelihood of confusion." However, the "fair use" of descriptive terms may be allowed. Mandatory use of a second "local" trademark (as Mexico once required) is banned. Mandatory use that reduces the function of trademarks as source indicators is also prohibited. Furthermore, compulsory licensing of trademarks is contrary to NAFTA, but contractual licensing and assignment of trademarks can be conditioned.

Trade Secrets

NAFTA was the first international agreement on trade secret protection. Its primary impact has been on Mexican law. At a minimum, each nation must ensure legal means to prevent trade secrets from being disclosed, acquired or used without consent "in a manner contrary to honest commercial practices." (Article 1711). Breach of contract, breach of confidence, and inducement to breach of contract are specifically listed as examples of dishonest commercial practices. Moreover, persons who acquire trade secrets knowing them to be the product of such practices, or who were grossly negligent in failing to know this, also engage in dishonest commercial practices. This is true even if they do not use the secrets in question. NAFTA does not mention, however, the practice of "reverse engineering". This practice is thought to be common and has been authoritatively endorsed by the U.S. Supreme Court. *See Kewanee Oil Co. v. Bicron Corp.*, 416 U.S. 470 (1974).

For NAFTA purposes, information is "secret" if it is not generally known or readily accessible to persons who normally deal with it, has commercial value because of its secrecy, and reasonable steps have been taken to keep it secret. This definition ought to cover, for example, the secret formula for making Coca–Cola. Nevertheless, trade secret holders may be required to produce evidence documenting the existence of the secret in order to secure protection. Release of such information to government authorities obviously involves risks that will need to be considered.

No NAFTA government may discourage or impede the voluntary licensing of trade secrets (often referred to as "knowhow licensing"). Imposing excessive or discriminatory conditions on knowhow licenses is prohibited. More specifically, in testing and licensing the sale of pharmaceutical and agricultural chemical products, there is a general duty to protect against disclosure of proprietary data.

In 1996, independently of NAFTA, the United States enacted the Economic Espionage Act. 18 U.S.C. § 1831 et seq. This Act creates criminal penalties for misappropriation of trade secrets. For these purposes, a "trade secret" is defined as "financial, business, scientific, technical, economic or engineering information" that the owner has taken reasonable measures to keep secret and whose "independent economic value derives from being closely held". All proceeds from the theft of trade secrets and all property used or intended for use in the misappropriation can be seized and forfeited.

CHAPTER 8

DISPUTE SETTLEMENT

NAFTA employs a range of dispute settlement procedures. Chapters 19 and 20 are the best known, most visible and most formal. Chapter 19 concerns antidumping and countervailing duty disputes. Chapter 20 creates general dispute settlement procedures that apply unless there are more specific provisions in the agreement. For example, Section B of Chapter 11 establishes investor-state arbitration procedures that operate outside Chapter 20. *See* Chapter 6. Environmental and labor cooperation disputes are governed by special procedures found in the two "side agreements" negotiated under the Clinton Administration. These procedures are covered in Chapters 9 and 10.

Not all dispute settlement under NAFTA is formal in character. Disputes are often avoided or settled informally by intergovernmental and advisory NAFTA committees and working groups. To name just a few, such committees range in focus from trade in goods to trade in worn clothing, from automotive standards to labeling of apparel, from agricultural subsidies to trade and competition policy, and from small business to financial services.

All of the NAFTA dispute settlement decisions, the Code of Conduct, and the procedural rules re-

ferred to in this chapter are reproduced and analyzed in R. Folsom, M. Gordon and J. A. Spanogle,
Handbook of NAFTA Dispute Settlement.

Selecting Panels—Conflicts of Interest

Under NAFTA, the use of binational panels and
extraordinary challenge committees as a substitute
for national judicial review of administrative determinations continues despite unanswered questions
of constitutionality under U.S. law. *See* B. A. Acker-
man and D. Golove, *Is NAFTA Constitutional?*
(1995). NAFTA does, however, seek to "profession-
alize" the process by adding judges and retired
judges to the roster of acceptable Chapter 19 panelists. The panelists under CFTA were more often
lawyers, economists or academicians. Each party to
the dispute chooses two panelists (invariably from
their home country). Each party may peremptorily
reject without cause four panelist selections. The
fifth panelist is chosen by agreement if that is
possible, or by lot if not. The panel then selects its
chair (who must be a lawyer) by majority vote or
failing that by lot. This panel selection procedure
differs significantly from the "reverse selection"
process used in Chapter 20 disputes (below).

All Chapter 19 and 20 panelists are governed by a
Code of Conduct. Panelists can be removed only by
mutual agreement if the Code of Conduct is breached. The Code broadly stipulates disclosure of any
circumstances that raise a conflict or an appearance
of conflict, with no time limits nor materiality requirements. Conflict issues have repeatedly delayed

the Chapter 19 dispute resolution process. Undisclosed conflicts of interest were alleged in the CFTA Chapter 19 *Softwood Lumber* dispute. ECC–94–1904–01 USA. *See* Chapter 2. Judge Wilkey's dissent in the *Softwood Lumber* Extraordinary Challenge made it perfectly clear that he believed the Code had not been followed by two Canadian attorney-panelists:

> This part of my opinion is much shorter than the first. Do not think that the issue addressed is one whit less important. Indeed, it may well be the more important of the two, the greater threat to the integrity of the whole process.

> * * *

> There is an obligation for a prospective panelist, at the time he is originally placed on a general list and at the time he is queried as to his willingness and his capacity to serve on a specific Panel, to disclose any and everything which might affect his impartial performance of his duties on the Panel, or affect the judgment of the contending parties as to whether to accept the particular panelist or reject him. The two governments do not send their investigative agencies to pry into the details of the prospective panelist's business and personal affiliations. There is no subpoena of the records of the panelist or his law firm, no review of his business contacts, public or private records to determine his sources of income for past years. The two governments rely exclusively on the honesty—and just as impor-

tantly, the diligence—of the prospective panelist to reveal any and everything which could seemingly have an impact on his being chosen to serve or not.

Attorney Homer E. Moyer, Jr. has presented an alternative and perhaps more persuasive perspective:

An analysis of panel decisions suggests that the level of bias in Chapter 19 binational panel decisions is very low. For example, almost no cases have involved a split among panelists along national lines. The presence of actual conflicts of interest (as distinguished from possible appearances of conflicts) has been rare; lawyers who have served as panelists and have subsequently described their experiences, with only rare exceptions, have highly praised the objectivity and fairness of panelists. Where sharp disagreements among panelists have emerged, they have tended to be the result of a panelist's ideological view of the panel process itself, rather than any conflicts of interest related to clients or panelists' nationality.

The *Softwood Lumber* case, which is the most celebrated case involving an allegation of conflict of interest, suggests the importance of separating issues of conflicts of interest from disagreements over substantive issues or the merits of a case. To many observers and participants, the claims of conflict of interest in the *Lumber* case appeared disingenuous: they were raised for the first time more than two years after the litigation had begun and only after the complaining parties had lost the case on the merits. Moreover, many of the after-the-fact conflict allegations were far-fetched, relating to work done years before, in some cases by firms with which panelists had long since severed their relationships.

Therefore, the Chapter 19 experience suggests that we should carefully differentiate between questions of possible conflicts of interest and dissatisfaction with judgments on the merits. 3 S.W.J. Law & Trade in the Americas 423, 425–26 (1996).

Chapter 19–Antidumping and Countervailing Duties

Chapter 19 of the NAFTA agreement is substantially similar to Chapter 19 of CFTA. Binational panels act as a substitute for national judicial review of final administrative determinations, subject only to extraordinary challenges taken to NAFTA "Committees" (ECC). *See* Chapter 2. Once again, the North Americans were unable to follow the European path and eliminate antidumping (AD) and countervailing (CVD) duties on internal trade. Canada and Chile, however, did so for AD (but not CVD) in their 1996 Free Trade Agreement. Canada no doubt hopes that it has established a precedent that will later be followed if Chile joins NAFTA. *See* Chapter 11.

National antidumping and countervailing duty laws continue to govern all proceedings, including decisions by Chapter 19 panels. However, these laws have generally been harmonized by common adoption of GATT/WTO codes. For example, each NAFTA nation adheres to the WTO Antidumping and Subsidies Codes (1995). United States implementation of these Codes was controversial. It is possible that Canada or Mexico might challenge this implementation by complaint and invocation of the WTO Dispute Settlement Understanding.

In addition, since NAFTA commits each nation to "effective and fair" AD and CVD rules, Canada or Mexico could conceivably challenge U.S. implementation of the Codes under NAFTA. In such a case, or any instance of ineffective or unfair rules, a "declaratory opinion" on the issue can be obtained from a duly constituted Chapter 19 panel. Any unilateral amendment of AD or CVD statutory law by a NAFTA nation can be similarly reviewed. This panel can recommend modifications and consultations, but has no power to resolve the dispute. If no resolution occurs, the complaining party can undertake comparable action or terminate application of Chapter 19.

NAFTA also creates the possibility of consultations and "special committee" review if "fundamental failures" occur in Chapter 19 dispute settlement. The prevention of the establishment of a Chapter 19 panel is one such failure. Blockage of a final decision or ineffective implementation of a panel decision is another. "Special committees" are to be primarily engaged in fact finding. If a systemic failure is found, use of Chapter 19 for antidumping and countervailing duty disputes can be suspended. Presumably, this would result in a return to national judicial review of AD and CVD determinations. From 1994 to date, no "declaratory opinion" or "special committee" review has taken place. This should not be taken, however, as a sign that all has been quiet on the antidumping and countervailing duty front.

United States administrative AD and CVD determinations (mostly annual reviews of pre–NAFTA proceedings) have been reviewed by NAFTA Chapter 19 panels more often than Canadian or Mexican determinations. Goods from Mexico have been involved in the U.S. determinations more than twice as frequently as Canadian goods. Leather apparel, porcelain-on-steel cookware, cement, oil country tubular goods and fresh cut flowers provide examples of U.S. imports from Mexico that have been the subject of Chapter 19 panel decisions. Live swine, concrete, color picture tubes and carbon steel imports from Canada have also been decided under Chapter 19. Nearly all of these decisions have concerned the imposition of U.S. antidumping duties. U.S. exports of synthetic baler twine, steel sheet, malt beverages and refined sugar to Canada, and flat coated steel, steel plate and polystyrene to Mexico, provide examples of Chapter 19 decisions reviewing Canadian and Mexican AD and CVD determinations.

No extraordinary challenges to NAFTA Chapter 19 panel decisions have as yet been raised. This record contrasts with CFTA where three provocative ECC proceedings were pursued. *See* Chapter 2.

Standards of Review—Judge Wilkey Dissents

Some CFTA Chapter 19 panels were accused of ignoring or poorly implementing their duty to apply Canadian and U.S. standards of review for administrative determinations. This was especially true in the *Softwood Lumber* dispute. ECC–19–1904–01 USA. Judge Wilkey of the U.S. Federal Court of Appeals served on the Extraordinary Challenge Committee in that dispute. He concluded that the Panel had produced "egregiously erroneous results." Judge Wilkey did not mince his words:

I submit that the well intentioned system of Extraordinary Challenge Committees, as a substitute for the standard appellate review under United States law, has failed. It has failed both at the Panel and the Committee level to apply United States law, substantively, and most clearly in regard to the United States standard of review of administrative agency actions. The system runs the risk, not only of producing egregiously erroneous results as in the instant three to two Panel decision, but also of creating a body of law—even though formally without precedential value—which will be divergent from United States law applied to countries not members of NAFTA.

I believe that I have demonstrated that this is so in this particular case, and I suggest that analysis demonstrates that this should be no surprise.

Consider the position of the Binational Panels. The members are to be experts, distinguished practitioners in the esoteric field of trade law. Surely, a better mechanism for review of agency action than a single judge from the Court of International Trade or a three judge panel of a Circuit Court of Appeals? Not necessarily. The record shows that five (or in this case three) distinguished "experts" have shown no deference whatsoever to the "experts" in the ITA of the Commerce Department.

Psychologically, why should they be expected to show the deference to administrative agency action which is required as a fundamental tenet of U.S. judicial review of agency action? The panel members are experts; they know better than the lowly paid "experts" over the Commerce Department, and they have felt inclined to say so. Repeatedly, most vividly in this particular case, they seem to have substituted their judgment for that of the agency. They have not hesitated to say that the agency was wrong on its methodology, wrong in the choice of alternate economic analyses, wrong in its conclusions, and that the Panel of five experts knows far better how to do it. All of this of course is directly contrary to long-standing

United States law concepts of review of agency action.

Why do these distinguished Panel experts make this type of error? The answer is, I suggest, that they are experts in trade law; they are not experts in the field of judicial review of agency action; they do not necessarily have any familiarity whatsoever with the standards of judicial review under United States law. This would particularly be true of the Canadian members. . . .

While not all agree with Judge Wilkey, his opinion certainly helped push Canada and the United States into a dialogue on standards of review. As a result of this dialogue, NAFTA created a specific example of a binational panel that manifestly exceeds its powers, authority or jurisdiction (one of the grounds for reversal before an Extraordinary Challenge Committee). Any failure "to apply the appropriate standard of review" is the example. Article 1904.13(a)(iii).

"Standards of review" for each country are defined in Annex 1911 by reference to national statutes, which the parties are free to amend. For Canada and the United States these are the same standards stipulated by CFTA and discussed in Chapter 2. *See* Subsection 181(4) of the Federal Court Act of Canada; Sections 516A(b)(1)(A) and (B) of the U.S. Tariff Act of 1930. Thus, despite the heated rhetoric, there was no change in the U.S. or Canadian statutory standards of review nor in the grounds for reversal by Extraordinary Challenge

Committees. At a minimum, however, the United States hoped that this example would drive home the obligation of binational panels to apply its standards in Chapter 19 disputes challenging U.S. administrative determinations, and the obligation of ECCs to consider such issues when panel decisions are challenged. This obligation was anticipated by extending the ECC review period from 30 to 90 days and by adding a requirement that the ECC examine the legal and factual analysis underlying the panel's findings and conclusions. *See* Annex 1904.13(3).

For Mexico, Article 238 of the Federal Fiscal Code is the source of the standard of review that NAFTA panels must apply in Chapter 19 proceedings. Article 238, drafted specifically for NAFTA and amended several times since 1994, provides (in rough very simplified translation) that SECOFI* antidumping and countervailing duty "resolutions" will be declared illegal if there is: (1) Official "incompetence" (lack of authority); (2) omissions of formal legal requirements or procedural errors affecting individual defenses and the result of the resolution; (3) mistaken facts underlying the resolution; (4) issuance of resolutions in violation of law or incorrect application of law; and (5) exercises of discretion not corresponding to the purposes behind discretionary powers.

* Secretaria de Comercio y Fomento Industrial (Ministry of Commerce and Industrial Development). SECOFI makes dumping and subsidy determinations as well as domestic industry injury determinations under Mexican law.

The competence issue has been central to several Panel reviews of SECOFI determinations. *See* MEX–94–1904–01, 02 and 03. In Case 02, for example, a U.S. attorney and a U.S. law professor joined with a Mexican attorney to conclude that SECOFI lacked competence to levy antidumping duties because it had not been established in strict accordance with Mexican procedural formalities. A Mexican and U.S. attorney dissented; they wanted to undertake a substantive examination of SECOFI's determinations.

Mexico and Chapter 19

In Mexico, antidumping and countervailing duty law is very new, as is judicial (Federal Fiscal Tribunal) and NAFTA panel review of trade agency actions. For all concerned, Chapter 19 has been a learning process. Professor Robert Lutz has analyzed some of the early issues and differences in approach that Chapter 19 panels must follow according to Mexican law. *See* 3 S.W. J. Law & Trade in the Americas 391 (1996). Professor Lutz emphasizes that Mexican *constitutional* law (specifically Articles 14 and 16 guaranteeing "legal security" and "legality") govern administrative action. NAFTA panels reviewing SECOFI determinations have split on whether these provisions apply. One reason for this split is that the national "law" that Chapter 19 panels must apply is defined in the NAFTA agreement as consisting of "relevant statutes, legislative history, regulations, administrative practice and judicial precedents" (Article 1904). This definition does not reference constitutional law.

As Professor David Gantz has noted, there are additional conflicts and uncertainties in Mexican law as applied in the first five binational panel decisions reviewing SECOFI determinations. *See* 29 Law & Policy Int'l Bus. 297 (1988). These include counsel access to confidential information with or without powers of attorney and bonding, the direct applicability of the GATT/WTO Antidumping Code in panel proceedings, and the power of the panel to dismiss SECOFI proceedings.

Professor Lutz also notes that Mexican doctrine on precedent ("jurisprudencia") depends upon five consecutive appellate decisions agreeing on the same issue, and that "writ of amparo" proceedings may be used to challenge NAFTA panel decisions in the Mexican federal courts. Indeed, two U.S. companies successfully initiated amparo proceedings against the Panel in MEX–94–1904–1 notwithstanding the NAFTA provisions eliminating national judicial review of AD and CVD proceedings and the alternative of Extraordinary Challenge Committee review of panel decisions.

The writ of amparo is a uniquely Mexican lawsuit which is the source of great pride in the Mexican legal community. The writ asserts infringement of rights. It is constitutionally based (see Articles 103 and 107 of the Mexican Constitution). The writ of amparo allows individuals and legal entities to challenge virtually all state acts or omissions when ordinary remedies have been exhausted or are not available. Such challenges can be raised against federal, state or local authorities, including legislative, executive, administrative or judicial authorities. Writs of amparo, for example, are frequently used to challenge judicial decisions.

The Tomatoes Dispute

There have been a number of Chapter 19 antidumping and countervailing duty panels involving U.S.-Mexico trade. The most prominent dispute, however, never got that far. This dispute concerned Mexican exports of tomatoes at prices that were rapidly taking market share from U.S. growers.

After failing to persuade the U.S. International Trade Commission to pursue escape clause relief, Florida growers alleged dumping by Mexican tomato producers early in 1996. This politically high profile petition eventually led to a "suspension agreement" between the U.S. Commerce Department and Mexican growers. The Department promised to suspend its antidumping probe (dumping at a 17.56 percent margin had been found) in return for a commitment by Mexican growers not to sell at less than a specified "reference price." This price was based on the lowest average import price in a recent period not involving dumping. It amounted in 1996 to 20.68 cents per pound. At that price, there is no limit on the volume of Mexican tomatoes that may be shipped to the U.S. market.

Critics from states like Arizona alleged "political blackmail" as the settlement came just days before the 1996 Presidential election vote. President Clinton carried Florida in 1996, something he had failed to do in 1992. The suspension agreement remains in force, fixing prices and managing trade in a most remarkable manner. It has not, however, significantly slowed Mexico's market penetration. Prior to NAFTA, Mexican tomatoes held about 30 percent of the U.S. market. At this point, Mexican tomatoes enjoy at least a 65 percent U.S. market share.

Chapter 20 Dispute Settlement

The intergovernmental dispute resolution procedures found in Chapter 20 of the NAFTA agreement apply absent more specific NAFTA provisions. As was the case with CFTA, these procedures were intended to be an alternative to GATT 1947 dispute settlement (since replaced by much more effective World Trade Organization (WTO) procedures). *See* Chapter 2. Private parties do not participate in Chapter 20 dispute settlement. Moreover, Article 2021 expressly prohibits rights of action asserting inconsistency with NAFTA against a member state. The United States Trade Representative (USTR), however, does afford interested persons the opportunity to comment on Chapter 20 proceedings. Private parties can and have lodged complaints with the USTR about member state measures that adversely affect them. Whether to proceed to Chapter 20 dispute settlement is strictly a matter of USTR discretion.

The right of each member state to elect between NAFTA or WTO dispute settlement is generally preserved. However, once made, the election is final. Use of Chapter 20 under NAFTA will be denied if the complainant takes the issue to the WTO. That said, as part of a broad evaluation of NAFTA/WTO choice of forum opportunities and risks, Professor David Gantz has noted that nations may sometimes judiciously frame their disputes so as to gain access to both NAFTA and WTO fora. *See* 14 American U. Law. Rev. 1025 (1999) (citing Mexico-U.S. sugar/corn syrup trade complaints and the Canada-U.S. farm products blockade dispute). In Chapter 2 we noted that preserving the option of WTO dispute settlement allows the U.S. to challenge Canadian cultural industry trade restraints that have been excluded from CFTA and NAFTA. For any complaint that the remaining NAFTA nation wishes to join, the two complainants must resolve the choice of forum. Absent resolution, the dispute "normally" will be heard under NAFTA.

The right to elect as between NAFTA or WTO dispute settlement is qualified. If the dispute falls in certain categories, the responding nation may force the issue to be heard under Chapter 20. This is the case when the dispute concerns:

1. Specified environmental or conservation agreements (listed at page 72);

2. sanitary and phytosanitary (SPS) health regulations (*See* Chapter 4); or

3. environmental, health, safety or conservation product or service standards (SRM) (*Id.*).

Why are these the only disputes where the responding nation may insist on the NAFTA forum? One reason may be the perception that these areas involve unusually sensitive trade matters. Another may be the desire to ensure that national standards are absolutely respected (as NAFTA requires) and insulated from potentially global challenges at the WTO. A third may be the "lessons" learned in the pre-NAFTA challenge by Mexico under GATT 1947 of the U.S. Marine Mammal Protection Act (dolphin-safe tuna). *See* BISD 39 Supp. 155 (1993). The United States certainly wanted no repetition of that adverse GATT Panel ruling, which it "blocked" by pressuring Mexico into a negotiated settlement.

Recourse to Chapter 20 dispute settlement may ordinarily be had if an actual or proposed act is or would be inconsistent with NAFTA obligations. Canada and Mexico have, for example, threatened to carry to arbitration their challenge of the 1996 U.S. "Helms–Burton" law (110 Stat. 785, *see* Chapter 5) against trafficking in U.S. property confiscated by Cuba. For some provisions of the agreement, Chapter 20 can also be used to challenge measures that are consistent with the NAFTA but cause "nullification or impairment" of expected benefits. But the government procurement, investment, telecommunications, financial services, competition law and monopolies, temporary entry of business persons, and automotive trading (Annex 300–A) provisions in NAFTA typically *cannot* be challenged in this way.

Any member state with a substantial interest in a Chapter 20 dispute can join as a complaining party and thereby participate in solutions to the dispute. However, in all cases, NAFTA's general dispute settlement procedures are *not* binding. Consultations are followed by mediation efforts of the NAFTA Free Trade Commission followed by arbitration before a 5–member panel. A "reverse selection" process is used to select the arbitration panel from a roster (yet to be finalized) of acceptable panelists. It is possible to propose a panelist from off the roster, but such nominees can be vetoed without cause by the other side.

First, the chair is selected by consensus or by lot. The chair cannot be from the selecting country, but can come from outside NAFTA. For example, in the first Chapter 20 panel the chair came from Britain and the second from Australia. Two panelists are chosen by both parties. Each side must select persons who are citizens of the *other* country.

Chapter 20 Arbitrations

A Chapter 20 report should be completed 120 days after the request for arbitration. There is no appeal to a higher body such as the Extraordinary Challenge Committee under Chapter 19. If the dispute is not resolved, the prevailing party can pursue equivalent compensatory action within 30 days. Normally this should be in the same economic sector and can be challenged by panel review only if "manifestly excessive." Compensatory action cannot be undertaken by a member state that failed to join the dispute as a complaining party. The third NAFTA partner may not "normally" commence WTO or NAFTA proceedings on substantially equivalent grounds absent a significant change in economic or commercial circumstances.

Professor David Lopez has provided a revealing portrait of early Chapter 20 dispute settlement, one which emphasizes just how few disputes are pushed to arbitration. *See* 32 Texas Int'l Law J. 163 (1997). Of the eight complaints he cites as lodged by the end of 1996, only three have gone to arbitration ... Canadian agricultural tariffication (*see* Chapter 2), U.S. escape clause restraints on Mexican brooms (*see* Chapter 4), and U.S. refusal to admit Mexican trucks and buses (pending, *see* Chapter 5). Professor Lopez suggests that complaints linger at the consultation/mediation stages of Chapter 20 dispute settlement because there is no compulsion to move the dispute forward and because political realities temper that decision. Some disputes are settled (e.g., tomatoes above) while others just keep on lingering (Helms–Burton).

Private Commercial Disputes

The NAFTA Advisory Committee on Private Commercial Disputes has been very active. The Committee has developed model mediation and arbitration clauses for international contracts. The promotion of mediation and arbitration as an alternative to litigation of NAFTA commercial disputes rests partly on the absence of an agreement on enforcement of judgments. This contrasts with adherence by all NAFTA member states to the New York Convention on Recognition and Enforcement of Arbitral Awards. It also rests, although not explicitly so, on a desire to avoid problems associated with Mexican linkages between penal and civil commercial dispute proceedings.

Mexican law permits civil litigants to file criminal charges, obtain judicial detention orders and dispute bail while the other party remains in jail. *See Camp*, 5 U.S. Mexico L.J. 85 (Symposium 1997). Needless to say, a negotiated settlement often arrives in short order. U.S. attorneys and clients doing business in Mexico have been on both sides of such a strategy. Back in the United States, settlements agreed to in Mexico in this manner may be void as the product of the crime of "compounding." The Texas Supreme Court has so ruled. *Lewkowicz v. El Paso Apparel Corp.*, 625 S.W.2d 301 (Tex. 1981).

CHAPTER 9

THE ENVIRONMENT

Environmental concerns appear very selectively in the NAFTA agreement negotiated by President Bush. No chapter of NAFTA is dedicated exclusively to the environment. This absence of focus and priority offended many environmentalists. Public Citizen even filed suit to enjoin NAFTA for lack of an accompanying environmental impact statement. *See Public Citizen v. USTR*, 5 F.3d 549 (D.C.Cir.1993). If the environmentalists were upset, labor was outraged. Nowhere in the NAFTA agreement is there any coverage of labor rights and protections. NAFTA's pro-business tilt activated organized labor in Canada and the United States.

Bill Clinton made NAFTA's inadequacies on labor and the environment an election campaign issue in his defeat of President Bush in 1992. Once in office President Clinton proceeded to negotiate several "side agreements" to NAFTA: The North American Agreement on Environmental Cooperation (NAEC), the Mexico–United States Border Environmental Cooperation Agreement (BECA), and the North American Agreement on Labor Cooperation (NALC). These Agreements helped assure U.S. ratification of NAFTA.

NAFTA Provisions on the Environment

NAFTA's supremacy is subordinated to the "specific trade obligations" of five pre-existing environmental and conservation agreements. The least NAFTA-inconsistent manner of implementing these trade obligations must be selected:

1. The Convention on International Trade in Endangered Species of Wild Flora and Fauna (Washington, 1973, amended 1979);

2. The Protocol on Substances That Deplete the Ozone Layer (Montreal, 1987, amended 1990);

3. The Convention on the Control of Transboundary Movement of Hazardous Wastes and Their Disposal (Basel, 1989) (which the United States has not yet ratified);

4. The Canada–U.S. Agreement Concerning Transboundary Movement of Hazardous Waste (Ottawa, 1986); and

5. The Mexico–U.S. Agreement on Cooperation for the Protection and Improvement of the Environment of the Border Area (La Paz, 1983).

It is noteworthy that NAFTA's supremacy was subordinated to no other types of international agreements.

Under the NAFTA agreement, each member state retains the right to establish its own levels of environmental protection. For example, "sustainable development" is specifically recognized as a legitimate objective for environmental regulation of trade goods. *See* Chapter 4. NAFTA also prioritizes the need for scientific evaluation of environmental risks in establishing environmental product and SPS (food) standards. *Id.* Furthermore, if environmentally-related trade disputes emerge, there is heavy emphasis on employment of scientific experts to resolve them. *See* Chapter 8. Most significantly, NAFTA forces disputes about environmental standards or the pre-existing agreements listed above into NAFTA dispute settlement. Such issues, if taken to the WTO by the complainant, can be brought back to NAFTA Chapter 20 by the respondent. *Id.*

The NAFTA agreement also articulates a commitment not to lower environmental standards for purposes of attracting investment ("pollution havens"). *See* Chapter 6. However, since this promise is not subject to NAFTA dispute settlement and possible sanctions under Chapter 20, it is not exactly a ringing endorsement of environmental concerns.

The North American Agreement on Environmental Cooperation

A trilateral Commission for Environmental Cooperation (CEC) was established under the NAEC side agreement. The Commission's Council of Ministers is comprised of cabinet-level officers from each member state. The Council can discuss, recommend and settle environmental disputes publicly by consensus. The Commission's Secretariat (located in Montreal) investigates, reviews and reports with recommendations to the Council on environmental matters. The Executive Director of the Secretariat rotates every three years among the NAEC countries. He or she chooses the staff of the Secretariat on the basis of "competence and integrity." However, "due regard" must be given to recruiting "equitable proportions" from each NAEC country. (Article 11). The CEC Council of Ministers and Secretariat are advised, especially on technical and scientific matters, by a 15–person Joint Public Advisory Committee.

Under the NAEC, each member state agreed to maintain "high" levels of environmental protection, but this commitment is not enforceable through NAEC dispute settlement. Rather, NAEC focuses on enforcement of the individual environmental protection standards of each nation. This focus, politically speaking, targeted Mexico. There was a widespread perception in the United States that Mexican enforcement of its environmental laws states was inadequate. It is perhaps ironic therefore that many of the more than 20 complaints lodged under NAEC to date have challenged Canadian and U.S. environmental law enforcement.

Article 13 Reports

Article 13 authorizes the CEC Secretariat to issue reports on virtually any environmental matter not involving law enforcement. Notice of an intent to issue such a report must first be given to the CEC Council of Ministers. If the Council objects by a two-thirds vote, no report can be undertaken. Nongovernmental organizations (NGOs) and others can and have petitioned for Article 13 reports by the Secretariat. The two first Article 13 reports concerned long range transport of air pollutants and the death of 40,000 migratory birds at the Silva Reservoir in Guanajuato. The latter report determined that avian botulism was the cause of the deaths and fostered a clean up and cooperative information exchanges.

The third Article 13 report concerns water use in the Fort Huachuca, Arizona region. It was undertaken at the initiative of the CEC Secretariat after an Article 14 complaint (below) concerning riparian areas for migratory birds was dismissed. (The Secretariat determined that preparation of a factual record was not warranted.) Thus Article 13 reports can serve as an alternative to direct challenges raised under Article 14.

Article 14 Citizen and NGO Submissions

The NAEC, under Article 14, contains its own submission, response and dispute resolution process. Complaints can be filed with the CEC Secretariat by any person or nongovernmental organization (NGO) concerning workplaces, enterprises or sectors that produce NAEC-traded or NAEC-competitive goods or services. Article 14 submissions must allege that a NAEC nation is not "effectively enforcing" *its* environmental law. See SEM–97–005 (submission challenging Canada's ratification [but not implementation by statute] of Biodiversity Convention did not concern effective enforcement of *Canadian* law). SEM stands for Submissions on

Enforcement Matters. Guidelines for such submissions have been issued by the CEC Secretariat. They can be found at the Secretariat's excellent web site, www.cec.org.

The Secretariat can dismiss Article 14 submissions on a variety of grounds. For example, the NAEC agreement stipulates that no ineffective enforcement of environmental law exists when the action or inaction reflects a reasonable exercise of official discretion in investigatory, prosecutorial, regulatory or compliance matters. Furthermore, since "environmental law" is defined in NAEC as excluding occupational safety and health laws, and laws that primarily manage the harvest or exploitation of natural resources, such complaints can also be dismissed. *See* SEM–98–002 (submission concerning Mexican commercial forestry dispute dismissed). The submission must "appear to be aimed at promoting enforcement rather than harassing industry." (Article 14(1)(d)). It must also be filed in a timely manner. *See* SEM–97–004 (submission filed three years after Canadian environmental decision not timely).

The CEC Secretariat determines if the submission merits a response from the nation whose environmental law enforcement practices are being challenged. Private remedies available under national law must have been pursued and pending administrative or judicial proceedings will keep the CEC from moving forward on the complaint. *See Canadian Wetlands* and *Canadian Fisheries Act*

SEM–96–002 and 003 (CEC rejects citizen and NGO submissions). The NAEC requires extensive private access to environmental remedies, including the ability to file complaints with administrative authorities, access to administrative, quasi-judicial and judicial proceedings, and the right to sue for damages, mitigating relief and injunctions. Exhausting national remedies first is therefore a major prerequisite. In evaluating whether a submission merits a response, the Secretariat is also to be "guided" by whether the submission alleges "harm" to the complaining party. Proof of such harm is not mandatory, merely a relevant issue. Several of the Secretariat's early decisions suggest that it takes a liberal view of this "standing to submit" question. *See Cozumel Pier*, SEM–96–001 (discussed below).

In addition, as the rejection by the Secretariat of the first two Article 14 submissions made clear, legislative actions that diminish environmental law enforcement cannot be challenged. SEM–95–001 and 002. Thus complaints by various NGOs against the suspension of enforcement of the U.S. Endangered Species Act listing provisions and the elimination of private remedies to review U.S. timber salvage sales (both alleged to have been accomplished in appropriations bills) failed to proceed under Article 14.

With or without a response from the member state alleged to be inadequately enforcing its law, the Secretariat must decide whether development of a factual record is warranted and inform the Council of its reasons. The Council must approve development of a factual record by a two-thirds vote. If there are past, pending, or possible national administrative or judicial proceedings, the Secretariat or Council are unlikely to allow this to occur. NAEC governments are obliged to submit relevant information throughout the factual record process, but the Secretariat cannot enforce this obligation.

The third submission under Article 14 was made by Mexican NGOs alleging that the Mexican government had failed to conduct an environmental impact review before authorizing a cruise ship pier at Cozumel Island. SEM–96–001. The CEC Secretariat ruled that this complaint passed muster under Article 14 and compiled the first factual record under NAEC. Factual Record No. 1 (1997). After summarizing the submission and Mexican response, the CEC "presented" facts with respect to the "matters raised in the submissions." In this record, the CEC adopts the role of a neutral finder of facts. A second Factual Record is being developed concerning a submission that alleges that the Canadian government is failing to enforce the Fisheries Act to ensure protection of fish and fish habitat in connection with hydroelectric dams in British Columbia. SEM–97–001.

The Secretariat's factual record goes to the Environmental Council of Ministers. By a two-thirds vote, the Council can release it to the public, as was done in the *Cozumel Pier* dispute. After this release, the Mexican government abandoned the project.

Such releases are the only available "sanction" unless there has been a "persistent pattern of failure" (from January 1, 1994) to effectively enforce environmental law. For these purposes, persistent pattern is defined as a "sustained or recurring course of action or inaction". (Article 45). If (and only if) there is such a pattern does formal NAEC dispute settlement commence. The *Cozumel Pier* dispute, for example, did not get beyond preparation by the CEC of a factual record.

Formal dispute settlement starts with consultations which are followed by Council mediation and conciliation. Ultimately, the Council by a two-thirds vote can forward the dispute to arbitration.

Environmental Arbitrations

Environmental specialists will be the arbitrators chosen from a roster of 45 persons previously selected by consensus. The arbitration panel consists of five members, with the chair chosen first by consensus or lot. Each nation then chooses two arbitrators from the opposite side. This "reverse selection" process is also used under NAFTA Chapter 20. *See* Chapter 8. Thereafter, the panel's procedures and report largely track the process used under Chapter 20.

If a NAEC arbitration panel finds a persistent failure pattern, the parties may agree on a mutually satisfactory "action plan." If not, the panel is authorized to establish a plan. It may also impose monetary penalties for failure to implement an action plan. Annex 34 to the NAEC authorizes penalties up to a maximum of .007 percent of the *total* trade in goods between the disputing countries. Hence, very large monetary penalties may be imposed. Such penalties are paid into a separate fund of the Environmental Council to improve or enhance the environment or environmental law enforcement of the offending member state. If the penalty is not paid, the complaining party may raise tariffs sufficiently to collect the monetary penalty. If Canada is the offending party, however, the Commission for Environmental Cooperation must seek enforcement of the penalty in the Canadian courts under special procedures outlined in Annex 36A.

Summary

In sum, the NAEC establishes five environmental dispute settlement mechanisms. *First*, the Secretariat may report on almost any environmental matter. *Second*, the Secretariat may develop a factual record in trade-related law enforcement disputes. *Third*, the Council can release that record to the public. *Fourth*, if there is a persistent pattern of failure to enforce environmental law, the Council will mediate and conciliate. *Fifth*, if such efforts fail, the Council can send the matter to arbitration and awards can be enforced by monetary penalties.

The Mexico–United States Border Environmental Cooperation Agreement

Long before NAFTA or NAEC, Mexico and the United States negotiated an Agreement on Cooperation for the Protection and Improvement of the Environment in the Border Area (the 1983 La Paz Agreement). With rapid maquiladora growth along the border in the 1980s and 1990s, border environmental issues came to the forefront. In 1992, Mexico and the United States established and financed an integrated border environment cleanup program that prioritized drinking water, waste treatment, hazardous waste, and law enforcement.

In 1993, as a NAFTA side agreement, the two countries ratified the Mexico–U.S. Border Environment Cooperation Agreement. Under this agreement, the Border Environment Cooperation Commission (BECC) was created with offices in El Paso, Texas and Ciudad Juarez, Mexico. The BECC is intended to provide expertise on border environmental protection. If the BECC certifies infrastructure proposals as meeting technical and environmental criteria, funding (and assistance in obtaining funding) by the North American Development Bank (NADBank) is possible.

The NADBank was inaugurated by the 1993 Agreement and is funded and governed jointly by Mexico and the United States. It is located in San Antonio, Texas. Priority is given to water and solid waste initiatives that are self-sustaining, mostly through user fees. NADBank interest rates are not subsidized, generally Treasury Rates plus 2 percent. The NADBank has a cooperative agreement with the EPA to combine its financing with EPA grants. It also has partnered with export credit agencies, border states and the private sector in co-financings.

It is fair to say that the BECC and NADBank proceeded slowly in carrying out their missions. There have been lots of studies and strategizing. Gradually some environmental infrastructure projects were given the green light. By the end of 1996, the BECC had certified 16 projects, four of which garnered NADBank's approval for leveraged financing. All four involved water or wastewater treatment facilities. For the other certified projects, also for the most part concerned with water, NADBank provided technical and project finance advice. Although the pace of BECC and NADBank activity has increased, their capacities to meet the challenges of border pollution remain seriously in doubt.

CHAPTER 10

LABOR

The NAFTA agreement has virtually no coverage of labor standards, rights or regulations. Ordinary workers are also left out of the NAFTA provisions on temporary entry visas. *See* Chapter 5. The omission of labor from NAFTA became an issue in the 1992 presidential election. As he promised during his campaign, President Clinton negotiated a "side" labor agreement in 1993: The North American Agreement on Labor Cooperation (NALC). This supplemental agreement was helpful in securing passage of NAFTA through the U.S. Congress.

Mexico's presence drove the NALC negotiations. Ironically, the Mexican Constitution embraces workers, unions, working conditions and a host of labor-related rights. But the operational reality of Mexican labor law is debatable, especially given the longstanding alliance between the Confederacion de Trabajadores Mexicanos (CTM), Mexico's most powerful labor organization, and the ruling PRI party.

A number of commentators have suggested that Mexico's employer-dominated industrial relations are more "customary" than legal. Indeed many of the customs directly contravene Mexican labor law. For example, organization of "independent" unions (not affiliated with the CTM or sponsored by employers) is customarily opposed, sometimes by payoffs or violence, but more generally by CTM and PRI controlled labor tribunals charged with registering unions. Job security, paid leave, working hours, occupational safety and even the constitutionally enshrined Christmas bonus don't always conform in reality to the requirements of Mexican law.

The NALC agreement therefore centers on enforcement problems under Mexican law, but is not limited to Mexico. It is limited in its application to Canada because most labor matters in that country are governed by provincial not federal law. Canadian provinces can opt in or remain outside the NALC. For NALC to apply, the matter must be governed by Canadian federal labor law or designated percentages of the Canadian labor force as a result of provincial opt ins. Since only Alberta, Quebec, Manitoba and Prince Edward Island have to date agreed to respect the NALC, the agreement has had relatively little impact on Canada.

The North American Agreement on Labor Cooperation

The right of each NAFTA nation to establish different but "high" labor standards is preserved by the NALC. However, eleven "guiding labor principles" were recognized in Annex 1. These are reproduced at the end of this chapter. Annex 1 specifies that these principles are not to be construed as creating common minimum labor law standards for the region.

Under NALC, each member state promised "effective enforcement" by government action of its labor laws. This commitment extends to laws governing the eleven areas cited in the guiding labor principles: Occupational safety and health; equal pay for men and women; labor rights to organize; the right to strike; forced labor; employment standards; collective bargaining; child labor; workers' compensation; employment discrimination; migrant workers; and collectively bargained agreements. What laws fall in which of these areas matters because NALC remedies vary with the subject matter under dispute.

Each country undertook to ensure private rights of access to tribunals for the enforcement of its labor laws. Procedural guarantees to support fair, transparent and equitable legal processes of concern to interested parties are also established under NALC. These include promises to ensure due process of law, open meetings, the right to be heard, reasonable fees, time frames and procedures, written decisions based on evidence in the record, impartial review and effective remedies. A general commitment to publishing labor laws, regulations, procedures and administrative rulings was given.

Much of NALC's cooperation on labor matters is educational in focus. Conferences, seminars and workshops abound on everything from child labor to gender issues, the right to organize and occupational safety, and employment and job training. Just exactly what impact all these educational programs have had is hard to measure.

The NALC Law Enforcement System

The NALC created a North American Commission for Labor Cooperation. This Commission has a Council of Ministers and a Secretariat located in Dallas, Texas. Perhaps most importantly, in sharp contrast with NAEC, the Labor Secretariat cannot review individual or organizational complaints concerning effective labor law enforcement. The Labor Secretariat and Council are reduced largely to monitoring, study and report.

However, individual and organizational submissions about labor law, its administration or labor market conditions in a member state can be filed with "National Administrative Offices" (NAO) in each country. The U.S. NAO is located in the Bureau of International Affairs of the Department of Labor. All submissions must allege a failure to enforce national labor law in *another* member state. For example, complaints about Mexican labor law can only be filed with the Canadian or United States NAO. The three NAOs consult one another, but whether to review and report is a matter of discretion for the NAO receiving the complaint. *See* U.S. NAO Submission No. 9801 (handling of Aero-Mexico strike, dismissed as not furthering NALC objectives) and No. 9804 (collective bargaining for rural mail carriers at Canada Post, dismissed as not raising issues of application or enforcement of labor law).

Two NAOs can and have reviewed the same submission concerning labor law enforcement in the third NAFTA nation. There are no structured complaint and response procedures as in the Environmental Cooperation Agreement. Even so, there has been a surprising amount of NAO activity. Most NAO reports follow public hearings and end up recommending ministerial consultations (below).

Much of the NALC labor law enforcement system has yet to be tested. NAFTA nations can at any time request ministerial consultations on all labor principles (see the attachment to this chapter) covered by the NALC. If ministerial consultations fail, a three person Evaluation Committee of Experts (ECE) can be created in most trade-related instances, but not if the issues concern collective bargaining, strikes or union organizing. This means that the numerous disputes about union organizing (below) can never proceed to an ECE report.

The Labor Ministers Council selects the Committee which reports back with recommendations to the Council. Comparative assessments of the enforcement "patterns of practice" of NAFTA nations on mutually recognized labor laws are to be the focus of ECE reports. In the end, the ECE report is published unless the Council decides otherwise. To date, no Evaluation Committee of Experts has been created under NALC.

For certain issues, publication of the ECE report is all that can be done under NALC. This is the case for issues of employment discrimination, equal pay, occupational safety, workers compensation, minimum employment standards, migrant workers, forced labor and protection of children and youth. When, however, the issues concern enforcement of occupational safety and health, child labor or minimum wage laws, further consultations can occur. The Labor Ministers Council may attempt to mediate. Ultimately a two-thirds vote of the Council can send the matter to arbitration. But the arbitration cannot cover labor standards or levels of minimum wages, only the issue of a persistent pattern of enforcement failure. That will be hard to find since Article 49 of the NALC specifically provides that a Party has not failed to effectively enforce its law where the action or inaction by agencies or officials: (a) Reflects a reasonable exercise of discretion with respect to investigatory, prosecutorial, regulatory or compliance matters; or (b) results from *bona fide* decisions to allocate resources to enforcement of other labor matters determined to have higher priorities.

NALC arbitration panels are to be created and administered in much the same manner as environmental arbitration panels. The panels report, with dissenting opinions, on the issue. A mutually agreed corrective plan of action should follow. If not, monetary penalties can (as with NAEC) be imposed by the panel. Suspension of tariff benefits is the fallback "solution."

Summary

In sum, the NALC labor law enforcement system is a calibrated four-tier series of dispute resolution mechanisms. *First*, the NAOs may review and report on eleven designated labor law enforcement matters that correspond to the NALC Labor Principles. *Second*, ministerial consultations may follow when recommended by the NAO. *Third*, an Evaluation Committee of Experts can report on trade-related mutually recognized labor law enforcement patterns of practice concerning eight of the NALC Labor Principles (excluding strikes, union organizing and collective bargaining). *Fourth*, persistent patterns of failure to enforce occupational health and safety, child labor or minimum wage laws (only) can be arbitrated and awards enforced by monetary penalties.

Labor Law Enforcement Submissions—Union Organizing

Early U.S. organized labor submissions to the United States NAO alleged the firing by U.S. and Japanese maquiladora subsidiaries of Mexican workers due to union organizing activities. U.S. NAO Submission Nos. 940001, 2 and 3. Public hearings were held at which Mexican workers, their attorneys and U.S. union supporters gave testimony. Honeywell, General Electric and Sony boycotted these hearings. The NAO Report in the Honeywell and GE cases was generally uncertain as to the legality of the firings under Mexican law, particularly because some of the dismissed workers accepted severance pay which indemnified the employers. No ministerial consultations were recommended, but some employees were reinstated and both Honeywell and GE made it clear to their managers that they did not want a reoccurrence of these events.

With Sony, the NAO Report cited "serious questions" about the legality of the firings and recommended ministerial consultations. These consultations resulted in a series of workshops, conferences, studies and meetings (including Sony representatives) on union registration and certification (especially of independent unions) in Mexico. In due course, the U.S. Secretary of Labor requested a follow-up NAO report. This report put a positive spin on developments in Mexico concerning union organizing, a topic that NALC does not allow to proceed to the next dispute settlement tier (an Evaluation Committee of Experts).

On the other side of the border, the Telephone Workers Union of Mexico (collaborating with the Communications Workers of America) (CWA) filed a submission with the Mexican NAO about worker dismissals and a plant closing at Sprint's La Conexion Familiar in San Francisco. OAN Mex. Submission No. 9501. Again, the allegation involved denial of labor's right to organize. The NLRB eventually ruled against Sprint and ordered rehiring of the workers. 322 NLRB 774 (1996). On appeal, the D.C. Circuit found that the claim that plant was closed because of union organizing activities was not substantiated. *LCF, Inc. v. NLRB*, 129 F.3d 1276

(1997). More recently, the Mexican NAO has accepted submissions challenging U.S. labor law enforcement concerning workers in a solar panel plant in California, the Washington State apple industry, and in a Maine egg farm. OAN Mex. Nos. 9801, 9802, 9803.

In the *Sprint* submission, the Mexican NAO found "possible problems" in enforcement of U.S. labor law and recommended ministerial consultations. These consultations resulted in a public forum, a special report by the NALC Secretariat on *Plant Closings and Labor Rights* (1997) in all three NAFTA nations, and monitoring of the pending NLRB proceeding based upon Sprint's actions. The Secretariat's report highlights widespread use of anti-union plant closing tactics in the United States (but not Canada or Mexico):

U.S. labor law authorities actively prosecute unfair labor practice cases involving plant closings and threats of plant closing. They demonstrate a high level of success in litigation before the NLRB and the courts. However, despite this effective enforcement, the incidence of anti-union plant closings and threats of plant closing continues with some frequency. There appears to be significant variation in the types of statements employers are permitted to make about plant closings in connection with a union organizing effort.

The Secretariat examined all 89 federal appeals court decisions in cases involving plant closings and threats of plant closing published between 1986 and 1993. Of the cases, 70 arose in the context of a new union organizing campaign. Closings or partial closings prompted 32 cases, and 57 cases involved threats of closing. Courts of appeals upheld NLRB determinations that employers unlawfully closed or threatened to close plants in 84 of the 89 cases.

The Secretariat studied 319 decisions of the NLRB between 1990 and 1995 involving plant closings and the threats of closing. Of the total, 109 cases involved closings or partial closings, and 210 involved threats of closing. New union organizing campaigns in non-union workplaces were involved in 275 of these cases, while 44 involved existing unions. The NLRB found a violation by the employer in 283 of the 319 cases.

The Secretariat also looked at case files in two regional offices of the NLRB to determine the volume and disposition of cases that do not reach the level of a published determination by an adjudicator. Findings suggest that for every case that reaches a published decision, 10 cases are initiated at the regional office level. More than half of these are withdrawn or dismissed.

In more than 40 percent of cases where the regional office found merit in the charge, the NLRB General Counsel took the case to trial before an ALJ. This is 10 times the rate of enforcement in other cases of meritorious unfair labor practice charges against employers. These

findings indicate that the NLRB takes plant closing cases very seriously and actively pursues
them to a litigated conclusion. The General Counsel prevails in nearly 90 percent of such cases.

In the United States, resources were readily
available to conduct survey research for information that could not be gleaned from administrative and judicial records. Union representatives
surveyed reported what they believed to be plant
closing threats occurring in half of the sampled
union organizing campaigns during the 3–year
period studied, with a higher incidence in industries more susceptible to closing such as manufacturing, trucking, and warehousing. Perceived
plant closing threats were the largest single factor
identified by respondents who decided to withdraw an election petition they had earlier filed,
thus discontinuing the organizing campaign.
When unions proceeded to an election, the overall
union win rate where plant closing threats were
reported to have occurred was 33 percent, compared with 47 percent in elections where no
threats were reported to have taken place.

The fourth submission to an NAO was made by
U.S. labor and human rights groups and a Mexican
lawyers association. They claimed that an independent public sector Mexican union lost its representation rights to a rival union when the government
merged the Fisheries Ministry into a larger Ministry of the Environment, Natural Resources and
Fisheries. U.S. NAO Submission No. 9610 ("Pesca

Union"). After a public hearing at which many testified, the NAO Report recommended ministerial consultations on the effect of International Labor Organization (ILO) Conventions (No. 87 was cited) on Mexican labor law, particularly the prohibition against more than one union in a governmental entity. The independent union subsequently had its registration restored by Mexican court order.

Another union organizing case came to the U.S. NAO in 1996. Submission No. 9602. The Communications Workers of America and its Mexican ally (the STRM) alleged that Taiwan-owned Maxi–Switch had a "protection contract" with a CTM union that was not employee approved. CTM is closely allied with the ruling PRI party. After scheduling public testimony, the complaint was withdrawn when registration was granted to a STRM-affiliated "independent" union in the Maxi–Switch maquiladora plant.

Perhaps the most bitter of all the union organizing complaints was that filed against Han Young, a Hyundai Corporation maquiladora making truck chassis in Tijuana, Mexico. U.S. NAO Submission No. 9702. Unions and labor groups from all three NAFTA nations alleged a brutal and blatant pattern of employer-CTM opposition to an independent union organizing effort. The U.S. NAO report documents threats, bribes, harassment, intimidation and dismissals. Moreover, the independent union's election victory was inexplicably nullified by the local Mexican labor Conciliation and Arbitration Board

(CAB). At this point, with outrage and embarrassment evident in the NAO investigation, the Mexican federal and state governments intervened and negotiated a settlement allowing a second supervised election which the independents also won. The local CAB then delayed notifying the election results to Han Young which in turn refused to collectively bargain. Indeed, Han Young hired a large number of new workers just in time for the CTM to petition for a third union representation election.

NAO Submission Strategies

One pattern that emerges in early NALC dispute settlement is the cross-border alliance of U.S. organized labor with Mexican labor groups, particularly those that are part of the "forista" movement for independent unions. This development is particularly notable since U.S. and Mexican unions have traditionally viewed NAFTA as a zero–sum game in which the winner takes all. Another pattern of note is the absence of any need to exhaust national administrative remedies, which is required under the NAEC. Indeed, there are essentially no "standing to submit" requirements under NALC. The NAOs can investigate and report at their discretion.

One example of creative use of the NALC involves double barrel submissions. In at least two instances, organized labor and NGOs have filed complaints with both available NAOs. In one case, the U.S. NAO and the Canada NAO received essentially the same submission concerning union organizing and occupational safety at an auto parts plant in Ciudad de los Reyes, Mexico. U.S. Submission No. 9703 and Canada Submission No. 98–1. Each NAO then proceeded to review and report on inadequate Mexican labor law enforcement. Both NAOs recommended ministerial consultations.

Likewise, in the Fall of 1998, a coalition of NGOs headed by a Yale Law School group filed submissions with the Canadian and Mexican NAOs alleging ineffective enforcement of U.S. minimum wage and overtime pay laws against employers of foreign nationals. Submission Nos. Canada 98–2 and Mexico 9804. These complaints seek to challenge U.S. Labor Department reporting of suspected immigration violations to the U.S. Immigration and Naturalization Service. They allege that such practices deter immigrant workers from filing wage and hour complaints under U.S. law. On the same day that the Mexican NAO accepted the submission (Nov. 23, 1998), the U.S. government announced that an interagency Memorandum of Understanding had been signed with the intent of dealing with these issues.

Employers are also starting to find NAO submissions strategic. In April of 1999, a United States *employer* group representing over 250 companies filed a submission with the Canadian NAO challenging U.S. labor law enforcement regarding employee participation in labor-management committees in nonunion workplaces. The employer group alleges a failure on the part of the U.S. to effectively enforce Section 8(a)(2) of the NLRA, which makes it an unfair labor practice for employers to "dominate or interfere" with the formation or administration of any "labor organization" or contribute financial or other support to such organizations. This submission was made after an NLRB decision that EFCO Corp. "employee participation committees" formed to consider employee benefits, policies and safety were labor organizations illegally dominated by EFCO. The NLRB decision has been appealed by EFCO to the Fourth Circuit. The submission also hopes to spur legislative change that would dilute Section 8(a)(2).

The Pregnancy Discrimination Case

As the number, scope and creativity of the submissions and reports continue to grow, NALC appears to be more than the toothless tiger many have alleged it to be. For example, the U.S. NAO investigated allegations of widespread state-tolerated sex discrimination against pregnant women in maquiladora plants. Submission No. 9701. This complaint could have resulted (but did not) in a report by an Evaluation Committee of Experts (discussed above).

Human Rights Watch/Americas, the International Labor Rights Fund and the Association Nacional de Abogados Democraticos (the same complainants in the *Pesca Union* case above) filed this submission. They maintained that employers regularly used pregnancy tests to avoid the 6 weeks paid maternity leave required under Mexican law. The Mexican NAO challenged these complaints as beyond the scope of the NALC, asserted that Mexican law adequately protects women from gender discrimination, and argued that there is no Mexican law against pre-employment pregnancy screening. The U.S. NAO hired an expert on Mexican labor law and gender issues and held public hearings in Brownsville, Texas at which workers and expert witnesses testified.

The NAO, in its report, reviewed Mexican constitutional and labor law, their enforcement bodies, the Alliance for Equality (the Mexican National Program for Women, 1995–2000), the Mexican Human Rights Commission and relevant international conventions. Post-employment pregnancy discrimination is clearly illegal in Mexico. On pre-employment law, one decision of note that emerged from the investigation was that of the Human Rights Commission for the Federal District which found pre-employment pregnancy screening a violation of Articles 4 and 5 of the Mexican Constitution. Here is the U.S. NAO analysis on point. Note especially its implications concerning the credibility of the Mexican NAO submissions in response to the complaint:

[T]he Human Rights Commission for the Federal District offers a markedly different interpretation to that of the Mexican NAO on the legality of pre-employment pregnancy screening. The Commission found (1) that the federal agencies it investigated did, in fact, conduct pregnancy screening and, (2) this practice violated Mexico's Constitution.

The Mexican NAO has asserted that the recommendations of the Commission are not binding and do not establish jurisprudence. The enacting legislation for the Commission, however, imposes an obligation on the responding agencies to comply with the recommendations once they accept the findings of the report. Additionally, the Commission was created pursuant to the Mexican Constitution and implemented by Federal law. It is composed of prominent jurists, appointed by the President and confirmed by the legislature, and their recommendation, in this case, was complied with by Federal Government agencies. Further, though the case involved public sector agencies, in its recommendation the Commission made no distinction on the application of the appropriate constitutional guarantees between the public and private sectors.

The position of the Human Rights Commission on the legality of pregnancy screening is markedly different from that expressed by the Mexican NAO. Moreover, the *Alliance for Equality* recognized pregnancy screening as a problem and outlined a plan of action to address such discriminatory practices. That pregnancy screening occurs and is of concern is supported by information from companies conducting business in Mexico, women workers, and the submitters. It also appears that the intrusive nature of the questioning described in the submission goes beyond what is necessary to determine if an applicant for employment is pregnant.

An additional question is raised with regard to the lack of any legal procedure by which to bring cases of pre-employment gender discrimination. The Mexican NAO asserted that the FLL [Federal Labor Law] does not provide for the adjudication of cases involving pre-employment discrimination. CAB officials interviewed by HRW [Human Rights Watch] also indicated that the CABs had no jurisdiction over these cases as they involved issues that occurred prior to the establishment of the employment relationship. The Mexican NAO's position appears to go beyond the question of pre-employment pregnancy screening to also include the lack of a legal procedure for bringing any pre-employment discrimination issue. Since Mexican law clearly prohibits employers from discriminating in hiring for a variety of reasons, the Mexican NAO's response creates a question as to what process exists for bringing such pre-employment discrimination claims.

The NAO report issued in Submission No. 9701 recommended ministerial consultations. These resulted in a U.S.-Mexican agreement on an improved "action plan" to combat pregnancy discrimination in the workplace.

Trade Adjustment Assistance

There was a second Clinton Administration approach to labor issues and NAFTA. Worker training and trade adjustment assistance for persons displaced by NAFTA was adopted unilaterally as part of U.S. law. These provisions can be found in the NAFTA Implementation Act, Title V, entitled the

"NAFTA Worker Safety Act." (17 Stat. § 501 et seq.)

Under this Act, workers can petition the Secretary of Labor for assistance if a significant number of employees have been or are threatened with job losses. NAFTA imports must have "contributed importantly" to this result. Assistance is also available if production of like or directly competitive articles has been shifted to Mexico or Canada. Income support (extended beyond regular state unemployment benefits) and job search and relocation reimbursements are possible, but only if job training is undertaken.

In the first three years of operation, the Secretary of Labor certified nearly 100,000 U.S. workers as being "at risk" because of NAFTA imports or job shifts. Not all of these workers actually lost their jobs. Mexico was the source country in 60 percent of these certifications, Canada in 23 percent and 17 percent involved no single source. Of these 100,000 workers, only slightly more than 12,000 applied for NAFTA trade adjustment benefits. Another 20,000 certified workers opted for regular (non-NAFTA) trade adjustment benefits where job training requirements can be waived.

NALC

ANNEX 1

LABOR PRINCIPLES

The following are guiding principles that the Parties are committed to promote, subject to each Party's domestic law, but do not establish common minimum standards for their domestic law. They indicate broad areas of concern where the Parties have developed, each in its own way, laws, regulations, procedures and practices that protect the rights and interests of their respective workforces.

1. Freedom of association and protection of the right to organize

The right of workers exercised freely and without impediment to establish and join organizations of their own choosing to further and defend their interests.

2. The right to bargain collectively

The protection of the right of organized workers to freely engage in collective bargaining on matters concerning the terms and conditions of employment.

3. The right to strike

The protection of the right of workers to strike in order to defend their collective interests.

4. Prohibition of forced labor

The prohibition and suppression of all forms of forced or compulsory labor, except for types of compulsory work generally considered acceptable by the parties, such as compulsory military service, certain civic obligations, prison labor not for private purposes and work exacted in cases of emergency.

5. Labor protections for children and young persons

The establishment of restrictions on the employment of children and young persons that may vary taking into consideration relevant factors likely to jeopardize the full physical, mental and moral development of young persons, including schooling and safety requirements.

6. Minimum employment standards

The establishment of minimum employment standards, such as minimum wages and overtime pay, for wage earners, including those not covered by collective agreements.

7. Elimination of employment discrimination

Elimination of employment discrimination on such grounds as race, religion, age, sex or other grounds, subject to certain reasonable exceptions, such as, where applicable, bona fide occupational requirements or qualifications and established practices or rules governing retirement ages, and special measures of protection or assistance for particular groups designed to take into account the effects of discrimination.

8. Equal pay for women and men

Equal wages for women and men by applying the principle of equal pay for equal work in the same establishment.

9. Prevention of occupational injuries and illnesses

Prescribing and implementing standards to minimize the causes of occupational injuries and illnesses.

10. Compensation in cases of occupational injuries and illnesses

The establishment of a system providing benefits and compensation to workers or their dependents in cases of occupational injuries, accident or fatalities arising out of, linked with or occurring in the course of employment.

11. Protection of migrant workers

Providing migrant workers in a Party's territory with the same legal protection as the Party's nationals in respect of working conditions.

CHAPTER 11

FREE TRADE AND THE AMERICAS

When Canada and the United States agreed to free trade in 1989, there was no expectation of extension of that agreement to Mexico or any other country. The NAFTA agreement, on the other hand, specifically anticipates growth by accession. Article 2204 invites applications to join NAFTA by countries or groups of countries without regard to their geographic location or cultural background. This is unlike the European Union which only allows "European" nations to join. Australia, South Korea, New Zealand and Singapore have, for example, all expressed interest in NAFTA. Canada would also like to see European nations actively considered for membership.

The NAFTA Free Trade Commission is authorized to negotiate the terms and conditions of any new memberships. The resulting accession agreement must be approved and ratified by each NAFTA nation. Practically speaking, as in the European Union, this means that current members can veto NAFTA applicants.

Expanding NAFTA To Include Chile

In December of 1994 at the "Summit of the Americas" in Miami, Canada and Mexico joined the United States in formally inviting Chile to apply for NAFTA membership. This invitation has gone nowhere because Congress has repeatedly refused to authorize "fast track" negotiations by the President of the United States. Fast track negotiations would provide assurance to all concerned that Congress would not be able to alter the terms and conditions of Chile's accession. Under fast track, Congress would have to approve or disapprove the agreement by majority vote. Apart from partisan politics, one thorny issue is whether there will be side agreements with Chile on labor and the environment.

Absent fast track authority, Chile, Canada and Mexico have all steered different courses. Mexico and Chile have renegotiated and expanded their pre-NAFTA free trade agreement. Canada and Chile reached agreement in 1997 on free trade along with side agreements that are similar to NAEC and NALC. Chile in 1996 became a free trade associate of MERCOSUR, the Southern Cone common market of Brazil, Argentina, Paraguay and Uruguay. All these free trade commitments flow partly from want of U.S. fast track authority. They have already had an impact on trade and investment patterns. Some U.S. companies with Canadian subsidiaries, for example, are shifting production and exports to Canada in order to take advantage of Canada–Chile free trade.

Free Trade and The Americas

The "Enterprise for the Americas Initiative" (EAI) under President Bush raised hopes of economic integration against a background of competitive regionalism in trade relations, especially between the European Union and North America. At the Americas Summit in Miami, President Clinton and 33 Latin American heads of state (only Fidel Castro was absent) renewed this hope by agreeing to commence negotiations on a Free Trade Area of the Americas (FTAA). The year 2005 was targeted at the Summit for creation of the FTAA.

FTAA preparatory working groups have regularly met since 1995 to discuss the following topics: (1) Market Access; (2) Customs Procedures and Rules of Origin; (3) Investment; (4) Standards and Technical Barriers to Trade; (5) Sanitary and Phytosanitary Measures; (6) Subsidies, Antidumping and Countervailing Duties; (7) Smaller Economies; (8) Government Procurement; (9) Intellectual Property Rights; (10) Services; (11) Competition Policy; and (12) Dispute Settlement. It is expected that each of these areas would be covered in any FTAA agreement. Formal FTAA negotiations were delayed several times, particularly because of differences between Brazil-led MERCOSUR and U.S.-led NAFTA.

The absence of fast track authority and the general perception that political support for free trade in the United States is waning has clearly slowed FTAA developments. MERCOSUR and Brazil in particular have seized the opportunity to move towards a South American Free Trade Area (SAFTA). Presumably, SAFTA would be in a much better position to negotiate terms and conditions with NAFTA than individual countries or sub-groups within South America. To that end, Bolivia and Chile are already MERCOSUR free trade associates and negotiations with virtually all South American nations are in progress. Indeed, MERCOSUR is even negotiating along the same lines with Canada, Mexico, the Central American states, and the European Union. The EU, for its part, is expanding its European membership and is discussing a free trade agreement with Mexico!

Politics aside, Professor David Gantz has analyzed some of the technical challenges facing any alliance of the NAFTA and MERCOSUR trade blocs. 14 Ariz. J. Int'l & Comp. Law 381 (1997). He finds NAFTA's rules of origin too complex and ponderous to serve as a basis for expanded integration. While MERCOSUR's rules of origin are easier to work with, they are headed towards extinction if MERCOSUR successfully implements its much postponed plans for a common external tariff (CET). In his opinion, a full CET is unlikely since Canada, Mexico and MERCOSUR would be unwilling to reduce their tariffs to anything approximating U.S. levels. Professor Gantz suggests that a hybrid free trade area/customs union system with a CET for trade in major product sectors may be needed to resolve these conflicts. Other challenges to a MERCOSUR–NAFTA alliance concern investor-state arbitrations, intergovernmental dispute settlement, procurement, trade in services, and antidumping and countervailing duty actions (none of which are covered by MERCOSUR).

Quebec and NAFTA

The Canadian Constitution of 1982 was adopted by an Act of the British Parliament. As such, the Act and Constitution of 1982 are thought to bind all Canadian provinces including Quebec. That province, however, has never formally ratified the Constitution of Canada. Since 1982 a series of negotiations have attempted to secure Quebec's ratification, and all have failed miserably.

In 1987, the "Meech Lake Accord" was reached. This agreement recognized Quebec as a "distinct society" in Canada. What the practical consequences of this recognition would have been will never be known. Quebec's adherence to the Meech Lake Accord was nullified when Manitoba, New Brunswick and ultimately Newfoundland failed to ratify the Accord.

A second set of negotiations led in 1992 to the Charlottetown Accord which also acknowledged Quebec as a distinct society with its French language, unique culture and Civil Law tradition. This time a national referendum was held and its defeat was overwhelming. Quebec, five English-speaking Canadian provinces, and the Yukon territory voted against the Charlottetown Accord.

The failure of these Accords has moved Quebec towards separation from Canada. In 1994, the Parti

Quebecois came to power. It held a provincial referendum on separation in 1995. By the narrowest of margins, the people of Quebec rejected separation from Canada. Just exactly what "separation" would have meant was never entirely clear during the debate, perhaps deliberately so.

In 1998, Canada's Supreme Court ruled that Quebec could not "under the Constitution" withdraw unilaterally. To secede, Quebec would need to negotiate a constitutional amendment with the rest of Canada. *See* Reference re. Secession of Quebec, File No. 25506, Can.Sup.Ct. (Aug. 20, 1998). The rest of Canada would, likewise, be obliged to enter into such negotiations if a "clear majority" of Quebec's voters approved a "clear question" on secession in a referendum.

If Quebec separates from Canada this will raise fundamental issues about Quebec and NAFTA. Would Quebec be forced to negotiate for membership in NAFTA? If so, would English-speaking Canada veto its application? Might Quebec's relationship to Canada continue in some limited manner (such as for defense and international trade purposes) such that NAFTA is not an issue at all? Might Quebec automatically "succeed" to the NAFTA treaty, thus becoming a member without application?

Article 34(1) of The Vienna Convention of Succession of States in Respect of Treaties (1978) (not in force) supports the succession alternative. *See* 17 Int'l Legal Mats. 1488. Customary international practice maintains existing treaties when nations sub-divide. This practice was applied recently to the Czech Republic, Slovakia, and various states of the former Yugoslavia. Thus custom suggests that fears in Quebec about losing NAFTA benefits are exaggerated.

Conclusion

The future of free trade in the Americas is uncertain. NAFTA's expansion is stalled, and the FTAA proposal is barely maintaining momentum. Congress could change these prospects overnight by authorizing fast track negotiations, but the rainbow coalition of interests against free trade has held firm since 1995. Meanwhile Canada, Chile, Mexico, MERCOSUR and the European Union have seized the opportunity to advance their trade relations while Congress deliberates.

Quebec may well end up becoming the fourth member of NAFTA. All of these trends suggest a rethinking of U.S. free trade objectives and outcomes. Perhaps the old idea of a transatlantic free trade agreement should be revived. Recent dialogues between European Union leaders and United States officials have explored this possibility.

James Lawrence, a social scientist, has crunched the numbers and provocatively concluded that a free trade agreement between NAFTA and Japan would harvest much more economic benefit than integration of the Americas. 20 Md. J. Int'l Law &

Trade 61 (1996). Now there is an idea whose time has certainly not arrived.

We conclude this Nutshell with a NAFTA timeline:

1986	Canada–U.S. free trade negotiations commence. Mexico joins the GATT. Uruguay Round of GATT negotiations launched.
1989	CFTA enters into effect.
1991	Congress extends fast track authority to NAFTA and Uruguay Round.
1992	NAFTA signed by Presidents Bush and Salinas, Prime Minister Mulroney.
1993 (August)	Side agreements on North American Labor and Environmental Cooperation concluded under President Clinton.
1993 (October)	Vice President Gore "defeats" Ross Perot in nationally televised NAFTA debate.
1993 (November)	U.S. Congress ratifies NAFTA.
1993 (December)	Uruguay Round agreements concluded.
1994	NAFTA enters into effect.
1994 (December)	Miami Summit supports creation by 2005 of a Free Trade Area of the Americas (FTAA).
1994–95	Mexican peso crashes, U.S. organizes rescue package.
1995	Uruguay Round agreements enter into effect. WTO created. Negotiations commence for Chile to join NAFTA. Quebec voters barely reject separation from Canada.
1997	Canada and Chile agree on free trade with side agreements. Mexico revises its free trade agreement with Chile.

1995–date   Congress refuses to authorize fast track negotiations for FTAA or accession of Chile to NAFTA. FTAA negotiations ongoing in 12 working groups.

APPENDIX I

NORTH AMERICAN FREE TRADE AGREEMENT (1994)

PART ONE—GENERAL PART

Chapter One—Objectives

Article 101: Establishment of the Free Trade Area

The Parties to this Agreement, consistent with Article XXIV of the General Agreement on Tariffs and Trade, hereby establish a free trade area.

Article 102: Objectives

1. The objectives of this Agreement, as elaborated more specifically through its principles and rules, including national treatment, most-favored-nation treatment and transparency, are to: (a) eliminate barriers to trade in, and facilitate the cross border movement of, goods and services between the territories of the Parties; (b) promote conditions of fair competition in the free trade area; (c) increase substantially investment opportunities in the territories of the Parties; (d) provide adequate and effective protection and enforcement of intellectual property rights in each Party's territory; (e) create effective procedures for the implementation and application of this Agreement, for its joint administration and for the resolution of disputes; and (f) establish a framework for further trilateral, regional and multilateral cooperation to expand and enhance the benefits of this Agreement.

2. The Parties shall interpret and apply the provisions of this Agreement in the light of its objectives set out in paragraph 1 and in accordance with applicable rules of international law.

Article 103: Relation to Other Agreements

1. The Parties affirm their existing rights and obligations with respect to each other under the General Agreement on Tariffs and Trade and other agreements to which such Parties are party.

2. In the event of any inconsistency between this Agreement and such other agreements, this Agreement shall prevail to the extent of the inconsistency, except as otherwise provided in this Agreement.

Article 104: Relation to Environmental and Conservation Agreements

1. In the event of any inconsistency between this Agreement and the specific trade obligations set out in: (a) the Convention on International Trade in Endangered Species of Wild Fauna and Flora, done at Washington, March 3, 1973, as amended June 22, 1979; (b) the Montreal Protocol on Substances that Deplete the Ozone Layer, done at Montreal, September 16, 1987, as amended June 29, 1990; (c) the Basel Convention on the Control of Transboundary Movements of Hazardous Wastes and Their Disposal, done at Basel, March 22, 1989, on its entry into force for Canada, Mexico and the United States; or (d) the agreements set out in Annex 104.1, such obligations shall prevail to the extent of the inconsistency, provided that where a Party has a choice among equally effective and reasonably available means of complying with such obligations, the Party chooses the alternative that is the least inconsistent with the other provisions of this Agreement.

2. The Parties may agree in writing to modify Annex 104.1 to include any amendment to an agreement re-

ferred to in paragraph 1, and any other environmental or conservation agreement.

Article 105: Extent of Obligations

The Parties shall ensure that all necessary measures are taken in order to give effect to the provisions of this Agreement, including their observance, except as otherwise provided in this Agreement, by state and provincial governments.

Annex 104.1

Bilateral and Other Environmental and Conservation Agreements

1. The Agreement Between the Government of Canada and the Government of the United States of America Concerning the Transboundary Movement of Hazardous Waste, signed at Ottawa, October 28, 1986.

2. The Agreement Between the United States of America and the United Mexican States on Cooperation for the Protection and Improvement of the Environment in the Border Area, signed at La Paz, Baja California Sur, August 14, 1983.

Chapter Two—General Definitions

* * *

enterprise means any entity constituted or organized under applicable law, whether or not for profit, and whether privately-owned or governmentally-owned, including any corporation, trust, partnership, sole proprietorship, joint venture or other association;

enterprise of a Party means an enterprise constituted or organized under the law of a Party;

* * *

measure includes any law, regulation, procedure, requirement or practice;

national means a natural person who is a citizen or permanent resident of a Party and any other natural person referred to in Annex 201.1;

originating means qualifying under the rules of origin set out in Chapter Four (Rules of Origin);

person means a natural person or an enterprise;

* * *

state enterprise means an enterprise that is owned, or controlled through ownership interests, by a Party; and

PART TWO—TRADE IN GOODS

Chapter Three—National Treatment and Market Access for Goods

Section A—National Treatment

Article 300: Scope and Coverage

This Chapter applies to trade in goods of a Party, including: (a) goods covered by Annex 300-A (Trade and Investment in the Automotive Sector); (b) goods covered by Annex 300-B (Textile and Apparel Goods); and (c) goods covered by another Chapter in this Part, except as provided in such Annex or Chapter.

Article 301: National Treatment

1. Each Party shall accord national treatment to the goods of another Party in accordance with Article III of the General Agreement on Tariffs and Trade (GATT), including its interpretative notes, and to this end Article III of the GATT and its interpretative notes, or any equivalent provision of a successor agreement to which all Parties are party, are incorporated into and made part of this Agreement.

2. The provisions of paragraph 1 regarding national treatment shall mean, with respect to a state or province, treatment no less favorable than the most favorable treatment accorded by such state or province to any like, directly competitive or substitutable goods, as the case may be, of the Party of which it forms a part.

3. Paragraphs 1 and 2 do not apply to the measures set out in Annex 301.3.

Section B—Tariffs

Article 302: Tariff Elimination

1. Except as otherwise provided in this Agreement, no Party may increase any existing customs duty, or adopt any customs duty, on an originating good.

2. Except as otherwise provided in this Agreement, each Party shall progressively eliminate its customs duties on originating goods in accordance with its Schedule to Annex 302.2 or as otherwise indicated in Annex 300–B.

3. At the request of any Party, the Parties shall consult to consider accelerating the elimination of customs duties set out in their Schedules. An agreement between two or more Parties to accelerate the elimination of a customs duty on a good shall supersede any duty rate or staging category in their Schedules for such good when approved by each such Party in accordance with Article 2202(2) (Amendments).

4. (a) Each Party may adopt or maintain import measures to allocate in-quota imports made pursuant to a tariff rate quota set out in Annex 302.2, provided that such measures do not have trade restrictive effects on imports additional to those caused by the imposition of the tariff rate quota.

(b) On written request of any Party, a Party applying or intending to apply measures pursuant to subparagraph

(a) shall consult to review the administration of those measures.

Article 303: Restriction on Drawback and Duty Deferral Programs

1. Except as otherwise provided in this Article, no Party may refund the amount of customs duties paid, or waive or reduce the amount of customs duties owed, on a good imported into its territory, on condition that the good is: (a) subsequently exported to the territory of another Party, (b) used as a material in the production of another good that is subsequently exported to the territory of another Party, or (c) substituted by an identical or similar good used as a material in the production of another good that is subsequently exported to the territory of another Party, in an amount that exceeds the lesser of the total amount of customs duties paid or owed on the good on importation into its territory, and the total amount of customs duties paid to another Party on the good that has been subsequently exported to the territory of that other Party.

2. No Party may, by reason of an exportation described in paragraph 1, refund, waive or reduce: (a) an antidumping or countervailing duty that is applied pursuant to a Party's domestic law and that is not applied inconsistently with Chapter Nineteen (Review and Dispute Settlement in Antidumping and Countervailing Duty Matters); (b) a premium offered or collected on an imported good arising out of any tendering system in respect of the administration of quantitative import restrictions, tariff rate quotas or tariff preference levels; (c) a fee applied pursuant to section 22 of the U.S. Agricultural Adjustment Act, subject to Chapter Seven (Agriculture and Sanitary and Phytosanitary Measures); or (d) customs duties paid or owed on a good imported into its territory and substituted by an identical or similar good

that is subsequently exported to the territory of another Party.

3. Where a good is imported into the territory of a Party pursuant to a duty deferral program and is subsequently exported to the territory of another Party, or is used as a material in the production of another good that is subsequently exported to the territory of another Party, or is substituted by an identical or similar good used as a material in the production of another good that is subsequently exported to the territory of another Party, the Party from whose territory the good is exported: (a) shall assess the customs duties as if the exported good had been withdrawn for domestic consumption; and (b) may waive or reduce such customs duties to the extent permitted under paragraph 1.

4. In determining the amount of customs duties that may be refunded, waived or reduced pursuant to paragraph 1 on a good imported into its territory, each Party shall require presentation of satisfactory evidence of the amount of customs duties paid to another Party on the good that has been subsequently exported to the territory of that other Party.

5. Where satisfactory evidence of the customs duties paid to the Party to which a good is subsequently exported under a duty deferral program described in paragraph 3 is not presented within 60 days after the date of exportation, the Party from whose territory the good was exported: (a) shall collect customs duties as if the exported good had been withdrawn for domestic consumption; and (b) may refund such customs duties to the extent permitted under paragraph 1 upon the timely presentation of such evidence under the laws and regulations of the Party.

* * *

Article 304: Waiver of Customs Duties

1. Except as set out in Annex 304.1, no Party may adopt any new waiver of customs duties, or expand with respect to existing recipients or extend to any new recipient the application of an existing waiver of customs duties, where the waiver is conditioned, explicitly or implicitly, upon the fulfillment of a performance requirement.

2. Except as set out in Annex 304.2, no Party may, explicitly or implicitly, condition on the fulfillment of a performance requirement the continuation of any existing waiver of customs duties.

3. If a waiver or a combination of waivers of customs duties granted by a Party with respect to goods for commercial use by a designated person can be shown by another Party to have an adverse impact on the commercial interests of a person of that Party, or of a person owned or controlled by a person of that Party that is located in the territory of the Party granting the waiver, or on the other Party's economy, the Party granting the waiver shall either cease to grant it or make it generally available to any importer.

4. This Article shall not apply to measures covered by Article 303.

* * *

Section C—Non–Tariff Measures

Article 309: Import and Export Restrictions

1. Except as otherwise provided in this Agreement, no Party may adopt or maintain any prohibition or restriction on the importation of any good of another Party or on the exportation or sale for export of any good destined for the territory of another Party, except in accordance with Article XI of the GATT, including its interpretative notes, and to this end Article XI of the GATT and its

interpretative notes, or any equivalent provision of a successor agreement to which all Parties are party, are incorporated into and made part of this Agreement.

2. The Parties understand that the GATT rights and obligations incorporated by paragraph 1 prohibit, in any circumstances in which any other form of restriction is prohibited, export price requirements and, except as permitted in enforcement of countervailing and antidumping orders and undertakings, import price requirements.

3. In the event that a Party adopts or maintains a prohibition or restriction on the importation from or exportation to a non-Party of a good, nothing in this Agreement shall be construed to prevent the Party from: (a) limiting or prohibiting the importation from the territory of another Party of such good of that non-Party; or (b) requiring as a condition of export of such good of the Party to the territory of another Party, that the good not be re-exported to the non-Party, directly or indirectly, without being consumed in the territory of the other Party.

4. In the event that a Party adopts or maintains a prohibition or restriction on the importation of a good from a non-Party, the Parties, on request of any Party, shall consult with a view to avoiding undue interference with or distortion of pricing, marketing and distribution arrangements in another Party.

5. Paragraphs 1 through 4 shall not apply to the measures set out in Annex 301.3.

* * *

Article 314: Export Taxes

Except as set out in Annex 314, no Party may adopt or maintain any duty, tax or other charge on the export of any good to the territory of another Party, unless such duty, tax or charge is adopted or maintained on: (a) exports of any such good to the territory of all other Parties; and (b) any such good when destined for domestic consumption.

Article 315: Other Export Measures

1. Except as set out in Annex 315, a Party may adopt or maintain a restriction otherwise justified under Articles XI:2(a) or XX(g), (i) or (j) of the GATT with respect to the export of a good of the Party to the territory of another Party, only if:

(a) the restriction does not reduce the proportion of the total export shipments of the specific good made available to that other Party relative to the total supply of that good of the Party maintaining the restriction as compared to the proportion prevailing in the most recent 36–month period for which data are available prior to the imposition of the measure, or in such other representative period on which the Parties may agree;

(b) the Party does not impose a higher price for exports of a good to that other Party than the price charged for such good when consumed domestically, by means of any measure, such as licenses, fees, taxation and minimum price requirements. The foregoing provision does not apply to a higher price that may result from a measure taken pursuant to subparagraph (a) that only restricts the volume of exports; and

(c) the restriction does not require the disruption of normal channels of supply to that other Party or normal proportions among specific goods or categories of goods supplied to that other Party.

2. The Parties shall cooperate in the maintenance and development of effective controls on the export of each other's goods to a non-Party in implementing this Article.

* * *

Annex 311—Country of Origin Marking

1. The Parties shall establish by January 1, 1994, rules for determining whether a good is a good of a Party ("Marking Rules") for purposes of this Annex, Annex 300–B, Annex 302.2, and for such other purposes as the Parties may agree.

2. Each Party may require that a good of another Party, as determined in accordance with the Marking Rules, bear a country of origin marking, when imported into its territory, that indicates to the ultimate purchaser of that good the name of its country of origin.

3. Each Party shall permit the country of origin marking of a good of another Party to be indicated in English, French or Spanish, except that a Party may, as part of its general consumer information measures, require that an imported good be marked with its country of origin in the same manner as prescribed for goods of that Party.

4. Each Party shall, in adopting, maintaining and applying any measure relating to country of origin marking, minimize the difficulties, costs and inconveniences that the measure may cause to the commerce and industry of the other Parties.

* * *

Annex 312.2—Wine and Distilled Spirits

Section A—Canada and the United States

As between Canada and the United States, any measure related to the internal sale and distribution of wine and distilled spirits, other than a measure covered by Article 312(1) or Article 313, shall be governed under this Agreement exclusively in accordance with the relevant provisions of the Canada—United States Free Trade Agreement, which for this purpose are hereby incorporated into this Agreement.

Annex 313—Distinctive Products

1. Canada and Mexico shall recognize Bourbon Whiskey and Tennessee Whiskey, which is a straight Bourbon Whiskey authorized to be produced only in the State of Tennessee, as distinctive products of the United States. Accordingly, Canada and Mexico shall not permit the sale of any product as Bourbon Whiskey or Tennessee Whiskey, unless it has been manufactured in the United States in accordance with the laws and regulations of the United States governing the manufacture of Bourbon Whiskey and Tennessee Whiskey.

2. Mexico and the United States shall recognize Canadian Whisky as a distinctive product of Canada. Accordingly, Mexico and the United States shall not permit the sale of any product as Canadian Whisky, unless it has been manufactured in Canada in accordance with the laws and regulations of Canada governing the manufacture of Canadian Whisky for consumption in Canada.

3. Canada and the United States shall recognize Tequila and Mezcal as distinctive products of Mexico. Accordingly, Canada and the United States shall not permit the sale of any product as Tequila or Mezcal, unless it has been manufactured in Mexico in accordance with the laws and regulations of Mexico governing the manufacture of Tequila and Mezcal. This provision shall apply to Mezcal, either on the date of entry into force of this Agreement, or 90 days after the date when the official standard for this product is made obligatory by the Government of Mexico, whichever is later.

Annex 314—Export Taxes

Mexico

1. Mexico may adopt or maintain a duty, tax or other charge on the export of those basic foodstuffs set out in paragraph 4, on their ingredients, or on the goods from which such foodstuffs are derived, if such duty, tax or

other charge is adopted or maintained on the export of such goods to the territory of all other Parties, and is used: (a) to limit to domestic consumers the benefits of a domestic food assistance program with respect to such foodstuff; or (b) to ensure the availability of sufficient quantities of such foodstuff to domestic consumers or of sufficient quantities of its ingredients, or of the goods from which such foodstuffs are derived, to a domestic processing industry, when the domestic price of such foodstuff is held below the world price as part of a governmental stabilization plan, provided that such duty, tax, or other charge (i) does not operate to increase the protection afforded to such domestic industry, and (ii) is maintained only for such period of time as is necessary to maintain the integrity of the stabilization plan.

2.   Notwithstanding paragraph 1, Mexico may adopt or maintain a duty, tax, or other charge on the export of any foodstuff to the territory of another Party if such duty, tax, or other charge is temporarily applied to relieve critical shortages of that foodstuff. For purposes of this paragraph, "temporarily" means up to one year, or such longer period as the Parties may agree.

* * *

Annex 300–A—Trade and Investment in the Automotive Sector

1.   Each Party shall accord to all existing producers of vehicles in its territory treatment no less favorable than it accords to any new producer of vehicles in its territory under the measures referred to in this Annex, except that this obligation shall not be construed to apply to any differences in treatment specifically provided for in the Appendices to this Annex.

* * *

Canada—Existing Measures

1.   Canada and the United States may maintain the Agreement Concerning Automotive Products between the Government of Canada and the Government of the United States of America, signed at Johnson City, Texas, January 16, 1965 and entered into force on September 16, 1966, in accordance with Article 1001, and Article 1002(1) and (4) (as they refer to Annex 1002.1, Part One), Article 1005(1) and (3), and Annex 1002.1, Part One (Waivers of Customs Duties) of the Canada–United States Free Trade Agreement. For purposes of Article 1005(1) of that agreement, Chapter Four (Rules of Origin) of this Agreement shall be applied in the place of Chapter Three of the Canada–United States Free Trade Agreement.

2.   Canada may maintain the measures referred to in Article 1002(1) and (4) (as they refer to Annex 1002.1, Parts Two and Three), Article 1002(2) and (3), Article 1003 and Parts Two (Export–Based Waivers of Customs Duties) and Three (Production–Based Waivers of Customs Duties) of Annex 1002.1 of the Canada–United States Free Trade Agreement. Canada shall eliminate those measures in accordance with the terms set out in that agreement.

3.   For greater certainty, the differences in treatment pursuant to paragraphs 1 and 2 shall not be considered to be inconsistent with Article 1103 (Investment—Most–Favored–Nation Treatment).

* * *

Mexico—Auto Decree and Auto Decree Implementing Regulations

1.   Until January 1, 2004, Mexico may maintain the provisions of the Decree for Development and Modernization of the Automotive Industry ("Decreto para el Fomento y Modernizacion de la Industria Automotriz"), December 11, 1989, (the "Auto Decree") and the Resolution that

Establishes Rules for the Implementation of the Auto
Decree ("Acuerdo que Determina Reglas para la Aplica-
cion para el Fomento y Modernizacion de la Industria
Automotriz"), November 30, 1990, (the "Auto Decree
Implementing Regulations") that would otherwise be inconsistent with this Agreement, subject to the conditions
set out in paragraphs 2 through 18. No later than January 1, 2004, Mexico shall bring any inconsistent provision
of the Auto Decree and the Auto Decree Implementing
Regulations into conformity with the other provisions of
this Agreement.

*Autoparts Industry, National Suppliers and Independent
Maquiladoras*

2.   Mexico may not require that an enterprise attain a
level of national value added in excess of 20 percent of its
total sales as one of the conditions to qualify as a national
supplier or enterprise of the autoparts industry.

3.   Mexico may require that a national supplier or an
enterprise of the autoparts industry, in calculating its
national value added solely for purposes of paragraph 2,
include customs duties in the value of imports incorporated into the autoparts produced by such supplier or enterprise.

4.   Mexico shall grant national supplier status to an
independent maquiladora that requests such status and
meets the requirements for that status set out in the
existing Auto Decree, as modified by paragraphs 2 and 3.
Mexico shall continue to grant to all independent maquiladoras that request national supplier status all existing
rights and privileges accorded to independent maquiladoras under the existing Decree for the Promotion and
Operation of the Maquiladora Export Industry ("Decreto
para el Fomento y Operacion de la Industria Maquiladora
de Exportacion"), December 22, 1989 (the "Maquiladora
Decree").

National Value Added

5. Mexico shall provide that a manufacturer ("empresa de la industria terminal") calculate its required national value added from suppliers (VANp) as a percentage of: (a) the manufacturer's reference value as set out in paragraph 8; or (b) the manufacturer's total national value added (VANt), whichever is greater, except that Mexico shall provide that a manufacturer beginning production of motor vehicles in Mexico after model year 1991 calculate its required national value added from suppliers (VANp) as a percentage of its total national value added (VANt).

6. Mexico may not require that the percentage referred to in paragraph 5 be greater than: (a) 34 percent for each of the first five years beginning January 1, 1994; (b) 33 percent for 1999; (c) 32 percent for 2000; (d) 31 percent for 2001; (e) 30 percent for 2002; and (f) 29 percent for 2003.

7. Notwithstanding paragraph 6, Mexico shall allow a manufacturer that produced motor vehicles in Mexico before model year 1992 to use as its percentage referred to in paragraph 5 the ratio of actual national value added from suppliers (VANp) to total national value added (VANt) that the manufacturer attained in model year 1992, for so long as that ratio is lower than the applicable percentage specified under paragraph 6. In determining such ratio for model year 1992, purchases that the manufacturer made from independent maquiladoras that would have been eligible to receive national supplier status had paragraphs 2, 3 and 4 of this Appendix been in effect at that time, shall be included in the calculation of the manufacturer's national value added from suppliers (VANp), in the same manner as autoparts from any other national supplier or enterprise of the autoparts industry.

8. The annual reference value for a manufacturer ("reference value") shall be: (a) for each of the years 1994

through 1997, the base value for the manufacturer, plus no more than 65 percent of the difference between the manufacturer's total sales in Mexico in that year and its base value; (b) for each of the years 1998 through 2000, the base value for the manufacturer, plus no more than 60 percent of the difference between the manufacturer's total sales in Mexico in that year and its base value; and (c) for each of the years 2001 through 2003, the base value for the manufacturer, plus no more than 50 percent of the difference between the manufacturer's total sales in Mexico in that year and its base value.

9. Mexico shall provide that where a manufacturer's total sales in Mexico in a year are lower than its base value, the reference value for the manufacturer for that year shall be equal to the manufacturer's total sales in Mexico for the year.

10. In the event an abnormal production disruption affects a manufacturer's production capability, Mexico shall allow the manufacturer to seek a reduction in its reference value before the Intersecretariat Automotive Industry Commission, established under Chapter V of the Auto Decree. If the Commission finds that the production capability of the manufacturer has been impaired by such an abnormal production disruption, the Commission shall reduce the manufacturer's reference value in an amount commensurate to the event.

11. If, upon the request of a manufacturer, the Intersecretariat Automotive Industry Commission finds that the production capability of the manufacturer has been significantly disrupted as a result of a major retooling or plant conversion in the facilities of the manufacturer, the Commission shall reduce the manufacturer's reference value for that year in an amount commensurate with the disruption, provided that any reduction in that manufacturer's required national value added from suppliers (VANp) that may result from the Commission's determination to reduce the manufacturer's reference value shall

be fully made up by the manufacturer over the twenty-four months after the date on which the retooling or plant conversion is completed.

Trade Balance

12. Mexico may not require a manufacturer to include in the calculation of its trade balance (S) a percentage of the value of direct and indirect imports of autoparts that the manufacturer incorporated into that manufacturer's production in Mexico for sale in Mexico (VTVd) in the corresponding year, greater than the following:

(a) 80 percent for 1994; (b) 77.2 percent for 1995; (c) 74.4 percent for 1996; (d) 71.6 percent for 1997; (e) 68.9 percent for 1998; (f) 66.1 percent for 1999; (g) 63.3 percent for 2000; (h) 60.5 percent for 2001; (i) 57.7 percent for 2002; and (j) 55.0 percent for 2003.

13. Mexico shall provide that, for purposes of determining a manufacturer's total national value added (VANt), paragraph 12 shall not apply to the calculation of the manufacturer's trade balance (S).

14. Mexico shall allow a manufacturer with a surplus in its extended trade balance to divide its extended trade balance by the applicable percentages in paragraph 12 to determine the total value of new motor vehicles that it may import.

15. Mexico shall provide that a manufacturer's adjustment factor (Y), included in the calculation of such manufacturer's extended trade balance, shall be equal to (a) for a manufacturer that produced motor vehicles prior to model year 1992: (i) the greater of the manufacturer's reference value or the manufacturer's total national value added (VANt), minus (ii) the manufacturer's actual national value added from suppliers (VANp) divided by the appropriate percentage specified under paragraph 6 or 7 as appropriate; (b) for all other manufacturers:(i) the manufacturer's total national value added (VANt), minus

(ii) the manufacturer's actual national value added from suppliers (VANp) divided by the appropriate percentage specified under paragraph 6; except that the adjustment factor (Y) shall be zero if the amount resulting from subtracting (ii) from (i), under (a) or (b), is negative.

* * *

Other Restrictions in the Auto Decree

17. Mexico shall eliminate any restriction that limits the number of motor vehicles that a manufacturer may import into Mexico in relation to the total number of motor vehicles that such manufacturer sells in Mexico.

18. For greater certainty, the differences in treatment required under paragraphs 5, 7 and 15 shall not be considered to be inconsistent with Article 1103 (Investment–Most–Favored–Nation Treatment).

* * *

Import Licensing Measures

26. Mexico may adopt or maintain import licensing measures to the extent necessary to administer restrictions (a) pursuant to the Auto Decree and the Auto Decree Implementing Regulations, as modified by this Appendix, on the importation of motor vehicles; (b) pursuant to paragraph 19 of this Appendix on the importation of new automotive products provided for in item 8407.34.99 (gasoline engines of more than 1000cm<3>, except for motorcycles) or 8703.10.99 (other special vehicles) in the Tariff Schedule of the General Import Duty Act, (c) pursuant to paragraphs 22 and 23 of this Appendix on the importation of autotransportation vehicles; and (d) pursuant to subparagraphs (a) through (f) of paragraph 24 of this Appendix on the importation of used vehicles that are motor vehicles or autotransportation vehicles or of other used vehicles provided for in existing

items 8702.90.01, 8705.10.01, 8705.20.99, 8705.90.01 or 8705.90.99 in the Tariff Schedule of the General Import Duty Act; A–12 provided that such measures shall not have trade restrictive effects on the importation of such goods additional to those due to restrictions imposed in accordance with the provisions of this Appendix, and that a license shall be granted to any person that fulfills Mexico's legal requirements for the importation of the goods.

* * *

Annex 300–B—Textile and Apparel Goods

Section 1: Scope and Coverage

1. This Annex applies to the textile and apparel goods set out in Appendix 1.1.

2. In the event of any inconsistency between this Agreement and the Arrangement Regarding International Trade in Textiles (Multifiber Arrangement), as amended and extended, including any amendment or extension after January 1, 1994, or any other existing or future agreement applicable to trade in textile or apparel goods, this Agreement shall prevail to the extent of the inconsistency, unless the Parties agree otherwise.

Section 2: Tariff Elimination

1. Except as otherwise provided in this Agreement, each Party shall progressively eliminate its customs duties on originating textile and apparel goods in accordance with its Schedule to Annex 302.2 (Tariff Elimination), and as set out for ease of reference in Appendix 2.1.

2. For purposes of this Annex: (a) a textile or apparel good shall be considered an originating good if the applicable change in tariff classification set out in Chapter Four (Rules of Origin) has been satisfied in the territory of one or more of the Parties in accordance with Article

404 (Accumulation); and (b) for purposes of determining
which rate of customs duty and staging category is applicable to an originating textile or apparel good, a good
shall be considered a good of a Party (i) as determined by
each importing Party's regulations, practices or procedures, or (ii) in the event of an agreement between the
Parties pursuant to Annex 311(1) (Country of Origin
Marking), as determined by such agreement.

* * *

Section 4: Bilateral Emergency Actions (Tariff Actions)

* * *

Appendix 2.1—Tariff Elimination

For purposes of this Appendix, each Party shall apply
Section 2(2) to determine whether a textile or apparel
good is an originating good of a particular Party.

A. Trade between Canada and the United States

As required by Article 302, Canada and the United
States each shall progressively eliminate its respective
customs duties on originating textile and apparel goods of
the other Party in accordance with Annex 401.2, as
amended, of the Canada—United States Free Trade
Agreement, as incorporated into Annex 302.2 and as set
out in each Party's Schedule to that Annex.

B. Trade between Mexico and the United States

Except as provided in Schedule 2.1.B, and as required
by Article 302, Mexico and the United States each shall
progressively eliminate its respective customs duties on
originating textile and apparel goods of the other Party in
accordance with its respective Schedule to Annex 302.2,
as follows:

(a) duties on textile and apparel goods provided for in the items in staging category A in a Party's Schedule shall be eliminated entirely and such goods shall be duty-free, effective January 1, 1994;

(b) duties on textile and apparel goods provided for in the items in staging category B6 in a Party's Schedule shall be reduced on January 1, 1994, by an amount equal, in percentage terms, to the base rates. Thereafter, duties shall be removed in five equal annual stages beginning on January 1, 1995, and such goods shall be duty-free, effective January 1, 1999;

(c) duties on textile and apparel goods provided for in the items in staging category C in a Party's Schedule shall be removed in 10 equal annual stages beginning on January 1, 1994, and such goods shall be duty-free, effective January 1, 2003; and

(d) if the application of a formula provided in subparagraph (b) or (c) for staging category B or C results in a duty that exceeds 20 percent ad valorem during any annual stage, the rate of duty during that stage shall be 20 percent ad valorem instead of the rate that otherwise would have applied.

* * *

Chapter Four—Rules of Origin

Article 401: Originating Goods

Except as otherwise provided in this Chapter, a good shall originate in the territory of a Party where:

(a) the good is wholly obtained or produced entirely in the territory of one or more of the Parties, as defined in Article 415;

(b) each of the non-originating materials used in the production of the good undergoes an applicable change in tariff classification set out in Annex 401 as a result of production occurring entirely in the territory of one or more of the Parties, or otherwise satisfies the applicable requirements of that Annex where no change in tariff classification is required, and the good satisfies all other applicable requirements of this Chapter;

(c) the good is produced entirely in the territory of one or more of the Parties exclusively from originating materials; or

(d) except for a good provided for in Chapters 61 through 63 of the Harmonized System, the good is produced entirely in the territory of one or more of the Parties but one or more of the non-originating materials provided for as parts under the Harmonized System that are used in the production of the good does not undergo a change in tariff classification because

(i) the good was imported into the territory of a Party in an unassembled or a disassembled form but was classified as an assembled good pursuant to General Rule of Interpretation 2(a) of the Harmonized System, or

(ii) the heading for the good provides for and specifically describes both the good itself and its parts and is not further subdivided into subheadings, or the subheading for the good provides for and specifically describes both the good itself and its parts, 2 provided that the regional value content of the good, determined in accordance with Article 402, is not less than 60 percent where the transaction value method is used, or is not less than 50 percent where the net cost method is used, and that the good satisfies all other applicable requirements of this Chapter.

Article 402: Regional Value Content

1. Except as provided in paragraph 5, each Party shall provide that the regional value content of a good shall be calculated, at the choice of the exporter or producer of the

good, on the basis of either the transaction value method set out in paragraph 2 or the net cost method set out in paragraph 3.

2. Each Party shall provide that an exporter or producer may calculate the regional value content of a good on the basis of the following transaction value method:

$$RVC = TV–VNM / TV \times 100$$

where RVC is the regional value content, expressed as a percentage; TV is the transaction value of the good adjusted to a F.O.B. basis; and VNM is the value of non-originating materials used by the producer in the production of the good.

3. Each Party shall provide that an exporter or producer may calculate the regional value content of a good on the basis of the following net cost method:

$$RVC = NC–VNM / NC \times 100$$

where RVC is the regional value content, expressed as a percentage; NC is the net cost of the good; and VNM is the value of non-originating materials used by the producer in the production of the good.

4. Except as provided in Articles 403(1) and 403(2)(a)(i), the value of non-originating materials used by the producer in the production of a good shall not, for purposes of calculating the regional value content of the good under paragraph 2 or 3, include the value of non-originating materials used to produce originating materials that are subsequently used in the production of the good.

5. Each Party shall provide that an exporter or producer shall calculate the regional value content of a good solely on the basis of the net cost method set out in paragraph 3 where: (a) there is no transaction value for the good; (b) the transaction value of the good is unacceptable under Article 1 of the Customs Valuation Code; (c) the good is sold by the producer to a related person and

the volume, by units of quantity, of sales of identical or similar goods to related persons during the six-month period immediately preceding the month in which the good is sold exceeds 85 percent of the producer's total sales with respect to such goods; (d) the good is (i) a motor vehicle provided for in heading 8701 or 8702, subheadings 8703.21 through 8703.90, or heading 8704, 8705 or 8706, (ii) identified in Annex 403.1 or 403.2 and is for use in a motor vehicle provided for in headings 8701 through 8706, (iii) provided for in headings 64.01 through 64.05, or (iv) provided for in tariff item 8469.10.aa (word processing machines);

(e) the exporter or producer chooses to accumulate the regional value content of the good in accordance with Article 404; or (f) the good is designated as an intermediate material under paragraph 10 and is subject to a regional value-content requirement.

6. If an exporter or producer of a good calculates the regional value content of the good on the basis of the transaction value method set out in paragraph 2 and a Party subsequently notifies the exporter or producer, during the course of a verification pursuant to Chapter Five (Customs Procedures), that the transaction value of the good, or the value of any material used in the production of the good, is required to be adjusted or is unacceptable under Article 1 of the Customs Valuation Code, the exporter or producer may then also calculate the regional value content of the good on the basis of the net cost method set out in paragraph 3.

7. Nothing in paragraph 6 shall be construed to prevent any review or appeal available under Article 510 (Review and Appeal) of an adjustment to or a rejection of: (a) the transaction value of a good; or (b) the value of any material used in the production of a good.

8. For purposes of calculating the net cost of a good under paragraph 3, the producer of the good may:

(a) calculate the total cost incurred with respect to all goods produced by that producer, subtract any sales promotion, marketing and after-sales service costs, royalties, shipping and packing costs, and non-allowable interest costs that are included in the total cost of all such goods, and then reasonably allocate the resulting net cost of those goods to the good;

(b) calculate the total cost incurred with respect to all goods produced by that producer, reasonably allocate the total cost to the good, and then subtract any sales promotion, marketing and after-sales service costs, royalties, shipping and packing costs and non-allowable interest costs that are included in the portion of the total cost allocated to the good; or

(c) reasonably allocate each cost that forms part of the total cost incurred with respect to the good so that the aggregate of these costs does not include any 5 sales promotion, marketing and after-sales service costs, royalties, shipping and packing costs, and non-allowable interest costs, provided that the allocation of all such costs is consistent with the provisions regarding the reasonable allocation of costs set out in the Uniform Regulations, established under Article 511 (Customs Procedures—Uniform Regulations).

9. Except as provided in paragraph 11, the value of a material used in the production of a good shall:

(a) be the transaction value of the material determined in accordance with Article 1 of the Customs Valuation Code; or (b) in the event the transaction value of the material is unacceptable under Article 1 of the Customs Valuation Code, be determined in accordance with Articles 2 through 7 of the Customs Valuation Code; and

(c) where not included under subparagraph (a) or (b), include (i) freight, insurance, packing and all other costs incurred in transporting the material to the location of the producer, (ii) duties, taxes and customs brokerage fees on the material paid in the territory of one or more of the Parties, and (iii) the cost of waste and spoilage resulting from the use of the material in the production of the good, less the value of renewable scrap or by-product.

10. Except as provided in Article 403(1) and for a component identified in Annex 403.2, the producer of a good may, for purposes of calculating the regional value content of the good under paragraph (2) or (3), designate any self-produced material used in the production of the good as an intermediate material, provided that where the intermediate material is subject to a regional value-content requirement, no other self-produced material subject to a regional value-content requirement used in the production of that intermediate material may itself be designated by the producer as an intermediate material.

11. The value of an intermediate material shall be: (a) the total cost incurred with respect to all goods produced by the producer of the good that can be reasonably allocated to that intermediate material; or (b) the aggregate of each cost that forms part of the total cost incurred with respect to that intermediate material that can be reasonably allocated to that intermediate material.

12. The value of an indirect material shall be based on the Generally Accepted Accounting Principles applicable in the territory of the Party in which the good is produced.

Article 403: Automotive Goods

1. For purposes of calculating the regional value content under the net cost method set out in Article 402(3) for: (a) a good that is a motor vehicle provided for in subheading 8702.xx (vehicles for the transport of 15 or fewer persons), 8703.21 through 8703.90, 8704.21 or 8704.31, or (b) a good provided for in the tariff provisions listed in Annex 403.1 where the good is subject to a regional value-content requirement and is for use as

original equipment in the production of a good provided for in subheading 8702.xx, 8703.21 through 8703.90, 8704.21 or 8704.31, the value of non-originating materials used by the producer in the production of the good shall be the sum of the values of non-originating materials, determined in accordance with Article 402(9) at the time the non-originating materials are received by the first person in the territory of a Party who takes title to them, that are imported from outside the territories of the Parties under the tariff provisions listed in Annex 403.1 and that are used in the production of the good or that are used in the production of any material used in the production of the good.

2. For purposes of calculating the regional value content under the net cost method set out in Article 402(3) for a good that is a motor vehicle provided for in heading 8701, subheading 8702.yy (vehicles for the transport of 16 or more persons), 8704.10, 8704.22, 8704.23, 8704.32 or 8704.90, or heading 8705 or 8706, or for a component identified in Annex 403.2 for use as original equipment in the production of the motor vehicle, the value of non-originating materials used by the producer in the production of the good shall be the sum of:

(a) for each material used by the producer listed in Annex 403.2, whether or not produced by the producer, at the choice of the producer and determined in accordance with Article 402, either (i) the value of such material that is non-originating, or (ii) the value of non-originating materials used in the production of such material, and (b) the value of any other non-originating material used by the producer that is not listed in Annex 403.2, determined in accordance with Article 402.

3. For purposes of calculating the regional value content of a motor vehicle identified in paragraph 1 or 2, the producer may average its calculation over its fiscal year, using any one of the following categories, on the basis of either all motor vehicles in the category or only those

motor vehicles in the category that are exported to the territory of one or more of the other Parties:

(a) the same model line of motor vehicles in the same class of vehicles produced in the same plant in the territory of a Party; (b) the same class of motor vehicles produced in the same plant in the territory of a Party; (c) the same model line of motor vehicles produced in the territory of a Party; or (d) if applicable, the basis set out in Annex 403.3.

4. For purposes of calculating the regional value content for any or all goods provided for in a tariff provision listed in Annex 403.1, or a component or material identified in Annex 403.2, produced in the same plant, the producer of the good may: (a) average its calculation (i) over the fiscal year of the motor vehicle producer to whom the good is sold, (ii) over any quarter or month, or (iii) over its fiscal year, if the good is sold as an aftermarket part; (b) calculate the average referred to in subparagraph (a) separately for any or all goods sold to one or more motor vehicle producers; or (c) with respect to any calculation under this paragraph, calculate separately those goods that are exported to the territory of one or more of the Parties.

* * *

6. The regional value-content requirement for a motor vehicle identified in Article 403(1) or 403(2) shall be: (a) 50 percent for five years after the date on which the first motor vehicle prototype is produced in a plant by a motor vehicle assembler, if (i) it is a motor vehicle of a class, or marque, or, except for a motor vehicle identified in Article 403(5)(b)(i), size category and underbody, not previously produced by the motor vehicle assembler in the territory of any of the Parties, (ii) the plant consists of a new building in which the motor vehicle is assembled, and (iii) the plant contains substantially all new machinery that is used in the assembly of the motor vehicle; or (b) 50

percent for two years after the date on which the first motor vehicle prototype is produced at a plant following a refit, if it is a different motor vehicle of a class, or marque, or, except for a motor vehicle identified in Article 403(5)(b)(i), size category and underbody, than was assembled by the motor vehicle assembler in the plant before the refit.

Article 404: Accumulation

1. For purposes of determining whether a good is an originating good, the production of the good in the territory of one or more of the Parties by one or more producers shall, at the choice of the exporter or producer of the good for which preferential tariff treatment is claimed, be considered to have been performed in the territory of any of the Parties by that exporter or producer, provided that:

(a) all non-originating materials used in the production of the good undergo an applicable tariff classification change set out in Annex 401, and the good satisfies any applicable regional value-content requirement, entirely in the territory of one or more of the Parties; and (b) the good satisfies all other applicable requirements of this Chapter.

2. For purposes of Article 402(10), the production of a producer that chooses to accumulate its production with that of other producers under paragraph 1 shall be considered to be the production of a single producer.

Article 405: De Minimis

1. Except as provided in paragraphs 3 through 6, a good shall be considered to be an originating good if the value of all non-originating materials used in the production of the good that do not undergo an applicable change in tariff classification set out in Annex 401 is not more than seven percent of the transaction value of the good, adjusted to a F.O.B. basis, or, if the transaction value of the good is unacceptable under Article 1 of the Customs

Valuation Code, the value of all such non-originating materials is not more than seven percent of the total cost of the good, provided that: (a) if the good is subject to a regional value-content requirement, the value of such non-originating materials shall be taken into account in calculating the regional value content of the good; and (b) the good satisfies all other applicable requirements of this Chapter.

2. A good that is otherwise subject to a regional value-content requirement shall not be required to satisfy such requirement if the value of all non-originating materials used in the production of the good is not more than seven percent of the transaction value of the good, adjusted to a F.O.B. basis, or, if the transaction value of the good is unacceptable under Article 1 of the Customs Valuation Code, the value of all non-originating materials is not more than seven percent of the total cost of the good, provided that the good satisfies all other applicable requirements of this Chapter.

* * *

Article 411: Transshipment

A good shall not be considered to be an originating good by reason of having undergone production that satisfies the requirements of Article 401 if, subsequent to that production, the good undergoes further production or any other operation outside the territories of the Parties, other than unloading, reloading or any other operation necessary to preserve it in good condition or to transport the good to the territory of a Party.

Article 412: Non–Qualifying Operations

A good shall not be considered to be an originating good merely by reason of: (a) mere dilution with water or another substance that does not materially alter the characteristics of the good; or (b) any production or pricing practice in respect of which it may be demonstrated, on the basis of a preponderance of evidence, that the object was to circumvent this Chapter.

* * *

Article 413: Interpretation and Application

For purposes of this Chapter:

(a) the basis for tariff classification in this Chapter is the Harmonized System;

(b) where applying Article 401(d), the determination of whether a heading or subheading under the Harmonized System provides for and specifically describes both a good and its parts shall be made on the basis of the nomenclature of the heading or subheading, or the General Rules of Interpretation, the Chapter Notes or the Section Notes of the Harmonized System;

(c) in applying the Customs Valuation Code under this Chapter (i) the principles of the Customs Valuation Code shall apply to domestic transactions, with such modifications as may be required by the circumstances, as would apply to international transactions, (ii) the provisions of this Chapter shall take precedence over the Customs Valuation Code to the extent of any difference, and (iii) the definitions in Article 415 shall take precedence over the definitions in the Customs Valuation Code to the extent of any difference; and

(d) all costs referred to in this Chapter shall be recorded and maintained in accordance with the Generally Accepted Accounting Principles applicable in the territory of the Party in which the good is produced.

Chapter Five—Customs Procedures

Article 501: Certificate of Origin

1. The Parties shall establish a Certificate of Origin for the purpose of certifying that a good being exported

from the territory of a Party into the territory of another Party qualifies as an originating good, and may thereafter revise the Certificate by agreement.

2. Each Party may require that a Certificate of Origin for a good imported into its territory be completed in a language required under its law.

3. Each Party shall: (a) require an exporter in its territory to complete and sign a Certificate of Origin for any exportation of a good for which an importer may claim preferential tariff treatment on importation of the good into the territory of another Party; and (b) provide that where an exporter in its territory is not the producer of the good, the exporter may complete and sign a Certificate on the basis of (i) its knowledge of whether the good qualifies as an originating good, (ii) its reasonable reliance on the producer's written representation that the good qualifies as an originating good, or (iii) a completed and signed Certificate for the good voluntarily provided to the exporter by the producer.

4. Nothing in paragraph 3 shall be construed to require a producer to provide a Certificate of Origin to an exporter.

5. Each Party shall provide that a Certificate of Origin that has been completed and signed by an exporter or a producer in the territory of another Party that is applicable to: (a) a single importation of a good into the Party's territory; or (b) multiple importations of identical goods into the Party's territory that occur within a specified period, not exceeding 12 months, set out therein by the exporter or producer, shall be accepted by its customs administration for four years after the date on which the Certificate was signed.

Article 502: Obligations Regarding Importations

1. Except as otherwise provided in this Chapter, each Party shall require an importer in its territory that claims

preferential tariff treatment for a good imported into its
territory from the territory of another Party to:

(a) make a written declaration, based on a valid Certificate of Origin, that the good qualifies as an originating
good; (b) have the Certificate in its possession at the time
the declaration is made; (c) provide, on the request of that
Party's customs administration, a copy of the Certificate;
and (d) promptly make a corrected declaration and pay
any duties owing where the importer has reason to believe that a Certificate on which a declaration was based
contains information that is not correct.

2.   Except as otherwise provided in this Chapter, each
Party shall provide that, where an importer in its territory claims preferential tariff treatment for a good imported
into its territory from the territory of another Party:

(a) the Party may deny preferential tariff treatment to
the good if the importer fails to comply with any requirement of this Chapter; and (b) the importer shall not be
subject to penalties for the making of an incorrect declaration, if it voluntarily makes a corrected declaration
pursuant to paragraph (1)(d).

3.   Each Party shall provide that, where a good would
have qualified as an originating good when it was imported into the territory of that Party but no claim for
preferential tariff treatment was made at that time, the
importer of the good may, no later than one year after the
date on which the good was imported, apply for a refund
of any excess duties paid as the result of the good not
having been accorded preferential tariff treatment, on
presentation of:

(a) a written declaration that the good qualifies as an
originating good at the time of importation; (b) a copy of
the Certificate of Origin; and (c) such other documentation relating to the importation of the good as that Party
may require.

* * *

Article 504: Obligations Regarding Exportations

1. Each Party shall provide that:

(a) an exporter in its territory, or a producer in its territory that has provided a copy of a Certificate of Origin to that exporter pursuant to Article 501(3)(b)(iii), shall provide a copy of the Certificate to its customs administration on request; and

(b) an exporter or a producer in its territory that has completed and signed a Certificate of Origin, and that has reason to believe that the Certificate contains information that is not correct, shall promptly notify in writing all persons to whom the Certificate was given by the exporter or producer of any change that could affect the accuracy or validity of the Certificate.

2. Each Party:

(a) shall provide that a false certification by an exporter or a producer in its territory that a good to be exported to the territory of another Party qualifies as an originating good shall have the same legal consequences, with appropriate modifications, as would apply to an importer in its territory for a contravention of its customs laws and regulations regarding the making of a false statement or representation;

(b) may apply such measures as the circumstances may warrant where an exporter or a producer in its territory fails to comply with any requirement of this Chapter; and

(c) shall not impose penalties on an exporter or a producer in its territory that voluntarily provides written notification pursuant to paragraph (1)(b) with respect to the making of an incorrect certification.

Article 505: Records

Each Party shall provide that:

(a) an exporter or a producer in its territory that completes and signs a Certificate of Origin shall maintain

in its territory, for five years after the date on which the
Certificate was signed or for such longer period as the
Party may specify, all records relating to the origin of a
good for which preferential tariff treatment was claimed
in the territory of another Party, including records associated with (i) the purchase of, cost of, value of, and
payment for, the good that is exported from its territory,
(ii) the purchase of, cost of, value of, and payment for, all
materials, including indirect materials, used in the production of the good that is exported from its territory,
and (iii) the production of the good in the form in which
the good is exported from its territory; and

(b) an importer claiming preferential tariff treatment
for a good imported into the Party's territory shall maintain in that territory, for five years after the date of
importation of the good or for such longer period as the
Party may specify, a copy of the Certificate and all other
documentation required by the Party relating to the
importation of the good.

Article 506: Origin Verifications

1. For purposes of determining whether a good imported into its territory from the territory of another
Party qualifies as an originating good, a Party may,
through its customs administration, conduct a verification
solely by means of:

(a) written questionnaires to an exporter or a producer
in the territory of another Party; (b) visits to the premis-
es of an exporter or a producer in the territory of another
Party to review the records referred to in Article 505(a)
and observe the facilities used in the production of the
good; or (c) such other procedure as the Parties may
agree.

* * *

Articles 509: Advance Rulings

1. Each Party shall, through its customs administration, provide for the expeditious issuance of written advance rulings, prior to the importation of a good into its territory, to an importer in its territory or an exporter or a producer in the territory of another Party, on the basis of the facts and circumstances presented by such importer, exporter or producer of the good, concerning:

(a) whether materials imported from a non-Party used in the production of a good undergo an applicable change in tariff classification set out in Annex 401 as a result of production occurring entirely in the territory of one or more of the Parties;

(b) whether a good satisfies a regional value-content requirement under either the transaction value method or the net cost method set out in Chapter Four;

(c) for the purpose of determining whether a good satisfies a regional value-content requirement under Chapter Four, the appropriate basis or method for customs value to be applied by an exporter or a producer in the territory of another Party, in accordance with the principles of the Customs Valuation Code, for calculating the transaction value of the good or of the materials used in the production of the good;

(d) for the purpose of determining whether a good satisfies a regional value-content requirement under Chapter Four, the appropriate basis or method for reasonably allocating costs, in accordance with the allocation methods set out in the Uniform Regulations, for calculating the net cost of the good or the value of an intermediate material;

(e) whether a good qualifies as an originating good under Chapter Four;

(f) whether a good that re-enters its territory after the good has been exported from its territory to the territory of another Party for repair or alteration qualifies for duty-free treatment in accordance with Article 307 (Goods Re–Entered after Repair or Alteration);

(g) whether the proposed or actual marking of a good satisfies country of origin marking requirements under Article 311 (Country of Origin Marking);

(h) whether an originating good qualifies as a good of a Party under Annex 300–B (Textile and Apparel Goods), Annex 302.2 (Tariff Elimination) or Chapter Seven (Agriculture and Sanitary and Phytosanitary Measures); or (i) such other matters as the Parties may agree.

2.   Each Party shall adopt or maintain procedures for the issuance of advance rulings, including a detailed description of the information reasonably required to process an application for a ruling.

* * *

Article 510: Review and Appeal

1.   Each Party shall grant substantially the same rights of review and appeal of determinations of origin and advance rulings by its customs administration as it provides to importers in its territory to any person:

(a) who completes and signs a Certificate of Origin for a good that has been the subject of a determination of origin; (b) whose good has been the subject of a country of origin marking determination pursuant to Article 311 (Country of Origin Marking); or (c) who has received an advance ruling pursuant to Article 509(1).

2.   Further to Articles 1804 (Administrative Proceedings) and 1805 (Review and Appeal), each Party shall provide that the rights of review and appeal referred to in paragraph 1 shall include access to: (a) at least one level of administrative review independent of the official or office responsible for the determination under review; and (b) in accordance with its domestic law, judicial or quasi-

judicial review of the determination or decision taken at the final level of administrative review.

Article 511: Uniform Regulations

1. The Parties shall establish, and implement through their respective laws or regulations, Uniform Regulations regarding the interpretation, application and administration of Chapter Four, this Chapter and other matters as may be agreed by the Parties.

2. Each Party shall implement any modification of or addition to the Uniform Regulations no later than 180 days after the Parties agree on such modification or addition, or such other period as the Parties may agree.

* * *

Chapter Six—Energy and Basic Petrochemicals

Article 601: Principles

1. The Parties confirm their full respect for their Constitutions.

2. The Parties recognize that it is desirable to strengthen the important role that trade in energy and basic petrochemical goods play in the free trade area and to enhance this role through sustained and gradual liberalization.

3. The Parties recognize the importance of having viable and internationally competitive energy and petrochemical sectors to further their individual national interests.

Article 602: Scope and Coverage

1. This Chapter applies to measures relating to energy and basic petrochemical goods originating in the territories of the Parties and to measures relating to investment

and to the cross-border trade in services associated with such goods, as set forth in this Chapter.

* * *

Article 603: Import and Export Restrictions

1. Subject to the further rights and obligations of this Agreement, the Parties incorporate the provisions of the General Agreement on Tariffs and Trade (GATT), with respect to prohibitions or restrictions on trade in energy and basic petrochemical goods. The Parties agree that this language does not incorporate their respective protocols of provisional application to the GATT.

2. The Parties understand that the provisions of the GATT incorporated in paragraph 1 prohibit, in any circumstances in which any other form of quantitative restriction is prohibited, minimum or maximum export-price requirements and, except as permitted in enforcement of countervailing and antidumping orders and undertakings, minimum or maximum import-price requirements.

3. In circumstances where a Party adopts or maintains a restriction on importation from or exportation to a non-Party of an energy or basic petrochemical good, nothing in this Agreement shall be construed to prevent the Party from:

(a) limiting or prohibiting the importation from the territory of any Party of such energy or basic petrochemical good of the non-Party; or (b) requiring as a condition of export of such energy or basic petrochemical good of the Party to the territory of any other Party that the good be consumed within the territory of the other Party.

4. In the event that a Party adopts or maintains a restriction on imports of an energy or basic petrochemical good from non-Party countries, the Parties, upon request of any Party, shall consult with a view to avoiding undue

interference with or distortion of pricing, marketing and distribution arrangements in another Party.

5. Parties may administer a system of import and export licensing for energy and basic petrochemical goods provided that such system is operated in a manner consistent with the provisions of this Agreement, including paragraph 1 and Article 1502 (Monopolies and State Enterprises).

6. This Article is subject to the reservations set out in Annex 603.6.

Article 604: Export Taxes

No Party may adopt or maintain any duty, tax or other charge on the export of any energy or basic petrochemical good to the territory of another Party, unless such duty, tax or charge is adopted or maintained on: (a) exports of any such good to the territory of all other Parties; and (b) any such good when destined for domestic consumption.

Article 605: Other Export Measures

Subject to Annex 605, a Party may adopt or maintain a restriction otherwise justified under Articles XI:2(a) or XX(g), (i) or (j) of the GATT with respect to the export of an energy or basic petrochemical good to the territory of another Party, only if:

(a) the restriction does not reduce the proportion of the total export shipments of the specific energy or basic petrochemical good made available to that other Party relative to the total supply of that good of the Party maintaining the restriction as compared to the proportion prevailing in the most recent 36–month period for which data are available prior to the imposition of the measure, or in such other representative period on which the Parties may agree;

(b) the Party does not impose a higher price for exports of an energy or basic petrochemical good to that other

Party than the price charged for such energy good when consumed domestically, by means of any measure such as licenses, fees, taxation and minimum price requirements. The foregoing provision does not apply to a higher price that may result from a measure taken pursuant to subparagraph (a) that only restricts the volume of exports; and

(c) the restriction does not require the disruption of normal channels of supply to that other Party or normal proportions among specific energy or basic petrochemical goods supplied to that other Party, such as, for example, between crude oil and refined products and among different categories of crude oil and of refined products.

Article 606: Energy Regulatory Measures

1. The Parties recognize that energy regulatory measures are subject to the disciplines of:

(a) national treatment, as provided in Article 301; (b) import and export restrictions, as provided in Article 603; or (c) export taxes, as provided in Article 604.

2. Each Party shall seek to ensure that in the application of any energy regulatory measure, energy regulatory bodies within its territory avoid disruption of contractual relationships to the maximum extent practicable, and provide for orderly and equitable implementation appropriate to such measures.

Article 607: National Security Measures

Subject to Annex 607, no Party may adopt or maintain a measure restricting imports of an energy or basic petrochemical good from, or exports of an energy or basic petrochemical good to, another Party under Article XXI of the GATT or under Article 2102 (National Security), except to the extent necessary to:

(a) supply a military establishment of a Party or enable fulfillment of a critical defense contract of a Party; (b) respond to a situation of armed conflict involving the Party taking the measure; (c) implement national policies or international agreements relating to the non-proliferation of nuclear weapons or other nuclear explosive devices; or (d) respond to direct threats of disruption in the supply of nuclear materials for defense purposes.

* * *

Annex 602.3—Reservations

1. The Mexican State reserves to itself the following strategic activities, including investment in such activities and the provision of services in such activities:

(a) exploration and exploitation of crude oil and natural gas; refining or processing of crude oil and natural gas; and production of artificial gas, basic petrochemicals and their feedstocks and pipelines;

(b) foreign trade; transportation, storage and distribution, up to and including the first hand sales of the following goods: (i) crude oil, (ii) natural and artificial gas, (iii) goods covered by this Chapter obtained from the refining or processing of crude oil and natural gas, and (iv) basic petrochemicals;

(c) the supply of electricity as a public service in Mexico, including, except as provided in paragraph 5, the generation, transmission, transformation, distribution and sale of electricity; and

(d) exploration, exploitation and processing of radioactive minerals, the nuclear fuel cycle, the generation of nuclear energy, the transportation and storage of nuclear waste, the use and reprocessing of nuclear fuel and the regulation of their applications for other purposes and the production of heavy water.

In the event of an inconsistency between this paragraph and another provision of this Agreement, this paragraph shall prevail to the extent of that inconsistency.

2. Pursuant to Article 1102(2), private investment is not permitted in the activities listed in paragraph 1. Chapter Twelve (Cross–Border Trade in Services) shall only apply to 8 activities involving the provision of services covered in paragraph 1 when Mexico permits a contract to be granted in respect of such activities and only to the extent of that contract.

Trade in Natural Gas and Basic Petrochemicals

3. Where end-users and suppliers of natural gas or basic petrochemical goods consider that cross-border trade in such goods may be in their interests, each Party shall permit such end-users and suppliers, and any state enterprise of that Party as may be required under its domestic law, to negotiate supply contracts.

Each Party shall leave the modalities of the implementation of any such contract to the end-users, suppliers, and any state enterprise of the Party as may be required under its domestic law, which may take the form of individual contracts between the state enterprise and each of the other entities. Such contracts may be subject to regulatory approval.

Performance Clauses

4. Each Party shall allow its state enterprises to negotiate performance clauses in their service contracts.

Activities and Investment in Electricity Generation Facilities

5. (a) Production for Own Use

An enterprise of another Party may acquire, establish, and/or operate an electrical generating facility in Mexico to meet the enterprise's own supply needs. Electricity generated in excess of such needs must be sold to the Federal Electricity Commission (Comision Federal de Electricidad) (CFE) and CFE shall purchase such electricity under terms and conditions agreed to by CFE and the enterprise.

(b) Co-generation

An enterprise of another Party may acquire, establish, and/or operate a co-generation facility in Mexico that generates electricity using heat, steam or other energy sources associated with an industrial process. Owners of the industrial facility need not be the owners of the co-generating facility. Electricity generated in excess of the industrial facility's supply requirements must be sold to CFE and CFE shall purchase such electricity under terms and conditions agreed to by CFE and the enterprise.

(c) Independent Power Production

An enterprise of another Party may acquire, establish, and/or operate an electricity generating facility for independent power production (IPP) in Mexico. Electricity generated by such a facility for sale in Mexico shall be sold to CFE and CFE shall purchase such electricity under terms and conditions agreed to by CFE and the enterprise. Where an IPP located in Mexico and an electric utility of another Party consider that cross-border trade in electricity may be in their interests, each relevant Party shall permit these entities and CFE to negotiate terms and conditions of power purchase and power sale contracts. The modalities of implementing such supply contracts are left to the end users, suppliers and CFE and may take the form of individual contracts between CFE and each of the other entities. Each relevant Party shall determine whether such contracts are subject to regulatory approval.

* * *

Annex 608.2—Other Agreements

1. Canada and the United States shall act in accordance with the terms of Annexes 902.5 and 905.2 of the

Canada—United States Free Trade Agreement. This paragraph shall impose no obligations and confer no rights on Mexico.

2. Canada and the United States intend no inconsistency between this Chapter and the Agreement on an International Energy Program (IEP). In the event of any inconsistency between the IEP and this Chapter, the IEP shall prevail as between Canada and the United States to the extent of that inconsistency.

Chapter Seven—Agriculture and Sanitary and Phytosanitary Measures

Article 701: Scope and Coverage

1. This Section applies to measures adopted or maintained by a Party relating to agricultural trade.

2. In the event of any inconsistency between this Section and another provision of this Agreement, this Section shall prevail to the extent of the inconsistency.

Article 702: International Obligations

1. Annex 702.1 applies to the Parties specified in that Annex with respect to agricultural trade under certain agreements between them.

2. Prior to adopting pursuant to an intergovernmental commodity agreement, a measure that may affect trade in an agricultural good between the Parties, the Party proposing to adopt the measure shall consult with the other Parties with a view to avoiding nullification or impairment of a concession granted by that Party in its Schedule to Annex 302.2 (Tariff Elimination).

3. Annex 702.3 applies to the Parties specified in that Annex with respect to measures adopted or maintained pursuant to an intergovernmental coffee agreement.

Article 703: Market Access

1. The Parties shall work together to improve access to their respective markets through the reduction or elimination of import barriers to trade between them in agricultural goods.

* * *

Article 704: Domestic Support

The Parties recognize that domestic support measures can be of crucial importance to their agricultural sectors but may also have trade distorting and production effects and that domestic support reduction commitments may result from agricultural multilateral trade negotiations under the General Agreement on Tariffs and Trade (GATT). Accordingly, where a Party supports its agricultural producers, that Party should endeavor to work toward domestic support measures that:

(a) have minimal or no trade distorting or production effects; or (b) are exempt from any applicable domestic support reduction commitments that may be negotiated under the GATT.

The Parties further recognize that a Party may change its domestic support measures, including those that may be subject to reduction commitments, at the Party's discretion, subject to its rights and obligations under the GATT.

Article 705: Export Subsidies

1. The Parties share the objective of the multilateral elimination of export subsidies for agricultural goods and shall cooperate in an effort to achieve an agreement under the GATT to eliminate those subsidies.

2. The Parties recognize that export subsidies for agricultural goods may prejudice the interests of importing and exporting Parties and, in particular, may disrupt the

markets of importing Parties. Accordingly, in addition to the rights and obligations of the Parties specified in Annex 702.1, the Parties affirm that it is inappropriate for a Party to provide an export subsidy for an agricultural good exported to the territory of another Party where there are no other subsidized imports of that good into the territory of that other Party.

3.   Except as provided in Annex 702.1, where an exporting Party considers that a non-Party is exporting an agricultural good to the territory of another Party with the benefit of export subsidies, the importing Party shall, on written request of the exporting Party, consult with the exporting Party with a view to agreeing on specific measures that the importing Party may adopt to counter the effect of any such subsidized imports. If the importing Party adopts the agreed-upon measures, the exporting Party shall refrain from applying, or immediately cease to apply, any export subsidy to exports of such good to the territory of the importing Party.

4.   Except as provided in Annex 702.1, an exporting Party shall deliver written notice to the importing Party at least three days, excluding weekends, prior to adopting an export subsidy measure on an agricultural good exported to the territory of another Party. The exporting Party shall consult with the importing Party within 72 hours of receipt of the importing Party's written request, with a view to eliminating the subsidy or minimizing any adverse impact on the market of the importing Party for that good. The importing Party shall, when requesting consultations with the exporting Party, at the same time, deliver written notice to a third Party of the request. A third Party may request to participate in such consultations.

5.   Each Party shall take into account the interests of the other Parties in the use of any export subsidy on an agricultural good, recognizing that such subsidies may

have prejudicial effects on the interests of the other Parties.

* * *

Section B—Sanitary and Phytosanitary Measures

Article 709: Scope and Coverage

In order to establish a framework of rules and disciplines to guide the development, adoption and enforcement of sanitary and phytosanitary measures, this Section applies to any such measure of a Party that may, directly or indirectly, affect trade between the Parties.

Article 710: Relation to Other Chapters

Articles 301 (National Treatment) and 309 (Import and Export Restrictions), and the provisions of Article XX(b) of the GATT as incorporated into Article 2101(1) (General Exceptions), do not apply to any sanitary or phytosanitary measure.

Article 711: Reliance on Non–Governmental Entities

Each Party shall ensure that any non-governmental entity on which it relies in applying a sanitary or phytosanitary measure acts in a manner consistent with this Section.

Article 712: Basic Rights and Obligations

Right to Take Sanitary and Phytosanitary Measures

1. Each Party may, in accordance with this Section, adopt, maintain or apply any sanitary or phytosanitary measure necessary for the protection of human, animal or plant life or health in its territory, including a measure more stringent than an international standard, guideline or recommendation.

Right to Establish Level of Protection

2.   Notwithstanding any other provision of this Section, each Party may, in protecting human, animal or plant life or health, establish its appropriate level of protection in accordance with Article 715.

Scientific Principles

3.   Each Party shall ensure that any sanitary or phytosanitary measure that it adopts, maintains or applies is: (a) based on scientific principles, taking into account relevant factors including, where appropriate, different geographic conditions; (b) not maintained where there is no longer a scientific basis for it; and (c) based on a risk assessment, as appropriate to the circumstances.

Non-Discriminatory Treatment

4.   Each Party shall ensure that a sanitary or phytosanitary measure that it adopts, maintains or applies does not arbitrarily or unjustifiably discriminate between its goods and like goods of another Party, or between goods of another Party and like goods of any other country, where identical or similar conditions prevail.

Unnecessary Obstacles

5.   Each Party shall ensure that any sanitary or phytosanitary measure that it adopts, maintains or applies is applied only to the extent necessary to achieve its appropriate level of protection, taking into account technical and economic feasibility.

Disguised Restrictions

6.   No Party may adopt, maintain or apply any sanitary or phytosanitary measure with a view to, or with the effect of, creating a disguised restriction on trade between the Parties.

Article 713: International Standards and Standardizing Organizations

1. Without reducing the level of protection of human, animal or plant life or health, each Party shall use, as a basis for its sanitary and phytosanitary measures, relevant international standards, guidelines or recommendations with the objective, among others, of making its sanitary and phytosanitary measures equivalent or, where appropriate, identical to those of the other Parties.

2. A Party's sanitary or phytosanitary measure that conforms to a relevant international standard, guideline or recommendation shall be presumed to be consistent with Article 712. A measure that results in a level of sanitary or phytosanitary protection different from that which would be achieved by a measure based on a relevant international standard, guideline or recommendation shall not for that reason alone be presumed to be inconsistent with this Section.

3. Nothing in Paragraph 1 shall be construed to prevent a Party from adopting, maintaining or applying, in accordance with the other provisions of this Section, a sanitary or phytosanitary measure that is more stringent than the relevant international standard, guideline or recommendation.

4. Where a Party has reason to believe that a sanitary or phytosanitary measure of another Party is adversely affecting or may adversely affect its exports and the measure is not based on a relevant international standard, guideline or recommendation, it may request, and the other Party shall provide in writing, the reasons for the measure.

5. Each Party shall, to the greatest extent practicable, participate in relevant international and North American standardizing organizations, including the Codex Alimentarius Commission, the International Office of Epizootics, the International Plant Protection Convention, and the

North American Plant Protection Organization, with a view to promoting the development and periodic review of international standards, guidelines and recommendations.

Article 714: Equivalence

1. Without reducing the level of protection of human, animal or plant life or health, the Parties shall, to the greatest extent practicable and in accordance with this Section, pursue equivalence of their respective sanitary or phytosanitary measures.

2. Each importing Party: (a) shall treat a sanitary or phytosanitary measure adopted or maintained by an exporting Party as equivalent to its own where the exporting Party, in cooperation with the importing Party, provides to the importing Party scientific evidence or other information, in accordance with risk assessment methodologies agreed on by those Parties, to demonstrate objectively, subject to subparagraph (b), that the exporting Party's measure achieves the importing Party's appropriate level of protection;

(b) may, where it has a scientific basis, determine that the exporting Party's measure does not achieve the importing Party's appropriate level of protection; and (c) shall provide to the exporting Party, on request, its reasons in writing for a determination under subparagraph (b).

3. For purposes of establishing equivalency, each exporting Party shall, on the request of an importing Party, take such reasonable measures as may be available to it to facilitate access in its territory for inspection, testing and other relevant procedures.

4. Each Party should, in the development of a sanitary or phytosanitary measure, consider relevant actual or proposed sanitary or phytosanitary measures of the other Parties.

Article 715: Risk Assessment and Appropriate Level of Protection

1. In conducting a risk assessment, each Party shall take into account: (a) relevant risk assessment techniques and methodologies developed by international or North American standardizing organizations; (b) relevant scientific evidence; (c) relevant processes and production methods; (d) relevant inspection, sampling and testing methods; (e) the prevalence of relevant diseases or pests, including the existence of pest-free or disease-free areas or areas of low pest or disease prevalence; (f) relevant ecological and other environmental conditions; and (g) relevant treatments, such as quarantines.

2. Further to paragraph 1, each Party shall, in establishing its appropriate level of protection regarding the risk associated with the introduction, establishment or spread of an animal or plant pest or disease, and in assessing the risk, also take into account the following economic factors, where relevant: (a) loss of production or sales that may result from the pest or disease; (b) costs of control or eradication of the pest or disease in its territory; and (c) the relative cost-effectiveness of alternative approaches to limiting risks.

3. Each Party, in establishing its appropriate level of protection: (a) should take into account the objective of minimizing negative trade effects; and (b) shall, with the objective of achieving consistency in such levels, avoid arbitrary or unjustifiable distinctions in such levels in different circumstances, where such distinctions result in arbitrary or unjustifiable discrimination against a good of another Party or constitute a disguised restriction on trade between the Parties.

4. Notwithstanding paragraphs (1) through (3) and Article 712(3)(c), where a Party conducting a risk assessment determines that available relevant scientific evidence or other information is insufficient to complete the

assessment, it may adopt a provisional sanitary or phytosanitary measure on the basis of available relevant information, including from international or North American
standardizing organizations and from sanitary or phytosanitary measures of other Parties. The Party shall, within a reasonable period after information sufficient to
complete the assessment is presented to it, complete its
assessment, review and, where appropriate, revise the
provisional measure in the light of the assessment.

5. Where a Party is able to achieve its appropriate
level of protection through the phased application of a
sanitary or phytosanitary measure, it may, on the request
of another Party and in accordance with this Section,
allow for such a phased application, or grant specified
exceptions for limited periods from the measure, taking
into account the requesting Party's export interests.

Article 716: Adaptation to Regional Conditions

1. Each Party shall adapt any of its sanitary or phytosanitary measures relating to the introduction, establishment or spread of an animal or plant pest or disease, to
the sanitary or phytosanitary characteristics of the area
where a good subject to such a measure is produced and
the area in its territory to which the good is destined,
taking into account any relevant conditions, including
those relating to transportation and handling, between
those areas. In assessing such characteristics of an area,
including whether an area is, and is likely to 35 remain, a
pest-free or disease-free area or an area of low pest or
disease prevalence, each Party shall take into account,
among other factors:

(a) the prevalence of relevant pests or diseases in that
area; (b) the existence of eradication or control programs
in that area; and (c) any relevant international standard,
guideline or recommendation.

2. Further to paragraph 1, each Party shall, in determining whether an area is a pest-free or disease-free area or an area of low pest or disease prevalence, base its determination on factors such as geography, ecosystems, epidemiological surveillance and the effectiveness of sanitary or phytosanitary controls in that area.

3. Each importing Party shall recognize that an area in the territory of the exporting Party is, and is likely to remain, a pest-free or disease-free area or an area of low pest or disease prevalence, where the exporting Party provides to the importing Party scientific evidence or other information sufficient to so demonstrate to the satisfaction of the importing Party. For this purpose, each exporting Party shall provide reasonable access in its territory to the importing Party for inspection, testing and other relevant procedures.

4. Each Party may, in accordance with this Section: (a) adopt, maintain or apply a different risk assessment procedure for a pest-free or disease-free area than for an area of low pest or disease prevalence; or (b) make a different final determination for the disposition of a good produced in a pest-free or disease-free area than for a good produced in an area of low pest or disease prevalence, taking into account any relevant conditions, including those relating to transportation and handling.

5. Each Party shall, in adopting, maintaining or applying a sanitary or phytosanitary measure relating to the introduction, establishment or spread of an animal or plant pest or disease, accord a good produced in a pest-free or disease-free area in the territory of another Party no less favorably treatment than it accords a good produced in a pest-free or disease-free area, in another country, that poses the same level of risk. The Party shall use equivalent risk assessment techniques to evaluate relevant conditions and controls in the 36 pest-free or disease-free area and in the area surrounding that area

and take into account any relevant conditions, including those relating to transportation and handling.

6. Each importing Party shall pursue an agreement with an exporting Party, on request, on specific requirements the fulfillment of which allows a good produced in an area of low pest or disease prevalence in the territory of an exporting Party to be imported into the territory of the importing Party and achieves the importing Party's appropriate level of protection.

Article 717: Control, Inspection and Approval Procedures

1. Each Party, with respect to any control or inspection procedure that it conducts: (a) shall initiate and complete the procedure as expeditiously as possible and in no less favorable manner for a good of another Party than for a like good of the Party or of any other country; (b) shall publish the normal processing period for each such procedure or communicate the anticipated processing period to the applicant on request;

(c) shall ensure that the competent body (i) on receipt of an application, promptly examines the completeness of the documentation and informs the applicant in a precise and complete manner of any deficiency, (ii) transmits to the applicant as soon as possible the results of the procedure in a form that is precise and complete so that the applicant may take any necessary corrective action, (iii) where the application is deficient, proceeds as far as practicable with the procedure if the applicant so requests, and (iv) informs the applicant, on request, of the status of the application and the reasons for any delay; (d) shall limit the information the applicant is required to supply to that necessary for conducting the procedure;

(e) shall accord confidential or proprietary information arising from, or supplied in connection with, the procedure conducted for a good of another Party (i) treatment no less favorable than for a good of the Party, and (ii) in any event, treatment that protects the applicant's legitimate commercial interests, to the extent provided under the Party's law; (f) shall limit any requirement regarding individual specimens or samples of a good to that which is reasonable and necessary;

(g) should not impose a fee for conducting the procedure that is higher for a good of another Party than is equitable in relation to any such fee it imposes for its like goods or for like goods of any other country, taking into account communication, transportation and other related costs; (h) should use criteria for selecting the location of facilities at which a procedure is conducted that do not cause unnecessary inconvenience to an applicant or its agent;

(i) shall provide a mechanism to review complaints concerning the operation of the procedure and to take corrective action when a complaint is justified; (j) should use criteria for selecting samples of goods that do not cause unnecessary inconvenience to an applicant or its agent; and (k) shall limit the procedure, for a good modified subsequent to a determination that the good fulfills the requirements of the applicable sanitary or phytosanitary measure, to that necessary to determine that the good continues to fulfill the requirements of that measure.

2. Each Party shall apply, with such modifications as may be necessary, paragraphs 1(a) through (i) to its approval procedures.

3. Where an importing Party's sanitary or phytosanitary measure requires the conduct of a control or inspection procedure at the level of production, an exporting Party shall, on the request of the importing Party, take such reasonable measures as may be available to it to facilitate access in its territory and to provide assistance necessary to facilitate the conduct of the importing Party's control or inspection procedure.

4. A Party maintaining an approval procedure may require its approval for the use of an additive, or its establishment of a tolerance for a contaminant, in a food, beverage or feedstuff, under that procedure, prior to granting access to its domestic market for a food, beverage or feedstuff containing that additive or contaminant. Where such Party so requires, it shall consider using a relevant international standard, guideline or recommendation as the basis for granting access until it completes the procedure.

* * *

Article 724: Definitions

risk assessment means an evaluation of:

(a) the potential for the introduction, establishment or spread of a pest or disease and associated biological and economic consequences; or (b) the potential for adverse effects on human or animal life or health arising from the presence of an additive, contaminant, toxin or disease-causing organism in a food, beverage or feedstuff;

sanitary or phytosanitary measure means a measure that a Party adopts, maintains or applies to:

(a) protect animal or plant life or health in its territory from risks arising from the introduction, stablishment or spread of a pest or disease, (b) protect human or animal life or health in its territory from risks arising from the presence of an additive, contaminant, toxin or disease-causing organism in a food, beverage or feedstuff, (c) protect human life or health in its territory from risks arising from a disease-causing organism or pest carried by an animal or plant, or a product thereof, (d) prevent or limit other damage in its territory arising from the introduction, establishment or spread of a pest, including end product criteria; a product-related processing or production method; a testing, inspection, certification or approval procedure; a relevant statistical method; a sampling procedure; a method of risk assessment; a packaging and labelling requirement directly related to food safety; and a quarantine treatment, such as a relevant requirement associated with the transportation of animals or plants or with material necessary for their survival during transportation; and scientific basis means a reason based on data or information derived using scientific methods.

Chapter Eight—Emergency Action

Article 801: Bilateral Actions

1. Subject to paragraphs 2 through 4 and Annex 801.1, and during the transition period only, if a good originating in the territory of a Party, as a result of the reduction or elimination of a duty provided for in this Agreement, is being imported into the territory of another Party in such increased quantities, in absolute terms, and under such conditions that the imports of the good from that Party alone constitute a substantial cause of serious injury, or threat thereof, to a domestic industry producing a like or directly competitive good, the Party into whose territory the good is being imported may, to the minimum extent necessary to remedy or prevent the injury:

(a) suspend the further reduction of any rate of duty provided for under this Agreement on the good; (b) increase the rate of duty on the good to a level not to exceed the lesser of (i) the most-favored-nation (MFN) applied rate of duty in effect at the time the action is taken, and (ii) the MFN applied rate of duty in effect on the day immediately preceding the date of entry into force of this Agreement; or (c) in the case of a duty applied to a good on a seasonal basis, increase the rate of duty to a level not to exceed the MFN applied rate of duty that was in effect on the good for the corresponding season immediately preceding the date of entry into force of this Agreement.

* * *

3. A Party may take a bilateral emergency action after the expiration of the transition period to deal with cases of serious injury, or threat thereof, to a domestic industry arising from the operation of this Agreement only with the consent of the Party against whose good the action would be taken.

4. The Party taking an action under this Article shall provide to the Party against whose good the action is taken mutually agreed trade liberalizing compensation in the form of concessions having substantially equivalent trade effects or equivalent to the value of the additional duties expected to result from the action. If the Parties concerned are unable to agree on compensation, the Party against whose good the action is taken may take tariff action having trade effects substantially equivalent to the action taken under this Article. The Party taking the tariff action shall apply the action only for the minimum period necessary to achieve the substantially equivalent effects.

5. This Article does not apply to emergency actions respecting goods covered by Annex 300–B (Textile and Apparel Goods).

Article 802: Global Actions

1. Each Party retains its rights and obligations under Article XIX of the GATT or any safeguard agreement pursuant thereto except those regarding compensation or retaliation and exclusion from an action to the extent that such rights or obligations are inconsistent with this Article. Any Party taking an emergency action under Article XIX or any such agreement shall exclude imports of a good from each other Party from the action unless:

(a) imports from a Party, considered individually, account for a substantial share of total imports; and (b) imports from a Party, considered individually, or in exceptional circumstances imports from Parties considered collectively, contribute importantly to the serious injury, or threat thereof, caused by imports.

2. In determining whether:

(a) imports from a Party, considered individually, account for a substantial share of total imports, those imports normally shall not be considered to account for a substantial share of total imports if that Party is not among the top five suppliers of the good subject to the proceeding, measured in terms of import share during the most recent three-year period; and

(b) imports from a Party or Parties contribute importantly to the serious injury, or threat thereof, the competent investigating authority shall consider such factors as the change in the import share of each Party, and the level and change in the level of imports of each Party. In this regard, imports from a Party normally shall not be deemed to contribute importantly to serious injury, or the threat thereof, if the growth rate of imports from a Party during the period 4 in which the injurious surge in imports occurred is appreciably lower than the growth rate of total imports from all sources over the same period.

3. A Party taking such action, from which a good from another Party or Parties is initially excluded pursuant to paragraph 1, shall have the right subsequently to include that good from the other Party or Parties in the action in the event that the competent investigating authority determines that a surge in imports of such good from the other Party or Parties undermines the effectiveness of the action.

4. A Party shall, without delay, deliver written notice to the other Parties of the institution of a proceeding that may result in emergency action under paragraph 1 or 3.

5. No Party may impose restrictions on a good in an action under paragraph 1 or 3:

(a) without delivery of prior written notice to the Commission, and without adequate opportunity for consultation with the Party or Parties against whose good the action is proposed to be taken, as far in advance of taking the action as practicable; and

(b) that would have the effect of reducing imports of such good from a Party below the trend of imports of the good from that Party over a recent representative base period with allowance for reasonable growth.

6.   The Party taking an action pursuant to this Article shall provide to the Party or Parties against whose good the action is taken mutually agreed trade liberalizing compensation in the form of concessions having substantially equivalent trade effects or equivalent to the value of the additional duties expected to result from the action. If the Parties concerned are unable to agree on compensation, the Party against whose good the action is taken may take action having trade effects substantially equivalent to the action taken under paragraph 1 or 3.

Article 803: Administration of Emergency Action Proceedings

1.   Each Party shall ensure the consistent, impartial and reasonable administration of its laws, regulations, decisions and rulings governing all emergency action proceedings.

2.   Each Party shall entrust determinations of serious injury, or threat thereof, in emergency action proceedings to a competent investigating authority, subject to review by judicial or administrative tribunals, to the extent provided by domestic law. Negative injury 5 determinations shall not be subject to modification, except by such review. The competent investigating authority empowered under domestic law to conduct such proceedings should be provided with the necessary resources to enable it to fulfill its duties.

3. Each Party shall adopt or maintain equitable, timely, transparent and effective procedures for emergency action proceedings, in accordance with the requirements set out in Annex 803.3.

4. This Article does not apply to emergency actions taken under Annex 300–B (Textile and Apparel Goods).

Article 804: Dispute Settlement in Emergency Action Matters

No Party may request the establishment of an arbitral panel under Article 2008 (Request for an Arbitral Panel) regarding any proposed emergency action.

* * *

Annex 801.1—Bilateral Actions

1. Notwithstanding Article 801, bilateral emergency actions between Canada and the United States on goods originating in the territory of either Party, other than goods covered by Annex 300–B (Textile and Apparel Goods), shall be governed in accordance with the terms of Article 1101 of the Canada—United States Free Trade Agreement, which is hereby incorporated into and made a part of this Agreement for such purpose.

Chapter Nine—Standards–Related Measures

Article 901: Scope and Coverage

1. This Chapter applies to standards-related measures of a Party, other than those covered by Section B of Chapter Seven (Sanitary and Phytosanitary Measures), that may, directly or indirectly, affect trade in goods or services between the Parties, and to measures of the Parties relating to such measures.

2. Technical specifications prepared by governmental bodies for production or consumption requirements of

such bodies shall be governed exclusively by Chapter Ten (Government Procurement).

Article 902: Extent of Obligations

1. Article 105 (Extent of Obligations) does not apply to this Chapter.

2. Each Party shall seek, through appropriate measures, to ensure observance of Articles 904 through 908 by state or provincial governments and by non-governmental standardizing bodies in its territory.

Article 903: Affirmation of Agreement on Technical Barriers to Trade and Other Agreements

Further to Article 103 (Relation to Other Agreements), the Parties affirm with respect to each other their existing rights and obligations relating to standards-related measures under the GATT Agreement on Technical Barriers to Trade and all other international agreements, including environmental and conservation agreements, to which those Parties are party.

Article 904: Basic Rights and Obligations

Right to Take Standards–Related Measures

1. Each Party may, in accordance with this Agreement, adopt, maintain or apply any standards-related measure, including any such measure relating to safety, the protection of human, animal or plant life or health, the environment or consumers, and any measure to ensure its enforcement or implementation. Such measures include those to prohibit the importation of a good of another Party or the provision of a service by a service provider of another Party that fails to comply with the applicable requirements of those measures or to complete the Party's approval procedures.

Right to Establish Level of Protection

2. Notwithstanding any other provision of this Chapter, each Party may, in pursuing its legitimate objectives of safety or the protection of human, animal or plant life or health, the environment or consumers, establish the level of protection that it considers appropriate in accordance with Article 907(2).

Non-Discriminatory Treatment

3. Each Party shall, in respect of its standards-related measures, accord to goods and service providers of another Party:

(a) national treatment in accordance with Article 301 (Market Access) or Article 1202 (Cross–Border Trade in Services); and (b) treatment no less favorable than that it accords to like goods, or in like circumstances to service providers, of any other country.

Unnecessary Obstacles

4. No Party may prepare, adopt, maintain or apply any standards-related measure with a view to or with the effect of creating an unnecessary obstacle to trade between the Parties. An unnecessary obstacle to trade shall not be deemed to be created where: (a) the demonstrable purpose of the measure is to achieve a legitimate objective; and (b) the measure does not operate to exclude goods of another Party that meet that legitimate objective.

Article 905: Use of International Standards

1. Each Party shall use, as a basis for its standards-related measures, relevant international standards or international standards whose completion is imminent, except where such standards would be an ineffective or inappropriate means to fulfill its legitimate objectives, for example because of fundamental climatic, geographical, technological or infrastructural factors, scientific justifica-

tion or the level of protection that the Party considers appropriate.

2. A Party's standards-related measure that conforms to an international standard shall be presumed to be consistent with Article 904(3) and (4).

3. Nothing in paragraph 1 shall be construed to prevent a Party, in pursuing its legitimate objectives, from adopting, maintaining or applying any standards-related measure that results in a higher level of protection than would be achieved if the measure were based on the relevant international standard.

Article 906: Compatibility and Equivalence

1. Recognizing the crucial role of standards-related measures in achieving legitimate objectives, the Parties shall, in accordance with this Chapter, work jointly to enhance the level of safety and of protection of human, animal and plant life and health, the environment and consumers.

2. Without reducing the level of safety or of protection of human, animal or plant life or health, the environment or consumers, without prejudice to the rights of any Party under this Chapter, and taking into account international standardization activities, the Parties shall, to the greatest extent practicable, make compatible their respective standards-related measures, so as to facilitate trade in a good or service between the Parties.

3. Further to Articles 902 and 905, a Party shall, on request of another Party, seek, through appropriate measures, to promote the compatibility of a specific standard or conformity assessment procedure that is maintained in its territory with the standards or conformity assessment procedures maintained in the territory of the other Party.

4. Each importing Party shall treat a technical regulation adopted or maintained by an exporting Party as equivalent to its own where the exporting Party, in coop-

eration with the importing Party, demonstrates to the satisfaction of the importing Party that its technical regulation adequately fulfills the importing Party's legitimate objectives.

5. The importing Party shall provide to the exporting Party, on request, its reasons in writing for not treating a technical regulation as equivalent under paragraph 4.

6. Each Party shall, wherever possible, accept the results of a conformity assessment procedure conducted in the territory of another Party, provided that it is satisfied that the procedure offers an assurance, equivalent to that provided by a procedure it conducts or a procedure conducted in its territory the results of which it accepts, that the relevant good or service complies with the applicable technical regulation or standard adopted or maintained in the Party's territory.

7. Prior to accepting the results of a conformity assessment procedure pursuant to paragraph 6, and to enhance confidence in the continued reliability of each other's conformity assessment results, the Parties may consult on such matters as the technical competence of the conformity assessment bodies involved, including verified compliance with relevant international standards through such means as accreditation.

Article 907: Assessment of Risk

1. A Party may, in pursuing its legitimate objectives, conduct an assessment of risk. In conducting an assessment, a Party may take into account, among other factors relating to a good or service:

(a) available scientific evidence or technical information; (b) intended end uses; (c) processes or production, operating, inspection, sampling or testing methods; or (d) environmental conditions.

2. Where pursuant to Article 904(2) a Party establishes the level of protection that it considers appropriate

and conducts an assessment of risk, it should avoid arbitrary or unjustifiable distinctions between similar goods or services in the level of protection it considers appropriate, where the distinctions:

(a) result in arbitrary or unjustifiable discrimination against goods or service providers of another Party; (b) constitute a disguised restriction on trade between the Parties; or (c) discriminate between similar goods or services for the same use under the same conditions that pose the same level of risk and provide similar benefits.

3. Where a Party conducting an assessment of risk determines that available scientific evidence or other information is insufficient to complete the assessment, it may adopt a provisional technical regulation on the basis of available relevant information. The Party shall, within a reasonable period after information sufficient to complete the assessment of risk is presented to it, complete its assessment, review and, where appropriate, revise the provisional technical regulation in the light of that assessment.

Article 908: Conformity Assessment

1. The Parties shall, further to Article 906 and recognizing the existence of substantial differences in the structure, organization and operation of conformity assessment procedures in their respective territories, make compatible those procedures to the greatest extent practicable.

2. Recognizing that it should be to the mutual advantage of the Parties concerned and except as set out in Annex 908.2, each Party shall accredit, approve, license or otherwise recognize conformity assessment bodies in the territory of another Party on terms no less favorable than those accorded to conformity assessment bodies in its territory.

3. Each Party shall, with respect to its conformity assessment procedures:

(a) not adopt or maintain any such procedure that is stricter, nor apply the procedure more strictly, than necessary to give it confidence that a good or a service conforms with an applicable technical regulation or standard, taking into account the risks that non-conformity would create; (b) initiate and complete the procedure as expeditiously as possible;(c) in accordance with Article 904(3), undertake processing of applications in non-discriminatory order; (d) publish the normal processing period for each such procedure or communicate the anticipated processing period to an applicant on request; (e) ensure that the competent body (i) on receipt of an application, promptly examines the completeness of the documentation and informs the applicant in a precise and complete manner of any deficiency, (ii) transmits to the applicant as soon as possible the results of the conformity assessment procedure in a form that is precise and complete so that the applicant may take any necessary corrective action, (iii) where the application is deficient, proceeds as far as practicable with the procedure where the applicant so requests, and (iv) informs the applicant, on request, of the status of the application and the reasons for any delay; (f) limit the information the applicant is required to supply to that necessary to conduct the procedure and to determine appropriate fees; (g) accord confidential or proprietary information arising from, or supplied in connection with, the conduct of the procedure for a good of another Party or for a service provided by a person of another Party (i) the same treatment as that for a good of the Party or a service provided by a person of the Party, and (ii) in any event, treatment that protects an applicant's legitimate commercial interests to the extent provided under the Party's law; (h) ensure that any fee it imposes for conducting the procedure is no higher for a good of another Party or a service provider of another Party than is equitable in relation to any such fee imposed for its like goods or service providers or for like goods or service providers of any other country, taking into account communication, transportation and other related costs; (i) ensure that the location of facilities at which a conformity assessment procedure is conducted does not cause unnecessary inconvenience to an applicant or its agent; (j) limit the procedure, for a good or service modified subsequent to a determination that the good or service conforms to the applicable technical regulation or standard, to that necessary to determine that the good or service continues to conform to the technical regulation or standard; and (k) limit any requirement regarding samples of a good to that which is reasonable, and ensure that the selection of samples does not cause unnecessary inconvenience to an applicant or its agent.

4.   Each Party shall apply, with such modifications as may be necessary, the relevant provisions of paragraph 3 to its approval procedures.

5.   Each Party shall, on request of another Party, take such reasonable measures as may be available to it to facilitate access in its territory for conformity assessment activities.

6.   Each Party shall give sympathetic consideration to a request by another Party to negotiate agreements for the mutual recognition of the results of that other Party's conformity assessment procedures.

* * *

Article 915: Definitions

1.   For purposes of this Chapter:

approval procedure means any registration, notification or other mandatory administrative procedure for granting permission for a good or service to be produced, marketed or used for a stated purpose or under stated conditions;

assessment of risk means evaluation of the potential for adverse effects;

conformity assessment procedure means any procedure used, directly or indirectly, to determine that a technical regulation or standard is fulfilled, including sampling, testing, inspection, evaluation, verification, monitoring, auditing, assurance of conformity, accreditation, registration or approval used for such a purpose, but does not mean an approval procedure;

international standard means a standards-related measure, or other guide or recommendation, adopted by an international standardizing body and made available to the public;

international standardizing body means a standardizing body whose membership is open to the relevant bodies of at least all the parties to the GATT Agreement on Technical Barriers to Trade, including the International Organization for Standardization (ISO), the International Electrotechnical Commission (IEC), Codex Alimentarius Commission, the World Health Organization (WHO), the Food and Agriculture Organization (FAO), the International Telecommunication Union (ITU); or any other body that the Parties designate;

land transportation service means a transportation service provided by means of motor carrier or rail;

legitimate objective includes an objective such as: (a) safety, (b) protection of human, animal or plant life or health, the environment or consumers, including matters relating to quality and identifiability of goods or services, and (c) sustainable development, considering, among other things, where appropriate, fundamental climatic or other geographical factors, technological or infrastructural factors, or scientific justification but does not include the protection of domestic production;

make compatible means bring different standards-related measures of the same scope approved by different standardizing bodies to a level such that they are either identical, equivalent or have the effect of permitting goods or services to be used in place of one another or fulfill the same purpose;

services means land transportation services and telecommunication services;

standard means a document, approved by a recognized body, that provides, for common and repeated use, rules, guidelines or characteristics for products, or related processes and production methods, or for services or related operating methods, with which compliance is not mandatory. It may also include or deal exclusively with terminology, symbols, packaging, marking or labelling requirements as they apply to a product, process or production or operating method;

standardizing body means a body having recognized activities in standardization;

standards-related measure means a standard, technical regulation or conformity assessment procedure;

technical regulation means a document which lays down product characteristics or their related processes and production methods, or for services or operating methods, including the applicable administrative provisions, with which compliance is mandatory. It may also include or deal exclusively with terminology, symbols, packaging, marking or labelling requirements as they apply to a product, process or production or operating method; and

telecommunications service means a service provided by means of the transmission and reception of signals by any electromagnetic means, but does not mean the cable, broadcast or other electromagnetic distribution of radio or television programming to the public generally.

* * *

PART FOUR—GOVERNMENT PROCUREMENT

Chapter Ten—Government Procurement

Article 1001: Scope and Coverage

1.   This Chapter applies to measures adopted or maintained by a Party relating to procurement:

(a) by a federal government entity set out in Annex 1001.1a–1, a government enterprise set out in Annex 1001.1a–2, or a state or provincial government entity set out in Annex 1001.1a–3 in accordance with Article 1024;

(b) of goods in accordance with Annex 1001.1b–1, services in accordance with Annex 1001.1b–2, or construction services in accordance with Annex 1001.1b–3; and

(c) where the value of the contract to be awarded is estimated to be equal to or greater than a threshold, calculated and adjusted according to the U.S. inflation rate as set out in Annex 1001.1c, of (i) for federal government entities, US$50,000 for contracts for goods, services or any combination thereof, and US$6.5 million for contracts for construction services, (ii) for government enterprises, US$250,000 for contracts for goods, services or any combination thereof, and US$8.0 million for contracts for construction services, and (iii) for state and provincial government entities, the applicable threshold, as set out in Annex 1001.1a–3 in accordance with Article 1024.

2.   Paragraph 1 is subject to: (a) the transitional provisions set out in Annex 1001.2a;(b) the General Notes set out in Annex 1001.2b; and (c) Annex 1001.2c, for the Parties specified therein.

3.   Subject to paragraph 4, where a contract to be awarded by an entity is not covered by this Chapter, this Chapter shall not be construed to cover any good or service component of that contract.

4. No Party may prepare, design or otherwise structure any procurement contract in order to avoid the obligations of this Chapter.

5. Procurement includes procurement by such methods as purchase, lease or rental, with or without an option to buy. Procurement does not include: (a) non-contractual agreements or any form of government assistance, including cooperative agreements, grants, loans, equity infusions, guarantees, fiscal incentives, and government provision of goods and services to persons or state, provincial and regional governments; and (b) the acquisition of fiscal agency or depository services, liquidation and management services for regulated financial institutions and sale and distribution services for government debt.

* * *

Article 1003: National Treatment and Non–Discrimination

1. With respect to measures covered by this Chapter, each Party shall accord to goods of another Party, to the suppliers of such goods and to service suppliers of another Party, treatment no less favorable than the most favorable treatment that the Party accords to: (a) its own goods and suppliers; and (b) goods and suppliers of another Party.

2. With respect to measures covered by this Chapter, no Party may: (a) treat a locally established supplier less favorably than another locally established supplier on the basis of degree of foreign affiliation or ownership; or (b) discriminate against a locally established supplier on the basis that the goods or services offered by that supplier for the particular procurement are goods or services of another Party.

3. Paragraph 1 does not apply to measures respecting customs duties or other charges of any kind imposed on or in connection with importation, the method of levying

such duties or charges or other import regulations, including restrictions and formalities.

Article 1004: Rules of Origin

No Party may apply rules of origin to goods imported from another Party for purposes of government procurement covered by this Chapter that are different from or inconsistent with the rules of origin the Party applies in the normal course of trade, which may be the Marking Rules established under Annex 311 if they become the rules of origin applied by that Party in the normal course of its trade.

Article 1005: Denial of Benefits

1. Subject to prior notification and consultation in accordance with Articles 1803 (Notification and Provision of Information) and 2006 (Consultations), a Party may deny the benefits of this Chapter to a service supplier of another Party where the Party establishes that the service is being provided by an enterprise that is owned or controlled by persons of a non-Party and that has no substantial business activities in the territory of any Party.

2. A Party may deny to an enterprise of another Party the benefits of this Chapter if nationals of a non-Party own or control the enterprise and: (a) the circumstance set out in Article 1113(1)(a) (Denial of Benefits) is met; or (b) the denying Party adopts or maintains measures with respect to the non-Party that prohibit transactions with the enterprise or that would be violated or circumvented if the benefits of this Chapter were accorded to the enterprise.

Article 1006: Prohibition of Offsets

Each Party shall ensure that its entities do not, in the qualification and selection of suppliers, goods or services, in the evaluation of bids or the award of contracts, consider, seek or impose offsets. For purposes of this Article, offsets means conditions imposed or considered by an entity prior to or in the course of its procurement process that encourage local development or improve its Party's balance of payments accounts, by means of requirements of local content, licensing of technology, investment, counter-trade or similar requirements.

Article 1007: Technical Specifications

1. Each Party shall ensure that its entities do not prepare, adopt or apply any technical specification with the purpose or the effect of creating unnecessary obstacles to trade.

2. Each Party shall ensure that any technical specification prescribed by its entities is, where appropriate:(a) specified in terms of performance criteria rather than design or descriptive characteristics; and (b) based on international standards, national technical regulations, recognized national standards, or building codes.

3. Each Party shall ensure that the technical specifications prescribed by its entities do not require or refer to a particular trademark or name, patent, design or type, specific origin or producer or supplier unless there is no sufficiently precise or intelligible way of otherwise describing the procurement requirements and provided that, in such cases, words such as "or equivalent" are included in the tender documentation.

4. Each Party shall ensure that its entities do not seek or accept, in a manner that would have the effect of precluding competition, advice that may be used in the preparation or adoption of any technical specification for a specific procurement from a person that may have a commercial interest in that procurement.

Article 1008: Tendering Procedures

1. Each Party shall ensure that the tendering procedures of its entities are: (a) applied in a non-discrimina-

tory manner; and (b) consistent with this Article and Articles 1009 (Qualification of Suppliers) through 1016 (Limited Tendering).

2. In this regard, each Party shall ensure that its entities: (a) do not provide to any supplier information with regard to a specific procurement in a manner that would have the effect of precluding competition; and (b) provide all suppliers equal access to information with respect to a procurement during the period prior to the issuance of any notice or tender documentation.

Article 1009: Qualification of Suppliers

1. Further to Article 1003 (National Treatment and Non–Discrimination), no entity of a Party may, in the process of qualifying suppliers in a tendering procedure, discriminate between suppliers of the other Parties or between domestic suppliers and suppliers of the other Parties.

2. The qualification procedures followed by an entity shall be consistent with the following:

(a) conditions for participation by suppliers in tendering procedures shall be published sufficiently in advance so as to provide the suppliers adequate time to initiate and, to the extent that it is compatible with efficient operation of the procurement process, to complete the qualification procedures;

(b) conditions for participation by suppliers in tendering procedures, including financial guarantees, technical qualifications and information necessary for establishing the financial, commercial and technical capacity of suppliers, as well as the verification of whether a supplier meets those conditions, shall be limited to those that are essential to ensure the fulfillment of the contract in question;

(c) the financial, commercial and technical capacity of a supplier shall be judged both on the basis of that supplier's global business activity, including its activity in the territory of the Party of the supplier, and its activity, if any, in the territory of the Party of the procuring entity;

(d) an entity shall not misuse the process of, including the time required for, qualification in order to exclude suppliers of another Party from a suppliers' list or from being considered for a particular procurement;

(e) an entity shall recognize as qualified suppliers those suppliers of another Party that meet the conditions for participation in a particular procurement;

(f) an entity shall consider for a particular procurement those suppliers of another Party that request to participate in the procurement and that are not yet qualified, provided there is sufficient time to complete the qualification procedure;

(g) an entity that maintains a permanent list of qualified suppliers shall ensure that suppliers may apply for qualification at any time, that all qualified suppliers so requesting are included in the list within a reasonably short period of time and that all qualified suppliers included in the list are notified of the termination of the list or of their removal from it;

(h) where, after publication of a notice in accordance with Article 1010 (Invitation to Participate), a supplier that is not yet qualified requests to participate in a particular procurement, the entity shall promptly start the qualification procedure;

(i) an entity shall advise any supplier that requests to become a qualified supplier of its decision as to whether that supplier has become qualified; and

(j) where an entity rejects a supplier's application to qualify or ceases to recognize a supplier as qualified, the entity shall, on request of the supplier, promptly provide pertinent information concerning the entity's reasons for doing so.

3. Each Party shall:

(a) ensure that each of its entities uses a single qualification procedure, except that an entity may use additional qualification procedures where the entity determines the need for a different procedure and is prepared, on request of another Party, to demonstrate that need; and (b) endeavor to minimize differences in the qualification procedures of its entities.

4. Nothing in paragraphs 2 and 3 shall prevent an entity from excluding a supplier on grounds such as bankruptcy or false declarations.

Article 1010: Invitation to Participate

1. Except as otherwise provided in Article 1016 (Limited Tendering), an entity shall publish an invitation to participate for all procurements in accordance with paragraphs 2, 3 and 5, in the appropriate publication referred to in Annex 1010.1 (Publications).

* * *

Article 1011: Selective Tendering Procedures

1. To ensure optimum effective competition between the suppliers of the Parties under selective tendering procedures, an entity shall, for each procurement, invite tenders from the maximum number of domestic suppliers and suppliers of the other Parties, consistent with the efficient operation of the procurement system.

2. Subject to paragraph 3, an entity that maintains a permanent list of qualified suppliers may select suppliers to be invited to tender for a particular procurement from among those listed. In the process of making a selection, the entity shall provide for equitable opportunities for suppliers on the list.

3. Subject to Article 1009(2)(f) (Qualification of Suppliers), an·entity shall allow a supplier that requests to participate in a particular procurement to submit a ten-

der and shall consider the tender. The number of additional suppliers permitted to participate shall be limited only by the efficient operation of the procurement system.

4.   Where an entity does not invite or admit a supplier to tender, the entity shall, on request of the supplier, promptly provide pertinent information concerning its reasons for not doing so.

Article 1012: Time Limits for Tendering and Delivery

1.   An entity shall: (a) in prescribing a time limit, provide adequate time to allow suppliers of another Party to prepare and submit tenders before the closing of the tendering procedures;

* * *

Article 1014: Negotiation Disciplines

1.   An entity may conduct negotiations only: (a) in the context of procurement in which the entity has, in a notice published in accordance with Article 1010 (Invitation to Participate), indicated its intent to negotiate; or (b) where it appears to the entity from the evaluation of the tenders that no one tender is obviously the most advantageous in terms of the specific evaluation criteria set out in the notices or tender documentation.

2.   An entity shall use negotiations primarily to identify the strengths and weaknesses in the tenders.

3.   An entity shall treat all tenders in confidence. In particular, no entity may provide to any person information intended to assist any supplier to bring its tender up to the level of any other tender.

4.   No entity may, in the course of negotiations, discriminate between suppliers. In particular, an entity shall: (a) carry out any elimination of suppliers in accordance with the criteria set out in the notices and tender documentation; (b) provide in writing all modifications to

the criteria or technical requirements to all suppliers remaining in the negotiations; (c) permit all remaining suppliers to submit new or amended tenders on the basis of the modified criteria or requirements; and (d) when negotiations are concluded, permit all remaining suppliers to submit final tenders in accordance with a common deadline.

Article 1015: Submission, Receipt and Opening of Tenders and Awarding of Contracts

* * *

7. No later than 72 days after the award of a contract, an entity shall publish a notice in the appropriate publication referred to in Annex 1010.1 (Publications) that shall contain the following information:

(a) a description of the nature and quantity of goods or services included in the contract; (b) the name and address of the entity awarding the contract; (c) the date of the award; (d) the name and address of each winning supplier; (e) the value of the contract, or the highest-priced and lowest-priced tenders considered in the process of awarding the contract; and (f) the tendering procedure used.

* * *

Article 1017: Bid Challenge

1. In order to promote fair, open and impartial procurement procedures, each Party shall adopt and maintain bid challenge procedures for procurement covered by this Chapter in accordance with the following:

(a) each Party shall allow suppliers to submit bid challenges concerning any aspect of the procurement process, which for the purposes of this Article begins after 21 an entity has decided on its procurement requirement and continues through the contract award; (b) a Party may encourage a supplier to seek a resolution of any complaint with the entity concerned prior to initiating a bid challenge; (c) each Party shall ensure that its entities accord fair and timely consideration to any complaint regarding procurement covered by this Chapter;

(d) whether or not a supplier has attempted to resolve its complaint with the entity, or following an unsuccessful attempt at such a resolution, no Party may prevent the supplier from initiating a bid challenge or seeking any other relief; (e) a Party may require a supplier to notify the entity on initiation of a bid challenge; (f) a Party may limit the period within which a supplier may initiate a bid challenge, but in no case shall the period be less than 10 working days from the time when the basis of the complaint became known or reasonably should have become known to the supplier;

(g) each Party shall establish or designate a reviewing authority with no substantial interest in the outcome of procurements to receive bid challenges and make findings and recommendations concerning them; (h) on receipt of a bid challenge, the reviewing authority shall expeditiously investigate the challenge; (i) a Party may require its reviewing authority to limit its considerations to the challenge itself; (j) in investigating the challenge, the reviewing authority may delay the awarding of the proposed contract pending resolution of the challenge, except in cases of urgency or where the delay would be contrary to the public interest;

(k) the reviewing authority shall issue a recommendation to resolve the challenge, which may include directing the entity to re-evaluate offers, terminate or re-compete the contract in question; (*l*) entities normally shall follow the recommendations of the reviewing authority; (m) each Party should authorize its reviewing authority, following the conclusion of a bid challenge procedure, to make additional recommendations in writing to an entity respecting any facet of the entity's procurement process that is identified as problematic during the investigation of the challenge, including recommendations for changes in the procurement procedures of the entity to bring them into conformity with this Chapter;

(n) the reviewing authority shall provide its findings and recommendations respecting bid challenges in writing and in a timely manner, and shall make them available to the Parties and interested persons; (o) each Party shall specify in writing and shall make generally available all its bid challenge procedures; and (p) each Party shall ensure that each of its entities maintains complete documentation regarding each of its procurements, including a written record of all communications substantially affecting each procurement, for at least three years from the date the contract was awarded, to allow verification that the procurement process was carried out in accordance with this Chapter.

2. A Party may require that a bid challenge be initiated only after the notice of procurement has been published or, where a notice is not published, after tender documentation has been made available. Where a Party imposes such a requirement, the 10–working day period described in paragraph 1(f) shall begin no earlier than the date that the notice is published or the tender documentation is made available.

Article 1018: Exceptions

1. Nothing in this Chapter shall be construed to prevent a Party from taking any action or not disclosing any information which it considers necessary for the protection of its essential security interests relating to the procurement of arms, ammunition or war materials, or to procurement indispensable for national security or for national defense purposes.

2. Provided that such measures are not applied in a manner that would constitute a means of arbitrary or

unjustifiable discrimination between Parties where the same conditions prevail or a disguised restriction on trade between the Parties, nothing in this Chapter shall be construed to prevent any Party from adopting or maintaining measures: (a) necessary to protect public morals, order or safety; (b) necessary to protect human, animal or plant life or health; (c) necessary to protect intellectual property; or (d) relating to goods or services of handicapped persons, of philanthropic institutions or of prison labor.

* * *

Annex 1001.1a–3—State and Provincial Government Entities

Coverage under this Annex will be the subject of consultations with state and provincial governments in accordance with Article 1024 (Further Negotiations).

PART FIVE—INVESTMENT, SERVICES AND RELATED MATTERS

Chapter Eleven—Investment

Section A—Investment

Article 1101: Scope and Coverage

1. This Chapter applies to measures adopted or maintained by a Party relating to: (a) investors of another Party; (b) investments of investors of another Party in the territory of the Party; and (c) with respect to Article 1106, all investments in the territory of the Party.

2. A Party has the right to perform exclusively the economic activities set out in Annex III and to refuse to permit the establishment of investment in such activities.

3. This Chapter does not apply to measures adopted or maintained by a Party to the extent that they are covered by Chapter Fourteen (Financial Services).

4.   Nothing in this Chapter shall be construed to prevent a Party from providing a service or performing a function such as law enforcement, correctional services, income security or insurance, social security or insurance, social welfare, public education, public training, health, and child care, in a manner that is not inconsistent with this Chapter.

Article 1102: National Treatment

1.   Each Party shall accord to investors of another Party treatment no less favorable than that it accords, in like circumstances, to its own investors with respect to the establishment, acquisition, expansion, management, conduct, operation, and sale or other disposition of investments.

2.   Each Party shall accord to investments of investors of another Party treatment no less favorable than that it accords, in like circumstances, to investments of its own investors with respect to the establishment, acquisition, expansion, management, conduct, operation, and sale or other disposition of investments.

3.   The treatment accorded by a Party under paragraphs 1 and 2 means, with respect to a state or province, treatment no less favorable than the most favorable treatment accorded, in like circumstances, by that state or province to investors, and to investments of investors, of the Party of which it forms a part.

4.   For greater certainty, no Party may: (a) impose on an investor of another Party a requirement that a minimum level of equity in an enterprise in the territory of the Party be held by its nationals, other than nominal qualifying shares for directors or incorporators of corporations; or (b) require an investor of another Party, by reason of its nationality, to sell or otherwise dispose of an investment in the territory of the Party.

Article 1103: Most–Favored–Nation Treatment

1. Each Party shall accord to investors of another Party treatment no less favorable than that it accords, in like circumstances, to investors of another Party or of a non-Party with respect to the establishment, acquisition, expansion, management, conduct, operation, and sale or other disposition of investments.

2. Each Party shall accord to investments of investors of another Party treatment no less favorable than that it accords, in like circumstances, to investments of investors of another Party or of a non-Party with respect to the establishment, acquisition, expansion, management, conduct, operation, and sale or other disposition of investments.

Article 1104: Standard of Treatment

Each Party shall accord to investors of another Party and to investments of investors of another Party the better of the treatment required by Articles 1102 and 1103.

Article 1105: Minimum Standard of Treatment

1. Each Party shall accord to investments of investors of another Party treatment in accordance with international law, including fair and equitable treatment and full protection and security.

2. Without prejudice to paragraph 1 and notwithstanding Article 1108(7)(b), each Party shall accord to investors of another Party, and to investments of investors of another Party, non-discriminatory treatment with respect to measures it adopts or maintains relating to losses suffered by investments in its territory owing to armed conflict or civil strife.

3. Paragraph 2 does not apply to existing measures relating to subsidies or grants that are inconsistent with Article 1102.

Article 1106: Performance Requirements

1.   No Party may impose or enforce any of the following requirements, or enforce any commitment or undertaking, in connection with the establishment, acquisition, expansion, management, conduct or operation of an investment of an investor of a Party or of a non-Party in its territory:

(a) to export a given level or percentage of goods or services; (b) to achieve a given level or percentage of domestic content; (c) to purchase, use or accord a preference to goods produced or services provided in its territory, or to purchase goods or services from persons in its territory; (d) to relate in any way the volume or value of imports to the volume or value of exports or to the amount of foreign exchange inflows associated with such investment; (e) to restrict sales of goods or services in its territory that such investment produces or provides by relating such sales in any way to the volume or value of its exports or foreign exchange earnings; (f) to transfer technology, a production process or other proprietary knowledge to a person in its territory, except when the requirement is imposed or the 4 commitment or undertaking is enforced by a court, administrative tribunal or competition authority to remedy an alleged violation of competition laws or to act in a manner not inconsistent with other provisions of this Agreement; or (g) to act as the exclusive supplier of the goods it produces or services it provides to a specific region or world market.

2.   A measure that requires an investment to use a technology to meet generally applicable health, safety or environmental requirements shall not be construed to be inconsistent with paragraph (1)(f). For greater certainty, Articles 1102 and 1103 apply to the measure.

3.   No Party may condition the receipt or continued receipt of an advantage, in connection with an investment

in its territory of an investor of a Party or of a non-Party, on compliance with any of the following requirements:

(a) to purchase, use or accord a preference to goods produced in its territory, or to purchase goods from producers in its territory; (b) to achieve a given level or percentage of domestic content; (c) to relate in any way the volume or value of imports to the volume or value of exports or to the amount of foreign exchange inflows associated with such investment; or (d) to restrict sales of goods or services in its territory that such investment produces or provides by relating such sales in any way to the volume or value of its exports or foreign exchange earnings.

4. Nothing in paragraph 3 shall be construed to prevent a Party from conditioning the receipt or continued receipt of an advantage, in connection with an investment in its territory of an investor of a Party or of a non-Party, on compliance with a requirement to locate production, provide a service, train or employ workers, construct or expand particular facilities, or carry out research and development, in its territory.

5. Paragraphs 1 and 3 do not apply to any requirement other than the requirements set out in those paragraphs.

6. Provided that such measures are not applied in an arbitrary or unjustifiable manner, or do not constitute a disguised restriction on international trade or investment, nothing in 5 paragraph 1(b) or (c) or 3(a) or (b) shall be construed to prevent any Party from adopting or maintaining measures, including environmental measures: (a) necessary to secure compliance with laws and regulations that are not inconsistent with the provisions of this Agreement; (b) necessary to protect human, animal or plant life or health; or (c) necessary for the conservation of living or non-living exhaustible natural resources.

Article 1107: Senior Management and Boards of Directors

1. No Party may require that an enterprise of that
Party that is an investment of an investor of another
Party appoint to senior management positions individuals
of any particular nationality.

2. A Party may require that a majority of the board of
directors, or any committee thereof, of an enterprise of
that Party that is an investment of an investor of another
Party, be of a particular nationality, or resident in the
territory of the Party, provided that the requirement does
not materially impair the ability of the investor to exercise control over its investment.

Article 1108: Reservations and Exceptions

1. Articles 1102, 1103, 1106 and 1107 do not apply to:

(a) any existing non-conforming measure that is maintained by (i) a Party at the federal level, as set out in its
Schedule to Annex I or III, (ii) a state or province, for two
years after the date of entry into force of this Agreement,
and thereafter as set out by a Party in its Schedule to
Annex I, in accordance with paragraph 2, or (iii) a local
government;

(b) the continuation or prompt renewal of any non-
conforming measure referred to in subparagraph (a); or

(c) an amendment to any non-conforming measure referred to in subparagraph (a) to the extent that the
amendment does not decrease the conformity of the measure, as it existed immediately before the amendment,
with Articles 1102, 1103, 1106 and 1107.

2. Each Party may set out in its Schedule to Annex I
any existing non-conforming measure maintained by a
state or province, not including a local government, within two years of the date of entry into force of this
Agreement.

3. Articles 1102, 1103, 1106 and 1107 do not apply to any measure that a Party adopts or maintains with respect to sectors, subsectors or activities, as set out in its Schedule to Annex II.

4. No Party may, under any measure adopted after the date of entry into force of this Agreement and covered by its Schedule to Annex II, require an investor of another Party, by reason of its nationality, to sell or otherwise dispose of an investment existing at the time the measure becomes effective.

5. Articles 1102 and 1103 do not apply to any measure that is an exception to, or derogation from, the obligations under Article 1703 (Intellectual Property—National Treatment) as specifically provided for in that Article.

6. Article 1103 does not apply to treatment accorded by a Party pursuant to agreements, or with respect to sectors, set out in its Schedule to Annex IV.

7. Articles 1102, 1103 and 1107 do not apply to: (a) procurement by a Party or a state enterprise; or (b) subsidies or grants provided by a Party or a state enterprise, including government-supported loans, guarantees and insurance.

8. The provisions of: (a) Article 1106(1)(a), (b) and (c), and (3)(a) and (b) do not apply to qualification requirements for goods or services with respect to export promotion and foreign aid programs; (b) Article 1106(1)(b), (c), (f) and (g), and (3)(a) and (b) do not apply to procurement by a Party or a state enterprise; and (c) Article 1106(3)(a) and (b) do not apply to requirements imposed by an importing Party relating to the content of goods necessary to qualify for preferential tariffs or preferential quotas.

Article 1109: Transfers

1. Each Party shall permit all transfers relating to an investment of an investor of another Party in the territo-

ry of the Party to be made freely and without delay. Such transfers include:

(a) profits, dividends, interest, capital gains, royalty payments, management fees, technical assistance and other fees, returns in kind and other amounts derived from the investment; (b) proceeds from the sale of all or any part of the investment or from the partial or complete liquidation of the investment; (c) payments made under a contract entered into by the investor, or its investment, including payments made pursuant to a loan agreement; (d) payments made pursuant to Article 1110; and (e) payments arising under Section B.

2. Each Party shall permit transfers to be made in a freely usable currency at the market rate of exchange prevailing on the date of transfer with respect to spot transactions in the currency to be transferred.

3. No Party may require its investors to transfer, or penalize its investors that fail to transfer, the income, earnings, profits or other amounts derived from, or attributable to, investments in the territory of another Party.

4. Notwithstanding paragraphs 1 and 2, a Party may prevent a transfer through the equitable, non-discriminatory and good faith application of its laws relating to: (a) bankruptcy, insolvency or the protection of the rights of creditors; (b) issuing, trading or dealing in securities; (c) criminal or penal offenses; (d) reports of transfers of currency or other monetary instruments; or (e) ensuring the satisfaction of judgments in adjudicatory proceedings.

5. Paragraph 3 shall not be construed to prevent a Party from imposing any measure through the equitable, non-discriminatory and good faith application of its laws relating to the matters set out in subparagraphs (a) through (e) of paragraph 4.

6. Notwithstanding paragraph 1, a Party may restrict transfers of returns in kind in circumstances where it

could otherwise restrict such transfers under this Agreement.

Article 1110: Expropriation and Compensation

1. No Party may directly or indirectly nationalize or expropriate an investment of an investor of another Party in its territory or take a measure tantamount to nationalization or expropriation of such an investment ("expropriation"), except: (a) for a public purpose; (b) on a nondiscriminatory basis; (c) in accordance with due process of law and Article 1105(1); and (d) on payment of compensation in accordance with paragraphs 2 through 6.

2. Compensation shall be equivalent to the fair market value of the expropriated investment immediately before the expropriation took place ("date of expropriation"), and shall not reflect any change in value occurring because the intended expropriation had become known earlier. Valuation criteria shall include going concern value, asset value including declared tax value of tangible property, and other criteria, as appropriate, to determine fair market value.

3. Compensation shall be paid without delay and be fully realizable.

4. If payment is made in a G7 currency, compensation shall include interest at a commercially reasonable rate for that currency from the date of expropriation until the date of actual payment.

5. If a Party elects to pay in a currency other than a G7 currency, the amount paid on the date of payment, if converted into a G7 currency at the market rate of exchange prevailing on that date, shall be no less than if the amount of compensation owed on the date of expropriation had been converted into that G7 currency at the market rate of exchange prevailing on that date, and interest had accrued at a commercially reasonable rate for

that G7 currency from the date of expropriation until the date of payment.

6. On payment, compensation shall be freely transferable as provided in Article 1109.

7. This Article does not apply to the issuance of compulsory licenses granted in relation to intellectual property rights, or the revocation, limitation or creation of intellectual property rights, to the extent that such issuance, revocation, limitation or creation is consistent with Chapter Seventeen (Intellectual Property).

8. For purposes of this Article and for greater certainty, a non-discriminatory measure of general application shall not be considered a measure tantamount to an expropriation of a debt security or loan covered by this Chapter solely on the ground that the measure imposes costs on the debtor that cause it to default on the debt.

Article 1111: Special Formalities and Information Requirements

1. Nothing in Article 1102 shall be construed to prevent a Party from adopting or maintaining a measure that prescribes special formalities in connection with the establishment of investments by investors of another Party, such as a requirement that investors be residents of the Party or that investments be legally constituted under the laws or regulations of the Party, provided that such formalities do not materially impair the protections afforded by a Party to investors of another Party and investments of investors of another Party pursuant to this Chapter.

2. Notwithstanding Articles 1102 or 1103, a Party may require an investor of another Party, or its investment in its territory, to provide routine information concerning that investment solely for informational or statistical purposes. The Party shall protect such business information that is confidential from any disclosure that

would prejudice the competitive position of the investor or the investment. Nothing in this paragraph shall be construed to prevent a Party from otherwise obtaining or disclosing information in connection with the equitable and good faith application of its law.

Article 1112: Relation to Other Chapters

1. In the event of any inconsistency between a provision of this Chapter and a provision of another Chapter, the provision of the other Chapter shall prevail to the extent of the inconsistency.

2. A requirement by a Party that a service provider of another Party post a bond or other form of financial security as a condition of providing a service into its territory does not of itself make this Chapter applicable to the provision of that cross-border service. This Chapter applies to that Party's treatment of the posted bond or financial security.

Article 1113: Denial of Benefits

1. A Party may deny the benefits of this Chapter to an investor of another Party that is an enterprise of such Party and to investments of such investor if investors of a non-Party own or control the enterprise and the denying Party: (a) does not maintain diplomatic relations with the non-Party; or (b) adopts or maintains measures with respect to the non-Party that prohibit transactions with the enterprise or that would be violated or circumvented if the benefits of this Chapter were accorded to the enterprise or to its investments.

2. Subject to prior notification and consultation in accordance with Articles 1803 (Notification and Provision of Information) and 2006 (Consultations), a Party may deny the benefits of this Chapter to an investor of another Party that is an enterprise of such Party and to investments of such investors if investors of a non-Party own or control the enterprise and the enterprise has no

substantial business activities in the territory of the Party under whose law it is constituted or organized.

Article 1114: Environmental Measures

1. Nothing in this Chapter shall be construed to prevent a Party from adopting, maintaining or enforcing any measure otherwise consistent with this Chapter that it considers appropriate to ensure that investment activity in its territory is undertaken in a manner sensitive to environmental concerns.

2. The Parties recognize that it is inappropriate to encourage investment by relaxing domestic health, safety or environmental measures. Accordingly, a Party should not waive or otherwise derogate from, or offer to waive or otherwise derogate from, such measures as an encouragement for the establishment, acquisition, expansion or retention in its territory of an investment of an investor. If a Party considers that another Party has offered such an encouragement, it may request consultations with the other Party and the two Parties shall consult with a view to avoiding any such encouragement.

Section B—Settlement of Disputes between a Party and an Investor of Another Party

Article 1115: Purpose

Without prejudice to the rights and obligations of the Parties under Chapter Twenty (Institutional Arrangements and Dispute Settlement Procedures), this Section establishes a mechanism for the settlement of investment disputes that assures both equal treatment among investors of the Parties in accordance with the principle of international reciprocity and due process before an impartial tribunal.

Article 1116: Claim by an Investor of a Party on Its Own Behalf

1. An investor of a Party may submit to arbitration under this Section a claim that another Party has breach-

ed an obligation under: (a) Section A or Article 1503(2) (State Enterprises); or (b) Article 1502(3)(a) (Monopolies and State Enterprises) where the monopoly has acted in a manner inconsistent with the Party's obligations under Section A, and that the investor has incurred loss or damage by reason of, or arising out of, that breach.

2. An investor may not make a claim if more than three years have elapsed from the date on which the investor first acquired, or should have first acquired, knowledge of the alleged breach and knowledge that the investor has incurred loss or damage.

Article 1117: Claim by an Investor of a Party on Behalf of an Enterprise

1. An investor of a Party, on behalf of an enterprise of another Party that is a juridical person that the investor owns or controls directly or indirectly, may submit to arbitration under this Section a claim that the other Party has breached an obligation under:

(a) Section A or Article 1503(2) (State Enterprises); or (b) Article 1502(3)(a) (Monopolies and State Enterprises) where the monopoly has acted in a manner inconsistent with the Party's obligations under Section A, and that the enterprise has incurred loss or damage by reason of, or arising out of, that breach.

2. An investor may not make a claim on behalf of an enterprise described in paragraph 1 if more than three years have elapsed from the date on which the enterprise first acquired, or should have first acquired, knowledge of the alleged breach and knowledge that the enterprise has incurred loss or damage.

3. Where an investor makes a claim under this Article and the investor or a noncontrolling investor in the enterprise makes a claim under Article 1116 arising out of the same events that gave rise to the claim under this Article, and two or more of the claims are submitted to

arbitration under Article 1120, the claims should be heard together by a Tribunal established under Article 1126, unless the Tribunal finds that the interests of a disputing party would be prejudiced thereby.

4. An investment may not make a claim under this Section.

Article 1118: Settlement of a Claim through Consultation and Negotiation

The disputing parties should first attempt to settle a claim through consultation or negotiation.

Article 1119: Notice of Intent to Submit a Claim to Arbitration

The disputing investor shall deliver to the disputing Party written notice of its intention to submit a claim to arbitration at least 90 days before the claim is submitted, which notice shall specify: (a) the name and address of the disputing investor and, where a claim is made under Article 1117, the name and address of the enterprise; (b) the provisions of this Agreement alleged to have been breached and any other relevant provisions; (c) the issues and the factual basis for the claim; and (d) the relief sought and the approximate amount of damages claimed.

Article 1120: Submission of a Claim to Arbitration

1. Except as provided in Annex 1120.1, and provided that six months have elapsed since the events giving rise to a claim, a disputing investor may submit the claim to arbitration under: (a) the ICSID Convention, provided that both the disputing Party and the Party of the investor are parties to the Convention; (b) the Additional Facility Rules of ICSID, provided that either the disputing Party or the Party of the investor, but not both, is a party to the ICSID Convention; or (c) the UNCITRAL Arbitration Rules.

2. The applicable arbitration rules shall govern the arbitration except to the extent modified by this Section.

Article 1121: Conditions Precedent to Submission of a Claim to Arbitration

1. A disputing investor may submit a claim under Article 1116 to arbitration only if: (a) the investor consents to arbitration in accordance with the procedures set out in this Agreement; and (b) both the investor and an enterprise of another Party that is a juridical person that the investor owns or controls directly or indirectly, waive their right to initiate or continue before any administrative tribunal or court under the law of any Party any proceedings with respect to the measure of the disputing Party that is alleged to be a breach referred to in Article 1116, except for proceedings for injunctive, declaratory or other extraordinary relief, not involving the payment of damages, before an administrative tribunal or court under the law of the disputing Party.

2. A disputing investor may submit a claim under Article 1117 to arbitration only if both the investor and the enterprise: (a) consent to arbitration in accordance with the procedures set out in this Agreement; and (b) waive their right to initiate or continue before any administrative tribunal or court under the law of any Party any proceedings with respect to the measure of the disputing Party that is alleged to be a breach referred to in Article 1117, except for proceedings for injunctive, declaratory or other extraordinary relief, not involving the payment of damages, before an administrative tribunal or court under the law of the disputing Party.

3. A consent and waiver required by this Article shall be in writing, shall be delivered to the disputing Party and shall be included in the submission of a claim to arbitration.

Article 1122: Consent to Arbitration

1. Each Party consents to the submission of a claim to arbitration in accordance with the procedures set out in this Agreement.

2. The consent given by paragraph 1 and the submission by a disputing investor of a claim to arbitration shall satisfy the requirement of: (a) Chapter II of the ICSID Convention (Jurisdiction of the Centre) and the Additional Facility Rules for written consent of the parties; (b) Article II of the New York Convention for an agreement in writing; and (c) Article I of the Inter–American Convention for an agreement.

Article 1123: Number of Arbitrators and Method of Appointment

Except in respect of a Tribunal established under Article 1126, and unless the disputing parties otherwise agree, the Tribunal shall comprise three arbitrators, one arbitrator appointed by each of the disputing parties and the third, who shall be the presiding arbitrator, appointed by agreement of the disputing parties.

Article 1124: Constitution of a Tribunal When a Party Fails to Appoint an Arbitrator or the Disputing Parties Are Unable to Agree on a Presiding Arbitrator

1. The Secretary–General shall serve as appointing authority for an arbitration under this Section.

2. If a Tribunal, other than a Tribunal established under Article 1126, has not been constituted within 90 days from the date that a claim is submitted to arbitration, the Secretary–General, on the request of either disputing party, shall appoint, in his discretion, the arbitrator or arbitrators not yet appointed, except that the presiding arbitrator shall be appointed in accordance with paragraph 3.

3. The Secretary–General shall appoint the presiding arbitrator from the roster of presiding arbitrators referred to in paragraph 4, provided that the presiding arbitrator shall not be a national of the disputing Party or a national of the Party of the disputing investor. In the event that no such presiding arbitrator is available to serve, the Secretary–General shall appoint, from the ICSID Panel of Arbitrators, a presiding arbitrator who is not a national of any of the Parties.

4. On the date of entry into force of this Agreement, the Parties shall establish, and thereafter maintain, a roster of 45 presiding arbitrators meeting the qualifications of the Convention and rules referred to in Article 1120 and experienced in international law and investment matters. The roster members shall be appointed by consensus and without regard to nationality.

Article 1125: Agreement to Appointment of Arbitrators

For purposes of Article 39 of the ICSID Convention and Article 7 of Schedule C to the ICSID Additional Facility Rules, and without prejudice to an objection to an arbitrator based on Article 1124(3) or on a ground other than nationality:

(a) the disputing Party agrees to the appointment of each individual member of a Tribunal established under the ICSID Convention or the ICSID Additional Facility Rules;

(b) a disputing investor referred to in Article 1116 may submit a claim to arbitration, or continue a claim, under the ICSID Convention or the ICSID Additional Facility Rules, only on condition that the disputing investor agrees in writing to the appointment of each individual member of the Tribunal; and

(c) a disputing investor referred to in Article 1117(1) may submit a claim to arbitration, or continue a claim, under the ICSID Convention or the ICSID Additional

Facility Rules, only on condition that the disputing investor and the enterprise agree in writing to the appointment of each individual member of the Tribunal.

Article 1126: Consolidation

1.   A Tribunal established under this Article shall be
established under the UNCITRAL Arbitration Rules and
shall conduct its proceedings in accordance with those
Rules, except as modified by this Section.

* * *

Article 1128: Participation by a Party

On written notice to the disputing parties, a Party may
make submissions to a Tribunal on a question of interpretation of this Agreement.

Article 1129: Documents

1.   A Party shall be entitled to receive from the disputing Party, at the cost of the requesting Party a copy of:
(a) the evidence that has been tendered to the Tribunal;
and (b) the written argument of the disputing parties.

2.   A Party receiving information pursuant to paragraph 1 shall treat the information as if it were a disputing Party.

Article 1130: Place of Arbitration

Unless the disputing parties agree otherwise, a Tribunal shall hold an arbitration in the territory of a Party
that is a party to the New York Convention, selected in
accordance with: (a) the ICSID Additional Facility Rules
if the arbitration is under those Rules or the ICSID
Convention; or (b) the UNCITRAL Arbitration Rules if
the arbitration is under those Rules.

Article 1131: Governing Law

1.   A Tribunal established under this Section shall decide the issues in dispute in accordance with this Agreement and applicable rules of international law.

2.   An interpretation by the Commission of a provision of this Agreement shall be binding on a Tribunal established under this Section.

Article 1132: Interpretation of Annexes

1.   Where a disputing Party asserts as a defense that the measure alleged to be a breach is within the scope of a reservation or exception set out in Annex I, Annex II, Annex III or Annex IV, on request of the disputing Party, the Tribunal shall request the interpretation of the Commission on the issue. The Commission, within 60 days of delivery of the request, shall submit in writing its interpretation to the Tribunal.

2.   Further to Article 1131(2), a Commission interpretation submitted under paragraph 1 shall be binding on the Tribunal. If the Commission fails to submit an interpretation within 60 days, the Tribunal shall decide the issue.

Article 1133: Expert Reports

Without prejudice to the appointment of other kinds of experts where authorized by the applicable arbitration rules, a Tribunal, at the request of a disputing party or, unless the disputing parties disapprove, on its own initiative, may appoint one or more experts to report to it in writing on any factual issue concerning environmental, health, safety or other scientific matters raised by a disputing party in a proceeding, subject to such terms and conditions as the disputing parties may agree.

Article 1134: Interim Measures of Protection

A Tribunal may order an interim measure of protection to preserve the rights of a disputing party, or to ensure that the Tribunal's jurisdiction is made fully effective, including an order to preserve evidence in the possession or control of a disputing party or to protect the Tribunal's jurisdiction. A Tribunal may not order attachment or enjoin the application of the measure alleged to constitute a breach referred to in Article 1116 or 1117. For purposes of this paragraph, an order includes a recommendation.

Article 1135: Final Award

1. Where a Tribunal makes a final award against a Party, the Tribunal may award only: (a) monetary damages and any applicable interest; or (b) restitution of property, in which case the award shall provide that the disputing Party may pay monetary damages and any applicable interest in lieu of restitution.

2. Subject to paragraph 1, where a claim is made under Article 1117(1): (a) an award of restitution of property shall provide that restitution be made to the enterprise; (b) an award of monetary damages and any applicable interest shall provide that the sum be paid to the enterprise; and (c) the award shall provide that it is made without prejudice to any right that any person may have in the relief under applicable domestic law.

3. A Tribunal may not order a Party to pay punitive damages.

Article 1136: Finality and Enforcement of an Award

1. An award made by a Tribunal shall have no binding force except between the disputing parties and in respect of the particular case.

2. Subject to paragraph 3 and the applicable review procedure for an interim award, a disputing party shall abide by and comply with an award without delay.

3. A disputing party may not seek enforcement of a final award until: (a) in the case of a final award made under the ICSID Convention (i) 120 days have elapsed

from the date the award was rendered and no disputing party has requested revision or annulment of the award, or (ii) revision or annulment proceedings have been completed; and (b) in the case of a final award under the ICSID Additional Facility Rules or the UNCITRAL Arbitration Rules (i) three months have elapsed from the date the award was rendered and no disputing party has commenced a proceeding to revise, set aside or annul the award, or (ii) a court has dismissed or allowed an application to revise, set aside or annul the award and there is no further appeal.

4. Each Party shall provide for the enforcement of an award in its territory.

5. If a disputing Party fails to abide by or comply with a final award, the Commission, on delivery of a request by a Party whose investor was a party to the arbitration, shall establish a panel under Article 2008 (Request for an Arbitral Panel). The requesting Party may seek in such proceedings: (a) a determination that the failure to abide by or comply with the final award is inconsistent with the obligations of this Agreement; and (b) a recommendation that the Party abide by or comply with the final award.

6. A disputing investor may seek enforcement of an arbitration award under the ICSID Convention, the New York Convention or the Inter–American Convention regardless of whether proceedings have been taken under paragraph 5.

7. A claim that is submitted to arbitration under this Section shall be considered to arise out of a commercial relationship or transaction for purposes of Article I of the New York Convention and Article I of the Inter–American Convention.

* * *

Article 1138: Exclusions

1. Without prejudice to the applicability or non-applicability of the dispute settlement provisions of this Sec-

tion or of Chapter Twenty (Institutional Arrangements and Dispute Settlement Procedures) to other actions taken by a Party pursuant to Article 2102 (National Security), a decision by a Party to prohibit or restrict the acquisition of an investment in its territory by an investor of another Party, or its investment, pursuant to that Article shall not be subject to such provisions.

2. The dispute settlement provisions of this Section and of Chapter Twenty shall not apply to the matters referred to in Annex 1138.2.

Article 1139: Definitions

For purposes of this Chapter:

disputing investor means an investor that makes a claim under Section B;

disputing parties means the disputing investor and the disputing Party;

disputing party means the disputing investor or the disputing Party;

disputing Party means a Party against which a claim is made under Section B;

enterprise means an "enterprise" as defined in Article 201, and a branch of an enterprise;

enterprise of a Party means an enterprise constituted or organized under the law of a Party, and a branch located in the territory of a Party and carrying out business activities there;

equity or debt securities includes voting and non-voting shares, bonds, convertible debentures, stock options and warrants;

G7 Currency means the currency of Canada, France, Germany, Italy, Japan, the United Kingdom of Great Britain and Northern Ireland or the United States;

ICSID means the International Centre for Settlement of Investment Disputes;

ICSID Convention means the Convention on the Settlement of Investment Disputes between States and Nationals of other States, done at Washington, March 18, 1965;

Inter–American Convention means the Inter–American Convention on International Commercial Arbitration, done at Panama, January 30, 1975;

investment means: (a) an enterprise; (b) an equity security of an enterprise; (c) a debt security of an enterprise (i) where the enterprise is an affiliate of the investor, or (ii) where the original maturity of the debt security is at least three years, but does not include a debt security, regardless of original maturity, of a state enterprise; (d) a loan to an enterprise (i) where the enterprise is an affiliate of the investor, or (ii) where the original maturity of the loan is at least three years, but does not include a loan, regardless of original maturity, to a state enterprise; (e) an interest in an enterprise that entitles the owner to share in income or profits of the enterprise; (f) an interest in an enterprise that entitles the owner to share in the assets of that enterprise on dissolution, other than a debt security or a loan excluded from subparagraph (c) or (d); (g) real estate or other property, tangible or intangible, acquired in the expectation or used for the purpose of economic benefit or other business purposes; and (h) interests arising from the commitment of capital or other resources in the territory of a Party to economic activity in such territory, such as under (i) contracts involving the presence of an investor's property in the territory of the Party, including turnkey or construction contracts, or concessions, or (ii) contracts where remuneration depends substantially on the production, revenues or profits of an enterprise;

but investment does not mean, (i) claims to money that arise solely from (i) commercial contracts for the sale of goods or services by a national or enterprise in the territory of a Party to an enterprise in the territory of another Party, or (ii) the extension of credit in connection with a commercial transaction, such as trade financing, other than a loan covered by subparagraph (d); or (j) any other claims to money, that do not involve the kinds of interests set out in subparagraphs (a) through (h);

investment of an investor of a Party means an investment owned or controlled directly or indirectly by an investor of such Party;

investor of a Party means a Party or state enterprise thereof, or a national or an enterprise of such Party, that seeks to make, is making or has made an investment;

investor of a non-Party means an investor other than an investor of a Party, that seeks to make, is making or has made an investment;

New York Convention means the United Nations Convention on the Recognition and Enforcement of Foreign Arbitral Awards, done at New York, June 10, 1958;

Secretary–General means the Secretary–General of ICSID;

transfers means transfers and international payments;

Tribunal means an arbitration tribunal established under Article 1120 or 1126; and

UNCITRAL Arbitration Rules means the arbitration rules of the United Nations Commission on International Trade Law, approved by the United Nations General Assembly on December 15, 1976.

Annex 1120.1—Submission of a Claim to Arbitration

Mexico

With respect to the submission of a claim to arbitration: (a) an investor of another Party may not allege that Mexico has breached an obligation under: (i) Section A or

Article 1503(2) (State Enterprises), or (ii) Article 1502(3)(a) (Monopolies and State Enterprises) where the monopoly has acted in a manner inconsistent with the Party's obligations under Section A, both in an arbitration under this Section and in proceedings before a Mexican court or administrative tribunal; and

(b) where an enterprise of Mexico that is a juridical person that an investor of another Party owns or controls directly or indirectly alleges in proceedings before a Mexican court or administrative tribunal that Mexico has breached an obligation under:(i) Section A or Article 1503(2) (State Enterprises), or (ii) Article 1502(3)(a) (Monopolies and State Enterprises) where the monopoly has acted in a manner inconsistent with the Party's obligations under Section A, the investor may not allege the breach in an arbitration under this Section.

* * *

Annex 1138.2—Exclusions from Dispute Settlement

Canada

A decision by Canada following a review under the Investment Canada Act, with respect to whether or not to permit an acquisition that is subject to review, shall not be subject to the dispute settlement provisions of Section B or of Chapter Twenty (Institutional Arrangements and Dispute Settlement Procedures).

Mexico

A decision by the National Commission on Foreign Investment ("Comision Nacional de Inversiones Extranjeras") following a review pursuant to Annex I, page I–M–4, with respect to whether or not to permit an acquisition that is subject to review, shall not be subject to the dispute settlement provisions of Section B or of Chapter Twenty (Institutional Arrangements and Dispute Settlement Procedures).

Chapter Twelve—Cross-Border Trade in Services

Article 1201: Scope and Coverage

1. This Chapter applies to measures adopted or maintained by a Party relating to cross-border trade in services by service providers of another Party, including measures respecting: (a) the production, distribution, marketing, sale and delivery of a service; (b) the purchase or use of, or payment for, a service; (c) the access to and use of distribution and transportation systems in connection with the provision of a service; (d) the presence in its territory of a service provider of another Party; and (e) the provision of a bond or other form of financial security as a condition for the provision of a service.

2. This Chapter does not apply to: (a) financial services, as defined in Chapter Fourteen (Financial Services); or (b) air services, including domestic and international air transportation services, whether scheduled or non-scheduled, and related services in support of air services, other than (i) aircraft repair and maintenance services during which an aircraft is withdrawn from service, and (ii) specialty air services.

3. Nothing in this Chapter shall be construed to: (a) impose any obligation on a Party with respect to a national of another Party seeking access to its employment market, or employed on a permanent basis in 2 its territory, or to confer any right on that national with respect to that access or employment; (b) impose any obligation or confer any right on a Party with respect to procurement by a Party or a state enterprise;

(c) impose any obligation or confer any right on a Party with respect to subsidies or grants provided by a Party or a state enterprise, including government-supported loans, guarantees and insurance; or (d) prevent a Party from providing a service or performing a function, such as law enforcement, correctional services, income security or insurance, social security or insurance, social welfare, public education, public training, health, and child care, in a manner that is not inconsistent with this Chapter.

Article 1202: National Treatment

1. Each Party shall accord to service providers of another Party treatment no less favorable than that it accords, in like circumstances, to its own service providers.

2. The treatment accorded by a Party under paragraph 1 means, with respect to a state or province, treatment no less favorable than the most favorable treatment accorded, in like circumstances, by that state or province to service providers of the Party of which it forms a part.

Article 1203: Most–Favored–Nation Treatment

Each Party shall accord to service providers of another Party treatment no less favorable than that it accords, in like circumstances, to service providers of another Party or of a non-Party.

Article 1204: Standard of Treatment

Each Party shall accord to service providers of another Party the better of the treatment required by Articles 1202 and 1203.

Article 1205: Local Presence

No Party may require a service provider of another Party to establish or maintain a representative office or any form of enterprise, or to be resident, in its territory as a condition for the cross-border provision of a service.

Article 1206: Reservations

1. Articles 1202, 1203 and 1205 do not apply to (a) any existing non-conforming measure that is maintained

by (i) a Party at the federal level, as set out in its
Schedule to Annex I, (ii) a state or province, for two years
after the date of entry into force of this Agreement, and
thereafter as set out by a Party in its Schedule to Annex
I, in accordance with paragraph 2, or (iii) a local government; (b) the continuation or prompt renewal of any non-
conforming measure referred to in subparagraph (a); or
(c) an amendment to any non-conforming measure referred to in subparagraph (a) to the extent that the
amendment does not decrease the conformity of the measure, as it existed immediately before the amendment,
with Articles 1202, 1203 and 1205.

2. Each Party may set out in its Schedule to Annex I
any existing non-conforming measure maintained by a
state or province, not including a local government, within two years of the date of entry into force of this
Agreement.

3. Articles 1202, 1203 and 1205 do not apply to any
measure that a Party adopts or maintains with respect to
sectors, subsectors or activities, as set out in its Schedule
to Annex II.

Article 1207: Quantitative Restrictions

1. The Parties shall periodically, but in any event at
least every two years, endeavor to negotiate the liberalization or removal of: (a) existing quantitative restrictions

* * *

Article 1208: Liberalization of Non–Discriminatory Measures

Each Party shall set out in its Schedule to Annex VI its
commitments to liberalize quantitative restrictions, licensing requirements, performance requirements or other
non-discriminatory measures.

Article 1209: Procedures

The Commission shall establish procedures for: (a) a Party to notify and include in its relevant Schedule (i) state or provincial measures in accordance with Article 1206(2), (ii) quantitative restrictions in accordance with Article 1207(2) and (3), (iii) commitments pursuant to Article 1208, and (iv) amendments of measures referred to in Article 1206(1)(c); and (b) consultations on reservations, quantitative restrictions or commitments with a view to further liberalization.

Article 1210: Licensing and Certification

1.   With a view to ensuring that any measure adopted or maintained by a Party relating to the licensing or certification of nationals of another Party does not constitute an unnecessary barrier to trade, each Party shall endeavor to ensure that any such measure: (a) is based on objective and transparent criteria, such as competence and the ability to provide a service; (b) is not more burdensome than necessary to ensure the quality of a service; and (c) does not constitute a disguised restriction on the cross-border provision of a service.

2.   Where a Party recognizes, unilaterally or by agreement, education, experience, licenses or certifications obtained in the territory of another Party or of a non-Party: (a) nothing in Article 1203 shall be construed to require the Party to accord such recognition to education, experience, licenses or certifications obtained in the territory of another Party; and (b) the Party shall afford another Party an adequate opportunity to demonstrate that education, experience, licenses or certifications obtained in that other Party's territory should also be recognized or to conclude an agreement or arrangement of comparable effect.

3.   Each Party shall, within two years of the date of entry into force of this Agreement, eliminate any citizen-

ship or permanent residency requirement set out in its Schedule to Annex I that it maintains for the licensing or certification of professional service providers of another Party. Where a Party does not comply with this obligation with respect to a particular sector, any other Party may, in the same sector and for such period as the non-complying Party maintains its requirement, solely have recourse to maintaining an equivalent requirement set out in its Schedule to Annex I or reinstating: (a) any such requirement at the federal level that it eliminated pursuant to this Article; or (b) on notification to the non-complying Party, any such requirement at the state or provincial level existing on the date of entry into force of this Agreement.

4. The Parties shall consult periodically with a view to determining the feasibility of removing any remaining citizenship or permanent residency requirement for the licensing or certification of each other's service providers.

5. Annex 1210.5 applies to measures adopted or maintained by a Party relating to the licensing or certification of professional service providers.

Article 1211: Denial of Benefits

1. A Party may deny the benefits of this Chapter to a service provider of another Party where the Party establishes that: (a) the service is being provided by an enterprise owned or controlled by nationals of a non-Party, and (i) the denying Party does not maintain diplomatic relations with the non-Party, or (ii) the denying Party adopts or maintains measures with respect to the non-Party that prohibit transactions with the enterprise or that would be violated or circumvented if the benefits of this Chapter were accorded to the enterprise; or (b) the cross-border provision of a transportation service covered by this Chapter is provided using equipment not registered by any Party.

2. Subject to prior notification and consultation in accordance with Articles 1803 (Notification and Provision of Information) and 2006 (Consultations), a Party may deny the benefits of this Chapter to a service provider of another Party where the Party establishes 7 that the service is being provided by an enterprise that is owned or controlled by persons of a non-Party and that has no substantial business activities in the territory of any Party.

Article 1213: Definitions

1. For purposes of this Chapter, a reference to a federal, state or provincial government includes any non-governmental body in the exercise of any regulatory, administrative or other governmental authority delegated to it by that government.

2. For purposes of this Chapter:

cross-border provision of a service or cross-border trade in services means the provision of a service: (a) from the territory of a Party into the territory of another Party; (b) in the territory of a Party by a person of that Party to a person of another Party; or (c) by a national of a Party in the territory of another Party, but does not include the provision of a service in the territory of a Party by an investment, as defined in Article 1138 (Investment—Definitions), in that territory;

enterprise means an "enterprise" as defined in Article 201 (Definitions of General Application), and a branch of an enterprise;

enterprise of a Party means an enterprise constituted or organized under the law of a Party, and a branch located in the territory of a Party and carrying out business activities there;

professional services means services, the provision of which requires specialized post-secondary education, or equivalent training or experience, and for which the right to practice is granted or restricted by a Party, but does not include services provided by trades-persons or vessel and aircraft crew members;

quantitative restriction means a non-discriminatory measure that imposes limitations on: (a) the number of service providers, whether in the form of a quota, a monopoly or an economic needs test, or by any other quantitative means; or (b) the operations of any service provider, whether in the form of a quota or an economic needs test, or by any other quantitative means;

service provider of a Party means a person of a Party that seeks to provide or provides a service; and

specialty air services means aerial mapping, aerial surveying, aerial photography, forest fire management, fire fighting, aerial advertising, glider towing, parachute jumping, aerial construction, heli-logging, aerial sightseeing, flight training, aerial inspection and surveillance, and aerial spraying services.

Annex 1210.5: Professional Services

Section A—General Provisions

Processing of Applications for Licenses and Certifications

1. Each Party shall ensure that its competent authorities, within a reasonable time after the submission by a national of another Party of an application for a license or certification: (a) where the application is complete, make a determination on the application and inform the applicant of that determination; or (b) where the application is not complete, inform the applicant without undue delay of the status of the application and the additional information that is required under the Party's law.

Development of Professional Standards

2. The Parties shall encourage the relevant bodies in their respective territories to develop mutually acceptable

standards and criteria for licensing and certification of professional service providers and to provide recommendations on mutual recognition to the Commission.

* * *

4. On receipt of a recommendation referred to in paragraph 2, the Commission shall review the recommendation within a reasonable time to determine whether it is consistent with this Agreement. Based on the Commission's review, each Party shall encourage its respective competent authorities, where appropriate, to implement the recommendation within a mutually agreed time.

* * *

Section B—Foreign Legal Consultants

1. Each Party shall, in implementing its obligations and commitments regarding foreign legal consultants as set out in its relevant Schedules and subject to any reservations therein, ensure that a national of another Party is permitted to practice or advise on the law of any country in which that national is authorized to practice as a lawyer.

Consultations With Professional Bodies

2. Each Party shall consult with its relevant professional bodies to obtain their recommendations on: (a) the form of association or partnership between lawyers authorized to practice in its territory and foreign legal consultants; (b) the development of standards and criteria for the authorization of foreign legal consultants in conformity with Article 1210; and (c) other matters relating to the provision of foreign legal consultancy services.

3. Prior to initiation of consultations under paragraph 7, each Party shall encourage its relevant professional bodies to consult with the relevant professional bodies designated by each of the other Parties regarding the

development of joint recommendations on the matters referred to in paragraph 2.

Future Liberalization

4. Each Party shall establish a work program to develop common procedures throughout its territory for the authorization of foreign legal consultants.

5. Each Party shall promptly review any recommendation referred to in paragraphs 2 and 3 to ensure its consistency with this Agreement. If the recommendation is consistent with this Agreement, each Party shall encourage its competent authorities to implement the recommendation within one year.

6. Each Party shall report to the Commission within one year of the date of entry into force of this Agreement, and each year thereafter, on its progress in implementing the work program referred to in paragraph 4.

7. The Parties shall meet within one year of the date of entry into force of this Agreement with a view to: (a) assessing the implementation of paragraphs 2 through 5; (b) amending or removing, where appropriate, reservations on foreign legal consultancy services; and (c) assessing further work that may be appropriate regarding foreign legal consultancy services.

Chapter Thirteen—Telecommunications

Article 1301: Scope and Coverage

1. This Chapter applies to: (a) measures adopted or maintained by a Party relating to access to and use of public telecommunications transport networks or services by persons of another Party, including access and use by such persons operating private networks; (b) measures adopted or maintained by a Party relating to the provision of enhanced or value-added services by persons of another Party in the territory, or across the borders, of a

Party; and (c) standards-related measures relating to attachment of terminal or other equipment to public telecommunications transport networks.

2. Except to ensure that persons operating broadcast stations and cable systems have continued access to and use of public telecommunications transport networks and services, this Chapter does not apply to any measure adopted or maintained by a Party relating to cable or broadcast distribution of radio or television programming.

3. Nothing in this Chapter shall be construed to: (a) require a Party to authorize a person of another Party to establish, construct, acquire, lease, operate or provide telecommunications transport networks or telecommunications transport services; (b) require a Party, or require a Party to compel any person, to establish, construct, acquire, lease, operate or provide telecommunications transport networks or telecommunications transport services not offered to the public generally; (c) prevent a Party from prohibiting persons operating private networks from using their networks to provide public telecommunications transport networks or services to third persons; or (d) require a Party to compel any person engaged in the cable or broadcast distribution of radio or television programming to make available its cable or broadcast facilities as a public telecommunications transport network.

Article 1302: Access to and Use of Public Telecommunications Transport Networks and Services

1. Each Party shall ensure that persons of another Party have access to and use of any public telecommunications transport network or service, including private leased circuits, offered in its territory or across its borders for the conduct of their business, on reasonable and non-discriminatory terms and conditions, including as set out in paragraphs 2 through 8.

2. Subject to paragraphs 6 and 7, each Party shall ensure that such persons are permitted to: (a) purchase or lease, and attach terminal or other equipment that interfaces with the public telecommunications transport network; (b) interconnect private leased or owned circuits with public telecommunications transport networks in the territory, or across the borders, of that Party, including for use in providing dial-up access to and from their customers or users, or with circuits leased or owned by another person on terms and conditions mutually agreed by those persons; (c) perform switching, signalling and processing functions; and (d) use operating protocols of their choice.

3. Each Party shall ensure that: (a) the pricing of public telecommunications transport services reflects economic costs directly related to providing the services; and (b) private leased circuits are available on a flat-rate pricing basis.

Nothing in this paragraph shall be construed to prevent cross-subsidization between public telecommunications transport services.

4. Each Party shall ensure that persons of another Party may use public telecommunications transport networks or services for the movement of information in its territory or across its borders, including for intracorporate communications, and for access to information contained in data bases or otherwise stored in machine-readable form in the territory of any Party.

5. Further to Article 2101 (General Exceptions), nothing in this Chapter shall be construed to prevent a Party from adopting or enforcing any measure necessary to: (a) ensure the security and confidentiality of messages; or (b) protect the privacy of subscribers to public telecommunications transport networks or services.

6. Each Party shall ensure that no condition is imposed on access to and use of public telecommunications

transport networks or services, other than that necessary to: (a) safeguard the public service responsibilities of providers of public telecommunications transport networks or services, in particular their ability to make their networks or services available to the public generally; or (b) protect the technical integrity of public telecommunications transport networks or services.

7.　Provided that conditions for access to and use of public telecommunications transport networks or services satisfy the criteria set out in paragraph 6, such conditions may include: (a) a restriction on resale or shared use of such services; (b) a requirement to use specified technical interfaces, including interface protocols, for interconnection with such networks or services; (c) a restriction on interconnection of private leased or owned circuits with such networks or services or with circuits leased or owned by another person, where the circuits are used in the provision of public telecommunications transport networks or services; and (d) a licensing, permit, registration or notification procedure which, if adopted or maintained, is transparent and applications filed thereunder are processed expeditiously.

8.　For purposes of this Article, "non-discriminatory" means on terms and conditions no less favorable than those accorded to any other customer or user of like public telecommunications transport networks or services in like circumstances.

Article 1303: Conditions for the Provision of Enhanced or Value–Added Services

1.　Each Party shall ensure that: (a) any licensing, permit, registration or notification procedure that it adopts or maintains relating to the provision of enhanced or value-added services is transparent and non-discriminatory, and that applications filed thereunder are processed expeditiously; and (b) information required under such procedures is limited to that necessary to demonstrate that the applicant has the financial solvency to begin providing services or to assess conformity of the applicant's terminal or other equipment with the Party's applicable standards or technical regulations.

2. A Party shall not require a person providing enhanced or value-added services to: (a) provide those services to the public generally; (b) cost-justify its rates; (c) file a tariff; (d) interconnect its networks with any particular customer or network; or (e) conform with any particular standard or technical regulation for interconnection other than for interconnection to a public telecommunications transport network.

3. Notwithstanding paragraph 2(c), a Party may require the filing of a tariff by: (a) such provider to remedy a practice of that provider that the Party has found in a particular case to be anticompetitive under its law; or (b) a monopoly to which Article 1305 applies.

Article 1304: Standards–Related Measures

1. Further to Article 904(4) (Unnecessary Obstacles), each Party shall ensure that its standards-related measures relating to the attachment of terminal or other equipment to the public telecommunications transport networks, including those measures relating to the use of testing and measuring equipment for conformity assessment procedures, are adopted or maintained only to the extent necessary to: (a) prevent technical damage to public telecommunications transport networks; (b) prevent technical interference with, or degradation of, public telecommunications transport services; (c) prevent electromagnetic interference, and ensure compatibility, with other uses of the electromagnetic spectrum; (d) prevent billing equipment malfunction; or (e) ensure users' safety and access to public telecommunications transport networks or services.

2. A Party may require approval for the attachment to the public telecommunications transport network of terminal or other equipment that is not authorized, provided that the criteria for that approval are consistent with paragraph 1.

3. Each Party shall ensure that the network termination points for its public telecommunications transport networks are defined on a reasonable and transparent basis.

4. No Party may require separate authorization for equipment that is connected on the customer's side of authorized equipment that serves as a protective device fulfilling the criteria of paragraph 1.

5. Further to Article 904(3) (Non–Discriminatory Treatment), each Party shall: (a) ensure that its conformity assessment procedures are transparent and non-discriminatory and that applications filed thereunder are processed expeditiously; (b) permit any technically qualified entity to perform the testing required under the Party's conformity assessment procedures for terminal or other equipment to be attached to the public telecommunications transport network, subject to the Party's right to review the accuracy and completeness of the test results; and (c) ensure that any measure that it adopts or maintains requiring persons to be authorized to act as agents for suppliers of telecommunications equipment before the Party's relevant conformity assessment bodies is non-discriminatory.

6. No later than one year after the date of entry into force of this Agreement, each Party shall adopt, as part of its conformity assessment procedures, provisions necessary to accept the test results from laboratories or testing facilities in the territory of another Party for tests performed in accordance with the accepting Party's standards-related measures and procedures.

7. The Telecommunications Standards Subcommittee established under Article 913(5) (Committee on Standards–Related Measures) shall perform the functions set out in Annex 913.5.a2.

Article 1305: Monopolies

1. Where a Party maintains or designates a monopoly to provide public telecommunications transport networks or services, and the monopoly, directly or through an affiliate, competes in the provision of enhanced or value-added services or other telecommunications-related services or telecommunications-related goods, the Party shall ensure that the monopoly does not use its monopoly position to engage in anticompetitive conduct in those markets, either directly or through its dealings with its affiliates, in such a manner as to affect adversely a person of another Party. Such conduct may include cross-subsidization, predatory conduct and the discriminatory provision of access to public telecommunications transport networks or services.

2. To prevent such anticompetitive conduct, each Party shall adopt or maintain effective measures, such as: (a) accounting requirements; (b) requirements for structural separation; (c) rules to ensure that the monopoly accords its competitors access to and use of its public telecommunications transport networks or services on terms and conditions no less favorable than those it accords to itself or its affiliates; or (d) rules to ensure the timely disclosure of technical changes to public telecommunications transport networks and their interfaces.

Article 1306: Transparency

Further to Article 1802, each Party shall make publicly available its measures relating to access to and use of public telecommunications transport networks or services, including measures relating to: (a) tariffs and other terms and conditions of service; (b) specifications of technical interfaces with the networks or services; (c) information on bodies responsible for the preparation and adoption of standards-related measures affecting such access and use; (d) conditions applying to attachment of terminal or other equipment to the networks; and (e) notification, permit, registration or licensing requirements.

Article 1307: Relation to Other Chapters

In the event of any inconsistency between a provision of this Chapter and a provision of another Chapter, the provision of this Chapter shall prevail to the extent of the inconsistency.

Article 1308: Relation to International Organizations and Agreements

The Parties recognize the importance of international standards for global compatibility and interoperability of telecommunication networks or services and undertake to promote those standards through the work of relevant international bodies, including the International Telecommunication Union and the International Organization for Standardization.

Article 1309: Technical Cooperation and Other Consultations

1. To encourage the development of interoperable telecommunications transport services infrastructure, the Parties shall cooperate in the exchange of technical information, the development of government-to-government training programs and other related activities. In implementing this obligation, the Parties shall give special emphasis to existing exchange programs.

2. The Parties shall consult with a view to determining the feasibility of further liberalizing trade in all

telecommunications services, including public telecommunications transport networks and services.

* * *

Chapter Fourteen—Financial Services

Article 1401: Scope and Coverage

1. This Chapter applies to measures adopted or maintained by a Party relating to: (a) financial institutions of another Party; (b) investors of another Party, and investments of such investors, in financial institutions in the Party's territory; and (c) cross-border trade in financial services.

2. Articles 1109 through 1111, 1113, 1114 and 1211 are hereby incorporated into and made a part of this Chapter. Articles 1115 through 1137 are hereby incorporated into and made a part of this Chapter solely for breaches by a Party of Articles 1109 through 1111, 1113 and 1114, as incorporated into this Chapter.

3. Nothing in this Chapter shall be construed to prevent a Party, or its public entities, from exclusively conducting or providing in its territory: (a) activities or services forming part of a public retirement plan or statutory system of social security; or (b) activities or services for the account or with the guarantee or using the financial resources of the Party or its public entities.

4. Annex 1401.4 applies to the Parties specified in that Annex.

Article 1402: Self–Regulatory Organizations

Where a Party requires a financial institution or a cross-border financial service provider of another Party to be a member of, participate in, or have access to, a self-regulatory organization to provide a financial service in or into the territory of that Party, the 2 Party shall ensure observance of the obligations of this Chapter by such self-regulatory organization.

Article 1403: Establishment of Financial Institutions

1. The Parties recognize the principle that an investor of another Party should be permitted to establish a financial institution in the territory of a Party in the juridical form chosen by such investor.

2. The Parties also recognize the principle that an investor of another Party should be permitted to participate widely in a Party's market through the ability of such investor to: (a) provide in that Party's territory a range of financial services through separate financial institutions as may be required by that Party; (b) expand geographically in that Party's territory; and (c) own financial institutions in that Party's territory without being subject to ownership requirements specific to foreign financial institutions.

3. Subject to Annex 1403.3, at such time as the United States permits commercial banks of another Party located in its territory to expand through subsidiaries or direct branches into substantially all of the United States market, the Parties shall review and assess market access provided by each Party in relation to the principles in paragraphs 1 and 2 with a view to adopting arrangements permitting investors of another Party to choose the juridical form of establishment of commercial banks.

4. Each Party shall permit an investor of another Party that does not own or control a financial institution in the Party's territory to establish a financial institution in that territory. A Party may: (a) require an investor of another Party to incorporate under the Party's law any financial institution it establishes in the Party's territory; or (b) impose terms and conditions on establishment that are consistent with Article 1405.

5. For purposes of this Article, "investor of another Party" means an investor of another Party engaged in the business of providing financial services in the territory of that Party.

Article 1404: Cross–Border Trade

1. No Party may adopt any measure restricting any type of cross-border trade in financial services by cross-border financial service providers of another Party that the Party permits on the date of entry into force of this Agreement, except to the extent set out in Section B of the Party's Schedule to Annex VII.

2. Each Party shall permit persons located in its territory, and its nationals wherever located, to purchase financial services from cross-border financial service providers of another Party located in the territory of that other Party or of another Party. This obligation does not require a Party to permit such providers to do business or solicit in its territory. Subject to paragraph 1, each Party may define "doing business" and "solicitation" for purposes of this obligation.

3. Without prejudice to other means of prudential regulation of cross-border trade in financial services, a Party may require the registration of cross-border financial service providers of another Party and of financial instruments.

4. The Parties shall consult on future liberalization of cross-border trade in financial services as set out in Annex 1404.4.

Article 1405: National Treatment

1. Each Party shall accord to investors of another Party treatment no less favorable than that it accords to its own investors, in like circumstances, with respect to the establishment, acquisition, expansion, management, conduct, operation and sale or other disposition of finan-

cial institutions and investments in financial institutions in its territory.

2.   Each Party shall accord to financial institutions of another Party and to investments of investors of another Party in financial institutions treatment no less favorable than that it accords to its own financial institutions and to investments of its own investors in financial institutions, in like circumstances, with respect to the establishment, acquisition, expansion, management, conduct, operation, and sale or other disposition of financial institutions and investments.

3.   Subject to Article 1404, where a Party permits the cross-border provision of a financial service it shall accord to the cross-border financial service providers of another Party treatment no less favorable than that it accords to its own financial service providers, in like circumstances, with respect to the provision of such service.

4.   The treatment that a Party is required to accord under paragraphs 1, 2 and 3 means, with respect to a measure of any state or province:

(a) in the case of an investor of another Party with an investment in a financial institution, an investment of such investor in an institution or an institution of such investor located in a state or province, treatment no less favorable than the treatment accorded to an investor of the Party in a financial institution, an investment of such investor in an institution or an institution of such investor located in that state or province, in like circumstances; and

(b) in any other case, treatment no less favorable than the most favorable treatment accorded to an investor of the Party in a financial institution, its financial institution or its investment in a financial institution, in like circumstances.

For greater certainty, in the case of an investor of another Party with investments in financial institutions or institutions located in more than one state or province, the treatment required under subparagraph (a) means: (c) treatment of the investor that is no less favorable than the most favorable treatment accorded to an investor of the Party with an investment located in such states, in like circumstances; and (d) with respect to an investment of the investor in a financial institution or a financial institution of such investor located in a state or province, treatment no less favorable than that accorded to an investment of an investor of the Party or a financial institution of such investor located in that state or province, in like circumstances.

5. A Party's treatment of financial institutions and cross-border financial service providers of another Party, whether different or identical to that accorded to its own institutions or providers in like circumstances, is consistent with paragraphs 1 through 3 if the treatment affords equal competitive opportunities.

6. A Party's treatment affords equal competitive opportunities if it does not disadvantage financial institutions and cross-border financial services providers of another Party in their ability to provide financial services as compared with the ability of the Party's own financial institutions and financial services providers, in like circumstances.

7. Differences in market share, profitability or size do not in themselves establish a denial of equal competitive opportunities, but such differences may be used as evidence regarding whether a Party's treatment affords equal competitive opportunities.

Article 1406: Most–Favored–Nation Treatment

1. Each Party shall accord to investors of another Party, financial institutions of another Party, investments of investors in financial institutions and cross-border financial service providers of another Party treat-

ment no less favorable than that it accords to the investors, financial institutions, investments of investors in financial institutions and cross-border financial service providers of any other Party or of a non-Party, in like circumstances.

2. A Party may recognize prudential measures of another Party or of a non-Party in the application of measures covered by this Chapter. Such recognition may be: (a) accorded unilaterally; (b) achieved through harmonization or other means; or (c) based upon an agreement or arrangement with the other Party or non-Party.

3. A Party according recognition of prudential measures under paragraph 2 shall provide adequate opportunity to another Party to demonstrate that circumstances exist in which there are or would be equivalent regulation, oversight, implementation of regulation, and if appropriate, procedures concerning the sharing of information between the Parties.

4. Where a Party accords recognition of prudential measures under paragraph 2(c) and the circumstances set out in paragraph 3 exist, the Party shall provide adequate opportunity to another Party to negotiate accession to the agreement or arrangement, or to negotiate a comparable agreement or arrangement.

Article 1407: New Financial Services and Data Processing

1. Each Party shall permit a financial institution of another Party to provide any new financial service of a type similar to those services that the Party permits its own financial institutions, in like circumstances, to provide under its domestic law. A Party may determine the institutional and juridical form through which the service may be provided and may require authorization for the provision of the service. Where such authorization is 6 required, a decision shall be made within a reasonable

time and the authorization may only be refused for prudential reasons.

2. Each Party shall permit a financial institution of another Party to transfer information in electronic or other form, into and out of the Party's territory, for data processing where such processing is required in the ordinary course of such institution's business.

Article 1408: Senior Management and Boards of Directors

1. No Party may require financial institutions of another Party to engage individuals of any particular nationality as senior managerial or other essential personnel.

2. No Party may require that more than a simple majority of the board of directors of a financial institution of another Party be composed of nationals of the Party, persons residing in the territory of the Party, or a combination thereof.

Article 1409: Reservations and Specific Commitments

1. Articles 1403 through 1408 do not apply to: (a) any existing non-conforming measure that is maintained by (i) a Party at the federal level, as set out in Section A of its Schedule to Annex VII, (ii) a state or province, for the time set out for the Parties specified in Annex 1409.1 for that state or province, and thereafter as described by the Party in Section A of its Schedule to Annex VII in accordance with Annex 1409.1, or (iii) a local government;

(b) the continuation or prompt renewal of any non-conforming measure referred to in subparagraph (a); or (c) an amendment to any non-conforming measure referred to in subparagraph (a) to the extent that the amendment does not decrease the conformity of the measure, as it existed immediately before the amendment, with Articles 1403 7 through 1408.

2. Articles 1403 through 1408 do not apply to any non-conforming measure that a Party adopts or maintains in accordance with Section B of its Schedule to Annex VII.

3. Section C of each Party's Schedule to Annex VII sets out certain specific commitments by that Party.

4. Where a Party has set out a reservation to Article 1102, 1103, 1202 or 1203 in its Schedule to Annex I, II, III or IV, the reservation shall be deemed to constitute a reservation to Article 1405 or 1406, as the case may be, to the extent that the measure, sector, subsector or activity set out in the reservation is covered by this Chapter.

Article 1410: Exceptions

1. Nothing in this Part shall be construed to prevent a Party from adopting or maintaining reasonable measures for prudential reasons, such as: (a) the protection of investors, depositors, financial market participants, policy-holders, policy-claimants, or persons to whom a fiduciary duty is owed by a financial institution or cross-border financial service provider; (b) the maintenance of the safety, soundness, integrity or financial responsibility of financial institutions or cross-border financial service providers; and (c) ensuring the integrity and stability of a Party's financial system.

2. Nothing in this Part applies to non-discriminatory measures of general application taken by any public entity in pursuit of monetary and related credit policies or exchange rate policies. This paragraph shall not affect a Party's obligations under Article 1106 (Investment–Performance Requirements) with respect to measures covered by Chapter Eleven (Investment) or Article 1109 (Investments–Transfers).

3. Article 1405 shall not apply to the granting by a Party to a financial institution of an exclusive right to

provide a financial service referred to in Article 1401(3)(a).

4. Notwithstanding Article 1109(1), (2) and (3), as incorporated into this Chapter, a Party may prevent or limit transfers by a financial institution or cross-border financial services provider to, or for the benefit of, an affiliate of or person related to such institution or provider, through the equitable, non-discriminatory and good faith application of measures relating to maintenance of the safety, soundness, integrity or financial responsibility of financial institutions or cross-border financial service providers. This paragraph does not prejudice any other provision of this Agreement that permits a Party to restrict transfers.

* * *

Article 1412: Financial Services Committee

1. The Parties hereby establish the Financial Services Committee. The principal representative of each Party shall be an official of the Party's authority responsible for financial services set out in Annex 1412.1.

2. Subject to Article 2001(2)(d) (Free Trade Commission), the Committee shall: (a) supervise the implementation of this Chapter and its further elaboration; (b) consider issues regarding financial services that are referred to it by a Party; and (c) participate in the dispute settlement procedures in accordance with Article 1415.

3. The Committee shall meet annually to assess the functioning of this Agreement as it applies to financial services. The Committee shall inform the Commission of the results of each annual meeting.

Article 1413: Consultations

1. A Party may request consultations with another Party regarding any matter arising under this Agreement

that affects financial services. The other Party shall give sympathetic consideration to the request. The consulting Parties shall report the results of their consultations to the Committee at its annual meeting.

* * *

Article 1414: Dispute Settlement

1.   Section B of Chapter Twenty (Institutional Arrangements and Dispute Settlement Procedures) applies as modified by this Article to the settlement of disputes arising under this Chapter.

2.   The Parties shall establish and maintain a roster of up to 15 individuals who are willing and able to serve as financial services panelists. Financial services roster members shall be appointed by consensus for terms of three years, and may be reappointed.

* * *

4.   Where a Party claims that a dispute arises under this Chapter, Article 2011 (Panel Selection) shall apply, except that: (a) where the disputing Parties so agree, the panel shall be composed entirely of panelists meeting the qualifications in paragraph 3; and (b) in any other case, (i) each disputing Party may select panelists meeting the qualifications set out in paragraph 3 or in Article 2010(1) (Qualifications of Panelists), and (ii) if the Party complained against invokes Article 1410, the chair of the panel shall meet the qualifications set out in paragraph 3.

5.   In any dispute where a panel finds a measure to be inconsistent with the obligations of this Agreement and the measure affects: (a) only the financial services sector, the complaining Party may suspend benefits only in the financial services sector; (b) the financial services sector and any other sector, the complaining Party may suspend benefits in the financial services sector that have an effect equivalent to the effect of the measure in the Party's

financial services sector; or (c) only a sector other than the financial services sector, the complaining Party may not suspend benefits in the financial services sector.

Article 1415: Investment Disputes in Financial Services

1. Where an investor of another Party submits a claim under Article 1116 or 1117 to arbitration under Section B of Chapter Eleven (Investment—Settlement of Disputes between a Party and an Investor of Another Party) against a Party and the disputing Party invokes Article 1410, on request of the disputing Party, the Tribunal shall refer the matter in writing to the Committee for a decision. The Tribunal may not proceed pending receipt of a decision or report under this Article.

2. In a referral pursuant to paragraph 1, the Committee shall decide the issue of whether and to what extent Article 1410 is a valid defense to the claim of the investor. The Committee shall transmit a copy of its decision to the Tribunal and to the Commission. The decision shall be binding on the Tribunal.

3. Where the Committee has not decided the issue within 60 days of the receipt of the referral under paragraph 1, the disputing Party or the Party of the disputing investor may request the establishment of an arbitral panel under Article 2008 (Request for an Arbitral Panel). The panel shall be constituted in accordance with Article 1414. Further to Article 2017 (Final Report), the panel shall transmit its final report to the Committee and to the Tribunal. The report shall be binding on the Tribunal.

4. Where no request for the establishment of a panel pursuant to paragraph 3 has been made within 10 days of the expiration of the 60–day period referred to in paragraph 3, the Tribunal may proceed to decide the matter.

Article 1416: Definitions

For purposes of this Chapter:

cross-border financial service provider of a Party means a person of a Party that is engaged in the business of providing a financial service within the territory of the Party and that seeks to provide or provides financial services through the cross-border provision of such services;

cross-border provision of a financial service or cross-border trade in financial services means the provision of a financial service: (a) from the territory of a Party into the territory of another Party; (b) in the territory of a Party by a person of that Party to a person of another Party; or (c) by a person of a Party in the territory of another Party; but does not include the provision of a service in the territory of a Party by an investment, as defined in Article 1138 (Investment—Definitions), in that territory;

financial institution means any financial intermediary or other enterprise that is authorized to do business and regulated or supervised as a financial institution under the law of the Party in whose territory it is located;

financial institution of another Party means a financial institution, including a branch, located in the territory of a Party that is controlled by persons of another Party;

financial service means a service of a financial nature, including insurance, and a service incidental or auxiliary to a service of a financial nature;

financial service provider of a Party means a person of a Party that is engaged in the business of providing a financial service within the territory of that Party;

investment means "investment" as defined in Article 1138, except that, with respect to "loans" and "debt securities" referred to in that Article: (a) a loan to or debt security issued by a financial institution is an investment only where it is treated as regulatory capital by the Party in whose territory the financial institution is located; and (b) a loan granted by or debt security owned by a financial institution, other than a loan to or debt security of a financial institution referred to in subparagraph (a), is not an investment;

For greater certainty: (c) a loan to, or debt security issued by, a Party or a state enterprise thereof is not a debt security; and (d) a loan granted by or debt security owned by a cross-border financial service provider, other than a loan to or debt security issued by a financial institution, is an investment as defined under Article 1138;

investor of a Party means a Party or state enterprise thereof, or a person of that Party, that seeks to make, makes, or has made an investment;

new financial service means a financial service not provided in the Party's territory that is provided within the territory of another Party, and includes any new form of delivery of a financial service or the sale of a financial product that is not sold in the Party's territory;

person of a Party means "person of a Party" as defined in Chapter Two (General Definitions) and, for greater certainty, does not include a branch of an enterprise of a non-Party;

public entity means a central bank or monetary authority of a Party, or any financial institution owned or controlled by a Party; and

self-regulatory organization means any non-governmental body, including any securities or futures exchange or market, clearing agency, or other organization or association, that exercises its own or delegated regulatory or supervisory authority over financial service providers or financial institutions.

Chapter Fifteen—Competition Policy, Monopolies and State Enterprises

Article 1501: Competition Law

1. Each Party shall adopt or maintain measures to proscribe anti-competitive business conduct and take ap-

propriate action with respect thereto, recognizing that such measures will enhance the fulfillment of the objectives of this Agreement. To this end the Parties shall consult from time to time about the effectiveness of measures undertaken by each Party.

2. Each Party recognizes the importance of cooperation and coordination among their authorities to further effective competition law enforcement in the free trade area. The Parties shall cooperate on issues of competition law enforcement policy, including mutual legal assistance, notification, consultation and exchange of information relating to the enforcement of competition laws and policies in the free trade area.

3. No Party may have recourse to dispute settlement under this Agreement for any matter arising under this Article.

Article 1502: Monopolies and State Enterprises

1. Nothing in this Agreement shall be construed to prevent a Party from designating a monopoly.

2. Where a Party intends to designate a monopoly and the designation may affect the interests of persons of another Party, the Party shall: (a) wherever possible, provide prior written notification to the other Party of the designation; and (b) endeavor to introduce at the time of the designation such conditions on the operation of the monopoly as will minimize or eliminate any nullification or impairment of benefits in the sense of Annex 2004 (Nullification and Impairment).

3. Each Party shall ensure, through regulatory control, administrative supervision or the application of other measures, that any privately-owned monopoly that it designates and any government monopoly that it maintains or designates:

(a) acts in a manner that is not inconsistent with the Party's obligations under this Agreement wherever such a monopoly exercises any regulatory, administrative or other governmental authority that the Party has delegated to it in connection with the monopoly good or service, such as the power to grant import or export licenses, approve commercial transactions or impose quotas, fees or other charges;

(b) except to comply with any terms of its designation that are not inconsistent with subparagraph (c) or (d), acts solely in accordance with commercial considerations in its purchase or sale of the monopoly good or service in the relevant market, including with regard to price, quality, availability, marketability, transportation and other terms and conditions of purchase or sale;

(c) provides non-discriminatory treatment to investments of investors, to goods and to service providers of another Party in its purchase or sale of the monopoly good or service in the relevant market; and

(d) does not use its monopoly position to engage, either directly or indirectly, including through its dealings with its parent, its subsidiary or other enterprise with common ownership, in anticompetitive practices in a non-monopolized market in its territory that adversely affect an investment of an investor of another Party, including through the discriminatory provision of the monopoly good or service, cross-subsidization or predatory conduct.

4. Paragraph 3 does not apply to procurement by governmental agencies of goods or services for governmental purposes and not with a view to commercial resale or with a view to use in the production of goods or the provision of services for commercial sale.

5. For purposes of this Article "maintain" means designate prior to the date of entry into force of this Agreement and existing on January 1, 1994.

Article 1503: State Enterprises

1. Nothing in this Agreement shall be construed to prevent a Party from maintaining or establishing a state enterprise.

2. Each Party shall ensure, through regulatory control, administrative supervision or the application of other measures, that any state enterprise that it maintains or establishes acts in a manner that is not inconsistent with the Party's obligations under Chapters Eleven (Investment) and Fourteen (Financial Services) wherever such enterprise exercises any regulatory, administrative or other governmental authority that the Party has delegated to it, such as the power to expropriate, grant licenses, approve commercial transactions or impose quotas, fees or other charges.

3. Each Party shall ensure that any state enterprise that it maintains or establishes accords non-discriminatory treatment in the sale of its goods or services to investments in the Party's territory of investors of another Party.

* * *

Chapter Sixteen—Temporary Entry for Business Persons

Article 1601: General Principles

Further to Article 102 (Objectives), this Chapter reflects the preferential trading relationship between the Parties, the desirability of facilitating temporary entry on a reciprocal basis and of establishing transparent criteria and procedures for temporary entry, and the need to ensure border security and to protect the domestic labor force and permanent employment in their respective territories.

Article 1602: General Obligations

1. Each Party shall apply its measures relating to the provisions of this Chapter in accordance with Article 1601 and, in particular, shall apply expeditiously those measures so as to avoid unduly impairing or delaying trade in

goods or services or conduct of investment activities under this Agreement.

2. The Parties shall endeavor to develop and adopt common criteria, definitions and interpretations for the implementation of this Chapter.

Article 1603: Grant of Temporary Entry

1. Each Party shall grant temporary entry to business persons who are otherwise qualified for entry under applicable measures relating to public health and safety and national security, in accordance with this Chapter, including the provisions of Annex 1603.

2. A Party may refuse to issue an immigration document authorizing employment to a business person where the temporary entry of that person might affect adversely: (a) the settlement of any labor dispute that is in progress at the place or intended place of employment; or (b) the employment of any person who is involved in such dispute.

3. When a Party refuses pursuant to paragraph 2 to issue an immigration document authorizing employment, it shall: (a) inform in writing the business person of the reasons for the refusal; and (b) promptly notify in writing the Party whose business person has been refused entry of the reasons for the refusal.

4. Each Party shall limit any fees for processing applications for temporary entry of business persons to the approximate cost of services rendered.

* * *

Article 1606: Dispute Settlement

1. A Party may not initiate proceedings under Article 2007 (Commission—Good Offices, Conciliation and Mediation) regarding a refusal to grant temporary entry under this Chapter or a particular case arising under Article

1602(1) unless: (a) the matter involves a pattern of practice; and (b) the business person has exhausted the available administrative remedies regarding the particular matter.

2. The remedies referred to in paragraph (1)(b) shall be deemed to be exhausted if a final determination in the matter has not been issued by the competent authority within one year of the institution of an administrative proceeding, and the failure to issue a determination is not attributable to delay caused by the business person.

* * *

Article 1608: Definitions

For purposes of this Chapter:

business person means a citizen of a Party who is engaged in trade in goods, the provision of services or the conduct of investment activities;

citizen means "citizen" as defined in Annex 1608 for the Parties specified in that Annex;

existing means "existing" as defined in Annex 1608 for the Parties specified in that Annex; and

temporary entry means entry into the territory of a Party by a business person of another Party without the intent to establish permanent residence.

Annex 1603—Temporary Entry for Business Persons

Section A—Business Visitors

* * *

Section B—Traders and Investors

* * *

Section C—Intra–Company Transferees

* * *

Section D—Professionals

* * *

PART SIX—INTELLECTUAL PROPERTY
Chapter Seventeen—Intellectual Property
Article 1701: Nature and Scope of Obligations

1. Each Party shall provide in its territory to the nationals of another Party adequate and effective protection and enforcement of intellectual property rights, while ensuring that measures to enforce intellectual property rights do not themselves become barriers to legitimate trade.

2. To provide adequate and effective protection and enforcement of intellectual property rights, each Party shall, at a minimum, give effect to this Chapter and to the substantive provisions of: (a) the Geneva Convention for the Protection of Producers of Phonograms Against Unauthorized Duplication of their Phonograms, 1971 (Geneva Convention); (b) the Berne Convention for the Protection of Literary and Artistic Works, 1971 (Berne Convention); (c) the Paris Convention for the Protection of Industrial Property, 1967 (Paris Convention); and (d) the International Convention for the Protection of New Varieties of Plants, 1978 (UPOV Convention), or the International Convention for the Protection of New Varieties of Plants, 1991 (UPOV Convention).

If a Party has not acceded to the specified text of any such Conventions on or before the date of entry into force of this Agreement, it shall make every effort to accede.

3. Annex 1701.3 applies to the Parties specified in that Annex.

Article 1702: More Extensive Protection

A Party may implement in its domestic law more extensive protection of intellectual property rights than is required under this Agreement, provided that such protection is not inconsistent with this Agreement.

Article 1703: National Treatment

1.   Each Party shall accord to nationals of another Party treatment no less favorable than that it accords to its own nationals with regard to the protection and enforcement of all intellectual property rights. In respect of sound recordings, each Party shall provide such treatment to producers and performers of another Party, except that a Party may limit rights of performers of another Party in respect of secondary uses of sound recordings to those rights its nationals are accorded in the territory of such other Party.

2.   No Party may, as a condition of according national treatment under this Article, require right holders to comply with any formalities or conditions in order to acquire rights in respect of copyright and related rights.

3.   A Party may derogate from paragraph 1 in relation to its judicial and administrative procedures for the protection of enforcement of intellectual property rights, including any procedure requiring a national of another Party to designate for service of process an address in the Party's territory or to appoint an agent in the Party's territory, if the derogation is consistent with the relevant Convention listed in Article 1701(2), provided that such derogation: (a) is necessary to secure compliance with measures that are not inconsistent with this Chapter; and (b) is not applied in a manner that would constitute a disguised restriction on trade.

4.   No Party shall have any obligation under this Article with respect to procedures provided in multilateral agreements concluded under the auspices of the World

Intellectual Property Organization relating to the acquisition or maintenance of intellectual property rights.

Article 1704: Control of Abusive or Anticompetitive Practices or Conditions

Nothing in this Chapter shall prevent a Party from specifying in its domestic law licensing practices or conditions that may in particular cases constitute an abuse of intellectual property rights having an adverse effect on competition in the relevant market. A Party may adopt or maintain, consistent with the other provisions of this Agreement, appropriate measures to prevent or control such practices or conditions.

Article 1705: Copyright

1. Each Party shall protect the works covered by Article 2 of the Berne Convention, including any other works that embody original expression within the meaning of that Convention. In particular: (a) all types of computer programs are literary works within the meaning of the Berne Convention and each Party shall protect them as such; and (b) compilations of data or other material, whether in machine readable or other form, which by reason of the selection or arrangement of their contents constitute intellectual creations, shall be protected as such.

The protection a Party provides under subparagraph (b) shall not extend to the data or material itself, or prejudice any copyright subsisting in that data or material.

2. Each Party shall provide to authors and their successors in interest those rights enumerated in the Berne Convention in respect of works covered by paragraph 1, including the right to authorize or prohibit: (a) the importation into the Party's territory of copies of the work made without the right holder's authorization; (b) the first public distribution of the original and each copy of

the work by sale, rental or otherwise; (c) the communication of a work to the public; and (d) the commercial rental of the original or a copy of a computer program.

Subparagraph (d) shall not apply where the copy of the computer program is not itself an essential object of the rental. Each Party shall provide that putting the original or a copy of a computer program on the market with the right holder's consent shall not exhaust the rental right.

3. Each Party shall provide that for copyright and related rights: (a) any person acquiring or holding economic rights may freely and separately transfer such rights by contract for purposes of their exploitation and enjoyment by the transferee; and (b) any person acquiring or holding such economic rights by virtue of a contract, including contracts of employment underlying the creation of works and sound recordings, shall be able to exercise those rights in its own name and enjoy fully the benefits derived from those rights.

4. Each Party shall provide that, where the term of protection of a work, other than a photographic work or a work of applied art, is to be calculated on a basis other than the life of a natural person, the term shall be not less than 50 years from the end of the calendar year of the first authorized publication of the work or, failing such authorized publication within 50 years from the making of the work, 50 years from the end of the calendar year of making.

5. Each Party shall confine limitations or exceptions to the rights provided for in this Article to certain special cases that do not conflict with a normal exploitation of the work and do not unreasonably prejudice the legitimate interests of the right holder.

6. No Party may grant translation and reproduction licenses permitted under the Appendix to the Berne Convention where legitimate needs in that Party's territory for copies or translations of the work could be met by the

right holder's voluntary actions but for obstacles created by the Party's measures.

7. Annex 1705.7 applies to the Parties specified in that Annex.

Article 1706: Sound Recordings

1. Each Party shall provide to the producer of a sound recording the right to authorize or prohibit: (a) the direct or indirect reproduction of the sound recording; (b) the importation into the Party's territory of copies of the sound recording made without the producer's authorization; (c) the first public distribution of the original and each copy of the sound recording by sale, rental or otherwise; and (d) the commercial rental of the original or a copy of the sound recording, except where expressly otherwise provided in a contract between the producer of the sound recording and the authors of the works fixed therein.

Each Party shall provide that putting the original or a copy of a sound recording on the market with the right holder's consent shall not exhaust the rental right.

2. Each Party shall provide a term of protection for sound recordings of at least 50 years from the end of the calendar year in which the fixation was made.

3. Each Party shall confine limitations or exceptions to the rights provided for in this Article to certain special cases that do not conflict with a normal exploitation of the sound recording and do not unreasonably prejudice the legitimate interests of the right holder.

Article 1707: Protection of Encrypted Program–Carrying Satellite Signals

Within one year from the date of entry into force of this Agreement, each Party shall make it: (a) a criminal offense to manufacture, import, sell, lease or otherwise make available a device or system that is primarily of assistance in decoding an encrypted program-carrying satellite signal without the authorization of the lawful distributor of such signal; and (b) a civil offense to receive, in connection with commercial activities, or further distribute, an encrypted program-carrying satellite signal that has been decoded without the authorization of the lawful distributor of the signal or to engage in any activity prohibited under subparagraph (a).

Each Party shall provide that any civil offense established under subparagraph (b) shall be actionable by any person that holds an interest in the content of such signal.

Article 1708: Trademarks

1. For purposes of this Agreement, a trademark consists of any sign, or any combination of signs, capable of distinguishing the goods or services of one person from those of another, including personal names, designs, letters, numerals, colors, figurative elements, or the shape of goods or of their packaging. Trademarks shall include service marks and collective marks, and may include certification marks. A Party may require, as a condition for registration that a sign be visually perceptible.

2. Each Party shall provide to the owner of a registered trademark the right to prevent all persons not having the owner's consent from using in commerce identical or similar signs for goods or services that are identical or similar to those goods or services in respect of which the owner's trademark is registered, where such use would result in a likelihood of confusion. In the case of the use of an identical sign for identical goods or services, a likelihood of confusion shall be presumed. The rights described above shall not prejudice any prior rights, nor shall they affect the possibility of a Party making rights available on the basis of use.

3. A Party may make registrability depend on use. However, actual use of a trademark shall not be a condition for filing an application for registration. No Party may refuse an application solely on the ground that intended use has not taken place before the expiry of a period of three years from the date of application for registration.

4. Each Party shall provide a system for the registration of trademarks, which shall include: (a) examination of applications; (b) notice to be given to an applicant of the reasons for the refusal to register a trademark; (c) a reasonable opportunity for the applicant to respond to the notice; (d) publication of each trademark either before or promptly after it is registered; and (e) a reasonable opportunity for interested persons to petition to cancel the registration of a trademark.

A Party may provide for a reasonable opportunity for interested persons to oppose the registration of a trademark.

5. The nature of the goods or services to which a trademark is to be applied shall in no case form an obstacle to the registration of the trademark.

6. Article 6<bis> of the Paris Convention shall apply, with such modifications as may be necessary, to services. In determining whether a trademark is well-known, account shall be taken of the knowledge of the trademark in the relevant sector of the public, including knowledge in the Party's territory obtained as a result of the promotion of the trademark. No Party may require that the reputation of the trademark extend beyond the sector of the public that normally deals with the relevant goods or services.

7. Each Party shall provide that the initial registration of a trademark be for a term of at least 10 years and that the registration be indefinitely renewable for terms

of not less than 10 years when conditions for renewal have been met.

8.   Each Party shall require the use of a trademark to maintain a registration. The registration may be canceled for the reason of non-use only after an uninterrupted period of at least two years of non-use, unless valid reasons based on the existence of obstacles to such use are shown by the trademark owner. Each Party shall recognize, as valid reasons for non-use, circumstances arising independently of the will of the trademark owner that constitute an obstacle to the use of the trademark, such as import restrictions on, or other government requirements for, goods or services identified by the trademark.

9.   Each Party shall recognize use of a trademark by a person other than the trademark owner, where such use is subject to the owner's control, as use of the trademark for purposes of maintaining the registration.

10.   No Party may encumber the use of a trademark in commerce by special requirements, such as a use that reduces the trademark's function as an indication of source or a use with another trademark.

11.   A Party may determine conditions on the licensing and assignment of trademarks, it being understood that the compulsory licensing of trademarks shall not be permitted and that the owner of a registered trademark shall have the right to assign its trademark with or without the transfer of the business to which the trademark belongs.

12.   A Party may provide limited exceptions to the rights conferred by a trademark, such as fair use of descriptive terms, provided that such exceptions take into account the legitimate interests of the trademark owner and of other persons.

13.   Each Party shall prohibit the registration as a trademark of words, at least in English, French or Span-

ish, that generically designate goods or services or types of goods or services to which the trademark applies.

14. Each Party shall refuse to register trademarks that consist of or comprise immoral, deceptive or scandalous matter, or matter that may disparage or falsely suggest a connection with persons, living or dead, institutions, beliefs or any Party's national symbols, or bring them into contempt or disrepute.

Article 1709: Patents

1. Subject to paragraphs 2 and 3, each Party shall make patents available for any inventions, whether products or processes, in all fields of technology, provided that such inventions are new, result from an inventive step and are capable of industrial application. For purposes of this Article, a Party may deem the terms "inventive step" and "capable of industrial application" to be synonymous with the terms "non-obvious" and "useful", respectively.

2. A Party may exclude from patentability inventions if preventing in its territory the commercial exploitation of the inventions is necessary to protect ordre public or morality, including to protect human, animal or plant life or health or to avoid serious prejudice to nature or the environment, provided that the exclusion is not based solely on the ground that the Party prohibits commercial exploitation in its territory of the subject matter of the patent.

3. A Party may also exclude from patentability: (a) diagnostic, therapeutic and surgical methods for the treatment of humans or animals; (b) plants and animals other than microorganisms; and (c) essentially biological processes for the production of plants or animals, other than non-biological and microbiological processes for such production.

Notwithstanding subparagraph (b), each Party shall provide for the protection of plant varieties through patents, an effective scheme of sui generis protection, or both.

4. If a Party has not made available product patent protection for pharmaceutical or agricultural chemicals commensurate with paragraph 1: (a) as of January 1, 1992, for subject matter that relates to naturally occurring substances prepared or produced by, or significantly derived from, microbiological processes and intended for food or medicine, and (b) as of July 1, 1991, for any other subject matter, that Party shall provide to the inventor of any such product or its assignee the means to obtain product patent protection for such product for the unexpired term of the patent for such product granted in another Party, as long as the product has not been marketed in the Party providing protection under this paragraph and the person seeking such protection makes a timely request.

5. Each Party shall provide that: (a) where the subject matter of a patent is a product, the patent shall confer on the patent owner the right to prevent other persons from making, using or selling the subject matter of the patent, without the patent owner's consent; and (b) where the subject matter of a patent is a process, the patent shall confer on the patent owner the right to prevent other persons from using that process and from using, selling, or importing at least the product obtained directly by that process, without the patent owner's consent.

6. A Party may provide limited exceptions to the exclusive rights conferred by a patent, provided that such exceptions do not unreasonably conflict with a normal exploitation of the patent and do not unreasonably prejudice the legitimate interests of the patent owner, taking into account the legitimate interests of other persons.

7. Subject to paragraphs 2 and 3, patents shall be available and patent rights enjoyable without discrimination as to the field of technology, the territory of the

Party where the invention was made and whether products are imported or locally produced.

8. A Party may revoke a patent only when: (a) grounds exist that would have justified a refusal to grant the patent; or (b) the grant of a compulsory license has not remedied the lack of exploitation of the patent.

9. Each Party shall permit patent owners to assign and transfer by succession their patents, and to conclude licensing contracts.

10. Where the law of a Party allows for use of the subject matter of a patent, other than that use allowed under paragraph 6, without the authorization of the right holder, including use by the government or other persons authorized by the government, the Party shall respect the following provisions: (a) authorization of such use shall be considered on its individual merits;

(b) such use may only be permitted if, prior to such use, the proposed user has made efforts to obtain authorization from the right holder on reasonable commercial terms and conditions and such efforts have not been successful within a reasonable period of time. The requirement to make such efforts may be waived by a Party in the case of a national emergency or other circumstances of extreme urgency or in cases of public non-commercial use. In situations of national emergency or other circumstances of extreme urgency, the right holder shall, nevertheless, be notified as soon as reasonably practicable. In the case of public non-commercial use, where the government or contractor, without making a patent search, knows or has demonstrable grounds to know that a valid patent is or will be used by or for the government, the right holder shall be informed promptly;

(c) the scope and duration of such use shall be limited to the purpose for which it was authorized; (d) such use shall be non-exclusive; (e) such use shall be non-assignable, except with that part of the enterprise or goodwill that enjoys such use; (f) any such use shall be authorized predominantly for the supply of the Party's domestic market;

(g) authorization for such use shall be liable, subject to adequate protection of the legitimate interests of the persons so authorized, to be terminated if and when the circumstances that led to it cease to exist and are unlikely to recur. The competent authority shall have the authority to review, on motivated request, the continued existence of these circumstances;

(h) the right holder shall be paid adequate remuneration in the circumstances of each case, taking into account the economic value of the authorization; (i) the legal validity of any decision relating to the authorization shall be subject to judicial or other independent review by a distinct higher authority; (j) any decision relating to the remuneration provided in respect of such use shall be subject to judicial or other independent review by a distinct higher authority;

(k) the Party shall not be obliged to apply the conditions set out in subparagraphs (b) and (f) where such use is permitted to remedy a practice determined after judicial or administrative process to be anticompetitive. The need to correct anticompetitive practices may be taken into account in determining the amount of remuneration in such cases. Competent authorities shall have the authority to refuse termination of authorization if and when the conditions that led to such authorization are likely to recur;

(*l*) the Party shall not authorize the use of the subject matter of a patent to permit the exploitation of another patent except as a remedy for an adjudicated violation of domestic laws regarding anticompetitive practices.

11. Where the subject matter of a patent is a process for obtaining a product, each Party shall, in any infringement proceeding, place on the defendant the burden of

establishing that the allegedly infringing product was made by a process other than the patented process in one of the following situations: (a) the product obtained by the patented process is new; or (b) a substantial likelihood exists that the allegedly infringing product was made by the process and the patent owner has been unable through reasonable efforts to determine the process actually used.

In the gathering and evaluation of evidence, the legitimate interests of the defendant in protecting its trade secrets shall be taken into account.

12.   Each Party shall provide a term of protection for patents of at least 20 years from the date of filing or 17 years from the date of grant. A Party may extend the term of patent protection, in appropriate cases, to compensate for delays caused by regulatory approval processes.

Article 1710: Layout Designs of Semiconductor Integrated Circuits

* * *

Article 1711: Trade Secrets

1.   Each Party shall provide the legal means for any person to prevent trade secrets from being disclosed to, acquired by, or used by others without the consent of the person lawfully in control of the information in a manner contrary to honest commercial practices, in so far as:

(a) the information is secret in the sense that it is not, as a body or in the precise configuration and assembly of its components, generally known among or readily accessible to persons that normally deal with the kind of information in question; (b) the information has actual or potential commercial value because it is secret; and (c) the person lawfully in control of the information has taken reasonable steps under the circumstances to keep it secret.

2. A Party may require that to qualify for protection a trade secret must be evidenced in documents, electronic or magnetic means, optical discs, microfilms, films or other similar instruments.

3. No Party may limit the duration of protection for trade secrets, so long as the conditions in paragraph 1 exist.

4. No Party may discourage or impede the voluntary licensing of trade secrets by imposing excessive or discriminatory conditions on such licenses or conditions that dilute the value of the trade secrets.

5. If a Party requires, as a condition for approving the marketing of pharmaceutical or agricultural chemical products that utilize new chemical entities, the submission of undisclosed test or other data necessary to determine whether the use of such products is safe and effective, the Party shall protect against disclosure of the data of persons making such submissions, where the origination of such data involves considerable effort, except where the disclosure is necessary to protect the public or unless steps are taken to ensure that the data is protected against unfair commercial use.

6. Each Party shall provide that for data subject to paragraph 5 that are submitted to the Party after the date of entry into force of this Agreement, no person other than the person that submitted them may, without the latter's permission, rely on such data in support of an application for product approval during a reasonable period of time after their submission. For this purpose, a reasonable period shall normally mean not less than five years from the date on which the Party granted approval to the person that produced the data for approval to market its product, taking account of the nature of the data and the person's efforts and expenditures in produc-

ing them. Subject to this provision, there shall be no limitation on any Party to implement abbreviated approval procedures for such products on the basis of bioequivalence and bioavailability studies.

7. Where a Party relies on a marketing approval granted by another Party, the reasonable period of exclusive use of the data submitted in connection with obtaining the approval relied on shall begin with the date of the first marketing approval relied on.

Article 1712: Geographical Indications

* * *

Article 1713: Industrial Designs

* * *

Article 1714: Enforcement of Intellectual Property Rights: General Provisions

1. Each Party shall ensure that enforcement procedures, as specified in this Article and Articles 1715 through 1718, are available under its domestic law so as to permit effective action to be taken against any act of infringement of intellectual property rights covered by this Chapter, including expeditious remedies to prevent infringements and remedies to deter further infringements. Such enforcement procedures shall be applied so as to avoid the creation of barriers to legitimate trade and to provide for safeguards against abuse of the procedures.

2. Each Party shall ensure that its procedures for the enforcement of intellectual property rights are fair and equitable, are not unnecessarily complicated or costly, and do not entail unreasonable time-limits or unwarranted delays.

3. Each Party shall provide that decisions on the merits of a case in judicial and administrative enforce-

ment proceedings shall: (a) preferably be in writing and preferably state the reasons on which the decisions are based; (b) be made available at least to the parties in a proceeding without undue delay; and (c) be based only on evidence in respect of which such parties were offered the opportunity to be heard.

4.   Each Party shall ensure that parties in a proceeding have an opportunity to have final administrative decisions reviewed by a judicial authority of that Party and, subject to jurisdictional provisions in its domestic laws concerning the importance of a case, to have reviewed at least the legal aspects of initial judicial decisions on the merits of a case. Notwithstanding the above, no Party shall be required to provide for judicial review of acquittals in criminal cases.

5.   Nothing in this Article or Articles 1715 through 1718 shall be construed to require a Party to establish a judicial system for the enforcement of intellectual property rights distinct from that Party's system for the enforcement of laws in general.

6.   For the purposes of Articles 1715 through 1718, the term "right holder" includes federations and associations having legal standing to assert such rights.

Article 1715: Specific Procedural and Remedial Aspects of Civil and Administrative Procedures

1.   Each Party shall make available to right holders civil judicial procedures for the enforcement of any intellectual property right covered by this Chapter. Each Party shall provide that: (a) defendants have the right to written notice that is timely and contains sufficient detail, including the basis of the claims; (b) parties in a proceeding are allowed to be represented by independent legal counsel; (c) the procedures do not include imposition of overly burdensome requirements concerning mandatory personal appearances; (d) all parties in a proceeding are

duly entitled to substantiate their claims and to present relevant evidence; and (e) the procedures include a means to identify and protect confidential information.

2.   Each Party shall provide that its judicial authorities shall have the authority:

(a) where a party in a proceeding has presented reasonably available evidence sufficient to support its claims and has specified evidence relevant to the substantiation of its claims that is within the control of the opposing party, to order the opposing party to produce such evidence, subject in appropriate cases to conditions that ensure the protection of confidential information;

(b) where a party in a proceeding voluntarily and without good reason refuses access to, or otherwise does not provide relevant evidence under that party's control within a reasonable period, or significantly impedes a proceeding relating to an enforcement action, to make preliminary and final determinations, affirmative or negative, on the basis of the evidence presented, including the complaint or the allegation presented by the party adversely affected by the denial of access to evidence, subject to providing the parties an opportunity to be heard on the allegations or evidence;

(c) to order a party in a proceeding to desist from an infringement, including to prevent the entry into the channels of commerce in their jurisdiction of imported goods that involve the infringement of an intellectual property right, which order shall be enforceable at least immediately after customs clearance of such goods;

(d) to order the infringer of an intellectual property right to pay the right holder damages adequate to compensate for the injury the right holder has suffered because of the infringement where the infringer knew or had reasonable grounds to know that it was engaged in an infringing activity;

(e) to order an infringer of an intellectual property right to pay the right holder's expenses, which may include appropriate attorney's fees; and

(f) to order a party in a proceeding at whose request measures were taken and who has abused enforcement procedures to provide adequate compensation to any party wrongfully enjoined or restrained in the proceeding for the injury suffered because of such abuse and to pay that party's expenses, which may include appropriate attorney's fees.

3. With respect to the authority referred to in subparagraph 2(c), no Party shall be obliged to provide such authority in respect of protected subject matter that is acquired or 20 ordered by a person before that person knew or had reasonable grounds to know that dealing in that subject matter would entail the infringement of an intellectual property right.

4. With respect to the authority referred to in subparagraph 2(d), a Party may, at least with respect to copyrighted works and sound recordings, authorize the judicial authorities to order recovery of profits or payment of pre-established damages, or both, even where the infringer did not know or had no reasonable grounds to know that it was engaged in an infringing activity.

5. Each Party shall provide that, in order to create an effective deterrent to infringement, its judicial authorities shall have the authority to order that:

(a) goods that they have found to be infringing be, without compensation of any sort, disposed of outside the channels of commerce in such a manner as to avoid any injury caused to the right holder or, unless this would be contrary to existing constitutional requirements, destroyed; and

(b) materials and implements the predominant use of which has been in the creation of the infringing goods be, without compensation of any sort, disposed of outside the channels of commerce in such a manner as to minimize the risks of further infringements.

In considering whether to issue such an order, judicial authorities shall take into account the need for proportionality between the seriousness of the infringement and the remedies ordered as well as the interests of other persons. In regard to counterfeit goods, the simple removal of the trademark unlawfully affixed shall not be sufficient, other than in exceptional cases, to permit release of the goods into the channels of commerce.

6. In respect of the administration of any law pertaining to the protection or enforcement of intellectual property rights, each Party shall only exempt both public authorities and officials from liability to appropriate remedial measures where actions are taken or intended in good faith in the course of the administration of such laws.

7. Notwithstanding the other provisions of Articles 1714 through 1718, where a Party is sued with respect to an infringement of an intellectual property right as a result of its use of that right or use on its behalf, that Party may limit the remedies available against it to the payment to the right holder of adequate remuneration in the circumstances of each case, taking into account the economic value of the use.

8. Each Party shall provide that, where a civil remedy can be ordered as a result of administrative procedures on the merits of a case, such procedures shall conform to principles equivalent in substance to those set out in this Article.

Article 1716: Provisional Measures

1. Each Party shall provide that its judicial authorities shall have the authority to order prompt and effective provisional measures:

(a) to prevent an infringement of any intellectual property right, and in particular to prevent the entry into the channels of commerce in their jurisdiction of allegedly infringing goods, including measures to prevent the entry of imported goods at least immediately after customs clearance; and (b) to preserve relevant evidence in regard to the alleged infringement.

* * *

Article 1717: Criminal Procedures and Penalties

1. Each Party shall provide criminal procedures and penalties to be applied at least in cases of willful trademark counterfeiting or copyright piracy on a commercial scale. Each Party shall provide that penalties available include imprisonment or monetary fines, or both, sufficient to provide a deterrent, consistent with the level of penalties applied for crimes of a corresponding gravity.

2. Each Party shall provide that, in appropriate cases, its judicial authorities may order the seizure, forfeiture and destruction of infringing goods and of any materials and implements the predominant use of which has been in the commission of the offense.

3. A Party may provide criminal procedures and penalties to be applied in cases of infringement of intellectual property rights, other than those in paragraph 1, where they are committed wilfully and on a commercial scale.

Article 1718: Enforcement of Intellectual Property Rights at the Border

1. Each Party shall, in conformity with this Article, adopt procedures to enable a right holder, who has valid grounds for suspecting that the importation of counterfeit trademark goods or pirated copyright goods may take place, to lodge an application in writing with its competent authorities, whether administrative or judicial, for the suspension by the customs administration of the

release of such goods into free circulation. No Party shall be obligated to apply such procedures to goods in transit. A Party may permit such an application to be made in respect of goods that involve other infringements of intellectual property rights, provided that the requirements of this Article are met. A Party may also provide for corresponding procedures concerning the suspension by the customs administration of the release of infringing goods destined for exportation from its territory.

2. Each Party shall require any applicant who initiates procedures under paragraph 1 to provide adequate evidence: (a) to satisfy that Party's competent authorities that, under the domestic laws of the country of importation, there is prima facie an infringement of its intellectual property right; and (b) to supply a sufficiently detailed description of the goods to make them readily recognizable by the customs administration. 24 The competent authorities shall inform the applicant within a reasonable period whether they have accepted the application and, if so, the period for which the customs administration will take action.

3. Each Party shall provide that its competent authorities shall have the authority to require an applicant under paragraph 1 to provide a security or equivalent assurance sufficient to protect the defendant and the competent authorities and to prevent abuse. Such security or equivalent assurance shall not unreasonably deter recourse to these procedures.

4. Each Party shall provide that, where pursuant to an application under procedures adopted pursuant to this Article, its customs administration suspends the release of goods involving industrial designs, patents, integrated circuits or trade secrets into free circulation on the basis of a decision other than by a judicial or other independent authority, and the period provided for in paragraphs 6 through 8 has expired without the granting of provisional relief by the duly empowered authority, and provided that

all other conditions for importation have been complied with, the owner, importer or consignee of such goods shall be entitled to their release on the posting of a security in an amount sufficient to protect the right holder against any infringement. Payment of such security shall not prejudice any other remedy available to the right holder, it being understood that the security shall be released if the right holder fails to pursue its right of action within a reasonable period of time.

5. Each Party shall provide that its customs administration shall promptly notify the importer and the applicant when the customs administration suspends the release of goods pursuant to paragraph 1.

6. Each Party shall provide that its customs administration shall release goods from suspension if within a period not exceeding 10 working days after the applicant under paragraph 1 has been served notice of the suspension: (a) the customs administration has not been informed that a party other than the defendant has initiated proceedings leading to a decision on the merits of the case, or (b) a competent authority has taken provisional measures prolonging the suspension, provided that all other conditions for importation or exportation have been met. Each Party shall provide that, in appropriate cases, the customs administration may extend the suspension by another 10 working days.

7. Each Party shall provide that if proceedings leading to a decision on the merits of the case have been initiated, a review, including a right to be heard, shall take place on request of the defendant with a view to deciding, within a reasonable period, whether the measures shall be modified, revoked or confirmed.

8. Notwithstanding paragraphs 6 and 7, where the suspension of the release of goods is carried out or continued in accordance with a provisional judicial measure, Article 1716(6) shall apply.

9. Each Party shall provide that its competent authorities shall have the authority to order the applicant under paragraph 1 to pay the importer, the consignee and the owner of the goods appropriate compensation for any injury caused to them through the wrongful detention of goods or through the detention of goods released pursuant to paragraph 6.

10. Without prejudice to the protection of confidential information, each Party shall provide that its competent authorities shall have the authority to give the right holder sufficient opportunity to have any goods detained by the customs administration inspected in order to substantiate its claims. Each Party shall also provide that its competent authorities have the authority to give the importer an equivalent opportunity to have any such goods inspected. Where the competent authorities have made a positive determination on the merits of a case, a Party may provide the competent authorities the authority to inform the right holder of the names and addresses of the consignor, the importer and the consignee, and of the quantity of the goods in question.

11. Where a Party requires its competent authorities to act on their own initiative and to suspend the release of goods in respect of which they have acquired prima facie evidence that an intellectual property right is being infringed:

(a) the competent authorities may at any time seek from the right holder any information that may assist them to exercise these powers; (b) the importer and the right holder shall be promptly notified of the suspension by the Party's competent authorities, and where the importer lodges an appeal against the suspension with competent authorities, the suspension shall be subject to the conditions, with such modifications as may be necessary, set out in paragraphs 6 through 8; and (c) the Party shall only exempt both public authorities and officials from liability to appropriate remedial measures where actions are taken or intended in good faith.

12.   Without prejudice to other rights of action open to the right holder and subject to the defendant's right to seek judicial review, each Party shall provide that its competent authorities shall have the authority to order the destruction or disposal of infringing goods in accordance with the principles set out in Article 1715(5). In regard to counterfeit goods, the authorities shall not allow the re-exportation of the infringing goods in an unaltered state or subject them to a different customs procedure, other than in exceptional circumstances.

13.   A Party may exclude from the application of paragraphs 1 through 12 small quantities of goods of a non-commercial nature contained in travellers' personal luggage or sent in small consignments that are not repetitive.

14.   Annex 1718.14 applies to the Parties specified in that Annex.

* * *

Article 1721: Definitions

1.   For purposes of this Chapter:

confidential information includes trade secrets, privileged information and other materials exempted from disclosure under the Party's domestic law.

2.   For purposes of this Agreement:

encrypted program-carrying satellite signal means a program-carrying satellite signal that is transmitted in a form whereby the aural or visual characteristics, or both, are modified or altered for the purpose of preventing the unauthorized reception, by persons without the authorized equipment that is designed to eliminate the effects of such modification or alteration, of a program carried in that signal;

geographical indication means any indication that identifies a good as originating in the territory of a Party, or a region or locality in that territory, where a particular quality, reputation or other characteristic of the good is essentially attributable to its geographical origin;

in a manner contrary to honest commercial practices means at least practices such as breach of contract, breach of confidence and inducement to breach, and includes the acquisition of undisclosed information by other persons who knew, or were grossly negligent in failing to know, that such practices were involved in the acquisition;

intellectual property rights refers to copyright and related rights, trademark rights, patent rights, rights in layout designs of semiconductor integrated circuits, trade secret rights, plant breeders' rights, rights in geographical indications and industrial design rights;

nationals of another Party means, in respect of the relevant intellectual property right, persons who would meet the criteria for eligibility for protection provided for in the Paris Convention (1967), the Berne Convention (1971), the Geneva Convention (1971), the International Convention for the Protection of Performers, Producers of Phonograms and Broadcasting Organizations (1961), the UPOV Convention (1978), the UPOV Convention (1991) or the Treaty on Intellectual Property in Respect of Integrated Circuits, as if each Party were a party to those Conventions, and with respect to intellectual property rights that are not the subject of these Conventions, "nationals of another Party" shall be understood to be at least individuals who are citizens or permanent residents of that Party and also includes any other natural person referred to in Annex 201.1 (Country–Specific Definitions);

public includes, with respect to rights of communication and performance of works provided for under Articles 11, 11<bis>(1) and 14(1)(ii) of the Berne Convention, with respect to dramatic, dramatico-musical, musical and cinematographic works, at least, any aggregation of individuals intended to be the object of, and capable of perceiving, communications or performances of works, regardless of whether they can do so at the same or different times or in the same or different places, provided that such an aggregation is larger than a family and its immediate circle of acquaintances or is not a group comprising a limited number of individuals having similarly close ties that has not been formed for the principal purpose of receiving such performances and communications of works; and

secondary uses of sound recordings means the use directly for broadcasting or for any other public communication of a sound recording.

* * *

PART SEVEN—ADMINISTRATIVE AND INSTITUTIONAL PROVISIONS

Chapter Eighteen—Publication, Notification and Administration of Laws

* * *

Chapter Nineteen—Review and Dispute Settlement in Antidumping and Countervailing Duty Matters

Article 1901: General Provisions

1. Article 1904 applies only with respect to goods that the competent investigating authority of the importing Party, applying the importing Party's antidumping or countervailing duty law to the facts of a specific case, determines are goods of another Party.

2. For purposes of Articles 1903 and 1904, panels shall be established in accordance with the provisions of Annex 1901.2.

3. Except for Article 2203 (Entry into Force), no provision of any other Chapter of this Agreement shall be construed as imposing obligations on a Party with respect to the Party's antidumping law or countervailing duty law.

Article 1902: Retention of Domestic Antidumping Law and Countervailing Duty Law

1. Each Party reserves the right to apply its antidumping law and countervailing duty law to goods imported from the territory of any other Party. Antidumping law and countervailing duty law include, as appropriate for each Party, relevant statutes, legislative history, regulations, administrative practice and judicial precedents.

2. Each Party reserves the right to change or modify its antidumping law or countervailing duty law, provided that in the case of an amendment to a Party's antidumping or countervailing duty statute:

(a) such amendment shall apply to goods from another Party only if the amending statute specifies that it applies to goods from that Party or from the Parties to this Agreement; (b) the amending Party notifies in writing the Parties to which the amendment applies of the amending statute as far in advance as possible of the date of enactment of such statute; (c) following notification, the amending Party, on request of any Party to which the amendment applies, consults with that Party prior to the enactment of the amending statute; and

(d) such amendment, as applicable to that other Party, is not inconsistent with (i) the General Agreement on Tariffs and Trade (GATT), the Agreement on Implementation of Article VI of the General Agreement on Tariffs and Trade (the Antidumping Code) or the Agreement on the Interpretation and Application of Articles VI, XVI and XXIII of the General Agreement on Tariffs and Trade (the Subsidies Code), or any successor agreement to which all the original signatories to this Agreement are party, or (ii) the object and purpose of this Agreement and this Chapter, which is to establish fair and predictable conditions for the progressive liberalization of trade between the Parties to this Agreement while maintaining effective and fair disciplines on unfair trade practices, such object and purpose to be ascertained from the provisions of this Agreement, its preamble and objectives, and the practices of the Parties.

Article 1903: Review of Statutory Amendments

1. A Party to which an amendment of another Party's antidumping or countervailing duty statute applies may request in writing that such amendment be referred to a binational panel for a declaratory opinion as to whether: (a) the amendment does not conform to the provisions of Article 1902(2)(d)(i) or (ii); or (b) such amendment has the function and effect of overturning a prior decision of a panel made pursuant to Article 1904 and does not conform to the provisions of Article 1902(2)(d)(i) or (ii).

Such declaratory opinion shall have force or effect only as provided in this Article.

2. The panel shall conduct its review in accordance with the procedures of Annex 1903.2.

3. In the event that the panel recommends modifications to the amending statute to remedy a non-conformity that it has identified in its opinion:

(a) the two Parties shall immediately begin consultations and shall seek to achieve a mutually satisfactory solution to the matter within 90 days of the issuance of the panel's final declaratory opinion. Such solution may include seeking corrective legislation with respect to the statute of the amending Party;

(b) if corrective legislation is not enacted within nine months from the end of the 90–day consultation period referred to in subparagraph (a) and no other mutually satisfactory solution has been reached, the Party that requested the panel may (i) take comparable legislative or equivalent executive action, or (ii) terminate this Agreement with regard to the amending Party upon 60–day written notice to that Party.

Article 1904: Review of Final Antidumping and Countervailing Duty Determinations

1. As provided in this Article, each Party shall replace judicial review of final antidumping and countervailing duty determinations with binational panel review.

2. An involved Party may request that a panel review, based upon the administrative record, a final antidumping or countervailing duty determination of a competent investigating authority of an importing Party to determine whether such determination was in accordance with the antidumping or countervailing duty law of the importing Party. For this purpose, the antidumping or countervailing duty law consists of the relevant statutes, legislative history, regulations, administrative practice and judicial precedents to the extent that a court of the importing Party would rely on such materials in reviewing a final determination of the competent investigating authority. Solely for purposes of the panel review provided for in this Article, the antidumping and countervailing duty statutes of the Parties, as those statutes may be amended from time to time, are incorporated into and made part of this Agreement.

3. The panel shall apply the standard of review set out in Annex 1911 and the general legal principles that a court of the importing Party otherwise would apply to a

review of a determination of the competent investigating authority.

4. A request for a panel shall be made in writing to the other involved Party within 30 days following the date of publication of the final determination in question in the official journal of the importing Party. In the case of final determinations that are not published in the official journal of the importing Party, the importing Party shall immediately notify the other involved Party of such final determination where it involves goods from the other involved Party, and the other involved Party may request a panel within 30 days of receipt of such notice. Where the competent investigating authority of the importing Party has imposed provisional measures in an investigation, the other involved Party may provide notice of its intention to request a panel under this Article, and the Parties shall begin to establish a panel at that time. Failure to request a panel within the time specified in this paragraph shall preclude review by a panel.

5. An involved Party on its own initiative may request review of a final determination by a panel and shall, on request of a person who would otherwise be entitled under the law of the importing Party to commence domestic procedures for judicial review of that final determination, request such review.

6. The panel shall conduct its review in accordance with the procedures established by the Parties pursuant to paragraph 14. Where both involved Parties request a panel to review a final determination, a single panel shall review that determination.

7. The competent investigating authority that issued the final determination in question shall have the right to appear and be represented by counsel before the panel. Each Party shall provide that other persons who, pursuant to the law of the importing Party, otherwise would have had the right to appear and be represented in a

domestic judicial review proceeding concerning the determination of the competent investigating authority, shall
have the right to appear and be represented by counsel
before the panel.

8. The panel may uphold a final determination, or
remand it for action not inconsistent with the panel's
decision. Where the panel remands a final determination,
the panel shall establish as brief a time as is reasonable
for compliance with the remand, taking into account the
complexity of the factual and legal issues involved and the
nature of the panel's decision. In no event shall the time
permitted for compliance with a remand exceed an
amount of time equal to the maximum amount of time
(counted from the date of the filing of a petition, complaint or application) permitted by statute for the competent investigating authority in question to make a final
determination in an investigation. If review of the action
taken by the competent investigating authority on remand is needed, such review shall be before the same
panel, which shall normally issue a final decision within
90 days of the date on which such remand action is
submitted to it.

9. The decision of a panel under this Article shall be
binding on the involved Parties with respect to the particular matter between the Parties that is before the panel.

10. This Agreement shall not affect: (a) the judicial
review procedures of any Party; or (b) cases appealed
under those procedures, with respect to determinations
other than final determinations.

11. A final determination shall not be reviewed under
any judicial review procedures of the importing Party if
an involved Party requests a panel with respect to that
determination within the time limits set out in this
Article. No Party may provide in its domestic legislation
for an appeal from a panel decision to its domestic courts.

12. This Article shall not apply where: (a) neither
involved Party seeks panel review of a final determination; (b) a revised final determination is issued as a direct
result of judicial review of the original final determination
by a court of the importing Party in cases where neither
involved Party sought panel review of that original final
determination; or (c) a final determination is issued as a
direct result of judicial review that was commenced in a
court of the importing Party before the date of entry into
force of this Agreement.

13. Where, within a reasonable time after the panel
decision is issued, an involved Party alleges that: (a)(i) a
member of the panel was guilty of gross misconduct, bias,
or a serious conflict of interest, or otherwise materially
violated the rules of conduct, (ii) the panel seriously
departed from a fundamental rule of procedure, or (iii)
the panel manifestly exceeded its powers, authority or
jurisdiction set out in this Article, for example by failing
to apply the appropriate standard of review, and (b) any
of the actions set out in subparagraph (a) has materially
affected the panel's decision and threatens the integrity
of the binational panel review process, that Party may
avail itself of the extraordinary challenge procedure set
out in Annex 1904.13.

14. To implement the provisions of this Article, the
Parties shall adopt rules of procedure by January 1, 1994.
Such rules shall be based, where appropriate, upon judicial rules of appellate procedure, and shall include rules
concerning the content and service of requests for panels;
a requirement that the competent investigating authority
transmit to the panel the administrative record of the
proceeding; the protection of business proprietary, government classified, and other privileged information (including sanctions against persons participating before
panels for improper release of such information); participation by private persons; limitations on panel review to
errors alleged by the Parties or private persons; filing and

service; computation and extensions of time; the form and content of briefs and other papers; pre-and post-hearing conferences; motions; oral argument; requests for rehearing; and voluntary terminations of panel reviews. The rules shall be designed to result in final decisions within 315 days of the date on which a request for a panel is made, and shall allow:

(a) 30 days for the filing of the complaint; (b) 30 days for designation or certification of the administrative record and its filing with the panel; (c) 60 days for the complainant to file its brief; (d) 60 days for the respondent to file its brief; (e) 15 days for the filing of reply briefs; (f) 15 to 30 days for the panel to convene and hear oral argument; and (g) 90 days for the panel to issue its written decision.

15. In order to achieve the objectives of this Article, the Parties shall amend their antidumping and countervailing duty statutes and regulations with respect to antidumping or countervailing duty proceedings involving goods of the other Parties, and other statutes and regulations to the extent that they apply to the operation of the antidumping and countervailing duty laws. In particular, without limiting the generality of the foregoing, each Party shall:

(a) amend its statutes or regulations to ensure that existing procedures concerning the refund, with interest, of antidumping or countervailing duties operate to give effect to a final panel decision that a refund is due;

(b) amend its statutes or regulations to ensure that its courts shall give full force and effect, with respect to any person within its jurisdiction, to all sanctions imposed pursuant to the laws of the other Parties to enforce provisions of any protective order or undertaking that such other Party has promulgated or accepted in order to permit access for purposes of panel review or of the extraordinary challenge procedure to confidential, personal, business proprietary or other privileged information;

(c) amend its statutes or regulations to ensure that (i) domestic procedures for judicial review of a final determination may not be commenced until the time for requesting a panel under paragraph 4 has expired, and (ii) as a prerequisite to commencing domestic judicial review procedures to review a final determination, a Party or other person intending to commence such procedures shall provide notice of such intent to the Parties concerned and to other persons entitled to commence such review procedures of the same final determination no later than 10 days prior to the latest date on which a panel may be requested; and (d) make the further amendments set out in its Schedule to Annex 1904.15.

Article 1905: Safeguarding the Panel Review System

1. Where a Party alleges that the application of another Party's domestic law: (a) has prevented the establishment of a panel requested by the complaining Party; (b) has prevented a panel requested by the complaining Party from rendering a final decision; (c) has prevented the implementation of the decision of a panel requested by the complaining Party or denied it binding force and effect with respect to the particular matter that was before the panel; or

(d) has resulted in a failure to provide opportunity for review of a final determination by a panel or court of competent jurisdiction that is independent of the competent investigating authorities, that examines the basis for the competent investigating authority's determination and whether the competent investigating authority properly applied domestic antidumping and countervailing duty law in reaching the challenged determination, and that employs the relevant standard of review identified in Article 1911, the Party may request in writing consultations with the other Party regarding the allegations. The consultations shall begin within 15 days of the date of the request.

2. If the matter has not been resolved within 45 days of the request for consultations, or such other period as the consulting Parties may agree, the complaining Party may request the establishment of a special committee.

3. Unless otherwise agreed by the disputing Parties, the special committee shall be established within 15 days of a request and perform its functions in a manner consistent with this Chapter.

4. The roster for special committees shall be that established under Annex 1904.13.

5. The special committee shall comprise three members selected in accordance with the procedures set out in Annex 1904.13.

6. The Parties shall establish rules of procedure in accordance with the principles set out in Annex 1905.6.

7. Where the special committee makes an affirmative finding in respect of one of the grounds specified in paragraph 1, the complaining Party and the Party complained against shall begin consultations within 10 days thereafter and shall seek to achieve a mutually satisfactory solution within 60 days of the issuance of the committee's report.

8. If, within the 60–day period, the Parties are unable to reach a mutually satisfactory solution to the matter, or the Party complained against has not demonstrated to the satisfaction of the special committee that it has corrected the problem or problems with respect to which the committee has made an affirmative finding, the complaining Party may suspend: (a) the operation of Article 1904 with respect to the Party complained against; or (b) the application to the Party complained against of such bene-

fits under this Agreement as may be appropriate under the circumstances.

9.   In the event that a complaining Party suspends the operation of Article 1904 with respect to the Party complained against, the latter Party may reciprocally suspend the operation of Article 1904. If either Party decides to suspend the operation of Article 1904, it shall provide written notice of such suspension to the other Party.

10.   At the request of the Party complained against, the special committee shall reconvene to determine whether: (a) the suspension of benefits by the complaining Party pursuant to subparagraph 8(b) is manifestly excessive; or (b) the Party complained against has corrected the problem or problems with respect to which the committee has made an affirmative finding.

The special committee shall, within 45 days of the request, present a report to both Parties containing its determination. Where the special committee determines that the Party complained against has corrected the problem or problems, any suspension effected by the complaining Party or the Party complained against, or both, pursuant to paragraph 8 or 9 shall be terminated.

11.   If the special committee makes an affirmative finding in respect of one of the grounds specified in paragraph 1, then effective as of the day following the date of issuance of the special committee's report:

(a) binational panel or extraordinary challenge committee review under Article 1904 shall be stayed (i) in the case of review of any final determination of the complaining Party requested by the Party complained against, if such review was 10 requested after the date on which consultations were requested pursuant to paragraph 1, and in no case later than 150 days prior to an affirmative finding by the special committee, or (ii) in the case of review of any final determination of the Party complained against requested by the complaining Party, at the request of the complaining Party; and (b) the time set out in Article 1904(4) or Annex 1904.13 for requesting panel or committee review shall not run unless and until resumed in accordance with paragraph 12.

12. If either Party suspends the operation of Article 1904 pursuant to paragraph 8(a), the panel or committee review stayed under paragraph 11(a) shall be terminated and the challenge to the final determination shall be irrevocably referred to the appropriate domestic court for decision, as provided below:

(a) in the case of review of any final determination of the complaining Party requested by the Party complained against, at the request of either Party, or of a party to the panel review under Article 1904; or (b) in the case of review of any final determination of the Party complained against requested by the complaining Party, at the request of the complaining Party, or of a person of the complaining Party that is a party to the panel review under Article 1904.

If either Party suspends the operation of Article 1904 pursuant to paragraph 8(a), any running of time suspended under paragraph 11(b) shall resume. If the suspension of Article 1904 does not become effective, panel or committee review stayed under paragraph 11(a), and any running of time suspended under paragraph 11(b), shall resume.

* * *

Annex 1901.2: Establishment of Binational Panels

1. On the date of entry into force of this Agreement, the Parties shall establish and thereafter maintain a roster of individuals to serve as panelists in disputes under this Chapter. The roster shall include judges or former judges to the fullest extent practicable. The Parties shall consult in developing the roster, which shall include at least 75 candidates. Each Party shall select at

least 25 candidates, and all candidates shall be citizens of Canada, Mexico or the United States. Candidates shall be of good character, high standing and repute, and shall be chosen strictly on the basis of objectivity, reliability, sound judgment and general familiarity with international al trade law. Candidates shall not be affiliated with a Party, and in no event shall a candidate take instructions from a Party. The Parties shall maintain the roster, and may amend it, when necessary, after consultations.

2.　A majority of the panelists on each panel shall be lawyers in good standing. Within 30 days of a request for a panel, each involved Party shall appoint two panelists, in consultation with the other involved Party. The involved Parties normally shall appoint panelists from the roster. If a panelist is not selected from the roster, the panelist shall be chosen in accordance with and be subject to the criteria of paragraph 1. Each involved Party shall have the right to exercise four peremptory challenges, to be exercised simultaneously and in confidence, disqualifying from appointment to the panel up to four candidates proposed by the other involved Party. Peremptory challenges and the selection of alternative panelists shall occur within 45 days of the request for the panel. If an involved Party fails to appoint its members to a panel within 30 days or if a panelist is struck and no alternative panelist is selected within 45 days, such panelist shall be selected by lot on the 31st or 46th day, as the case may be, from that Party's candidates on the roster.

3.　Within 55 days of the request for a panel, the involved Parties shall agree on the selection of a fifth panelist. If the involved Parties are unable to agree, they shall decide by lot which of them shall select, by the 61st day, the fifth panelist from the roster, excluding candidates eliminated by peremptory challenges.

4.　Upon appointment of the fifth panelist, the panelists shall promptly appoint a chairman from among the lawyers on the panel by majority vote of the panelists. If there is no majority vote, the chairman shall be appointed by lot from among the lawyers on the panel.

5.   Decisions of the panel shall be by majority vote and based upon the votes of all members of the panel. The panel shall issue a written decision with reasons, together with any dissenting or concurring opinions of panelists.

6.   Panelists shall be subject to the code of conduct established pursuant to Article 1909. If an involved Party believes that a panelist is in violation of the code of conduct, the involved Parties shall consult and if they agree, the panelist shall be removed and a new panelist shall be selected in accordance with the procedures of this Annex.

7.   When a panel is convened pursuant to Article 1904 each panelist shall be required to sign: (a) an application for protective order for information supplied by the United States or its persons covering business proprietary and other privileged information; (b) an undertaking for information supplied by Canada or its persons covering confidential, personal, business proprietary and other privileged information; or (c) an undertaking for information supplied by Mexico or its persons covering confidential, business proprietary and other privileged information.

8.   Upon a panelist's acceptance of the obligations and terms of an application for protective order or disclosure undertaking, the importing Party shall grant access to the information covered by such order or disclosure undertaking. Each Party shall establish appropriate sanctions for violations of protective orders or disclosure undertakings issued by or given to any Party. Each Party shall enforce such sanctions with respect to any person within its jurisdiction. Failure by a panelist to sign a protective order or disclosure undertaking shall result in disqualification of the panelist.

9.   If a panelist becomes unable to fulfill panel duties or is disqualified, proceedings of the panel shall be sus-

pended pending the selection of a substitute panelist in accordance with the procedures of this Annex.

10. Subject to the code of conduct established pursuant to Article 1909, and provided that it does not interfere with the performance of the duties of such panelist, a panelist may engage in other business during the term of the panel.

11. While acting as a panelist, a panelist may not appear as counsel before another panel.

12. With the exception of violations of protective orders or disclosure undertakings, signed pursuant to paragraph 7, panelists shall be immune from suit and legal process relating to acts performed by them in their official capacity.

Annex 1903.2: Panel Procedures Under Article 1903

1. The panel shall establish its own rules of procedure unless the Parties otherwise agree prior to the establishment of that panel. The procedures shall ensure a right to at least one hearing before the panel, as well as the opportunity to provide written submissions and rebuttal arguments. The proceedings of the panel shall be confidential, unless the two Parties otherwise agree. The panel shall base its decisions solely upon the arguments and submissions of the two Parties.

2. Unless the Parties to the dispute otherwise agree, the panel shall, within 90 days after its chairman is appointed, present to the two Parties an initial written declaratory opinion containing findings of fact and its determination pursuant to Article 1903.

3. If the findings of the panel are affirmative, the panel may include in its report its recommendations as to the means by which the amending statute could be brought into conformity with the provisions of Article 1902(2)(d). In determining what, if any, recommendations are appropriate, the panel shall consider the extent to

which the amending statute affects interests under this Agreement. Individual panelists may provide separate opinions on matters not unanimously agreed. The initial opinion of the panel shall become the final declaratory opinion, unless a Party to the dispute requests a reconsideration of the initial opinion pursuant to paragraph 4.

4.   Within 14 days of the issuance of the initial declaratory opinion, a Party to the dispute disagreeing in whole or in part with the opinion may present a written statement of its objections and the reasons for those objections to the panel. In such event, the panel shall request the views of both Parties and shall reconsider its initial opinion. The panel shall conduct any further examination that it deems appropriate, and shall issue a final written opinion, together with dissenting or concurring views of individual panelists, within 30 days of the request for reconsideration.

5.   Unless the Parties to the dispute otherwise agree, the final declaratory opinion of the panel shall be made public, along with any separate opinions of individual panelists and any written views that either Party may wish to be published.

6.   Unless the Parties to the dispute otherwise agree, meetings and hearings of the panel shall take place at the office of the amending Party's Section of the Secretariat.

Annex 1904.13: Extraordinary Challenge Procedure

1.   The involved Parties shall establish an extraordinary challenge committee, composed of three members, within 15 days of a request pursuant to Article 1904(13). The members shall be selected from a 15–person roster comprised of judges or former judges of a federal judicial court of the United States or a judicial court of superior jurisdiction of Canada, or a federal judicial court of Mexico. Each Party shall name five persons to this roster. Each involved Party shall select one member from this

roster and the involved Parties shall decide by lot which of them shall select the third member from the roster.

2. The Parties shall establish by the date of entry into force of the Agreement rules of procedure for committees. The rules shall provide for a decision of a committee within 90 days of its establishment.

3. Committee decisions shall be binding on the Parties with respect to the particular matter between the Parties that was before the panel. After examination of the legal and factual analysis underlying the findings and conclusions of the panel's decision in order to determine whether one of the grounds set out in Article 1904(13) has been established, and upon finding that one of those grounds has been established, the committee shall vacate the original panel decision or remand it to the original panel for action not inconsistent with the committee's decision; if the grounds are not established, it shall deny the challenge and, therefore, the original panel decision shall stand affirmed. If the original decision is vacated, a new panel shall be established pursuant to Annex 1901.2.

* * *

Chapter Twenty—Institutional Arrangements and Dispute Settlement Procedures

Section A—Institutions

Article 2001: The Free Trade Commission

1. The Parties hereby establish the Free Trade Commission, comprising cabinet-level representatives of the Parties or their designees.

2. The Commission shall: (a) supervise the implementation of this Agreement; (b) oversee its further elaboration; (c) resolve disputes that may arise regarding its interpretation or application; (d) supervise the work of all committees and working groups established under this

Agreement, referred to in Annex 2001.2; and (e) consider any other matter that may affect the operation of this Agreement.

3.   The Commission may: (a) establish, and delegate responsibilities to, ad hoc or standing committees, working groups or expert groups; (b) seek the advice of non-governmental persons or groups; and (c) take such other action in the exercise of its functions as the Parties may agree.

4.   The Commission shall establish its rules and procedures. All decisions of the Commission shall be taken by consensus, except as the Commission may otherwise agree.

5.   The Commission shall convene at least once a year in regular session. Regular sessions of the Commission shall be chaired successively by each Party.

Article 2002: The Secretariat

1.   The Commission shall establish and oversee a Secretariat comprising national Sections.

2.   Each Party shall: (a) establish a permanent office of its Section; (b) be responsible for (i) the operation and costs of its Section, and (ii) the remuneration and payment of expenses of panelists and members of committees and scientific review boards established under this Agreement, as set out in Annex 2002.2; (c) designate an individual to serve as Secretary for its Section, who shall be responsible for its administration and management; and (d) notify the Commission of the location of its Section's office.

3.   The Secretariat shall: (a) provide assistance to the Commission; (b) provide administrative assistance to (i) panels and committees established under Chapter Nineteen (Review and Dispute Settlement in Antidumping and Countervailing Duty Matters), in accordance with the procedures established pursuant to Article 1908, and (ii)

panels established under this Chapter, in accordance with procedures established pursuant to Article 2012; and (c) as the Commission may direct (i) support the work of other committees and groups established under this Agreement, and (ii) otherwise facilitate the operation of this Agreement.

Section B—Dispute Settlement

Article 2003: Cooperation

The Parties shall at all times endeavor to agree on the interpretation and application of this Agreement, and shall make every attempt through cooperation and consultations to arrive at a mutually satisfactory resolution of any matter that might affect its operation.

Article 2004: Recourse to Dispute Settlement Procedures

Except for the matters covered in Chapter Nineteen (Review and Dispute Settlement in Antidumping and Countervailing Duty Matters) and as otherwise provided in this Agreement, the dispute settlement provisions of this Chapter shall apply with respect to the avoidance or settlement of all disputes between the Parties regarding the interpretation or application of this Agreement or wherever a Party considers that an actual or proposed measure of another Party is or would be inconsistent with the obligations of this Agreement or cause nullification or impairment in the sense of Annex 2004.

Article 2005: GATT Dispute Settlement

1. Subject to paragraphs 2, 3 and 4, disputes regarding any matter arising under both this Agreement and the General Agreement on Tariffs and Trade, any agreement negotiated thereunder, or any successor agreement (GATT), may be settled in either forum at the discretion of the complaining Party.

2. Before a Party initiates a dispute settlement proceeding in the GATT against another Party on grounds
that are substantially equivalent to those available to that
Party under this Agreement, that Party shall notify any
third Party of its intention. If a third Party wishes to
have recourse to dispute settlement procedures under this
Agreement regarding the matter, it 4 agreement on a
single forum. If those Parties cannot agree, the dispute
normally shall be settled under this Agreement.

3. In any dispute referred to in paragraph 1 where the
responding Party claims that its action is subject to
Article 104 (Relation to Environmental and Conservation
Agreements) and requests in writing that the matter be
considered under this Agreement, the complaining Party
may, in respect of that matter, thereafter have recourse
to dispute settlement procedures solely under this Agreement.

4. In any dispute referred to in paragraph 1 that
arises under Section B of Chapter Seven (Sanitary and
Phytosanitary Measures) or Chapter Nine (Standards–
Related Measures):

(a) concerning a measure adopted or maintained by a
Party to protect its human, animal or plant life or health,
or to protect its environment, and (b) that raises factual
issues concerning the environment, health, safety or conservation, including directly related scientific matters,

where the responding Party requests in writing that
the matter be considered under this Agreement, the complaining Party may, in respect of that matter, thereafter
have recourse to dispute settlement procedures solely
under this Agreement.

5. The responding Party shall deliver a copy of a
request made pursuant to paragraph 3 or 4 to the other
Parties and to its Section of the Secretariat. Where the
complaining Party has initiated dispute settlement proceedings regarding any matter subject to paragraph 3 or

4, the responding Party shall deliver its request no later than 15 days thereafter. On receipt of such request, the complaining Party shall promptly withdraw from participation in those proceedings and may initiate dispute settlement procedures under Article 2007.

6. Once dispute settlement procedures have been initiated under Article 2007 or dispute settlement proceedings have been initiated under the GATT, the forum selected shall be used to the exclusion of the other, unless a Party makes a request pursuant to paragraph 3 or 4.

7. For purposes of this Article, dispute settlement proceedings under the GATT are deemed to be initiated by a Party's request for a panel, such as under Article XXIII:2 of the General Agreement on Tariffs and Trade 1947, or for a committee investigation, such as under Article 20.1 of the Customs Valuation Code.

Article 2006: Consultations

1. Any Party may request in writing consultations with any other Party regarding any actual or proposed measure or any other matter that it considers might affect the operation of this Agreement.

2. The requesting Party shall deliver the request to the other Parties and to its Section of the Secretariat.

3. Unless the Commission otherwise provides in its rules and procedures established under Article 2001(4), a third Party that considers it has a substantial interest in the matter shall be entitled to participate in the consultations on delivery of written notice to the other Parties and to its Section of the Secretariat.

4. Consultations on matters regarding perishable agricultural goods shall commence within 15 days of the date of delivery of the request.

5. The consulting Parties shall make every attempt to arrive at a mutually satisfactory resolution of any matter

through consultations under this Article or other consultative provisions of this Agreement. To this end, the consulting Parties shall: (a) provide sufficient information to enable a full examination of how the actual or proposed measure or other matter might affect the operation of this Agreement; (b) treat any confidential or proprietary information exchanged in the course of consultations on the same basis as the Party providing the information; and (c) seek to avoid any resolution that adversely affects the interests under this Agreement of any other Party.

Article 2007: Commission—Good Offices, Conciliation and Mediation

1. If the consulting Parties fail to resolve a matter pursuant to Article 2006 within: (a) 30 days of delivery of a request for consultations, (b) 45 days of delivery of such request if any other Party has subsequently requested or has participated in consultations regarding the same matter, (c) 15 days of delivery of a request for consultations in matters regarding perishable agricultural goods, or (d) such other period as they may agree, any such Party may request in writing a meeting of the Commission.

2. A Party may also request in writing a meeting of the Commission where: (a) it has initiated dispute settlement proceedings under the GATT regarding any matter subject to Article 2005(3) or (4), and has received a request pursuant to Article 2005(5) for recourse to dispute settlement procedures under this Chapter; or (b) consultations have been held pursuant to Article 513 (Working Group on Rules of Origin), Article 723 (Sanitary and Phytosanitary Measures—Technical Consultations) and Article 914 (Standards–Related Measures—Technical Consultations).

3. The requesting Party shall state in the request the measure or other matter complained of and indicate the provisions of this Agreement that it considers relevant,

and shall deliver the request to the other Parties and to its Section of the Secretariat.

4. Unless it decides otherwise, the Commission shall convene within 10 days of delivery of the request and shall endeavor to resolve the dispute promptly.

5. The Commission may: (a) call on such technical advisers or create such working groups or expert groups as it deems necessary, (b) have recourse to good offices, conciliation, mediation or such other dispute resolution procedures, or (c) make recommendations, as may assist the consulting Parties to reach a mutually satisfactory resolution of the dispute.

6. Unless it decides otherwise, the Commission shall consolidate two or more proceedings before it pursuant to this Article regarding the same measure. The Commission may consolidate two or more proceedings regarding other matters before it pursuant to this Article that it determines are appropriate to be considered jointly.

Article 2008: Request for an Arbitral Panel

1. If the Commission has convened pursuant to Article 2007(4), and the matter has not been resolved within: (a) 30 days thereafter, (b) 30 days after the Commission has convened in respect of the matter most recently referred to it, where proceedings have been consolidated pursuant to Article 2007(6), or (c) such other period as the consulting Parties may agree, any consulting Party may request in writing the establishment of an arbitral panel. The requesting Party shall deliver the request to the other Parties and to its Section of the Secretariat.

2. On delivery of the request, the Commission shall establish an arbitral panel.

3. A third Party that considers it has a substantial interest in the matter shall be entitled to join as a complaining Party on delivery of written notice of its intention to participate to the disputing Parties and its

Section of the Secretariat. The notice shall be delivered at the earliest possible time, and in any event no later than seven days after the date of delivery of a request by a Party for the establishment of a panel.

4.   If a third Party does not join as a complaining Party in accordance with paragraph 3, it normally shall refrain thereafter from initiating or continuing: (a) a dispute settlement procedure under this Agreement, or (b) a dispute settlement proceeding in the GATT on grounds that are substantially equivalent to those available to that Party under this Agreement, 8 regarding the same matter in the absence of a significant change in economic or commercial circumstances.

5.   Unless otherwise agreed by the disputing Parties, the panel shall be established and perform its functions in a manner consistent with the provisions of this Chapter.

Article 2009: Roster

1.   The Parties shall establish and maintain a roster of up to 30 individuals who are willing and able to serve as panelists. The roster members shall be appointed by consensus for terms of three years, and may be reappointed.

2.   Roster members shall: (a) have expertise or experience in law, international trade, other matters covered by this Agreement or the resolution of disputes arising under international trade agreements, and shall be chosen strictly on the basis of objectivity, reliability and sound judgment; (b) be independent of, and not be affiliated with or take instructions from, any Party; and (c) comply with a code of conduct to be established by the Commission.

Article 2010: Qualifications of Panelists

1.   All panelists shall meet the qualifications set out in Article 2009(2).

2. Individuals may not serve as panelists for a dispute in which they have participated pursuant to Article 2007(5).

Article 2011: Panel Selection

1. Where there are two disputing Parties, the following procedures shall apply: (a) The panel shall comprise five members. (b) The disputing Parties shall endeavor to agree on the chair of the panel within 15 days of the delivery of the request for the establishment of the panel. If the disputing Parties are unable to agree on the chair within this period, the disputing Party chosen by lot shall select within five days as chair an individual who is not a citizen of that Party. (c) Within 15 days of selection of the chair, each disputing Party shall select two panelists who are citizens of the other disputing Party. (d) If a disputing Party fails to select its panelists within such period, such panelists shall be selected by lot from among the roster members who are citizens of the other disputing Party.

2. Where there are more than two disputing Parties, the following procedures shall apply: (a) The panel shall comprise five members. (b) The disputing Parties shall endeavor to agree on the chair of the panel within 15 days of the delivery of the request for the establishment of the panel. If the disputing Parties are unable to agree on the chair within this period, the Party or Parties on the side of the dispute chosen by lot shall select within 10 days a chair who is not a citizen of such Party or Parties. (c) Within 15 days of selection of the chair, the Party complained against shall select two panelists, one of whom is a citizen of a complaining Party, and the other of whom is a citizen of another complaining Party. The complaining Parties shall select two panelists who are citizens of the Party complained against. (d) If any disputing Party fails to select a panelist within such period, such panelist shall be selected by lot in accordance with the citizenship criteria of subparagraph (c).

3. Panelists shall normally be selected from the roster. Any disputing Party may exercise a peremptory challenge against any individual not on the roster who is proposed as a panelist by a disputing Party within 15 days after the individual has been proposed.

4. If a disputing Party believes that a panelist is in violation of the code of conduct, the disputing Parties shall consult and if they agree, the panelist shall be removed and a new panelist shall be selected in accordance with this Article.

Article 2012: Rules of Procedure

1. The Commission shall establish Model Rules of Procedure, in accordance with the following principles: (a) the procedures shall assure a right to at least one hearing before the panel as well as the opportunity to provide initial and rebuttal written submissions; and (b) the panel's hearings, deliberations and initial report, and all written submissions to and communications with the panel shall be confidential.

2. Unless the disputing Parties otherwise agree, the panel shall conduct its proceedings in accordance with the Model Rules of Procedure.

3. Unless the disputing Parties otherwise agree within 20 days from the date of the delivery of the request for the establishment of the panel, the terms of reference shall be:

"To examine, in the light of the relevant provisions of the Agreement, the matter referred to the Commission (as set out in the request for a Commission meeting) and to make findings, determinations and recommendations as provided in Article 2016(2)."

4. If a complaining Party wishes to argue that a matter has nullified or impaired benefits, the terms of reference shall so indicate.

5. If a disputing Party wishes the panel to make findings as to the degree of adverse trade effects on any Party of any measure found not to conform with the obligations of the Agreement or to have caused nullification or impairment in the sense of Annex 2004, the terms of reference shall so indicate.

Article 2013—Third Party Participation

A Party that is not a disputing Party, on delivery of a written notice to the disputing Parties and to its Section of the Secretariat, shall be entitled to attend all hearings, to make written and oral submissions to the panel and to receive written submissions of the disputing Parties.

Article 2014: Role of Experts

On request of a disputing Party, or on its own initiative, the panel may seek information and technical advice from any person or body that it deems appropriate, provided that the disputing Parties so agree and subject to such terms and conditions as such Parties may agree.

Article 2015: Scientific Review Boards

1. On request of a disputing Party or, unless the disputing Parties disapprove, on its own initiative, the panel may request a written report of a scientific review board on any factual issue concerning environmental, health, safety or other scientific matters raised by a disputing Party in a proceeding, subject to such terms and conditions as such Parties may agree.

2. The board shall be selected by the panel from among highly qualified, independent experts in the scientific matters, after consultations with the disputing Parties and the scientific bodies set out in the Model Rules of Procedure established pursuant to Article 2012(1).

3. The participating Parties shall be provided: (a) advance notice of, and an opportunity to provide comments

to the panel on, the proposed factual issues to be referred to the board; and (b) a copy of the board's report and an opportunity to provide comments on the report to the panel.

4. The panel shall take the board's report and any comments by the Parties on the report into account in the preparation of its report.

Article 2016: Initial Report

1. Unless the disputing Parties otherwise agree, the panel shall base its report on the submissions and arguments of the Parties and on any information before it pursuant to Article 2014 or 2015.

2. Unless the disputing Parties otherwise agree, the panel shall, within 90 days after the last panelist is selected or such other period as the Model Rules of Procedure established 12 pursuant to Article 2012(1) may provide, present to the disputing Parties an initial report containing: (a) findings of fact, including any findings pursuant to a request under Article 2012(5); (b) its determination as to whether the measure at issue is or would be inconsistent with the obligations of this Agreement or cause nullification or impairment in the sense of Annex 2004, or any other determination requested in the terms of reference; and (c) its recommendations, if any, for resolution of the dispute.

3. Panelists may furnish separate opinions on matters not unanimously agreed.

4. A disputing Party may submit written comments to the panel on its initial report within 14 days of presentation of the report.

5. In such an event, and after considering such written comments, the panel, on its own initiative or on the request of any disputing Party, may: (a) request the views of any participating Party; (b) reconsider its report; and (c) make any further examination that it considers appropriate.

Article 2017: Final Report

1. The panel shall present to the disputing Parties a final report, including any separate opinions on matters not unanimously agreed, within 30 days of presentation of the initial report, unless the disputing Parties otherwise agree.

2. No panel may, either in its initial report or its final report, disclose which panelists are associated with majority or minority opinions.

3. The disputing Parties shall transmit to the Commission the final report of the panel, including any report of a scientific review board established under Article 2015, as well as any written views that a disputing Party desires to be appended, on a confidential basis within a reasonable period of time after it is presented to them.

4. Unless the Commission decides otherwise, the final report of the panel shall be published 15 days after it is transmitted to the Commission.

Article 2018: Implementation of Final Report

1. On receipt of the final report of a panel, the disputing Parties shall agree on the resolution of the dispute, which normally shall conform with the determinations and recommendations of the panel, and shall notify their Sections of the Secretariat of any agreed resolution of any dispute.

2. Wherever possible, the resolution shall be non-implementation or removal of a measure not conforming with this Agreement or causing nullification or impairment in the sense of Annex 2004 or, failing such a resolution, compensation.

Article 2019: Non–Implementation—Suspension of Benefits

1. If in its final report a panel has determined that a measure is inconsistent with the obligations of this Agree-

ment or causes nullification or impairment in the sense of Annex 2004 and the Party complained against has not reached agreement with any complaining Party on a mutually satisfactory resolution pursuant to Article 2018(1) within 30 days of receiving the final report, such complaining Party may suspend the application to the Party complained against of benefits of equivalent effect until such time as they have reached agreement on a resolution of the dispute.

2. In considering what benefits to suspend pursuant to paragraph 1: (a) a complaining Party should first seek to suspend benefits in the same sector or sectors as that affected by the measure or other matter that the panel has found to be inconsistent with the obligations of this Agreement or to have caused nullification or impairment in the sense of Annex 2004; and (b) a complaining Party that considers it is not practicable or effective to suspend benefits in the same sector or sectors may suspend benefits in other sectors.

3. On the written request of any disputing Party delivered to the other Parties and its Section of the Secretariat, the Commission shall establish a panel to determine whether the level of benefits suspended by a Party pursuant to paragraph 1 is manifestly excessive.

4. The panel proceedings shall be conducted in accordance with the Model Rules of Procedure. The panel shall present its determination within 60 days after the last panelist is selected or such other period as the disputing Parties may agree.

Section C—Domestic Proceedings and Private Commercial Dispute Settlement

Article 2020: Referrals of Matters from Judicial or Administrative Proceedings

1. If an issue of interpretation or application of this Agreement arises in any domestic judicial or administra-

tive proceeding of a Party that any Party considers would merit its intervention, or if a court or administrative body solicits the views of a Party, that Party shall notify the other Parties and its Section of the Secretariat. The Commission shall endeavor to agree on an appropriate response as expeditiously as possible.

2.   The Party in whose territory the court or administrative body is located shall submit any agreed interpretation of the Commission to the court or administrative body in accordance with the rules of that forum.

3.   If the Commission is unable to agree, any Party may submit its own views to the court or administrative body in accordance with the rules of that forum.

Article 2021: Private Rights

No Party may provide for a right of action under its domestic law against any other Party on the ground that a measure of another Party is inconsistent with this Agreement.

Article 2022: Alternative Dispute Resolution

1.   Each Party shall, to the maximum extent possible, encourage and facilitate the use of arbitration and other means of alternative dispute resolution for the settlement of international commercial disputes between private parties in the free trade area.

2.   To this end, each Party shall provide appropriate procedures to ensure observance of agreements to arbitrate and for the recognition and enforcement of arbitral awards in such disputes.

3.   A Party shall be deemed to be in compliance with paragraph 2 if it is a party to and is in compliance with the 1958 United Nations Convention on the Recognition and Enforcement of Foreign Arbitral Awards or the 1975 Inter–American Convention on International Commercial Arbitration.

4. The Commission shall establish an Advisory Committee on Private Commercial Disputes comprising persons with expertise or experience in the resolution of private international commercial disputes. The Committee shall report and provide recommendations to the Commission on general issues referred to it by the Commission respecting the availability, use and effectiveness of arbitration and other procedures for the resolution of such disputes in the free trade area.

* * *

Annex 2004—Nullification and Impairment

1. If any Party considers that any benefit it could reasonably have expected to accrue to it under any provision of: (a) Part Two (Trade in Goods), except for those provisions of Annex 300–A (Automotive Sector) or Chapter Six (Energy) relating to investment, (b) Part Three (Technical Barriers to Trade), (c) Chapter Twelve (Cross–Border Trade in Services), or (d) Part Six (Intellectual Property), is being nullified or impaired as a result of the application of any measure that is not inconsistent with this Agreement, the Party may have recourse to dispute settlement under this Chapter.

2. A Party may not invoke: (a) paragraph (1)(a) or (b), to the extent that the benefit arises from any cross-border trade in services provision of Part Two, or (b) paragraph (1)(c) or (d), with respect to any measure subject to an exception under Article 2101 (General Exceptions).

PART EIGHT—OTHER PROVISIONS

Chapter Twenty–One—Exceptions

Article 2101: General Exceptions

1. For purposes of:

(a) Part Two (Trade in Goods), except to the extent that a provision of that Part applies to services or investment, and (b) Part Three (Technical Barriers to Trade), except to the extent that a provision of that Part applies to services,

GATT Article XX and its interpretative notes, or any equivalent provision of a successor agreement to which all Parties are party, are incorporated into and made part of this Agreement. The Parties understand that the measures referred to in GATT Article XX(b) include environmental measures necessary to protect human, animal or plant life or health, and that GATT Article XX(g) applies to measures relating to the conservation of living and non-living exhaustible natural resources.

2. Provided that such measures are not applied in a manner that would constitute a means of arbitrary or unjustifiable discrimination between countries where the same conditions prevail or a disguised restriction on trade between the Parties, nothing in:

(a) Part Two (Trade in Goods), to the extent that a provision of that Part applies to services, (b) Part Three (Technical Barriers to Trade), to the extent that a provision of that Part applies to services, (c) Chapter Twelve (Cross–Border Trade in Services), and (d) Chapter Thirteen (Tele-communications), 2 shall be construed to prevent the adoption or enforcement by any Party of measures necessary to secure compliance with laws or regulations that are not inconsistent with the provisions of this Agreement, including those relating to health and safety and consumer protection.

Article 2102: National Security

1. Subject to Articles 607 (Energy—National Security Measures) and 1018 (Government Procurement—Exceptions), nothing in this Agreement shall be construed:

(a) to require any Party to furnish or allow access to any information the disclosure of which it determines to be contrary to its essential security interests; (b) to prevent any Party from taking any actions that it considers necessary for the protection of its essential security interests (i) relating to the traffic in arms, ammunition and implements of war and to such traffic and transactions in other goods, materials, services and technology undertaken directly or indirectly for the purpose of supplying a military or other security establishment, (ii) taken in time of war or other emergency in international relations, or (iii) relating to the implementation of national policies or international agreements respecting the non-proliferation of nuclear weapons or other nuclear explosive devices; or (c) to prevent any Party from taking action in pursuance of its obligations under the United Nations Charter for the maintenance of international peace and security.

Article 2103: Taxation

1. Except as set out in this Article, nothing in this Agreement shall apply to taxation measures.

2. Nothing in this Agreement shall affect the rights and obligations of any Party under any tax convention. In the event of any inconsistency between the provisions of this Agreement and any such convention, the provisions of that convention shall prevail to the extent of the inconsistency.

3. Notwithstanding paragraph 2: (a) Article 301 (Market Access—National Treatment) and such other provisions of this Agreement as are necessary to give effect to that Article shall apply to taxation measures to the same extent as does Article III of the GATT; and (b) Article 314 (Market Access—Export Taxes) and Article 604 (Energy—Export Taxes) shall apply to taxation measures.

4. Subject to paragraph 2: (a) Article 1202 (Cross–Border Trade in Services—National Treatment) and Arti-

cle 1405 (Financial Services—National Treatment) shall apply to taxation measures on income, capital gains or on the taxable capital of corporations, and to those taxes listed in paragraph 1 of Annex 2103.4, that relate to the purchase or consumption of particular services, and

(b) Articles 1102 and 1103 (Investment—National Treatment and Most–Favored Nation Treatment), Articles 1202 and 1203 (Cross–Border Trade in Services—National Treatment and Most–Favored Nation Treatment) and Articles 1405 and 1406 (Financial Services—National Treatment and Most–Favored Nation Treatment) shall apply to all taxation measures, other than those on income, capital gains or on the taxable capital of corporations, taxes on estates, inheritances, gifts and generation-skipping transfers and those taxes listed in paragraph 1 of Annex 2103.4,

except that nothing in those Articles shall apply (c) any most-favored-nation obligation with respect to an advantage accorded by a Party pursuant to a tax convention, (d) to a non-conforming provision of any existing taxation measure, (e) to the continuation or prompt renewal of a non-conforming provision of any existing taxation measure, (f) to an amendment to a non-conforming provision of any existing taxation measure to the extent that the amendment does not decrease its conformity, at the time of the amendment, with any of those Articles, (g) to any new taxation measure aimed at ensuring the equitable and effective imposition or collection of taxes and that does not arbitrarily discriminate between persons, goods or services of the Parties or arbitrarily nullify or impair benefits accorded under those Articles, in the sense of Annex 2004, or (h) to the measures listed in paragraph 2 of Annex 2103.4.

5. Subject to paragraph 2 and without prejudice to the rights and obligations of the Parties under paragraph 3, Article 1106(3), (4) and (5) (Investment—Performance Requirements) shall apply to taxation measures.

6. Article 1110 (Investment—Expropriation) shall apply to taxation measures except that no investor may invoke that Article as the basis for a claim under Article 1116 or 1117, where it has been determined pursuant to this paragraph that the measure is not an expropriation. The investor shall refer the issue of whether the measure is not an expropriation for a determination to the appropriate competent authorities set out in Annex 2104.6 at the time that it gives notice under Article 1119. If the competent authorities do not agree to consider the issue or, having agreed to consider it, fail to agree that the measure is not an expropriation within a period of six months of such referral, the investor may submit its claim to arbitration under Article 1120.

Article 2104: Balance of Payments

1. Nothing in this Agreement shall be construed to prevent a Party from adopting or maintaining measures that restrict transfers where the Party experiences serious balance of payments difficulties, or the threat thereof, and such restrictions are consistent with paragraphs 2 through 4 and are: (a) consistent with paragraph 5 to the extent they are imposed on other transfers than cross-border trade in financial services; or (b) consistent with paragraphs 6 and 7 to the extent they are imposed on cross-border trade in financial services.

2. As soon as practicable after a Party imposes a measure under this Article, the Party shall: (a) submit any current account exchange restrictions to the IMF for review under Article VIII of the Articles of Agreement of the IMF; and (b) enter into good faith consultations with the IMF on economic adjustment measures to address the fundamental underlying economic problems causing the difficulties; and (c) adopt or maintain economic policies consistent with such consultations.

3. A measure adopted or maintained under this Article shall: (a) avoid unnecessary damage to the commer-

cial, economic or financial interests of another Party; (b) not be more burdensome than necessary to deal with the balance of payments difficulties or threat thereof; (c) be temporary and be phased out progressively as the balance of payments situation improves; (d) be consistent with paragraph 2(c) and with the Articles of Ágreement of the IMF; and (e) be applied on a national treatment or most-favored-nation treatment basis, whichever is better.

4. A Party may adopt or maintain a measure under this Article that gives priority to services that are essential to its economic program, provided that a Party may not impose a measure for the purpose of protecting a specific industry or sector unless the measure is consistent with paragraph 2(c) and with Article VIII(3) of the Articles of Agreement of the IMF.

* * *

Annex 2106—Cultural Industries

Notwithstanding any other provision of this Agreement, as between Canada and the United States, any measure adopted or maintained with respect to cultural industries, except as specifically provided in Article 302 (Market Access—Tariff Elimination), and any measure of equivalent commercial effect taken in response, shall be governed under this Agreement exclusively in accordance with the provisions of the Canada—United States Free Trade Agreement. The rights and obligations between Canada and any other Party with respect to such measures shall be identical to those applying between Canada and the United States.

Chapter Twenty–Two—Final Provisions

Article 2201: Annexes

The Annexes to this Agreement constitute an integral part of this Agreement.

Article 2202: Amendments

1. The Parties may agree on any modification of or addition to this Agreement.

2. When so agreed, and approved in accordance with the applicable legal procedures of each Party, a modification or addition shall constitute an integral part of this Agreement.

Article 2203: Entry into Force

This Agreement shall enter into force on January 1, 1994, on an exchange of written notifications certifying the completion of necessary legal procedures.

Article 2204: Accession

1. Any country or group of countries may accede to this Agreement subject to such terms and conditions as may be agreed between such country or countries and the Commission and following approval in accordance with the applicable legal procedures of each country.

2. This Agreement shall not apply as between any Party and any acceding country or group of countries if, at the time of accession, either does not consent to such application.

Article 2205: Withdrawal

A Party may withdraw from this Agreement six months after it provides written notice of withdrawal to the other Parties. If a Party withdraws, the Agreement shall remain in force for the remaining Parties.

Article 2206: Authentic Texts

The English, French and Spanish texts of this Agreement are equally authentic.

APPENDIX II

NORTH AMERICAN AGREEMENT ON ENVIRONMENTAL COOPER-ATION (1994)

* * *

PART ONE—OBJECTIVES

* * *

PART TWO—OBLIGATIONS

Article 2: General Commitments

1. Each Party shall, with respect to its territory: (a) periodically prepare and make publicly available reports on the state of the environment; (b) develop and review environmental emergency preparedness measures; (c) promote education in environmental matters, including environmental law; (d) further scientific research and technology development in respect of environmental matters; (e) assess, as appropriate, environmental impacts; and (f) promote the use of economic instruments for the efficient achievement of environmental goals.

2. Each Party shall consider implementing in its law any recommendation developed by the Council under Article 10(5)(b).

3. Each Party shall consider prohibiting the export to the territories of the other Parties of a pesticide or toxic substance whose use is prohibited within the Party's

territory. When a Party adopts a measure prohibiting or severely restricting the use of a pesticide or toxic substance in its territory, it shall notify the other Parties of the measure, either directly or through an appropriate international organization.

Article 3: Levels of Protection

Recognizing the right of each Party to establish its own levels of domestic environmental protection and environmental development policies and priorities, and to adopt or modify accordingly its environmental laws and regulations, each Party shall ensure that its laws and regulations provide for high levels of environmental protection and shall strive to continue to improve those laws and regulations.

Article 4: Publication

1. Each Party shall ensure that its laws, regulations, procedures and administrative rulings of general application respecting any matter covered by this Agreement are promptly published or otherwise made available in such a manner as to enable interested persons and Parties to become acquainted with them.

2. To the extent possible, each Party shall: (a) publish in advance any such measure that it proposes to adopt; and (b) provide interested persons and Parties a reasonable opportunity to comment on such proposed measures.

Article 5: Government Enforcement Action

1. With the aim of achieving high levels of environmental protection and compliance with its environmental laws and regulations, each Party shall effectively enforce its environmental laws and regulations through appropriate governmental action, subject to Article 37, such as: (a) appointing and training inspectors; (b) monitoring compliance and investigating suspected violations, including through on-site inspections; (c) seeking assurances of vol-

untary compliance and compliance agreements; (d) publicly releasing non-compliance information; (e) issuing bulletins or other periodic statements on enforcement procedures; (f) promoting environmental audits; (g) requiring record keeping and reporting; (h) providing or encouraging mediation and arbitration services; (i) using licenses, permits or authorizations; (j) initiating, in a timely manner, judicial, quasi-judicial or administrative proceedings to seek appropriate sanctions or remedies for violations of its environmental laws and regulations; (k) providing for search, seizure or detention; or (*l*) issuing administrative orders, including orders of a preventative, curative or emergency nature.

2.   Each Party shall ensure that judicial, quasi-judicial or administrative enforcement proceedings are available under its law to sanction or remedy violations of its environmental laws and regulations.

3.   Sanctions and remedies provided for a violation of a Party's environmental laws and regulations shall, as appropriate: (a) take into consideration the nature and gravity of the violation, any economic benefit derived from the violation by the violator, the economic condition of the violator, and other relevant factors; and (b) include compliance agreements, fines, imprisonment, injunctions, the closure of facilities, and the cost of containing or cleaning up pollution.

Article 6: Private Access to Remedies

1.   Each Party shall ensure that interested persons may request the Party's competent authorities to investigate alleged violations of its environmental laws and regulations and shall give such requests due consideration in accordance with law.

2.   Each Party shall ensure that persons with a legally recognized interest under its law in a particular matter have appropriate access to administrative, quasi-judicial

or judicial proceedings for the enforcement of the Party's environmental laws and regulations.

3. Private access to remedies shall include rights, in accordance with the Party's law, such as: (a) to sue another person under that Party's jurisdiction for damages; (b) to seek sanctions or remedies such as monetary penalties, emergency closures or orders to mitigate the consequences of violations of its environmental laws and regulations; (c) to request the competent authorities to take appropriate action to enforce that Party's environmental laws and regulations in order to protect the environment or to avoid environmental harm; or (d) to seek injunctions where a person suffers, or may suffer, loss, damage or injury as a result of conduct by another person under that Party's jurisdiction contrary to that Party's environmental laws and regulations or from tortious conduct.

Article 7: Procedural Guarantees

1. Each Party shall ensure that its administrative, quasi-judicial and judicial proceedings referred to in Articles 5(2) and 6(2) are fair, open and equitable, and to this end shall provide that such proceedings: (a) comply with due process of law; (b) are open to the public, except where the administration of justice otherwise requires; (c) entitle the parties to the proceedings to support or defend their respective positions and to present information or evidence; and (d) are not unnecessarily complicated and do not entail unreasonable charges or time limits or unwarranted delays.

2. Each Party shall provide that final decisions on the merits of the case in such proceedings are: (a) in writing and preferably state the reasons on which the decisions are based; (b) made available without undue delay to the parties to the proceedings and, consistent with its law, to the public; and (c) based on information or evidence in

respect of which the parties were offered the opportunity to be heard.

3. Each Party shall provide, as appropriate, that parties to such proceedings have the right, in accordance with its law, to seek review and, where warranted, correction of final decisions issued in such proceedings.

4. Each Party shall ensure that tribunals that conduct or review such proceedings are impartial and independent and do not have any substantial interest in the outcome of the matter.

PART THREE—COMMISSION FOR ENVIRONMENTAL COOPERATION

Article 8: The Commission

1. The Parties hereby establish the Commission for Environmental Cooperation.

2. The Commission shall comprise a Council, a Secretariat and a Joint Public Advisory Committee.

Article 9: Council Structure and Procedures

1. The Council shall comprise cabinet-level or equivalent representatives of the Parties, or their designees.

2. The Council shall establish its rules and procedures.

3. The Council shall convene: (a) at least once a year in regular session; and (b) in special session at the request of any Party.

Regular sessions shall be chaired successively by each Party.

4. The Council shall hold public meetings in the course of all regular sessions. Other meetings held in the course of regular or special sessions shall be public where the Council so decides.

5. The Council may: (a) establish, and assign respon-sibilities to, ad hoc or standing committees, working groups or expert groups; (b) seek the advice of non-governmental organizations or persons, including inde-pendent experts; and (c) take such other action in the exercise of its functions as the Parties may agree.

6. All decisions and recommendations of the Council shall be taken by consensus, except as the Council may otherwise decide or as otherwise provided in this Agree-ment.

7. All decisions and recommendations of the Council shall be made public, except as the Council may otherwise decide or as otherwise provided in this Agreement.

Article 10: Council Functions

1. The Council shall be the governing body of the Commission and shall: (a) serve as a forum for the dis-cussion of environmental matters within the scope of this Agreement; (b) oversee the implementation and develop recommendations on the further elaboration of this Agreement and, to this end, the Council shall, within four years after the date of entry into force of this Agreement, review its operation and effectiveness in the light of experience; (c) oversee the Secretariat; (d) address ques-tions and differences that may arise between the Parties regarding the interpretation or application of this Agree-ment; (e) approve the annual program and budget of the Commission; and (f) promote and facilitate cooperation between the Parties with respect to environmental mat-ters.

2. The Council may consider, and develop recommen-dations regarding: (a) comparability of techniques and methodologies for data gathering and analysis, data man-agement and electronic data communications on matters covered by this Agreement; (b) pollution prevention tech-niques and strategies; (c) approaches and common indica-

tors for reporting on the state of the environment; (d) the use of economic instruments for the pursuit of domestic and internationally agreed environmental objectives; (e) scientific research and technology development in respect of environmental matters; (f) promotion of public awareness regarding the environment; (g) transboundary and border environmental issues, such as the long-range transport of air and marine pollutants; (h) exotic species that may be harmful; (i) the conservation and protection of wild flora and fauna and their habitat, and specially protected natural areas; (j) the protection of endangered and threatened species; (k) environmental emergency preparedness and response activities; (*l*) environmental matters as they relate to economic development; (m) the environmental implications of goods throughout their life cycles; (n) human resource training and development in the environmental field; (*o*) the exchange of environmental scientists and officials; (p) approaches to environmental compliance and enforcement; (q) ecologically sensitive national accounts; (r) eco-labelling; and (s) other matters as it may decide.

3. The Council shall strengthen cooperation on the development and continuing improvement of environmental laws and regulations, including by: (a) promoting the exchange of information on criteria and methodologies used in establishing domestic environmental standards; and (b) without reducing levels of environmental protection, establishing a process for developing recommendations on greater compatibility of environmental technical regulations, standards and conformity assessment procedures in a manner consistent with the NAFTA.

4. The Council shall encourage: (a) effective enforcement by each Party of its environmental laws and regulations; (b) compliance with those laws and regulations; and (c) technical cooperation between the Parties.

5. The Council shall promote and, as appropriate, develop recommendations regarding: (a) public access to

information concerning the environment that is held by public authorities of each Party, including information on hazardous materials and activities in its communities, and opportunity to participate in decision-making processes related to such public access; and (b) appropriate limits for specific pollutants, taking into account differences in ecosystems.

6.   The Council shall cooperate with the NAFTA Free Trade Commission to achieve the environmental goals and objectives of the NAFTA by: (a) acting as a point of inquiry and receipt for comments from non-governmental organizations and persons concerning those goals and objectives; (b) providing assistance in consultations under Article 1114 of the NAFTA where a Party considers that another Party is waiving or derogating from, or offering to waive or otherwise derogate from, an environmental measure as an encouragement to establish, acquire, expand or retain an investment of an investor, with a view to avoiding any such encouragement; (c) contributing to the prevention or resolution of environment-related trade disputes by: (i) seeking to avoid disputes between the Parties, (ii) making recommendations to the Free Trade Commission with respect to the avoidance of such disputes, and (iii) identifying experts able to provide information or technical advice to NAFTA committees, working groups and other NAFTA bodies; (d) considering on an ongoing basis the environmental effects of the NAFTA; and (e) otherwise assisting the Free Trade Commission in environment-related matters.

7.   Recognizing the significant bilateral nature of many transboundary environmental issues, the Council shall, with a view to agreement between the Parties pursuant to this Article within three years on obligations, consider and develop recommendations with respect to: a) assessing the environmental impact of proposed projects subject to decisions by a competent government authority and likely to cause significant adverse transboundary effects,

including a full evaluation of comments provided by other Parties and persons of other Parties; b) notification, provision of relevant information and consultation between Parties with respect to such projects; and c) mitigation of the potential adverse effects of such projects.

8. The Council shall encourage the establishment by each Party of appropriate administrative procedures pursuant to its environmental laws to permit another Party to seek the reduction, elimination or mitigation of transboundary pollution on a reciprocal basis.

9. The Council shall consider and, as appropriate, develop recommendations on the provision by a Party, on a reciprocal basis, of access to and rights and remedies before its courts and administrative agencies for persons in another Party's territory who have suffered or are likely to suffer damage or injury caused by pollution originating in its territory as if the damage or injury were suffered in its territory.

Article 11: Secretariat Structure and Procedures

1. The Secretariat shall be headed by an Executive Director, who shall be chosen by the Council for a three-year term, which may be renewed by the Council for one additional three-year term. The position of Executive Director shall rotate consecutively between nationals of each Party. The Council may remove the Executive Director solely for cause.

2. The Executive Director shall appoint and supervise the staff of the Secretariat, regulate their powers and duties and fix their remuneration in accordance with general standards to be established by the Council. The general standards shall provide that: (a) staff shall be appointed and retained, and their conditions of employment shall be determined, strictly on the basis of efficiency, competence and integrity; (b) in appointing staff, the Executive Director shall take into account lists of candi-

dates prepared by the Parties and by the Joint Public Advisory Committee; (c) due regard shall be paid to the importance of recruiting an equitable proportion of the professional staff from among the nationals of each Party; and (d) the Executive Director shall inform the Council of all appointments.

3. The Council may decide, by a two-thirds vote, to reject any appointment that does not meet the general standards. Any such decision shall be made and held in confidence.

4. In the performance of their duties, the Executive Director and the staff shall not seek or receive instructions from any government or any other authority external to the Council. Each Party shall respect the international character of the responsibilities of the Executive Director and the staff and shall not seek to influence them in the discharge of their responsibilities.

5. The Secretariat shall provide technical, administrative and operational support to the Council and to committees and groups established by the Council, and such other support as the Council may direct.

6. The Executive Director shall submit for the approval of the Council the annual program and budget of the Commission, including provision for proposed cooperative activities and for the Secretariat to respond to contingencies.

7. The Secretariat shall, as appropriate, provide the Parties and the public information on where they may receive technical advice and expertise with respect to environmental matters.

8. The Secretariat shall safeguard: (a) from disclosure information it receives that could identify a non-governmental organization or person making a submission if the person or organization so requests or the Secretariat otherwise considers it appropriate; and (b) from public disclosure any information it receives from any non-

governmental organization or person where the information is designated by that non-governmental organization or person as confidential or proprietary.

Article 12: Annual Report of the Commission

1. The Secretariat shall prepare an annual report of the Commission in accordance with instructions from the Council. The Secretariat shall submit a draft of the report for review by the Council. The final report shall be released publicly.

2. The report shall cover: (a) activities and expenses of the Commission during the previous year; (b) the approved program and budget of the Commission for the subsequent year; (c) the actions taken by each Party in connection with its obligations under this Agreement, including data on the Party's environmental enforcement activities; (d) relevant views and information submitted by non-governmental organizations and persons, including summary data regarding submissions, and any other relevant information the Council deems appropriate; (e) recommendations made on any matter within the scope of this Agreement; and (f) any other matter that the Council instructs the Secretariat to include.

3. The report shall periodically address the state of the environment in the territories of the Parties.

Article 13: Secretariat Reports

1. The Secretariat may prepare a report for the Council on any matter within the scope of the annual program. Should the Secretariat wish to prepare a report on any other environmental matter related to the cooperative functions of this Agreement, it shall notify the Council and may proceed unless, within 30 days of such notification, the Council objects by a two-thirds vote to the preparation of the report. Such other environmental matters shall not include issues related to whether a Party has failed to enforce its environmental laws and regula-

tions. Where the Secretariat does not have specific expertise in the matter under review, it shall obtain the assistance of one or more independent experts of recognized experience in the matter to assist in the preparation of the report.

2. In preparing such a report, the Secretariat may draw upon any relevant technical, scientific or other information, including information: (a) that is publicly available; (b) submitted by interested non-governmental organizations and persons; (c) submitted by the Joint Public Advisory Committee; (d) furnished by a Party; (e) gathered through public consultations, such as conferences, seminars and symposia; or (f) developed by the Secretariat, or by independent experts engaged pursuant to paragraph 1.

3. The Secretariat shall submit its report to the Council, which shall make it publicly available, normally within 60 days following its submission, unless the Council otherwise decides.

Article 14: Submissions on Enforcement Matters

1. The Secretariat may consider a submission from any non-governmental organization or person asserting that a Party is failing to effectively enforce its environmental law, if the Secretariat finds that the submission: (a) is in writing in a language designated by that Party in a notification to the Secretariat; (b) clearly identifies the person or organization making the submission; (c) provides sufficient information to allow the Secretariat to review the submission, including any documentary evidence on which the submission may be based; (d) appears to be aimed at promoting enforcement rather than at harassing industry; (e) indicates that the matter has been communicated in writing to the relevant authorities of the Party and indicates the Party's response, if any; and (f) is filed by a person or organization residing or established in the territory of a Party.

2. Where the Secretariat determines that a submission meets the criteria set out in paragraph 1, the Secretariat shall determine whether the submission merits requesting a response from the Party. In deciding whether to request a response, the Secretariat shall be guided by whether: (a) the submission alleges harm to the person or organization making the submission; (b) the submission, alone or in combination with other submissions, raises matters whose further study in this process would advance the goals of this Agreement; (c) private remedies available under the Party's law have been pursued; and (d) the submission is drawn exclusively from mass media reports.

Where the Secretariat makes such a request, it shall forward to the Party a copy of the submission and any supporting information provided with the submission.

3. The Party shall advise the Secretariat within 30 days or, in exceptional circumstances and on notification to the Secretariat, within 60 days of delivery of the request: (a) whether the matter is the subject of a pending judicial or administrative proceeding, in which case the Secretariat shall proceed no further; and (b) of any other information that the Party wishes to submit, such as i) whether the matter was previously the subject of a judicial or administrative proceeding, and ii) whether private remedies in connection with the matter are available to the person or organization making the submission and whether they have been pursued.

Article 15: Factual Record

1. If the Secretariat considers that the submission, in the light of any response provided by the Party, warrants developing a factual record, the Secretariat shall so inform the Council and provide its reasons.

2. The Secretariat shall prepare a factual record if the Council, by a two-thirds vote, instructs it to do so.

3. The preparation of a factual record by the Secretariat pursuant to this Article shall be without prejudice to any further steps that may be taken with respect to any submission.

4. In preparing a factual record, the Secretariat shall consider any information furnished by a Party and may consider any relevant technical, scientific or other information: (a) that is publicly available; (b) submitted by interested non-governmental organizations or persons; (c) submitted by the Joint Public Advisory Committee; or (d) developed by the Secretariat or by independent experts.

5. The Secretariat shall submit a draft factual record to the Council. Any Party may provide comments on the accuracy of the draft within 45 days thereafter.

6. The Secretariat shall incorporate, as appropriate, any such comments in the final factual record and submit it to the Council.

7. The Council may, by a two-thirds vote, make the final factual record publicly available, normally within 60 days following its submission.

* * *

PART FOUR—COOPERATION AND PROVISION OF INFORMATION

Article 20: Cooperation

1. The Parties shall at all times endeavor to agree on the interpretation and application of this Agreement, and shall make every attempt through cooperation and Consultations to resolve any matter that might affect its operation.

2. To the maximum extent possible, each Party shall notify any other Party with an interest in the matter of any proposed or actual environmental measure that the Party considers might materially affect the operation of

this Agreement or otherwise substantially affect that other Party's interests under this Agreement.

3. On request of any other Party, a Party shall promptly provide information and respond to questions pertaining to any such actual or proposed environmental measure, whether or not that other Party has been previously notified of that measure.

4. Any Party may notify any other Party of, and provide to that Party, any credible information regarding possible violations of its environmental law, specific and sufficient to allow the other Party to inquire into the matter. The notified Party shall take appropriate steps in accordance with its law to so inquire and to respond to the other Party.

Article 21: Provision of Information

1. On request of the Council or the Secretariat, each Party shall, in accordance with its law, provide such information as the Council or the Secretariat may require, including: (a) promptly malting available any information in its possession required for the preparation of a report or factual record, including compliance and enforcement data; and (b) taking all reasonable steps to make available any other such information requested.

2. If a Party considers that a request for information from the Secretariat is excessive or otherwise unduly burdensome, it may so notify the Council. The Secretariat shall revise the scope of its request to comply with any limitations established by the Council by a two-thirds vote.

3. If a Party does not make available information requested by the Secretariat, as may be limited pursuant to paragraph 2, it shall promptly advise the Secretariat of its reasons in writing.

PART FIVE—CONSULTATION AND
RESOLUTION OF DISPUTES

Article 22: Consultations

1. Any Party may request in writing consultations with any other Party regarding whether there has been a persistent pattern of failure by that other Party to effectively enforce its environmental law.

2. The requesting Party shall deliver the request to the other Parties and to the Secretariat.

3. Unless the Council otherwise provides in its rules and procedures established under Article 9(2), a third Party that considers it has a substantial interest in the matter shall be entitled to participate in the consultations on delivery of written notice to the other Parties and to the Secretariat.

4. The consulting Parties shall make every attempt to arrive at a mutually satisfactory resolution of the matter through consultations under this Article.

Article 23: Initiation of Procedures

1. If the consulting Parties fail to resolve the matter pursuant to Article 22 within 60 days of delivery of a request for consultations, or such other period as the consulting Parties may agree, any such Party may request in writing a special session of the Council.

2. The requesting Party shall state in the request the matter complained of and shall deliver the request to the other Parties and to the Secretariat.

3. Unless it decides otherwise, the Council shall convene within 20 days of delivery of the request and shall endeavor to resolve the dispute promptly.

4. The Council may: (a) call on such technical advisers or create such working groups or expert groups as it deems necessary, (b) have recourse to good offices, concil-

iation, mediation or such other dispute resolution procedures, or (c) make recommendations, as may assist the consulting Parties to reach a mutually satisfactory resolution of the dispute. Any such recommendations shall be made public if the Council, by a two-thirds vote, so decides.

5. Where the Council decides that a matter is more properly covered by another agreement or arrangement to which the consulting Parties are party, it shall refer the matter to those Parties for appropriate action in accordance with such other agreement or arrangement.

Article 24: Request for an Arbitral Panel

1. If the matter has not been resolved within 60 days after the Council has convened pursuant to Article 23, the Council shall, on the written request of any consulting Party and by a two-thirds vote, convene an arbitral panel to consider the matter where the alleged persistent pattern of failure by the Party complained against to effectively enforce its environmental law relates to a situation involving workplaces, firms, companies or sectors that produce goods or provide services: (a) traded between the territories of the Parties; or (b) that compete, in the territory of the Party complained against, with goods or services produced or provided by persons of another Party.

2. A third Party that considers it has a substantial interest in the matter shall be entitled to join as a complaining Party on delivery of written notice of its intention to participate to the disputing Parties and the Secretariat. The notice shall be delivered at the earliest possible time, and in any event no later than seven days after the date of the vote of the Council to convene a panel.

3. Unless otherwise agreed by the disputing Parties, the panel shall be established and perform its functions in a manner consistent with the provisions of this Part.

Article 25: Roster

1. The Council shall establish and maintain a roster of up to 45 individuals who are willing and able to serve as panelists. The roster members shall be appointed by consensus for terms of three years, and may be reappointed.

2. Roster members shall: (a) have expertise or experience in environmental law or its enforcement, or in the resolution of disputes arising under international agreements, or other relevant scientific, technical or professional expertise or experience; (b) be chosen strictly on the basis of objectivity, reliability and sound judgment; (c) be independent of, and not be affiliated with or take instructions from, any Party, the Secretariat or the Joint Public Advisory Committee; and (d) comply with a code of conduct to be established by the Council.

Article 26: Qualifications of Panelists

1. All panelists shall meet the qualifications set out in Article 25(2).

2. Individuals may not serve as panelists for a dispute in which: (a) they have participated pursuant to Article 23(4); or (b) they have, or a person or organization with which they are affiliated has, an interest, as set out in the code of conduct established under Article 25(2)(d).

Article 27: Panel Selection

1. Where there are two disputing Parties, the following procedures shall apply: (a) The panel shall comprise five members. (b) The disputing Parties shall endeavor to agree on the chair of the panel within 15 days after the Council votes to convene the panel. If the disputing Parties are unable to agree on the chair within this period, the disputing Party chosen by lot shall select within five days a chair who is not a citizen of that Party. (c) Within 15 days of selection of the chair, each disput-

ing Party shall select two panelists who are citizens of the other disputing Party. (d) If a disputing Party fails to select its panelists within such period, such panelists shall be selected by lot from among the roster members who are citizens of the other disputing Party.

2.   Where there are more than two disputing Parties, the following procedures shall apply: (a) The panel shall comprise five members. (b) The disputing Parties shall endeavor to agree on the chair of the panel within 15 days after the Council votes to convene the panel. If the disputing Parties are unable to agree on the chair within this period, the Party or Parties on the side of the dispute chosen by lot shall select within 10 days a chair who is not a citizen of such Party or Parties. (c) Within 30 days of selection of the chair, the Party complained against shall select two panelists, one of whom is a citizen of a complaining Party, and the other of whom is a citizen of another complaining Party. The complaining Parties shall select two panelists who are citizens of the Party complained against. (d) If any disputing Party fails to select a panelist within such period, such panelist shall be selected by lot in accordance with the citizenship criteria of subparagraph (c).

3.   Panelists shall normally be selected from the roster. Any disputing Party may exercise a peremptory challenge against any individual not on the roster who is proposed as a panelist by a disputing Party within 30 days after the individual has been proposed.

4.   If a disputing Party believes that a panelist is in violation of the code of conduct, the disputing Parties shall consult and, if they agree, the panelist shall be removed and a new panelist shall be selected in accordance with this Article.

Article 28: Rules of Procedure

1.   The Council shall establish Model Rules of Procedure. The procedures shall provide: (a) a right to at least

one hearing before the panel; (b) the opportunity to make initial and rebuttal written submissions; and (c) that no panel may disclose which panelists are associated with majority or minority opinions.

2. Unless the disputing Parties otherwise agree, panels convened under this Part shall be established and conduct their proceedings in accordance with the Model Rules of Procedure.

3. Unless the disputing Parties otherwise agree within 20 days after the Council votes to convene the panel, the terms of reference shall be:

"To examine, in light of the relevant provisions of the Agreement, including those contained in Part Five, whether there has been a persistent pattern of failure by the Party complained against to effectively enforce its environmental law, and to make findings, determinations and recommendations in accordance with Article 31(2)."

Article 29: Third Party Participation

A Party that is not a disputing Party, on delivery of a written notice to the disputing Parties and to the Secretariat, shall be entitled to attend all hearings, to make written and oral submissions to the panel and to receive written submissions of the disputing Parties.

Article 30: Role of Experts

On request of a disputing Party, or on its own initiative, the panel may seek information and technical advice from any person or body that it deems appropriate, provided that the disputing Parties so agree and subject to such terms and conditions as such Parties may agree.

Article 31: Initial Report

1. Unless the disputing Parties otherwise agree, the panel shall base its report on the submissions and argu-

ments of the Parties and on any information before it pursuant to Article 30.

2. Unless the disputing Parties otherwise agree, the panel shall, within 180 days after the last panelist is selected, present to the disputing Parties an initial report containing: (a) findings of fact; (b) its determination as to whether there has been a persistent pattern of failure by the Party complained against to effectively enforce its environmental law, or any other determination requested in the terms of reference; and (c) in the event the panel makes an affirmative determination under subparagraph (b), its recommendations, if any, for the resolution of the dispute, which normally shall be that the Party complained against adopt and implement an action plan sufficient to remedy the pattern of non-enforcement.

3. Panelists may furnish separate opinions on matters not unanimously agreed.

4. A disputing Party may submit written comments to the panel on its initial report within 30 days of presentation of the report.

5. In such an event, and after considering such written comments, the panel, on its own initiative or on the request of any disputing Party, may: (a) request the views of any participating Party; (b) reconsider its report; and (c) make any further examination that it considers appropriate.

Article 32: Final Report

1. The panel shall present to the disputing Parties a final report, including any separate opinions on matters not unanimously agreed, within 60 days of presentation of the initial report, unless the disputing Parties otherwise agree.

2. The disputing Parties shall transmit to the Council the final report of the panel, as well as any written views that a disputing Party desires to be appended, on a

confidential basis within 15 days after it is presented to them.

3. The final report of the panel shall be published five days after it is transmitted to the Council.

Article 33: Implementation of Final Report

If, in its final report, a panel determines that there has been a persistent pattern of failure by the Party complained against to effectively enforce its environmental law, the disputing Parties may agree on a mutually satisfactory action plan, which normally shall conform with the determinations and recommendations of the panel. The disputing Parties shall promptly notify the Secretariat and the Council of any agreed resolution of the dispute.

Article 34: Review of Implementation

1. If, in its final report, a panel determines that there has been a persistent pattern of failure by the Party complained against to effectively enforce its environmental law, and: (a) the disputing Parties have not agreed on an action plan under Article 33 within 60 days of the date of the final report, or (b) the disputing Parties cannot agree on whether the Party complained against is fully implementing (i) an action plan agreed under Article 33, (ii) an action plan deemed to have been established by a panel under paragraph 2, or (iii) an action plan approved or established by a panel under paragraph 4, any disputing Party may request that the panel be reconvened. The requesting Party shall deliver the request in writing to the other Parties and to the Secretariat. The Council shall reconvene the panel on delivery of the request to the Secretariat.

2. No Party may make a request under paragraph 1(a) earlier than 60 days, or later than 120 days, after the date of the final report. If the disputing Parties have not agreed to an action plan and if no request was made under paragraph 1(a), the last action plan, if any, submit-

ted by the Party complained against to the complaining Party or Parties within 60 days of the date of the final report, or such other period as the disputing Parties may agree, shall be deemed to have been established by the panel 120 days after the date of the final report.

3. A request under paragraph 1(b) may be made no earlier than 180 days after an action plan has been: (a) agreed under Article 33; (b) deemed to have been established by a panel under paragraph 2; or (c) approved or established by a panel under paragraph 4; and only during the term of any such action plan.

4. Where a panel has been reconvened under paragraph 1(a), it: (a) shall determine whether any action plan proposed by the Party complained against is sufficient to remedy the pattern of non-enforcement and (i) if so, shall approve the plan, or (ii) if not, shall establish such a plan consistent with the law of the Party complained against, and (b) may, where warranted, impose a monetary enforcement assessment in accordance with Annex 34, within 90 days after the panel has been reconvened or such other period as the disputing Parties may agree.

5. Where a panel has been reconvened under paragraph 1(b), it shall determine either that: (a) the Party complained against is fully implementing the action plan, in which case the panel may not impose a monetary enforcement assessment, or (b) the Party complained against is not fully implementing the action plan, in which case the panel shall impose a monetary enforcement assessment in accordance with Annex 34, within 60 days after it has been reconvened or such other period as the disputing Parties may agree.

6. A panel reconvened under this Article shall provide that the Party complained against shall fully implement any action plan referred to in paragraph 4(a)(ii) or 5(b), and pay any monetary enforcement assessment imposed

under paragraph 4(b) or 5(b), and any such provision shall be final.

Article 35: Further Proceeding

A complaining Party may, at any time beginning 180 days after a panel determination under Article 34(5)(b), request in writing that a panel be reconvened to determine whether the Party complained against is fully implementing the action plan. On delivery of the request to the other Parties and the Secretariat, the Council shall reconvene the panel. The panel shall make the determination within 60 days after it has been reconvened or such other period as the disputing Parties may agree.

Article 36: Suspension of Benefits

1. Subject to Annex 36A, where a Party fails to pay a monetary enforcement assessment within 180 days after it is imposed by a panel: (a) under Article 34(4)(b), or (b) under Article 34(5)(b), except where benefits may be suspended under paragraph 2(a), any complaining Party or Parties may suspend, in accordance with Annex 36B, the application to the Party complained against of NAFTA benefits in an amount no greater than that sufficient to collect the monetary enforcement assessment.

2. Subject to Annex 36A, where a panel has made a determination under Article 34(5)(b) and the panel: (a) has previously imposed a monetary enforcement assessment under Article 34(4)(b) or established an action plan under Article 34(4)(a)(ii); or (b) has subsequently determined under Article 35 that a Party is not fully implementing an action plan; the complaining Party or Parties may, in accordance with Annex 36B, suspend annually the application to the Party complained against of NAFTA benefits in an amount no greater than the monetary enforcement assessment imposed by the panel under Article 34(5)(b).

3.   Where more than one complaining Party suspends benefits under paragraph 1 or 2, the combined suspension shall be no greater than the amount of the monetary enforcement assessment.

4.   Where a Party has suspended benefits under paragraph 1 or 2, the Council shall, on the delivery of a written request by the Party complained against to the other Parties and the Secretariat, reconvene the panel to determine whether the monetary enforcement assessment has been paid or collected, or whether the Party complained against is fully implementing the action plan, as the case may be. The panel shall submit its report within 45 days after it has been reconvened. If the panel determines that the assessment has been paid or collected, or that the Party complained against is fully implementing the action plan, the suspension of benefits under paragraph 1 or 2, as the case may be, shall be terminated.

5.   On the written request of the Party complained against, delivered to the other Parties and the Secretariat, the Council shall reconvene the panel to determine whether the suspension of benefits by the complaining Party or Parties pursuant to paragraph 1 or 2 is manifestly excessive. Within 45 days of the request, the panel shall present a report to the disputing Parties containing its determination.

PART SIX—GENERAL PROVISIONS

Article 37: Enforcement Principle

Nothing in this Agreement shall be construed to empower a Party's authorities to undertake environmental law enforcement activities in the territory of another Party.

Article 38: Private Rights

No Party may provide for a right of action under its law against any other Party on the ground that another Party has acted in a manner inconsistent with this Agreement.

Article 39: Protection of Information

1. Nothing in this Agreement shall be construed to require a Party to make available or allow access to information: (a) the disclosure of which would impede its environmental law enforcement; or (b) that is protected from disclosure by its law governing business or proprietary information, personal privacy or the confidentiality of governmental decision making.

2. If a Party provides confidential or proprietary information to another Party, the Council, the Secretariat or the Joint Public Advisory Committee, the recipient shall treat the information on the same basis as the Party providing the information.

3. Confidential or proprietary information provided by a Party to a panel under this Agreement shall be treated in accordance with the rules of procedure established under Article 28.

Article 40: Relation to Other Environmental Agreements

Nothing in this Agreement shall be construed to affect the existing rights and obligations of the Parties under other international environmental agreements, including conservation agreements, to which such Parties are party.

Article 41: Extent of Obligations

Annex 41 applies to the Parties specified in that Annex.

Article 42: National Security

Nothing in this Agreement shall be construed: (a) to require any Party to make available or provide access to information the disclosure of which it determines to be contrary to its essential security interests; or (b) to prevent any Party from taking any actions that it considers necessary for the protection of its essential security interests relating to (i) arms, ammunition and implements of war, or (ii) the implementation of national policies or international agreements respecting the non-proliferation of nuclear weapons or other nuclear explosive devices.

Article 43: Funding of the Commission

Each Party shall contribute an equal share of the annual budget of the Commission, subject to the availability of appropriated funds in accordance with the Party's legal procedures. No Party shall be obligated to pay more than any other Party in respect of an annual budget.

Article 44: Privileges and Immunities

The Executive Director and staff of the Secretariat shall enjoy in the territory of each Party such privileges and immunities as are necessary for the exercise of their functions.

Article 45: Definitions

1. For purposes of this Agreement:

A Party has not failed to "effectively enforce its environmental law" or to comply with Article 5(1) in a particular case where the action or inaction in question by agencies or officials of that Party: (a) reflects a reasonable exercise of their discretion in respect of investigatory, prosecutorial, regulatory or compliance matters; or (b) results from bona fide decisions to allocate resources to enforcement in respect of other environmental matters determined to have higher priorities;

"non-governmental organization" means any scientific, professional, business, non-profit, or public interest organization or association which is neither affilated with, nor under the direction of, a government;

"persistent pattern" means a sustained or recurring course of action or inaction beginning after the date of entry into force of this Agreement;

"province" means a province of Canada, and includes the Yukon Territory and the Northwest Territories and their successors; and "territory" means for a Party the territory of that Party as set out in Annex 45.

2. For purposes of Article 14(1) and Part Five: (a) "environmental law" means any statute or regulation of a Party, or provision thereof, the primary purpose of which is the protection of the environment, or the prevention of a danger to human life or health, through (i) the prevention, abatement or control of the release, discharge, or emission of pollutants or environmental contaminants, (ii) the control of environmentally hazardous or toxic chemicals, substances, materials and wastes, and the dissemination of information related thereto, or (iii) the protection of wild flora or fauna, including endangered species, their habitat, and specially protected natural areas in the Party's territory, but does not include any statute or regulation, or provision thereof, directly related to worker safety or health.

(b) For greater certainty, the term "environmental law" does not include any statute or regulation, or provision thereof, the primary purpose of which is managing the commercial harvest or exploitation, or subsistence or aboriginal harvesting, of natural resources.

(c) The primary purpose of a particular statutory or regulatory provision for purposes of subparagraphs (a) and (b) shall be determined by reference to its primary purpose, rather than to the primary purpose of the statute or regulation of which it is part.

3. For purposes of Article 14(3), "judicial or administrative proceeding" means: (a) a domestic judicial, quasi-judicial or administrative action pursued by the Party in a timely fashion and in accordance with its law. Such actions comprise: mediation; arbitration; the process of issuing a license, permit, or authorization; seeking an assurance of voluntary compliance or a compliance agreement; seeking sanctions or remedies in an administrative or judicial forum; and the process of issuing an adminis-

trative order; and (b) an international dispute resolution proceeding to which the Party is party.

PART SEVEN—FINAL PROVISIONS

* * *

Article 49: Accession

Any country or group of countries may accede to this Agreement subject to such terms and conditions as may be agreed between such country or countries and the Council and following approval in accordance with the applicable legal procedures of each country.

Article 50: Withdrawal

A Party may withdraw from this Agreement six months after it provides written notice of withdrawal to the other Parties. If a Party withdraws, the Agreement shall remain in force for the remaining Parties.

Article 51: Authentic Texts

The English, French, and Spanish texts of this Agreement are equally authentic.

ANNEX 34—MONETARY ENFORCEMENT ASSESSMENTS

1. For the first year after the date of entry into force of this Agreement, any monetary enforcement assessment shall be no greater than 20 million dollars (U.S.) or its equivalent in the currency of the Party complained against. Thereafter, any monetary enforcement assessment shall be no greater than .007 percent of total trade in goods between the Parties during the most recent year for which data are available.

2. In determining the amount of the assessment, the panel shall take into account: (a) the pervasiveness and duration of the Party's persistent pattern of failure to effectively enforce its environmental law; (b) the level of

enforcement that could reasonably be expected of a Party given its resource constraints; (c) the reasons, if any, provided by the Party for not fully implementing an action plan; (d) efforts made by the Party to begin remedying the pattern of non-enforcement after the final report of the panel; and (e) any other relevant factors.

3. All monetary enforcement assessments shall be paid in the currency of the Party complained against into a fund established in the name of the Commission by the Council and shall be expended at the direction of the Council to improve or enhance the environment or environmental law enforcement in the Party complained against, consistent with its law.

* * *

ANNEX 36B—SUSPENSION OF BENEFITS

1. Where a complaining Party suspends NAFTA tariff benefits in accordance with this Agreement, the Party may increase the rates of duty on originating goods of the Party complained against to levels not to exceed the lesser of: (a) the rate that was applicable to those goods immediately prior to the date of entry into force of the NAFTA, and (b) the Most–Favored–Nation rate applicable to those goods on the date the Party suspends such benefits, and such increase may be applied only for such time as is necessary to collect, through such increase, the monetary enforcement assessment.

2. In considering what tariff or other benefits to suspend pursuant to Article 36(1) or (2): (a) a complaining Party shall first seek to suspend benefits in the same sector or sectors as that in respect of which there has been a persistent pattern of failure by the Party complained against to effectively enforce its environmental law; and (b) a complaining Party that considers it is not practicable or effective to suspend benefits in the same sector or sectors may suspend benefits in other sectors.

* * *

APPENDIX III

NORTH AMERICAN AGREEMENT ON LABOR COOPERATION (1994)

* * *

PART ONE—OBJECTIVES

* * *

PART TWO—OBLIGATIONS

Article 2: Levels of Protection

Affirming full respect for each Party's constitution, and recognizing the right of each Party to establish its own domestic labor standards, and to adopt or modify accordingly its labor laws and regulations, each Party shall ensure that its labor laws and regulations provide for high labor standards, consistent with high quality and productivity workplaces, and shall continue to strive to improve those standards in that light.

Article 3: Government Enforcement Action

1. Each Party shall promote compliance with and effectively enforce its labor law through appropriate government action, subject to Article 42, such as: (a) appointing and training inspectors; (b) monitoring compliance and investigating suspected violations, including through on-site inspections; (c) seeking assurances of voluntary compliance; (d) requiring record keeping and reporting; (e) encouraging the establishment of worker-management committees to address labor regulation of

the workplace; (f) providing or encouraging mediation, conciliation and arbitration services; or (g) initiating, in a timely manner, proceedings to seek appropriate sanctions or remedies for violations of its labor law.

2. Each Party shall ensure that its competent authorities give due consideration in accordance with its law to any request by an employer, employee or their representatives, or other interested person, for an investigation of an alleged violation of the Party's labor law.

Article 4: Private Action

1. Each Party shall ensure that persons with a legally recognized interest under its law in a particular matter have appropriate access to administrative, quasi-judicial, judicial or labor tribunals for the enforcement of the Party's labor law.

2. Each Party's law shall ensure that such persons may have recourse to, as appropriate, procedures by which rights arising under: (a) its labor law, including in respect of occupational safety and health, employment standards, industrial relations and migrant workers, and (b) collective agreements, can be enforced.

Article 5: Procedural Guarantees

1. Each Party shall ensure that its administrative, quasi-judicial, judicial and labor tribunal proceedings for the enforcement of its labor law are fair, equitable and transparent and, to this end, each Party shall provide that: (a) such proceedings comply with due process of law; (b) any hearings in such proceedings are open to the public, except where the administration of justice otherwise requires; (c) the parties to such proceedings are entitled to support or defend their respective positions and to present information or evidence; and (d) such proceedings are not unnecessarily complicated and do not entail unreasonable charges or time limits or unwarranted delays.

2. Each Party shall provide that final decisions on the merits of the case in such proceedings are: (a) in writing and preferably state the reasons on which the decisions are based; (b) made available without undue delay to the parties to the proceedings and, consistent with its law, to the public; and (c) based on information or evidence in respect of which the parties were offered the opportunity to be heard.

3. Each Party shall provide, as appropriate, that parties to such proceedings have the right, in accordance with its law, to seek review and, where warranted, correction of final decisions issued in such proceedings.

4. Each Party shall ensure that tribunals that conduct or review such proceedings are impartial and independent and do not have any substantial interest in the outcome of the matter.

5. Each Party shall provide that the parties to administrative, quasi-judicial, judicial or labor tribunal proceedings may seek remedies to ensure the enforcement of their labor rights. Such remedies may include, as appropriate, orders, compliance agreements, fines, penalties, imprisonment, injunctions or emergency workplace closures.

6. Each Party may, as appropriate, adopt or maintain labor defense offices to represent or advise workers or their organizations.

7. Nothing in this Article shall be construed to require a Party to establish, or to prevent a Party from establishing, a judicial system for the enforcement of its labor law distinct from its system for the enforcement of laws in general.

8. For greater certainty, decisions by each Party's administrative, quasi-judicial, judicial or labor tribunals, or pending decisions, as well as related proceedings shall

not be subject to revision or reopened under the provisions of this Agreement.

* * *

PART THREE—COMMISSION FOR LABOR COOPERATION

Article 8: The Commission

1. The Parties hereby establish the Commission for Labor Cooperation.

2. The Commission shall comprise a ministerial Council and a Secretariat. The Commission shall be assisted by the National Administrative Office of each Party.

Section A: The Council

Article 9: Council Structure and Procedures

1. The Council shall comprise labor ministers of the Parties or their designees.

2. The Council shall establish its rules and procedures.

3. The Council shall convene: (a) at least once a year in regular session, and (b) in special session at the request of any Party.

Regular sessions shall be chaired successively by each Party.

4. The Council may hold public sessions to report on appropriate matters.

5. The Council may: (a) establish, and assign responsibilities to, committees, working groups or expert groups; and (b) seek the advice of independent experts.

6. All decisions and recommendations of the Council shall be taken by consensus, except as the Council may otherwise decide or as otherwise provided in this Agreement.

Article 10: Council Functions

1. The Council shall be the governing body of the Commission and shall: (a) oversee the implementation and develop recommendations on the further elaboration of this Agreement and, to this end, the Council shall, within four years after the date of entry into force of this Agreement, review its operation and effectiveness in the light of experience; (b) direct the work and activities of the Secretariat and of any committees or working groups convened by the Council; (c) establish priorities for cooperative action and, as appropriate, develop technical assistance programs on the matters set out in Article 11; (d) approve the annual plan of activities and budget of the Commission; (e) approve for publication, subject to such terms or conditions as it may impose, reports and studies prepared by the Secretariat, independent experts or working groups; (f) facilitate Party-to-Party consultations, including through the exchange of information; (g) address questions and differences that may arise between the Parties regarding the interpretation or application of this Agreement; and (h) promote the collection and publication of comparable data on enforcement, labor standards and labor market indicators.

2. The Council may consider any other matter within the scope of this Agreement and take such other action in the exercise of its functions as the Parties may agree.

Article 11: Cooperative Activities

* * *

Article 13: Secretariat Functions

1. The Secretariat shall assist the Council in exercising its functions and shall provide such other support as the Council may direct.

2. The Executive Director shall submit for the approval of the Council the annual plan of activities and budget

for the Commission, including provision for contingencies and proposed cooperative activities.

3. The Secretariat shall report to the Council annually on its activities and expenditures.

4. The Secretariat shall periodically publish a list of matters resolved under Part Four or referred to Evaluation Committees of Experts.

Article 14: Secretariat Reports and Studies

1. The Secretariat shall periodically prepare background reports setting out publicly available information supplied by each Party on: (a) labor law and administrative procedures; (b) trends and administrative strategies related to the implementation and enforcement of labor law; (c) labor market conditions such as employment rates, average wages and labor productivity; and (d) human resource development issues such as training and adjustment programs.

2. The Secretariat shall prepare a study on any matter as the Council may request. The Secretariat shall prepare any such study in accordance with terms of reference established by the Council, and may (a) consider any relevant information; (b) where it does not have specific expertise in the matter, engage one or more independent experts of recognized experience; and (c) include proposals on the matter.

3. The Secretariat shall submit a draft of any report or study that it prepares pursuant to paragraph 1 or 2 to the Council. If the Council considers that a report or study is materially inaccurate or otherwise deficient, the Council may remand it to the Secretariat for reconsideration or other disposition.

4. Secretariat reports and studies shall be made public 45 days after their approval by the Council, unless the Council otherwise decides.

Article 15: National Administrative Office Structure

1. Each Party shall establish a National Administrative Office (NAO) at the federal government level and notify the Secretariat and the other Parties of its location.

2. Each Party shall designate a Secretary for its NAO, who shall be responsible for its administration and management.

3. Each Party shall be responsible for the operation and costs of its NAO.

Article 16: NAO Functions

1. Each NAO shall serve as a point of contact with: (a) governmental agencies of that Party; (b) NAOs of the other Parties; and (c) the Secretariat.

2. Each NAO shall promptly provide publicly available information requested by: (a) the Secretariat for reports under Article 14(1); (b) the Secretariat for studies under Article 14(2); (c) a NAO of another Party; and (d) an ECE.

3. Each NAO shall provide for the submission and receipt, and periodically publish a list, of public communications on labor law matters arising in the territory of another Party. Each NAO shall review such matters, as appropriate, in accordance with domestic procedures.

* * *

PART FOUR—COOPERATIVE CONSULTATIONS AND EVALUATIONS

Article 20: Cooperation

The Parties shall at all times endeavor to agree on the interpretation and application of this Agreement, and shall make every attempt through cooperation and consultations to resolve any matter that might affect its operation.

Article 21: Consultations between NAOs

1. A NAO may request consultations, to be conducted in accordance with the procedures set out in paragraph 2, with another NAO in relation to the other Party's labor law, its administration, or labor market conditions in its territory. The requesting NAO shall notify the NAOs of the other Parties and the Secretariat of its request.

2. In such consultations, the requested NAO shall promptly provide such publicly available data or information, including: (a) descriptions of its laws, regulations, procedures, policies or practices, (b) proposed changes to such procedures, policies or practices, and (c) such clarifications and explanations related to such matters, as may assist the consulting NAOs to better understand and respond to the issues raised.

3. Any other NAO shall be entitled to participate in the consultations on notice to the other NAOs and the Secretariat.

Article 22: Ministerial Consultations

1. Any Party may request in writing consultations with another Party at the ministerial level regarding any matter within the scope of this Agreement. The requesting Party shall provide specific and sufficient information to allow the requested Party to respond.

2. The requesting Party shall promptly notify the other Parties of the request. A third Party that considers it has a substantial interest in the matter shall be entitled to participate in the consultations on notice to the other Parties.

3. The consulting Parties shall make every attempt to resolve the matter through consultations under this Article, including through the exchange of sufficient publicly available information to enable a full examination of the matter.

Section B: Evaluations

Article 23: Evaluation Committee of Experts

1. If a matter has not been resolved after ministerial consultations pursuant to Article 22, any consulting Party may request in writing the establishment of an Evaluation Committee of Experts (ECE). The requesting Party shall deliver the request to the other Parties and to the Secretariat. Subject to paragraphs 3 and 4, the Council shall establish an ECE on delivery of the request.

2. The ECE shall analyze, in the light of the objectives of this Agreement and in a non-adversarial manner, patterns of practice by each Party in the enforcement of its occupational safety and health or other technical labor standards as they apply to the particular matter considered by the Parties under Article 22.

3. No ECE may be convened if a Party obtains a ruling under Annex 23 that the matter: (a) is not trade-related; or (b) is not covered by mutually recognized labor laws.

4. No ECE may be convened regarding any matter that was previously the subject of an ECE report in the absence of such new information as would warrant a further report.

Article 24: Rules of Procedure

1. The Council shall establish rules of procedure for ECEs, which shall apply unless the Council otherwise decides. The rules of procedures shall provide that: (a) an ECE shall normally comprise three members; (b) the chair shall be selected by the Council from a roster of experts developed in consultation with the ILO pursuant to Article 45 and, where possible, other members shall be selected from a roster developed by the Parties; (c) ECE members shall (i) have expertise or experience in labor matters or other appropriate disciplines, (ii) be chosen strictly on the basis of objectivity, reliability and sound

judgment, (iii) be independent of, and not be affiliated with or take instructions from, any Party or the Secretariat, and (iv) comply with a code of conduct to be established by the Council; (d) an ECE may invite written submissions from the Parties and the public; (e) an ECE may consider, in preparing its report, any information provided by (i) the Secretariat, (ii) the NAO of each Party, (iii) organizations, institutions and persons with relevant expertise, and (iv) the public; and (f) each Party shall have a reasonable opportunity to review and comment on information that the ECE receives and to make written submissions to the ECE.

2. The Secretariat and the NAOs shall provide appropriate administrative assistance to an ECE, in accordance with the rules of procedure established by the Council under paragraph 1.

Article 25: Draft Evaluation Reports

1. Within 120 days after it is established, or such other period as the Council may decide, the ECE shall present a draft report for consideration by the Council, which shall contain: (a) a comparative assessment of the matter under consideration; (b) its conclusions; and (c) where appropriate, practical recommendations that may assist the Parties in respect of the matter.

2. Each Party may submit written views to the ECE on its draft report. The ECE shall take such views into account in preparing its final report.

Article 26: Final Evaluation Reports

1. The ECE shall present a final report to the Council within 60 days after presentation of the draft report, unless the Council otherwise decides.

2. The final report shall be published within 30 days after its presentation to the Council, unless the Council otherwise decides.

3.   The Parties shall provide to each other and the Secretariat written responses to the recommendations contained in the ECE report within 90 days of its publication.

4.   The final report and such written responses shall be tabled for consideration at the next regular session of the Council. The Council may keep the matter under review.

PART FIVE—RESOLUTION OF DISPUTES

Article 27: Consultations

1.   Following presentation to the Council under Article 26(1) of an ECE final report that addresses the enforcement of a Party's occupational safety and health, child labor or minimum wage technical labor standards, any Party may request in writing consultations with any other Party regarding whether there has been a persistent pattern of failure by that other Party to effectively enforce such standards in respect of the general subject matter addressed in the report.

2.   The requesting Party shall deliver the request to the other Parties and to the Secretariat.

3.   Unless the Council otherwise provides in its rules and procedures established under Article 9(2), a third Party that considers it has a substantial interest in the matter shall be entitled to participate in the consultations on delivery of written notice to the other Parties and to the Secretariat.

4.   The consulting Parties shall make every attempt to arrive at a mutually satisfactory resolution of the matter through consultations under this Article.

Article 28: Initiation of Procedures

1.   If the consulting Parties fail to resolve the matter pursuant to Article 27 within 60 days of delivery of a

request for consultations, or such other period as the consulting Parties may agree, any such Party may request in writing a special session of the Council.

2. The requesting Party shall state in the request the matter complained of and shall deliver the request to the other Parties and to the Secretariat.

3. Unless it decides otherwise, the Council shall convene within 20 days of delivery of the request and shall endeavor to resolve the dispute promptly.

4. The Council may: (a) call on such technical advisers or create such working groups or expert groups as it deems necessary, (b) have recourse to good offices, conciliation, mediation or such other dispute resolution procedures, or (c) make recommendations, as may assist the consulting Parties to reach a mutually satisfactory resolution of the dispute. Any such recommendations shall be made public if the Council, by a two-thirds vote, so decides.

5. Where the Council decides that a matter is more properly covered by another agreement or arrangement to which the consulting Parties are party, it shall refer the matter to those Parties for appropriate action in accordance with such other agreement or arrangement.

Article 29: Request for an Arbitral Panel

1. If the matter has not been resolved within 60 days after the Council has convened pursuant to Article 28, the Council shall, on the written request of any consulting Party and by a two-thirds vote, convene an arbitral panel to consider the matter where the alleged persistent pattern of failure by the Party complained against to effectively enforce its occupational safety and health, child labor or minimum wage technical labor standards is: (a) trade-related; and (b) covered by mutually recognized labor laws.

2. A third Party that considers it has a substantial interest in the matter shall be entitled to join as a complaining Party on delivery of written notice of its intention to participate to the disputing Parties and the Secretariat. The notice shall be delivered at the earliest possible time, and in any event no later than seven days after the date of the vote of the Council to convene a panel.

3. Unless otherwise agreed by the disputing Parties, the panel shall be established and perform its functions in a manner consistent with the provisions of this Part.

Article 30: Roster

1. The Council shall establish and maintain a roster of up to 45 individuals who are willing and able to serve as panelists. The roster members shall be appointed by consensus for terms of three years, and may be reappointed.

2. Roster members shall: (a) have expertise or experience in labor law or its enforcement, or in the resolution of disputes arising under international agreements, or other relevant scientific, technical or professional expertise or experience; (b) be chosen strictly on the basis of objectivity, reliability and sound judgment; (c) be independent of, and not be affiliated with or take instructions from, any Party or the Secretariat; and (d) comply with a code of conduct to be established by the Council.

Article 31: Qualifications of Panelists

1. All panelists shall meet the qualifications set out in Article 30.

2. Individuals may not serve as panelists for a dispute where: (a) they have participated pursuant to Article 28(4) or participated as members of an ECE that addressed the matter; or (b) they have, or a person or organization with which they are affiliated has, an inter-

est in the matter, as set out in the code of conduct established under Article 30(2)(d).

Article 32: Panel Selection

1. Where there are two disputing Parties, the following procedures shall apply: (a) The panel shall comprise five members. (b) The disputing Parties shall endeavor to agree on the chair of the panel within 15 days after the Council votes to convene the panel. If the disputing Parties are unable to agree on the chair within this period, the disputing Party chosen by lot shall select within five days a chair who is not a citizen of that Party. (c) Within 15 days of selection of the chair, each disputing Party shall select two panelists who are citizens of the other disputing Party. (d) If a disputing Party fails to select its panelists within such period, such panelists shall be selected by lot from among the roster members who are citizens of the other disputing Party.

2. Where there are more than two disputing Parties, the following procedures shall apply: (a) The panel shall comprise five members. (b) The disputing Parties shall endeavor to agree on the chair of the panel within 15 days after the Council votes to convene the panel. If the disputing Parties are unable to agree on the chair within this period, the Party or Parties on the side of the dispute chosen by lot shall select within 10 days a chair who is not a citizen of such Party or Parties. (c) Within 30 days of selection of the chair, the Party complained against shall select two panelists, one of whom is a citizen of a complaining Party, and the other of whom is a citizen of another complaining Party. The complaining Parties shall select two panelists who are citizens of the Party complained against. (d) If any disputing Party fails to select a panelist within such period, such panelist shall be selected by lot in accordance with the citizenship criteria of subparagraph (c).

3.   Panelists shall normally be selected from the roster. Any disputing Party may exercise a peremptory challenge against any individual not on the roster who is proposed as a panelist by a disputing Party within 30 days after the individual has been proposed.

4.   If a disputing Party believes that a panelist is in violation of the code of conduct, the disputing Parties shall consult and, if they agree, the panelist shall be removed and a new panelist shall be selected in accordance with this Article.

Article 33: Rules of Procedure

1.   The Council shall establish Model Rules of Procedure. The procedures shall provide: (a) a right to at least one hearing before the panel; (b) the opportunity to make initial and rebuttal written submissions; and (c) that no panel may disclose which panelists are associated with majority or minority opinions.

2.   Unless the disputing Parties otherwise agree, panels convened under this Part shall be established and conduct their proceedings in accordance with the Model Rules of Procedure.

3.   Unless the disputing Parties otherwise agree within 20 days after the Council votes to convene the panel, the terms of reference shall be:

"To examine, in light of the relevant provisions of the Agreement including those contained in Part Five, whether there has been a persistent pattern of failure by the Party complained against to effectively enforce its occupational safety and health, child labor or minimum wage technical labor standards, and to make findings, determinations and recommendations in accordance with Article 36(2)."

Article 34: Third Party Participation

A Party that is not a disputing Party, on delivery of a written notice to the disputing Parties and the Secretariat, shall be entitled to attend all hearings, to make written and oral submissions to the panel and to receive written submissions of the disputing Parties.

Article 35: Role of Experts

On request of a disputing Party, or on its own initiative, the panel may seek information and technical advice from any person or body that it deems appropriate, provided that the disputing Parties so agree and subject to such terms and conditions as such Parties may agree.

Article 36: Initial Report

1. Unless the disputing Parties otherwise agree, the panel shall base its report on the submissions and arguments of the disputing Parties and on any information before it pursuant to Article 35.

2. Unless the disputing Parties otherwise agree, the panel shall, within 180 days after the last panelist is selected, present to the disputing Parties an initial report containing: (a) findings of fact; (b) its determination as to whether there has been a persistent pattern of failure by the Party complained against to effectively enforce its occupational safety and health, child labor or minimum wage technical labor standards in a matter that is trade-related and covered by mutually recognized labor laws, or any other determination requested in the terms of reference; and (c) in the event the panel makes an affirmative determination under subparagraph (b), its recommendations, if any, for the resolution of the dispute, which normally shall be that the Party complained against adopt and implement an action plan sufficient to remedy the pattern of non-enforcement.

3. Panelists may furnish separate opinions on matters not unanimously agreed.

4. A disputing Party may submit written comments to the panel on its initial report within 30 days of presentation of the report.

5.   In such an event, and after considering such written comments, the panel, on its own initiative or on the request of any disputing Party, may: (a) request the views of any participating Party; (b) reconsider its report; and (c) make any further examination that it considers appropriate.

Article 37: Final Report

1.   The panel shall present to the disputing Parties a final report, including any separate opinions on matters not unanimously agreed, within 60 days of presentation of the initial report, unless the disputing Parties otherwise agree.

2.   The disputing Parties shall transmit to the Council the final report of the panel, as well as any written views that a disputing Party desires to be appended, on a confidential basis within 15 days after it is presented to them.

3.   The final report of the panel shall be published five days after it is transmitted to the Council.

Article 38: Implementation of Final Report

If, in its final report, a panel determines that there has been a persistent pattern of failure by the Party complained against to effectively enforce its occupational safety and health, child labor or minimum wage technical labor standards, the disputing Parties may agree on a mutually satisfactory action plan, which normally shall conform with the determinations and recommendations of the panel. The disputing Parties shall promptly notify the Secretariat and the Council of any agreed resolution of the dispute.

Article 39: Review of Implementation

1.   If, in its final report, a panel determines that there has been a persistent pattern of failure by the Party

complained against to effectively enforce its occupational safety and health, child labor or minimum wage technical labor standards, and: (a) the disputing Parties have not agreed on an action plan under Article 38 within 60 days of the date of the final report, or (b) the disputing Parties cannot agree on whether the Party complained against is fully implementing (i) an action plan agreed under Article 38, (ii) an action plan deemed to have been established by a panel under paragraph 2, or (iii) an action plan approved or established by a panel under paragraph 4, any disputing Party may request that the panel be reconvened. The requesting Party shall deliver the request in writing to the other Parties and to the Secretariat. The Council shall reconvene the panel on delivery of the request to the Secretariat.

2. No Party may make a request under paragraph 1(a) earlier than 60 days, or later than 120 days, after the date of the final report. If the disputing Parties have not agreed to an action plan and if no request was made under paragraph 1(a), the last action plan, if any, submitted by the Party complained against to the complaining Party or Parties within 60 days of the date of the final report, or such other period as the disputing Parties may agree, shall be deemed to have been established by the panel 120 days after the date of the final report.

3. A request under paragraph 1(b) may be made no earlier than 180 days after an action plan has been: (a) agreed under Article 38, (b) deemed to have been established by a panel under paragraph 2, or (c) approved or established by a panel under paragraph 4, and only during the term of any such action plan.

4. Where a panel has been reconvened under paragraph 1(a), it: (a) shall determine whether any action plan proposed by the Party complained against is sufficient to remedy the pattern of non-enforcement and (i) if so, shall approve the plan, or (ii) if not, shall establish such a plan consistent with the law of the Party com-

plained against, and (b) may, where warranted, impose a monetary enforcement assessment in accordance with Annex 39, within 90 days after the panel has been reconvened or such other period as the disputing Parties may agree.

5. Where a panel has been reconvened under paragraph 1(b), it shall determine either that: (a) the Party complained against is fully implementing the action plan, in which case the panel may not impose a monetary enforcement assessment, or (b) the Party complained against is not fully implementing the action plan, in which case the panel shall impose a monetary enforcement assessment in accordance with Annex 39, within 60 days after it has been reconvened or such other period as the disputing Parties may agree.

6. A panel reconvened under this Article shall provide that the Party complained against shall fully implement any action plan referred to in paragraph 4(a)(ii) or 5(b), and pay any monetary enforcement assessment imposed under paragraph 4(b) or 5(b), and any such provision shall be final.

Article 40: Further Proceeding

A complaining Party may, at any time beginning 180 days after a panel determination under Article 39(5)(b), request in writing that a panel be reconvened to determine whether the Party complained against is fully implementing the action plan. On delivery of the request to the other Parties and the Secretariat, the Council shall reconvene the panel. The panel shall make the determination within 60 days after it has been reconvened or such other period as the disputing Parties may agree.

Article 41: Suspension of Benefits

1. Subject to Annex 41A, where a Party fails to pay a monetary enforcement assessment within 180 days after it is imposed by a panel: (a) under Article 39(4)(b), or (b)

under Article 39(5)(b), except where benefits may be suspended under paragraph 2(a), any complaining Party or Parties may suspend, in accordance with Annex 41B, the application to the Party complained against of NAF-TA benefits in an amount no greater than that sufficient to collect the monetary enforcement assessment.

2. Subject to Annex 41A, where a panel has made a determination under Article 39(5)(b) and the panel: (a) has previously imposed a monetary enforcement assessment under Article 39(4)(b) or established an action plan under Article 39(4)(a)(ii), or (b) has subsequently determined under Article 40 that a Party is not fully implementing an action plan, the complaining Party or Parties may, in accordance with Annex 41B, suspend annually the application to the Party complained against of NAF-TA benefits in an amount no greater than the monetary enforcement assessment imposed by the panel under Article 39(5)(b).

3. Where more than one complaining Party suspends benefits under paragraph 1 or 2, the combined suspension shall be no greater than the amount of the monetary enforcement assessment.

4. Where a Party has suspended benefits under paragraph 1 or 2, the Council shall, on the delivery of a written request by the Party complained against to the other Parties and the Secretariat, reconvene the panel to determine whether the monetary enforcement assessment has been paid or collected, or whether the Party complained against is fully implementing the action plan, as the case may be. The panel shall submit its report within 45 days after it has been reconvened. If the panel determines that the assessment has been paid or collected, or that the Party complained against is fully implementing the action plan, the suspension of benefits under paragraph 1 or 2, as the case may be, shall be terminated.

5. On the written request of the Party complained against, delivered to the other Parties and the Secretariat, the Council shall reconvene the panel to determine whether the suspension of benefits by the complaining Party or Parties pursuant to paragraph 1 or 2 is manifestly excessive. Within 45 days of the request, the panel shall present a report to the disputing Parties containing its determination.

PART SIX—GENERAL PROVISIONS

Article 42: Enforcement Principle

Nothing in this Agreement shall be construed to empower a Party's authorities to undertake labor law enforcement activities in the territory of another Party.

Article 43: Private Rights

No Party may provide for a right of action under its domestic law against any other Party on the ground that another Party has acted in a manner inconsistent with this Agreement.

Article 44: Protection of Information

1. If a Party provides confidential or proprietary information to another Party, including its NAO, the Council or the Secretariat, the recipient shall treat the information on the same basis as the Party providing the information.

2. Confidential or proprietary information provided by a Party to an ECE or a panel under this Agreement shall be treated in accordance with the rules of procedure established under Articles 24 and 33.

Article 45: Cooperation with the ILO

The Parties shall seek to establish cooperative arrangements with the ILO to enable the Council and Parties to

draw on the expertise and experience of the ILO for
purposes of implementing Article 24(1).

* * *

Article 49: Definitions

1. For purposes of this Agreement:

A Party has not failed to "effectively enforce its occupational safety and health, child labor or minimum wage
technical labor standards" or comply with Article 3(1) in
a particular case where the action or inaction by agencies
or officials of that Party: (a) reflects a reasonable exercise
of the agency's or the official's discretion with respect to
investigatory, prosecutorial, regulatory or compliance
matters; or (b) results from bona fide decisions to allocate
resources to enforcement in respect of other labor matters
determined to have higher priorities;

"labor law" means laws and regulations, or provisions
thereof, that are directly related to: (a) freedom of association and protection of the right to organize; (b) the right
to bargain collectively; (c) the right to strike; (d) prohibition of forced labor; (e) labor protections for children and
young persons; (f) minimum employment standards, such
as minimum wages and overtime pay, covering wage
earners, including those not covered by collective agreements; (g) elimination of employment discrimination on
the basis of grounds such as race, religion, age, sex, or
other grounds as determined by each Party's domestic
laws; (h) equal pay for men and women; (i) prevention of
occupational injuries and illnesses; (j) compensation in
cases of occupational injuries and illnesses; (k) protection
of migrant workers;

"mutually recognized labor laws" means laws of both a
requesting Party and the Party whose laws were the
subject of ministerial consultations under Article 22 that
address the same general subject matter in a manner that
provides enforceable rights, protections or standards;

"pattern of practice" means a course of action or inaction beginning after the date of entry into force of the Agreement, and does not include a single instance or case;

"persistent pattern" means a sustained or recurring pattern of practice;

"province" means a province of Canada, and includes the Yukon Territory and the Northwest Territories and their successors;

"publicly available information" means information to which the public has a legal right under the statutory laws of the Party;

"technical labor standards" means laws and regulations, or specific provisions thereof, that are directly related to subparagraphs (d) through (k) of the definition of labor law. For greater certainty and consistent with the provisions of this Agreement, the setting of all standards and levels in respect of minimum wages and labor protections for children and young persons by each Party shall not be subject to obligations under this Agreement. Each Party's obligations under this Agreement pertain to enforcing the level of the general minimum wage and child labor age limits established by that Party;

"territory" means for a Party the territory of that Party as set out in Annex 49; and

"trade-related" means related to a situation involving workplaces, firms, companies or sectors that produce goods or provide services: (a) traded between the territories of the Parties; or (b) that compete, in the territory of the Party whose labor law was the subject of ministerial consultations under Article 22, with goods or services produced or provided by persons of another Party.

PART SEVEN—FINAL PROVISIONS

* * *

Article 53: Accession

Any country or group of countries may accede to this Agreement subject to such terms and conditions as may be agreed between such country or countries and the Council and following approval in accordance with the applicable legal procedures of each country.

Article 54: Withdrawal

A Party may withdraw from this Agreement six months after it provides written notice of withdrawal to the other Parties. If a Party withdraws, the Agreement shall remain in force for the remaining Parties.

Article 55: Authentic Texts

The English, French and Spanish texts of this Agreement are equally authentic.

ANNEX 1—LABOR PRINCIPLES (reproduced in Chapter 101)

ANNEX 39—MONETARY ENFORCEMENT ASSESSMENTS (see NAEC Annex 34)

ANNEX 41B—SUSPENSION OF BENEFITS (see NAEC Annex 36B)

INDEX

References are to Pages

A

509

B

BERNE CONVENTION, 181

BINATIONAL PANELS, 63–66, 190–200

BORDER COOPERATION AGREEMENT **(Mexico–U.S.),**
215–217

BRAZIL, 242–244

BUSINESS PERSONS
Business visitors, 147
CFTA entry rights, 51
Intra-company transferees, 149
Investors, 148
NAFTA entry rights, 147–149
Professionals, 149
Traders, 148

BUY AMERICAN ACT, 38, 94–96

C

CANADA
Auto Pact with U.S., 3, 42
Banking in, 46–49
Branch plants, 15
Broadcast rules, 32
Canada–U.S. Agreement on Transboundary Movement of Hazardous Waste, 72, 207
Canada–U.S. Free Trade Agreement, Chapter 2
Canada–Chile FTA, 241
Cultural industries, 32–38
Foreign Investment Review Act, 50
Investment Canada Act, 50
Quebec, 244–246

CANADA–UNITED STATES FREE TRADE AGREEMENT (CFTA)
Alcoholic beverages, 39–41
Antidumping disputes, 58–66
Automotive goods, 42
Auto Pact, 3, 42
Binational panels, 63–66
Business persons (entry), 51
Chapter 18 disputes, 54–58

S

SAFEGUARDS
CFTA (generally), 38
NAFTA (generally), 118–122

SAFETY REGULATION, 111–116

SANITARY AND PHYTOSANITARY REGULATIONS (SPS), 108–111
SERVICES
CFTA (generally), 43–49
Financial services, 136–145
Foreign legal consultants, 127–129
Land transport, 129–132
Licensing and certification, 125–127
NAFTA (generally), Chapter 5
Professionals, 125–127, 149
Telecommunications,132–135

SOFTWOOD LUMBER, 65, 188–197

STATE ENTERPRISES, 104–106

SUBMISSIONS
Environmental, 210–214
Labor, 221–224

SUBSIDIES
Dispute settlement, 58–66, 190–194

SUPREMACY, 20, 71

T

TARIFFS
Agricultural, 106–111
CFTA removal schedules, 23
Customs user fees, 24, 77
Drawback (tariff refunds), 24, 77
External, 77
NAFTA removal schedules, 76
Waivers, 78

TECHNOLOGY, see Chapter 7

TELECOMMUNICATIONS, 132–135